Thinking about Political Reform

Thinking about Political Reform

How to Fix, or Not Fix, American Government and Politics

by

JOHN R. JOHANNES
Professor of Political Science
Villanova University

New York   Oxford

OXFORD UNIVERSITY PRESS

Oxford University Press is a department of the University of Oxford.
It furthers the University's objective of excellence in research,
scholarship, and education by publishing worldwide.

Oxford   New York
Auckland   Cape Town   Dar es Salaam   Hong Kong   Karachi
Kuala Lumpur   Madrid   Melbourne   Mexico City   Nairobi
New Delhi   Shanghai   Taipei   Toronto

With offices in

Argentina   Austria   Brazil   Chile   Czech Republic   France   Greece
Guatemala   Hungary   Italy   Japan   Poland   Portugal   Singapore
South Korea   Switzerland   Thailand   Turkey   Ukraine   Vietnam

For titles covered by Section 112 of the US Higher Education
Opportunity Act, please visit www.oup.com/us/he for the
latest information about pricing and alternate formats.

Published by Oxford University Press
198 Madison Avenue, New York, New York 10016
http://www.oup.com

Library of Congress Cataloging-in-Publication Data
Johannes, John R., 1943-
    Thinking about political reform : how to fix, or not fix, American government
and politics / John R. Johannes, Professor of Political Science, Villanova University.
        pages cm
    ISBN 978-0-19-993799-8
    1. United States--Politics and government--21st century. 2. Representative
government and representation--United States. 3. Administrative agencies--
United States--Reorganization. 4. Executive departments--United States--
Reorganization. 5. Organizational change--United States. 6. Political planning--
United States. I. Title.
    JK275.J64 2016
    320.60973--dc23
                                                                    2015013689

Printing number: 9 8 7 6 5 4 3 2 1

Printed in the United States of America
on acid-free paper

DEDICATION

To Fran, without whom this would not be possible

CONTENTS

PART 4 **CONCLUSION: ISSUES AND PROSPECTS**

ACKNOWLEDGMENTS

I am indebted to the many scholars, organizations, and institutes on whose data and research I have drawn. The political science, think tank, and journalist communities are amazing in their diligence and hard work. I am grateful to Villanova University for the time and support I have received, especially for the sabbatical and reduced teaching loads that provided the time to work on this book. I cannot think of a better place for a project like this, or one with better colleagues, than the Villanova Department of Political Science. Undergraduate and graduate students provided ideas and inspiration; Ryan Shay's editorial assistance was superb. My greatest debt, as always, is to my wife, Fran, whose patience and support were essential to this undertaking. Now, for a while at least, weekends and evenings will be free to enjoy her company more fully.

Additionally, there are many others, who are unaffiliated with the author and editors, who contributed to this book's progress and development as well. We owe a debt of gratitude to the following people, who reviewed the manuscript in some capacity leading up to its publication, and have provided valuable insight and feedback:

Jeremy Busacca, *California Polytechnic University, Pomona*
Taylor E. Dark III, *California State University, Los Angeles*
John P. Forren, *Miami University*
Brian Frederick, *Bridgewater State University*
Rodd Freitag, *University of Wisconsin—Eau Claire*
Therese M. Hammond, *Penn State University—Lehigh Valley*
Rick D. Henderson, *Texas State University*
Stephen Kleinschmit, *Eastern Kentucky University*
Jennefer Mazza, *Ramapo College of New Jersey*
Scott Meinke, *Bucknell University*
Kristin O'Donovan, *Wayne State University*
Hong Min Park, *University of Alabama*
Liliokanaio Peaslee, *James Madison University*
Andrew Roberts, *Northwestern University*

PREFACE

This book has one goal: to stimulate thinking about how to make American government and politics function better. Although there are some optimists on the topic, skeptics dominate the debate, sometimes to the point of despair, and not for the wrong reasons. The argument of the book is simple: reforms are needed and may be possible, but reformers must proceed carefully and with a conceptual scheme in mind. They must know what values they want to promote and how those values interact. They must think clearly about how power is to be distributed and exercised to advance those values. Piecemeal reform can be dangerous. The task is formidable.

Writing a book of this sort is both a challenge and a reward. The challenge is to understand the myriad issues involved in reforming political and governmental institutions and processes. The reward is the same. In my case, 20 years in higher administration at two universities pulled me away from the study of politics and government. This book represents my return.

CHAPTER 1

A Framework for Thinking about Reform

> It has been frequently remarked that it seems to have been
> reserved to the people of this country, by their conduct and
> example, to decide the important question, whether societies of
> men are really capable or not of establishing good government
> from reflection and choice, or whether they are forever destined
> to depend for their political constitutions on accident and force.
>
> —ALEXANDER HAMILTON, *The Federalist No. 1*

Frustration is rampant, screaming a popular dissatisfaction with government and politics across the board. Although a good deal of the complaining derives from the tenor of the times—the deepest recession since the Great Depression, the greatest income inequality in memory, wars without resolution, health and medical problems, terrorism, scandals on Wall Street, government snooping on citizens and allies, and record-high government debt—much of the grousing reflects a sense that the American political system just does not function as it should. Political parties are too divided and too well reflect a polarized citizenry; Congress can't function; the presidency has become too strong or too weak; Congress and the president are in gridlock; the courts and bureaucrats are out of control; money dominates elections; lobbyists run Washington; citizens have no say; laws and policies are out of whack. One op-ed summarized a common view: "Let's Give Up on the Constitution."[1]

America's governmental structure was designed for a different era and for a country characterized by many varied interests but with no mechanism—no real political parties—to aggregate them into the sort of political forces of today. There is a massive mismatch between a polarized citizenry, media, and political party system, on the one hand, and the set of institutions described in the Constitution, on the other. It is not surprising that citizens have become jaundiced about politics, either because their side has lost and cannot control government or because their side controls government but is blocked and frustrated at every turn by the other side. A third group simply throws up its hands in hopelessness. The first instinct is to blame the office holders, "throw out the rascals," and put "good people" into government positions—a strange remedy in light of the 90 percent re-election rate of incumbent congressmen. A second response is typically American: fix the problem—reform government. The question that Alexander Hamilton posed in the *Federalist Papers* remains: can reforms emerge as the product of rational thought and choice, or is the country doomed to limp forward because of the accidents of history?

Reformers come in all varieties, from those seeking radical restructuring of political and governmental rules and practices to the "tinkerers" who think that a tweak here or there, or maybe just more patience, would get us past current tribulations. Reform proposals rest on many, often contradictory, presumptions and assessments. At one extreme there is a firm conviction that popular democracy has been frustrated; at the other, some wonder whether the country has become too democratic and participatory to function. Liberals find that government does not do what it should; conservatives see government overstepping its legitimate bounds. Reform proposals fill volumes.[2]

1.1 REFORMS: WHAT AND WHY?

Reform, literally, means to reshape and restructure, sometimes to return to basic values or practices that had been lost and sometimes to pursue new ones. It implies an improvement over the status quo in pursuit of some objective. Political reforms are directed toward either substantive (e.g., an improved economy) or procedural (e.g., a smoother-running and more participatory government) ends. Those ends often divide and trigger disagreements among reform advocates. *Thinking about reform requires that these purposes and goals be made explicit and prioritized.* For example, one does not argue for more democracy and equality in the U.S. House of Representatives if one's goal is efficiency. Most efforts at structural or procedural change benefit some people at the expense of others; reforms rarely are neutral. A second problem is that what may be a great idea in the abstract must be enacted and applied; and as the saying goes, "the devil's in the details." No one should bet the farm that a proposed reform, no matter how obviously good, will survive intact. A third difficulty is interconnectivity: reforms of one institution or process may affect others, sometimes in a fashion that makes the latter worse. If maintaining a strong two-party system is one's objective, eliminating the Electoral College would not be a smart move.

Fourth, as Mark E. Rush put it, "Political reform always comes at a price, usually in the form of unanticipated or unintended consequences."[3] Some reforms may prove surprisingly beneficial, whereas others may frustrate the intent of the reform or create new headaches. One thinks, for example, of campaign finance reforms to limit spending and curtail corruption only to result in the explosion of spending, the rise of political action committees, and the emergence of independent spending by outside organizations. The many efforts to open up, modernize, and make more democratic the operations of the House of Representatives in 1910, 1946, and the early to mid-1970 period altered the quality and efficiency of the legislative process and led to all sorts of new relationships and power shifts that, in retrospect, do not seem all that positive. Efforts to clean up politics during the Progressive Era had negative consequences for voting turnout. Finally, regardless of how well motivated or how well crafted any given alteration of structure or process is, "a whole army of people who are very clever, quite ingenious, and more than a little devious will work to undermine any reform."[4] The success and viability of virtually all political reforms are contingent on a host of factors.

What follows in this book is an analysis of structural and procedural reform proposals, examined in the context of seven criteria essential for "good government."

The analysis examines the causes, purposes, and benefits of the reforms, the practicality of enactment, likely consequences—insofar as consequences can be known—and their interconnectivity. The theme is that *fundamental choices must be made if reform is to make sense and achieve salutary ends.*

1.2 GUIDING PRINCIPLES

A lesson to be learned from the founding fathers who gathered in Philadelphia in 1787 is that reforming political institutions and processes requires serious thought, a methodical but bold approach, a good dose of skepticism, lots of humility, and no little courage. Ideally, one begins with the goals of government—the characteristics that give people faith in government and lead them to support it even in difficult times. In the American context, there is no more eloquent statement of the ends of civil government than the preamble to the Constitution, which proclaims that government is established to "form a more perfect union, establish justice, insure domestic tranquility, provide for the common defence [sic], promote the general Welfare, and secure the blessings of liberty. . . ." Attaining these objectives requires the enactment and implementation of good public policy. What constitutes "good policy," of course, has been grist for the political mills forever, and any definition must include not only the substance and results of policy but also the processes by which goals are identified and policy is enacted and implemented.[5] Among both scholars and politicians, the near-universal belief is that good policy, however defined, is most likely to emerge if the political institutions and procedures that produce policy are properly designed, function well, and are assiduously maintained and refined. That is the task of reform.

What criteria, values, or standards should characterize American political institutions and processes? How should those institutions be structured, empowered, and aligned to cope with today's polarized world? Begin with the issues confronting the framers of the Constitution in that summer of 1787. Their experience with state constitutions and the Articles of Confederation dictated a government that was strong enough to do what the people of the nation needed. To be sure, that was a much more limited agenda than faces the country today, with much of it focused on security, safety, and commerce; but it meant that government had to be able to act on important matters and act when action was needed, doing so effectively, efficiently, and with reasoned and deliberative judgment.

A second goal was to make sure that the government would not be inclined, and certainly not able, to do "bad things." They knew that governments can get out of hand, impose unjust hardships, pursue unwise plans, and ignore and oppress its citizens. They naturally feared a strong executive; but having experienced popular government in the states that seemed to some of them like mob rule, they didn't want anything that smacked of unrestrained democracy. Tyranny was feared whether it came from a king or from a mob. Their solution had several elements. First, they would rely on republican government with indirect and representative popular rule. The role of the citizens was crucial to empowering, guiding, and curtailing government. Second, they saw the virtues in an extended republic, by which Madison meant a large country with multiple interests spread widely, and in federalism, whereby power was divided vertically between a centralized national government and sovereign state governments. Last, they divided the federal government horizontally into three independent branches, creating the familiar system of separation of powers or, more accurately, of "separated institutions sharing powers."[6] That sharing implied a complex set of checks and balances to ensure that government would be limited in what it can do to protect people's safety and security *from* government.

They gave to the presidency limited and rather vague "executive" powers, making presidents independently elected and re-eligible for office. The veto power would help protect them against congressional intrusions. Congress was the representative body, linking people to government. That presented a problem, namely, the tension between the founders' fear of a run-wild legislature as found in some of the states on the one hand and the need, on the other, to make the legislature supreme, the prime policy maker and provider of funds for the government. According to Madison, writing in *Federalist No. 51*, in republican governments, "the legislative authority necessarily predominates." The arrangement meant that the presidency and Congress were destined to struggle over the direction of government and control over the departments and agencies of the executive branch. At different times, one or the other has had the upper hand, and that is one reason so many observers have proposed reforms. The judiciary, in addition to its function of deciding cases and interpreting the law, in some respects has become the referee in the congressional–presidential rivalry.

Utilizing the wisdom of the framers, and with due consideration to the historical development of the American polity and the thought of respected scholars, it is relatively easy to specify criteria that should characterize good government today.[7] Governments with such characteristics will be *legitimate*, that is, accepted as appropriate for the society and thus given due obedience and loyalty. On the foundation of legitimacy rest stability and the viability of government structures and actions. Although legitimacy over the centuries has been based on various sources such as the divine right of kings or perhaps the Communist Party's role as "vanguard of the proletariat," legitimacy in democracies and republics rests on the consent of the governed and, ultimately, on the government's ability to meet citizens' needs. Of late, threats to legitimacy in the United States are seen in the significant distrust in government, the suspicion that government is acting on behalf of the privileged few rather than the multitude of citizens, the frustration over gridlock in Washington, and a disgust at politics in the nation's capital. One example of a possible threat to legitimacy is the 2000 presidential election. The vote in Florida was ambiguous; there were recounts; and finally the Supreme Court had to step in to settle the matter. George W. Bush's victory in Florida was, according to many critics, erroneous, calling into question the legitimacy of the Electoral College system of choosing presidents and Bush's very presidency. Still, most Americans do support their political system and institutions, even as they dislike and distrust the politicians who function within them. Ensuring a continuation of that support may depend on fixing the problems that exist.

1.3 GOALS, VALUES, AND CRITERIA
FOR EVALUATING INSTITUTIONS

There are two sets of values or criteria for evaluating and then reforming government and politics in the United States. The first set pertains to the institutional structure of government: the Congress, presidency, bureaucracy, and judiciary, along with federalism. These institutions simply must work well if government is to succeed. The second set relates to the flip side of the coin: guiding and controlling government hurdles so that it remains faithful to the needs and desires of the citizenry.

1. First, government must be *effective*. *Effectiveness* is the ability of government to function, to make and carry out policies to solve the country's problems with reasonable dispatch and success. Effectiveness is likely when a government's structures, internal procedures, and political processes are not systemic roadblocks to the making of policy. Many governments today appear to be absolutely or relatively ineffective for a host of reasons. Recent examples might include Iraq, Afghanistan, some African countries, Greece, and Italy. They suffer from a plethora of political parties, from institutional rules that fail to foster cooperation and stability, and even from a political culture that does not support strength in government. In the United States, threats to effectiveness might include the filibuster in the Senate, bureaucratic "red tape," and harsh polarized partisan warfare in Washington. More basically, in terms of factors undermining effectiveness, one might go so far as to question the bedrock principles of separation of powers and federalism themselves.

2. Second, effectiveness is linked to *efficiency*: "the most bang for a buck" or the "fewest bucks for a given amount of bang" and the ability to get business done with dispatch. No one has ever accused American government of being efficient; indeed, it was not designed to be. Polls reveal the public's skepticism. For example, a 2012 Pew Research Center poll found that 59 percent of the public agreed that "when something is run by the government, it is usually inefficient and wasteful."[8] A 2011 Gallup poll showed that Americans thought that 51 percent of every dollar the government spent was wasted.[9]

3. A third criterion of good governmental institutions is *reasoned deliberative judgment*. Decisions should result from a process informed by rational argument, informed deliberation, and careful judgment.[10] Such decisions are characterized by claims that are falsifiable rather than merely asserted as true; by a willingness to listen, make every effort to understand other views, and engage in debate; by a careful weighing of evidence; by consideration of both long- and short-term consequences; by reliance on sound information and plausible assumptions; and by an openness to negotiate with adversaries. These stand in contrast to making decisions based on the whim of leaders, use of anecdotal and partial evidence, excessive haste, short-term political pressure, or ideological claims that cannot be tested for their validity. This process must be fair in that procedures and thus decisions should not be stacked *a priori* for or against any faction, as, for example, when the majority party in Congress denies the minority a reasonable opportunity to offer amendments or when hurdles in the voting process systematically affect certain groups of people more than others. Nor should the rules and procedures vary from case to case; what is sauce for the goose (e.g., Democrats) should be sauce for the gander (Republicans). Specifying the precise content of fairness in a given situation is not easy, but most would agree that "politics ought to be fair" and reasonable.

Decisions, in short, should result from a search for the truth, be based on evidence, be well thought out, and be made with appropriate but not necessarily absolute deference accorded to experts—who can be wrong. Careful compromise, when necessary, rather than mere logrolling or horse-trading would be the ideal.

1.4 THE NEED FOR LIMITS AND CONTROLS: SAFETY

Government that is effective, efficient, and characterized by reasoned decision making should produce the sort of policies, policy adjudication, and policy implementation that the country needs and a thoughtful citizenry wants. There is a catch, however: effectiveness and efficiency in government depend in large measure on concentration and centralization of power, and as Lord Acton claimed, power tends to corrupt. Concentrated power can be dangerous and frightening, jeopardizing the personal liberty that constitutes the foundation of the American Republic.

Limitations on government must be factored into the reformist equation. In the Western political tradition, some areas of government action simply are off limits to protect individual rights. Moreover, democratic governments are susceptible to short-term political pressures, leading to popular policies that have negative consequences over the long haul. The framers of the American Constitution wrestled with this issue. As Madison argued in *Federalist No. 10*, the dangers of a self-interested and potentially tyrannical political faction, whether a majority or minority, can be dealt with either by removing the causes of faction or by controlling them. Removing the causes would involve taking away basic rights such as freedom of speech, a free press, and freedom of assembly—a cure would be worse than the disease. Thus a constitutional bill of rights, a system of separate political institutions sharing powers and functions, and operational checks and balances serve to control dangerous factions. Indeed, some matters simply are taken off the table as a way to "protect us from ourselves."

Some actions, because of their heavy consequences, ought to be possible only under extraordinary circumstances. For example, in emergencies some rights may have to be curtailed temporarily, but to make sure such action is not taken frivolously or cavalierly, supermajorities might be required in the legislature to permit it. To assure that such intrusions on rights do not become permanent, sunset provisions, judicial remedies, and avenues to repeal and modify such policies must be available. States, indeed, often ask citizens to vote directly in referendums on controversial issues precisely to ensure that the resolution of important conflicts is not compromised by normal political procedures. At times, the basic institutional arrangements themselves may need alteration, but such surgery should be relatively difficult, as, in fact, the constitutional amending process makes it. The system of checks and balances and the institutional sharing of powers and functions were deemed by the framers to be absolutely essential to protect liberty. As Madison noted, however, these are *auxiliary* precautions designed to supplement the primary check on government excess: the power of the people to hold government accountable and force it to act in their interests.

1.5 GOALS, VALUES, AND CRITERIA
FOR EVALUATING POPULAR SOVEREIGNTY

4. A fourth criterion is *responsiveness*, which means that government ought to meet the needs and wants of the governed. Government officials can be responsive out of

their benevolence and wisdom; out of their representativeness of and alignment with constituents' preferences; or out of fear of being removed from office. Responsive governments listen to the views of the citizens and give due consideration to those views in reaching decisions. One can think of four types:[11]

(1) Policy responsiveness: government officials provide the citizens, especially their constituents, with public policies the people like (e.g., Medicare).

(2) "Pork barrel" responsiveness: officials steer government building projects, jobs, and contracts ("pork") to their constituencies. For example, note how the construction of a new military airplane relies on a vast system of subcontractors located in many congressional districts.

(3) Service responsiveness: legislators provide individual assistance to constituents who experience difficulties with government offices, such as getting someone transferred to a different military base near her fiancé.

(4) Symbolic responsiveness: making constituents feel good, such as when a senator is seen munching on corn dogs at an Iowa county fair.

Responsiveness can be individual or collective. That is, an individual senator or representative can advance the views and welfare of his or her constituents through clever maneuvering and bargaining to ensure that federal dollars flow back home or by direct intervention with the bureaucracy to address an individual's problems. Responsiveness might work collectively through the voters' selection of one political party and its platform over another at election time, with the resulting governing majority then implementing the issues that were salient during the election campaign. Individual and collective responsiveness can and do collide: responding to the needs of one's constituents may or may not be compatible with good policy for the whole nation.

5. Perhaps the most natural way to foster responsiveness is through *representation*, which can be a confusing and multifaceted concept.[12] Two types of representation are of concern here. One is *descriptive representation*, in which the sociodemographic characteristics (race, gender, age, religion, income) of officials who govern resemble the characteristics of the citizenry. Representatives bring to government the wishes and preferences that the represented would bring if they were directly involved. The argument is that a congruence of demographic characteristics between representatives and their constituents is likely to produce a correspondence between the views and preferences of the representatives and the represented. In some areas—particularly issues relevant to women and certain ethnic and racial groups—a growing body of social science evidence suggests that descriptive representation makes a difference in legislator-constituent relationships and in the sorts of policies and issues brought to the attention of policy makers and, ultimately, enacted in response to those groups' needs and wishes.[13]

Substantive or policy representation—acting in the interest of those represented and enacting policies they want—is usually considered more important than, and the goal of, descriptive representation. Such representation can come in two ways. One is literally standing in place of those who are not present, that is, *acting as their delegate* and doing what they say they want. The other version of substantive representation considers that elected officials represent and deliberate *on behalf of the interests* of their electors, sometimes regardless of, and sometimes in opposition to, their temporary or short-term wishes. Edmund Burke's famous "Speech to the Electors of Bristol," in which he reminds them that his job is to exercise his judgment on their behalf, is the classic statement of this view.[14]

Representation can be *dyadic* (one to one) or *collective*. In the former, a representative seeks to represent his or her constituents, or at least a segment of them. Collective representation refers to the notion that all legislators taken together represent the public at large, or at least a substantial segment of the public. A given representative or senator might represent the views of many citizens outside his or her constituency who disagree with their own members of Congress. Collective representation can in fact be more comprehensive and accurate than the dyadic form.[15] Congress as a whole consists, therefore, of an aggregation of dyadic representative relationships that has the benefit of ensuring that people not well represented (in terms of policy views) by their own representatives do gain a measure of policy representation through other senators and congressmen.

6. Representation of whatever form does not necessarily guarantee responsiveness to people's wants and, especially, needs. Another mechanism, *accountability*, can pick up the slack. Accountability is the ability of the governed to require the governors to answer (be accountable) for their actions and, when the governed so judge, to revoke the authority they had bestowed on the governors.[16] Those who act for the citizenry must never be totally free to do whatever they want; there must be a way to make sure that, ultimately, they act in the best interests of those they represent, at least as judged by those people—who of course need sufficient transparency in government to see what is happening. The usual vehicle for such accountability is periodic elections through which citizens can throw out of office officials whose performance has failed the expectations of the citizenry. This, indeed, is the very definition of modern democracy.[17] In other political systems, revolutions, assassinations, or *coups* sometimes provide accountability of a sort. In the United States, with its half million elected public officials, electoral accountability is taken for granted. Still, many critics see elections as a sham because they believe that campaign spending and the media dictate the results, because candidates cannot get their messages across, because candidates are so similar or so radically different as to afford no "real" choice to voters, because they are bought off by organized interests, because voters are fools incompetent to choose, because too few citizens actually exercise their right to vote, or because some unseen "power"—Wall Street, Communists, or a conspiracy—controls them. Democratic accountability comes in several ways. The U.S. system relies on a dyadic approach in which a single senator or representative is chosen by the voters in a given state or district. The elected official is thus accountable directly to his or her voters, as an individual. Other countries rely more on party accountability, wherein elected officials are instruments of parties that stand for clear sets of policies; voters at election time choose one or another party. Which of these systems one likes will determine his or her assessment of the role of political parties, which in turn affects one's preferred reforms of, for example, the Electoral College or voting systems.

7. Effective representation and electoral accountability ultimately depend on the citizen. If, as Aristotle suggested, politics makes one more "human," *participation* in political processes should be highly valued not only for its contribution to accountability, representation, and responsiveness but also for enriching the lives of the citizenry.

Political systems that invite and encourage citizens to take part in the political process ought, in principle, to be preferable to those that do not; and they would seem more likely to produce "good" policies. Democratic values would seem to require a good measure of political equality such that, at least in terms of voting, expressing one's views, and having access to government and judicial processes and services, no citizen should be prevented from participating. That does not imply that everyone will or should have equal influence or must enjoy equally the economic or social benefits of the political system; but, arguably, the more opportunities for participation, the better the system.

To summarize, there are seven general values or criteria for evaluating government and the political process—and therefore reform proposals. Governmental institutions and processes above all must be (1) *effective*, implying that government's actions must be determined by a well-functioning process of (2) *reasoned and fair deliberation and judgment*, and that its operations should be (3) *efficient*. At the same time, government must be controlled and limited, leading to the criteria that apply to the citizenry: (4) *responsiveness*, (5) *representativeness*, (6) *accountability*, and (7) *participation*. Governments meeting these criteria are likely to be perceived as legitimate by the governed and are likely to be safe and protect liberties.

1.6 BUT IT ISN'T SO SIMPLE

The Criteria Go Together

Several qualifications are in order. *First, these criteria are interrelated and often interdependent.* Take responsiveness, representation, and accountability. Governments are likely to be responsive to the citizenry if they are representative and/or accountable. It is of course possible for a government to be responsive without being either representative or accountable; think in terms of a benevolent "philosopher king" dictator who cares deeply and acts for his subjects. One could have a representative legislature, chosen by randomly picking names from a phone book, that is not accountable because there are no elections or other means of removing the officials. There could be a highly accountable group of legislators who, although voters may watch what they do and reward or punish them accordingly, are unrepresentative of their constituents. Starkly put, would one prefer a legislature of intelligent and accomplished—but not representative—members who are held accountable or a perfectly representative legislature that probably would be less talented?

Questions abound. Which is more important, for a legislature to be representative of the citizenry, to be responsive to the people, or to be accountable for its actions? To whom, through what mechanism, and how well is government responsive? A president or legislator cannot possibly be responsive to all his or her constituents who probably have radically different preferences and demands. In what sense and of whom is government representative? Which constituents' views should the representative represent—those who voted for him or her, loyal close supporters and financial backers, a "majority" of one's constituents, or one's fellow partisans? How, how easily, and how well do the people hold their representatives accountable?

These three standards have implications for effectiveness and efficiency. A truly responsive and representative government is likely to be judged effective, since by definition it mirrors the views and characteristics of its people and has considered and acted on their wishes and welfare. Conversely, systemic effectiveness and efficiency can make it easier for a legislative body to be responsive to constituents. Governments that are effective, especially those that concentrate power in the hands of only one party, can more easily and clearly be held accountable since the voters can easily assign praise or blame for government's achievements or failures. Reasonable deliberative judgment that prevents hasty decisions, weighs consequences of proposed actions, and discourages policies that unfairly benefit a few at a cost to many surely would contribute to effectiveness and to policy representation and responsiveness, at least in the "big picture" sense. It would limit dangerous actions as well.

The Criteria Are in Conflict

Second, there are contradictions among some of these criteria, making it impossible to maximize all of them simultaneously. Taken to their extremes, these standards are not all mutually compatible, thus calling for trade-offs. Broad-based citizen participation, manifested in multiple pressures on legislators to be responsive and accountable, may confound effectiveness, efficiency, and reasoned deliberation as members scramble trying to represent and respond to so many different voices. The individual responsiveness of a legislator to her constituents—whether for policy or for pork—can interfere with the collective responsiveness and accountability of the Congress to the nation, perhaps undermining the collective effectiveness and efficiency of the legislature.[18]

An effective and efficient government need not be accountable, and it could be anything but safe for the nation; Hitler provided cars and highways, and Mussolini made the trains run on time. Most members of Congress occasionally wish they did not have to face re-election and thus do all they can to avoid electoral challenges. Either unchecked power or the freedom from having to face demanding constituents could make Congress and the presidency more effective organizations, but at what cost in terms of responsiveness and accountability? There are other incompatibilities the reader should explore. Surely the founders understood these trade-offs as they constructed the intricate system that has survived 200 years of wear and tear.

The Criteria Are Versatile

Third, many of these criteria can be invoked to support an activist, expansive, and "liberal" political philosophy; others would seem to support a passive, restrictive, and "conservative" one; still others apply regardless of political preferences. Accountability and reasoned judgment, for example, should characterize all democratic regimes. However, the other criteria can be invoked to greater or lesser degrees, based on one's philosophy of government. Whereas a liberal seeking broader government activity opts for effectiveness, efficiency, and responsiveness in most cases, a conservative seeking to limit government prefers representative and deliberative institutional structures and processes that constrain activism. Libertarians seldom support the sorts of effectiveness favored by liberals (and conservatives in some policy areas) and might question aspects of representation and responsiveness if they meant bigger government. An extremely responsive government characterized by high voting participation is likely to legislate and spend actively, and thus a conservative might be inclined to favor institutional arrangements that reduce responsiveness and broad participation.

The Need to Prioritize

Fourth, students of American politics, and indeed all citizens, need to think through and develop their own political philosophies and then decide the appropriate mix and relative priorities of the criteria. One's priorities will determine one's views on reforms. Is Congress to be a microcosm of society, or is it to be an efficient policy-making machine? Which is more important: broad-based participation and fairness of the electoral system or its simplicity and certainty in producing accountability? Do mass participation and responsiveness trump government effectiveness and efficiency? Ultimately, do Americans want a government that can act, or do they fear that it could act unwisely?

In some countries and during certain eras, it may make sense to choose one or another criterion over the others. Italians and Germans, between the World Wars, in the midst of depression and chaos, seemed to prefer effectiveness to accountability. The voters of Venezuela, or at least most of them, wanted a more representative, responsive, and participatory government when they elected Hugo Chavez in 1998. At different times in American history, one or another of these criteria has been ascendant. When Lincoln violated provisions of the Constitution to wage the Civil War, when Franklin Roosevelt rammed through emergency legislation in 1933 and decided to trade American ships to England in return for naval bases, when the country breathlessly awaited the outcome of the Watergate scandal in 1973 and 1974, or when the franchise was extended to women and citizens under 21 years of age, some values—effectiveness, accountability, reasoned judgment, participation, or representation—were being emphasized. Nonetheless, to judge reform proposals requires a consistent and constant prioritization of these values.

Thinking Broadly and Narrowly

Finally, each of these criteria can be applied both to the government system as a whole and to its component parts. This is where matters get messy, given the constitutional system of distinct branches of government that share authority over most policies but nonetheless maintain their own separate powers. As President Kennedy once remarked concerning the Electoral College,

> It is not only the unit vote for the Presidency we are talking about, but a whole solar system of governmental power. If it is proposed to change the balance of power of one of the elements of the solar system, it is necessary to consider all the others. . . . What the effects of these various changes will be on the Federal system, the two-party system, the popular plurality system, and large-states and small-states checks and balances system, no one knows.[19]

One might consider the many reforms of the 1970s that made Congress more representative, more democratic, more transparent, and arguably more accountable—but weakened it as an institution relative to the presidency, rendering it less effective, deliberative, and efficient.

These examples invite questions. How should power be distributed among Congress, the presidency, the judiciary, and the executive bureaucracy? Should one be clearly paramount? How does that affect the seven criteria? Classically, believers in a strong presidency have stressed the institution's effectiveness, efficiency, and national accountability. Those arguing for greater power for the judiciary cite reasoned judgment while celebrating the Court's ability to check and limit dangerous actions of the president and Congress. Proponents of Congress focus on representation and on individual more than collective responsiveness and accountability. Efficiency, reasoned deliberative judgment, and arguably responsiveness to and representation of certain groups ("clients") should characterize a healthy bureaucracy. It is likely that any reform to strengthen any one of these institutions would affect the relative power of all the others and could affect how well they meet the seven criteria.

For example, might the watchfulness over the executive bureaucracy by a Congress focused on representing and responding to particular constituent wishes render the administrative system less effective, less efficient, and less dispassionately reasonable in how it serves the public? Might an effective and efficient presidency run roughshod over Congress, destroying its effectiveness and responsiveness? What is the effect on congressional responsiveness and effectiveness of an independent judiciary with the power to rule acts of Congress unconstitutional?

Consider voting systems, systems parties use to nominate candidates for office, terms of office, and elections. Making them more effective, efficient, representative, responsive to voters, or deliberative presumably would be beneficial, but doing so surely will affect how senators, representatives, and presidents behave once in office, how much freedom they think they have to "do the right thing," and how much attention they must give to the next election. The guiding principle of the chapters that follow is that in assessing political reform efforts and targets, one should prefer to maximize his or her preferred criteria at the macro, system-wide level insofar as possible, rather than focusing on how they apply to individual institutions and processes. Depending on one's hierarchy of values, it might be logical to advocate reforms of part of the political system that seem to conflict with many of the values to serve the broader interest of the system as a whole.

1.7 HOW TO THINK ABOUT REFORM

Reform proposals are a dime a dozen, or maybe cheaper, and the old maxim that "if it ain't broke, don't fix it" might be useful guidance. All reform suggestions are plausible from one perspective or another, and for some of them the consequences can be predicted with a degree of confidence. How does one evaluate various and sometimes competing reform proposals? One approach is to investigate past performance and events. Have these approaches been tried before at the federal level? Did they succeed or fail?

A second approach is to look at state governments, the "laboratories of democracy," or at the experiences of foreign nations to see how similar reforms fared in those circumstances. Although potentially enlightening, this tactic is difficult and potentially misleading, given the different sizes and scopes of government activities, different political and economic cultures, and different geopolitical and historical situations; but it might be a bit easier when comparing the federal system to state governmental systems.

Third, there is what might be called the speculative-logical approach, focusing on the inherent and internal logic of a proposal. Does a proposal have face validity; does it make sense; is it likely to achieve its goals? How does it stack up against one's criteria for good governance? Are there likely to be adverse consequences?

To judge government performance is, in large measure, to judge the structures and processes through which governing officials act. Those institutions affect what policies are enacted, their composition, when they are put into place, how much they cost, and how they are carried out—and, ultimately, their effectiveness and consequences. Rendering judgments on political structures and processes requires criteria that must be logical and consistent in their definitions and in their application. The discussion above offered one list of criteria and one set of definitions, along with several caveats. The reader must give careful thought to these criteria, thinking about their interdependencies and potential inconsistencies, prioritizing them, adding others, and perhaps dropping some. Indeed, approaching reform proposals without a clear array of priorities and value preferences makes no sense, could lead to poor choices, and would undermine the legitimacy and persuasiveness of one's proposals. The following chapters invite application of these criteria in an examination of some of the recent and current efforts to reform the political system.

Applying the criteria and values must be done systematically. There must be a conceptual scheme to guide one's thinking about these values, especially when thinking about the policy-making institutions: the presidency, Congress, judiciary, and executive bureaucracy. How do and how should they interact? Which, if any, should be preeminent? How should they operate and be governed internally so as to maximize one or more of the criteria discussed above? This discussion must wait until later chapters, but for now it is a question to be borne in the back of the mind.

QUESTIONS TO CONSIDER

1. Are there other criteria, values, or standards that you would include as being essential for good democratic government? What is your rationale for including them? Are they implicit in the seven criteria? Should any of the seven be discarded?
2. How do you prioritize these criteria, and why do you rank them as you do?
3. How, and in what areas of public policy, would conservatives, liberals, libertarians, and populists apply the criteria?
4. Can you think of a reform of one part of the political-governmental system that, if enacted, would create difficulties for another?

NOTES

1. Louis Michael Seidman, *New York Times*, December 31, 2012: A17.
2. Richard A. Clucas, *Encyclopedia of American Political Reform* (Santa Barbara, CA: ABC-CLIO, 1996): 2.
3. "The Hidden Costs of Electoral Reform," in Mark E. Rush and Richard L. Engstrom, *Fair and Effective Representation? Debating Electoral Reform and Minority Rights* (Lanham, MD: Rowman & Littlefield, 2001): 69–120, 71.
4. John C. McAdams, "Six Theses on Campaign Finance Reform," *Vox Pop: Newsletter of Political Organizations and Parties* 8 (1): 6.
5. Michael L. Mezey, "The Legislature, the Executive and Public Policy: The Futile Quest for Congressional Power," *Congress & the Presidency* 13 (1986): 1–20; Joseph Cooper, "Assessing Legislative Performance: A Reply to the Critics of Congress," *ibid.*: 21–40.

6. Richard E. Neustadt, *Presidential Power and the Modern Presidents: The Politics of Leadership from Roosevelt to Reagan* (New York: Free Press, 1990): 29.

7. Graham Smith, *Democratic Innovations: Designing Institutions for Citizen Participation* (New York: Cambridge University Press, 2009); Michael E. Merrell, *Empathy and Democracy: Feeling, Thinking, and Deliberation* (University Park: Pennsylvania State University Press, 2010).

8. Pew Research Center for the People & the Press, "American Values Survey," http://www.people-press.org/values-questions/q30k/government-is-usually-inefficient-and-wasteful/#total/.

9. Jeffrey M. Jones, "Americans Say Federal Gov't Wastes over Half of Every Dollar," *Gallup Politics*, http://www.gallup.com/poll/149543/Americans-Say-Federal-Gov-Wastes-Half-Every-dollar.aspx/.

10. Jon Elster, ed., *Deliberative Democracy* (Cambridge, UK: Cambridge University Press, 1998).

11. Heinz Eulau and Paul D. Karps, "The Puzzle of Representation: Specifying the Components of Responsiveness," *Legislative Studies Quarterly* 2 (1977): 233–54.

12. Hanna Fenichel Pitkin, *The Concept of Representation* (Berkeley: University of California Press, 1967).

13. Michele L. Swers, *The Difference Women Make: The Policy Impact of Women in Congress* (Chicago: University of Chicago Press, 2002); Katherine Tate, *Black Faces in the Mirror: African Americans and Their Representatives in the U.S. Congress* (Princeton, NJ: Princeton University Press, 2003); Debra L. Dodson, *The Impact of Women in Congress* (New York: Oxford University Press, 2006); Andrew Reynolds, "Representation and Rights: The Impact of LGBT Legislators in Comparative Perspective," *American Political Science Review* 107 (2013): 259–74; Daniel C. Bowen and Christopher J. Clark, "Revisiting Descriptive Representation in Congress: Assessing the Effect of Race on the Constituent-Legislator Relationship," *Political Research Quarterly* 67 (2014): 695–707.

14. *The Works of the Right Honorable Edmund Burke* (New York: Harper, 1851). See Iain McLean, "Forms of Representation and Systems of Voting," in David Held, ed., *Political Theory Today* (Cambridge, UK: Polity Press, 1991), and Richard S. Katz, *Democracy and Elections* (Oxford, UK: Oxford University Press, 1997).

15. Robert Weissberg, "Collective vs. Dyadic Representation in Congress," *American Political Science Review* 72 (1978): 535–47.

16. Anthony H. Birch, *The Concepts and Theories of Modern Democracy* (London: Routledge, 1993), chap. 5.

17. Joseph A. Schumpeter, *Capitalism, Socialism, and Democracy*, 2nd ed. (New York: Harper & Brothers, 1947), chap. 22.

18. Justin Grimmer, "Appropriators Not Position Takers: The Distorting Effects of Electoral Incentives on Congressional Representation," *American Journal of Political Science* 57 (2013): 624–42.

19. Quoted by Arthur M. Schlesinger Jr. in "Not the People's Choice: How to Democratize American Democracy," in Robert E. DiClerico and Allan S. Hammock, *Points of View*, 9th ed. (Boston: McGraw-Hill, 2004): 123.

CHAPTER 2

⟁

Radical Reform

> In the compound republic of America, the power surrendered by
> the people is first divided between two distinct governments, and
> then the portion allotted to each subdivided among distinct and
> separate departments. . . . Hence a double security arises to the
> rights of the people. The different governments will control each
> other, at the same time that each will be controlled by itself.
>
> —James Madison, *The Federalist No. 51*

Reformers want to improve the performance of political institutions and those who labor within them, but some go further, questioning the very structure or wisdom of the institutions established by the framers and challenging the assumptions and premises on which they were built. From their perspective, the American federal separation-of-powers system no longer works, perhaps because it was the wrong answer to the wrong questions in the first place. Were the framers wrong in stressing limited government and deliberation as much as they did, arguably to the detriment of effectiveness and efficiency? Has the evolution toward greater democracy and citizen involvement—and even more so today's polarization between left and right—rendered the institutional arrangements obsolete? Have today's political parties undermined the relationships expected by the founders? In the words of one critic, do we suffer from "Our Imbecilic Constitution"?[1] Fundamental reform is a far-fetched notion, but it is worth considering for its perspective on the particular problems discussed in subsequent chapters. One message of this book is simple: the United States has a constitutional system predicated on certain assumptions—fragmentation, localism, multiple interest groups, and limited participation in national politics. Yet today's American society seems just the opposite: intensely involved voters divided into what seems like two rigid camps; 24/7 political information from all sorts of media; a uniformity of commercial and cultural life across the 50 states; unequal power among interest groups; and a strong central government.

The questions of 1787 were simple: (1) how to link 13 essentially sovereign entities into a single nation with a central government that would function in collaboration with the state governments; (2) how to make sure that such a government would be strong enough to foster security, growth, and commerce; and (3) how to ensure that it would not be so strong as to trample on people's liberties and the primacy of the states. The constitutional solutions, explained in the *Federalist Papers*, were federalism and the separation of powers. In constructing a government that would be widely accepted, the founders wanted effectiveness with limits. At the same time, they saw the states as the primary engines of policy responsiveness and public participation. Accountability and representation there would be, in multiple modes: the president would be chosen by electors selected by the state governments; the Senate would be composed of delegates from the states; the House would be more or less representative in terms of population and chosen by propertied adult white males. All would have fixed terms. Efficiency was not high on the agenda, if only because the national government would not be heavily engaged in policy making and administration. Reasoned deliberative judgment, with which they had considerable experience in colonial legislatures, on the other hand, topped the list.

Fast forward 225 years and ask whether those eighteenth-century constitutional institutions and political processes, modified over the years to be sure, now meet the seven standards of good government. The American political system divides power geographically and functionally, thus reducing effectiveness and efficiency. Government divided between two warring political parties, one dominating the presidency and the other the Congress, now seems to be the rule; little gets done; and deliberative judgment about policy seems rare. Accountability is fragmented. How does the average voter, who seems to love his or her own representative but despises a Congress controlled by the other party, hold that body as a whole accountable when the only means to do so might be to vote against one's own fellow partisan member of Congress? Individual legislators, fearing electoral defeat, seem obsessively responsive to their own constituents and powerful interest groups. Meanwhile, policy battles shift from the political arena into the world of bureaucratic regulation and judicial judgments. Adversarial litigation replaces political deliberation. No wonder voting turnout is low. Later chapters provide more detail on these problems.

Most of the recent battles over federalism—relying on the Tenth Amendment's dictate that "powers not delegated to the United States by the Constitution, nor prohibited by it to the States, are reserved to the States, respectively, or to the people"—have been over efforts to reduce the reach of the federal government and to return power to the states. The opposite view is that federalism is anachronistic; national policy making is frustrated by a system of 51 sovereign governing entities that use different taxation systems and goals, enact inconsistent laws, and administer them in a fashion that varies from state to state.

So much for the charges; what are the solutions? For decades, some commentators have argued that what the United States needs is a fundamentally different alignment of institutions. Their ideal alternative is the parliamentary form of government that is common in most other democracies and would seem to fit our current political parties. Short of that, they argue that with a few constitutional amendments and changes in federal and state laws, American democracy could gain many of the advantages of the parliamentary system. The solution brings with it the devil's bargain that fuses rather than divides power and responsibility.

2.1 PARLIAMENTARY GOVERNMENT IN WASHINGTON—WITH OR WITHOUT A KING?

How It Works
Parliamentary government rests on the principle of concentrating political power, fusing legislative and executive authority, to make government more effective and

efficient while making it easier for voters to hold it accountable. Key to the system is an elected legislature like the British *Parliament* or the Japanese *Diet* that chooses the executive, commonly called "the government," and holds it responsible for running the country. Most parliaments are bicameral, but the lower, popularly elected, and typically more representative and accountable chamber enjoys the most power. Parliamentary systems differ with respect to the strength and independence of the judiciary, but ultimate authority rests with the legislators and cabinet.

A strong political party system that structures elections is essential. Each party promulgates a party platform (or manifesto, as it sometimes is called), pledging that if elected, it will implement those promises. In a single-member district election system, candidates representing and selected by the competing parties contest as they do in the United States, with one emerging victorious. As explained in chapter 4, some systems use multimember districts, electing three, four, or more legislators per district. The important distinction is that the voters base their choices on partisan considerations rather than focusing on the individual candidate, as Americans often do. If a party earns a majority of seats in the parliament, it selects a prime minister, who serves as head of "the government." In turn, the prime minister, with the approval of his party leadership, appoints members of the cabinet, each of whom serves as the head of an executive department, leading it according to the overall directives set by the prime minister and the cabinet. In collaboration with the cabinet (or, sometimes, regardless of the cabinet), the prime minister governs as long as he or she retains the confidence of a majority of the parliament. If no one party wins a majority of parliamentary seats, two or more parties form a coalition to produce a majority, with the leader of the largest party in the coalition usually becoming prime minister. Under such circumstances, policies are more likely to be negotiated compromises rather than a fulfillment of the promises of the leading party.

Elections must be held at regular intervals, usually four, five, or six years, but the prime minister can dissolve parliament and call for elections whenever it seems appropriate or if it would be strategically advantageous to maintain or strengthen his party's margins. Should the government and prime minister lose the support of a majority of the parliament, expressed by means of a "vote of no confidence" or the failure to pass a major bill, the prime minister dissolves parliament. Until then, the prime minister and the majority party or coalition essentially have a free hand. He knows, when proposing a bill to the legislature, that it will pass. When needed, party unity is virtually absolute and enforced by party discipline. Parliamentarians who vote against their party on key issues risk not being allowed to run under the party label next time, and they know that their careers in the party are in jeopardy. Major threats occur (a) when one or more of the coalition partners is willing to bring down the government by abandoning it or (b) when individual members of the majority decide that they simply cannot support their party. In some cases, internal rebellions replace a prime minister, but the party retains its parliamentary majority. This is the textbook, "Westminster," or British model of how parliamentary systems work; in reality, there are numerous variations.

Pros and Cons

Parliamentary governments are likely to score high on effectiveness and efficiency, but there are vulnerabilities. The sole constraint on the government is the electorate;

typically there are no institutions with the power of the U.S. Supreme Court, or no practices such as the U.S. Senate's filibuster, to check the majority. Accountability comes relatively easily because everyone knows which party or coalition of parties is in charge; it is easy to "throw the bums out." Because individual legislators have little power, they tend to be less able to be responsive in terms of "bringing home the bacon" or voting along with local preferences; what many of them spend time on is personalized constituency service, helping citizens handle problems with the bureaucracy. Citizens can participate in politics quite readily in their local party organizations, ideally bringing demographic and policy representation into the parties. In a presidential separation-of-powers system, the responsibility for reasoned decision making lies with both the executive and the legislative branches. In parliamentary systems, decision making tends to be concentrated in the cabinet; parliamentary sessions sometimes offer opportunities for discussion of pending issues. The primary function of parliament is found in the meaning of its root word, the French "*parler*," to talk or to speak. Parliaments are known for their debates, through which the public learns about political matters, and for their ability to challenge and hold prime ministers and cabinets accountable. Sessions of parliament can be rowdy affairs (especially at what the British call their "Question Hour," during which the prime minister responds to, or often ducks, charges from the opposition party or parties) or dull, poorly attended sessions in which the outcomes of votes are preordained. Depending on the nature of the committees of a parliament—typically not as strong as in the U.S. Congress—one can find policy discussion there. Generally, however, parliaments do not come close to what Americans have in Congress or state legislatures.

In parliamentary governments the prime minister heads the government, whereas the largely ceremonial function of head of state devolves on a king, queen, or elected president. In the U.S. presidential system, the president plays both roles, which carries its own complications and contradictions. How can he be the nonpartisan, nonpolitical head of state representing the nation and simultaneously lead his party in pushing a specific political agenda? In some hybrid systems, such as those in France and Russia, presidents hold real power and can dissolve parliament, decide which party among several will be asked to form a government, and/or hold diplomatic and national security authority.[2] In yet others, such as Iran, religious leaders hold the trump card while presidents and prime ministers struggle with each other.

Would a parliamentary system be preferable to the American presidential system? If beauty lies in the eye of the beholder, so surely does the superiority of a parliamentary or a presidential system. Driving one's judgment should be the values listed in chapter 1. Does one favor effectiveness, efficiency, and collective party accountability above other criteria? Then parliamentary democracy has the advantage. Is there greater concern with limited government and the individual accountability and responsiveness of legislators to their constituents? Then the implications of a parliamentary system would cause nightmares, and a separation-of-powers system would be more attractive.

There are two items to focus on: the fusion rather than separation of institutional powers and the nature of political parties. Parties are "responsible" in the sense that they clearly tell the voters what they intend to do and, if elected, carry out their pledges, asking voters to hold them accountable. Parties are "disciplined" in the sense that, on issues important to the party, parliamentary members fall in line behind their leadership—or else pay a price for bolting. The justifications for moving in the parliamentary direction, along with the reforms, will become clear in subsequent chapters; the focus here now turns to the vertical or geographical division of political power.[3]

2.2 A FLAG WITHOUT 50 STARS?—UNITARY GOVERNMENT RATHER THAN FEDERALISM

The other distinctive characteristic of American government is federalism, the division of sovereign power between the states and the federal government. Other countries have forms of federalism, but the particular division of powers between the central and regional governments varies from Chile to Russia to Canada to Switzerland. Over the centuries, American federalism has evolved from what textbooks variously refer to as "dual" or "layer-cake" federalism, in which states and the federal government dealt with separate matters and generally stayed out of each other's hair, to cooperative federalism, wherein both levels of government deal with many overlapping issues and engage in various degrees of cooperation and rivalry. The evolution continues as judicial rulings and governmental initiatives alter the political landscape. Politicians, scholars, and pundits question the degree to which states do and should cooperate with each other. Debates rage over the wisdom and practicality of revenue sharing, the arrangement whereby the federal government sends some of its funds—about $600 billion, or about 17 percent of federal spending—to the states, providing them with about a quarter of their revenues. More specifically, there is disagreement over which form of revenue sharing—categorical grants aimed at specific problems, such as school lunches or sewage systems, or block grants (large chunks of money aimed at broad problems like crime, housing, or environment)—is more effective and efficient. Difference of opinion also emerges over the usual requirement that states match a portion of federal grants because compliance can distort state and local priorities. Experts disagree on whether specific conditions ("strings") should be attached to grants to constrain or incentivize state and local officials to bring their actions into accord with national policies; whether giving money raised by senators and representatives to state officials who take credit for building bridges and highways blurs the lines of accountability; whether reliance on variable federal largess causes unpredictability in many state and local programs; and whether states depend too much on Washington.

What almost no one discusses is whether the very concept of federalism makes sense today. Consider the arguments in favor of those 50 stars in the flag.

- The United States is too big for a single unitary government, so decentralized political organization is necessary to facilitate effectiveness, efficiency, participation, and responsiveness.
- Federalism recognizes and celebrates the geographical, cultural, political, and ethnic diversity of America and thus is essential for a representative and responsive government.
- State governments are closer to the people, and local problems should be handled locally to maximize effectiveness, efficiency, responsiveness, representation, and accountability of government to the citizenry.

- Federalism allows and encourages experimentation and new programs, as seen in the records of California on pollution, Wisconsin on labor laws, Minnesota on nuclear safety, North Dakota, Minnesota, and Wisconsin on voter registration, and Massachusetts on health insurance.
- As Madison argued in *Federalist No. 51*, dispersal of political power geographically ensures moderation, sound judgment, and restrained public policy. Major policy breakthroughs require a national consensus or at least acquiescence, making it difficult for a single regional majority or interest group to dominate. Policy making is slower, giving citizens and a wide array of interest groups the chance for access and influence.

These arguments are simple, self-evidently true, and compelling. Or, come to think of it, are they?

Federalism Causes Problems

Size. Is size really a factor? One can fly from New York to San Diego in a fraction of the time the founding fathers needed for travel from New York to Philadelphia or Boston. Although those distances paralyzed government 200 years ago, they make no difference today. Communication is instant, easy, and universal. Geography matters not in professional sports or in marketing national brand merchandise. A Walmart or Target store is the same from coast to coast; each of them can tell you what you bought last week and send you ads and coupons for what it thinks you will buy next.

Diversity. Does any identifiable form of diversity (other than, perhaps, religion in Utah or college football loyalties everywhere) align with state boundaries? Do Americans think of themselves first as Vermonters, Georgians, Iowans, or Kansans and only then as Americans? Or are they Americans first and state residents second? Even if any reasonable aspect of diversity were to align with state or any other regional boundaries, there might be dangers in accommodating it. If what is a small group relative to the national population constituted a majority or significant minority in a state, it could enact and implement policies that violate or frustrate national policies as applied to the state. The lengthy and torturous path of civil rights legislation was the product of conservative southern senators from a dozen or so states. How is it that one state can provide easy access to abortions while the state next door enacts strict pro-life laws? Should state or regional dissenters carry the day against the national common good? Does accommodating diversity make sense with respect to such things as the definition of marriage, the drinking age, divorce laws, trucking regulations, prison terms, consumer and environmental protection, welfare payments and rules, educational standards, licensing for pharmacists, the death penalty, or regulation of insurance?

Suppose that accommodating regional diversities is in fact desirable; do federalism and state boundaries do the job? Not at all; state lines are more or less arbitrary and thus do not delineate meaningful geographical territories for the groups that constitute American diversity. State lines frequently divide what may be naturally homogeneous groups: southern Wisconsin and northern Illinois; North Dakota, South Dakota, and eastern Montana; east Texas and Louisiana; or north Texas and Oklahoma. One can point to just about anywhere on the map and find regional commonalities and subcultures split by state borders. Moreover, many state lines capture widely diverse groups. Florida and New York could each be three different states; Texas and California could be four or five.

Local Problems Solved Locally. Although local problems obviously should be handled locally, and although Americans have higher opinions of their state and local governments than of the federal government,[4] where do people look for help to control pollution, fight narcotics and terrorism, create jobs, and promote agriculture—or just about any major problem? What level of government stimulates more interest or attracts heavier voter turnout? Indeed, what is a "local" problem that calls for a local solution? Many so-called local problems are in fact common nationwide problems that merely appear locally but require coordinated national solutions: air and water pollution, health care, poverty, transportation, energy, and education. States are not local in the same sense as neighborhoods, cities, or counties; yet states hold life-or-death authority over these units of government. Many state laws actually prevent local governments from dealing with local problems as they think best. Terms of police chiefs, control of a city's ability to incorporate surrounding towns and villages within the city (the power of annexation), mandatory roadway standards, school zone speed limits, regulations of school boards, local tax policies, and many other matters are regulated by legislators and executives in state capitals—frustrating local self-government, pressuring their treasuries, and preventing flexibility.

Boundary lines sometimes cut through otherwise coherent metropolitan areas, confounding local solutions to local problems. Consider the two Kansas Cities or, in somewhat broader terms, New York and some of its New Jersey suburbs; Augusta, Georgia, and North Augusta, South Carolina; St. Louis, Missouri, and East St. Louis, Illinois; Superior, Wisconsin, and Duluth, Minnesota; or Fargo, North Dakota, and Moorhead, Minnesota. These border anomalies have produced some interesting stories, such as the case of the farmer whose property included pieces of Colorado and Nebraska and who was forbidden by Nebraska law to pump water from a well in Nebraska to irrigate his crops located in Colorado.[5]

Laboratories of Democracy. Federalism allows and encourages experimentation with new program initiatives and policy implementation, but this is not an unmixed blessing. Experimental policies can harm innocent people or prevent coordination across states. For example, more than half the states exceed federal standards for proving eligibility to vote, perhaps depressing turnout among poor minority citizens and the elderly. Some states pass laws to frustrate federal gun control policies. A few states, claiming that the federal government has failed to implement immigration controls, established their own policies. Alabama and Arizona, for example, allowed police and school officials to question suspected illegal immigrants, scaring legal immigrants, causing many minority students in Alabama to stop going to schools, and inducing immigrant workers to flee to other states. Sometimes, when one state reduces welfare support, another state may become relatively attractive, causing residents of the former state to migrate to the latter.[6] Experimentation and innovation are important, but there is no reason why the federal government cannot run controlled policy experiments, holding constant different variables, even comparing regions to each other. Indeed, such has been the case in many areas, such as the Obama administration's "Race to the Top" program that encourages states to compete to produce the greatest improvements in student test scores and teacher assessment, thus developing programs to be replicated nationwide.

Moderation versus Efficiency. It is likewise true that federalism brings moderation, slowness, and safety into the political arena—if only because, before tackling a problem, decision makers must decide which level of government will do so and bear the costs. The benefits of moderation come at the cost of effectiveness and efficiency. This country is blessed, or cursed, with 51 separate sovereign taxing authorities, school systems, highway departments, agriculture departments, health and welfare systems, consumer protection agencies, and so on—not counting those in the U.S. territories and possessions. State autonomy works at cross purposes with Washington: in a recession, the national government pursues an expansionary Keynesian strategy, reducing taxes and increasing spending to stimulate the economy. Many states, however, are constitutionally or legally bound to protect themselves by doing just the opposite so as not to run in the red. Federalism's inefficiencies exact significant costs from American taxpayers.[7]

Consider trade policy. Instead of acting as a single American entity, each of the 50 states seeks to win foreign contracts, investments, even the Olympics—undercutting each other and, sometimes, the national interest. Or take the tax system. The progressivity of the national tax structure is undermined by flat, less progressive, or regressive state income, sales, and property taxes. Then there is the pork barrel. To pass almost any program in Congress, representatives and senators insist on "something" for their districts and states; unless benefits are widely distributed, not much can be accomplished. Then follow battles over the formulas or bureaucratic decisions that distribute federal money, all stimulated and supported by heavy and costly lobbying by governors, mayors, and other state and local officials and their lobbyists in Washington. The notion of state governments' having to spend taxpayer funds to get Washington to send some other taxpayers' money back to their states might strike some as bizarre.

The examples make for fun reading. The Montana Housing Authority has little public housing to construct or manage, but the agency remains in business, seeking federal funds—$2,603,000 in 2015—that are said to do little more than keep the program operational from year to year.[8] Federal funding for poor school districts often goes to wealthy school districts as well; more than two in three school districts nationwide receive "antipoverty" money.[9] Antiterrorism legislation was drafted to send 90 percent of the funding to communities in the greatest danger, but the Senate in 2005 chose to divide the money differently. Thus, on a per capita basis, Wyoming got more money than New York! The 2009 federal fiscal stimulus legislation allocated funding strangely. In 2010, Alaska got $1,718 per capita, South Dakota $1,123, Montana $1,128, Vermont $1,320, and North Dakota $1,164—amounts exceeding those for many more populous and troubled states. Never mind that these five states had jobless rates below, and three of them well below, the national average.[10]

State interests conflict with national ones. Despite a nationwide need for energy, some states tried to block federal oil and gas leasing and offshore oil drilling programs, first by banning them and later by taxing or imposing heavy liability burdens. Under pressure from states, Congress gave them the right to veto decisions regarding nuclear waste disposal. Thus, in February 2011, New York, Connecticut, and Vermont sued the Nuclear Regulatory Commission over the NRC's ruling that would allow storage of nuclear fuel waste at a power plant site for 60 years.[11] Nevada went so far as to create a new county ("Bullfrog") with no people but high taxes to discourage the United States from choosing that open land as a nuclear waste dump.[12]

Defense and national security are not immune. Colorado sued the United States over placement of MX missiles in Nebraska and Wyoming to prevent a "negative environmental impact" on Colorado.[13] Colorado also has aggressively resisted the federal government on coal mining and storage of nerve gas.[14] Nevada passed laws to prevent the government from burying chemical weapons there.[15] Alaska sued in 1987 to block shipments of plutonium from Europe to Japan from crossing Alaskan land and air space.[16] In 2004 Alaska skirted an Environmental Protection Agency rule by allowing a company to use less effective antipollution equipment.[17]

States go after each other, using antiunion laws and low taxes to lure industry from others, sometimes in strange ways. The Briggs and Stratton Corporation was lured from Milwaukee to Missouri using a federal grant. Given the shares of state-generated income that went to Washington, it is likely that the grant was financed more by Wisconsin than by Missouri taxpayers![18] Kansas and Missouri for years have enacted tax breaks and other incentives to steal businesses from each other; only recently has the possibility of a truce emerged.[19] According to one count, states, cities, and counties annually provide more than $80 billion in incentives to lure businesses from one location to another.[20] A perennial bone of contention is the precise location of state boundary lines because those borders can mean money. New Hampshire and Maine have long squabbled over water rights for lobster fishing and over ownership of Seavey Island in the Piscataqua River, where the Portsmouth Naval Shipyard is located. The conflict concerned which state could tax the workers on the island.[21] South Carolina and Georgia feuded over control of border marshlands that were eligible for up to $1.3 billion in federal aid and which, at the time, were thought possibly to contain oil.[22] Mississippi has battled with Louisiana concerning "Stack Island" in the Mississippi River, real estate that a shift in the course of the river pushed to the Louisiana shore.[23] States regularly try to prevent others from dumping garbage in their landfills.

Nebraska, fearing a drop in the water table to which South Dakota had access, sued South Dakota over water it sold to Wyoming to make coal slurry for transport elsewhere. Colorado sued Wyoming for seeding clouds to prevent it from "stealing" water that might have fallen in Colorado.[24] New Jersey recently fought Pennsylvania's efforts to dredge the Delaware River, but Pennsylvania won out.[25] Florida sued to stop Georgia from restricting the flow of water from two Georgia rivers into Apalachicola Bay because restrictions deprived the bay of fresh water and thus harmed the oyster industry.[26] New Hampshire sought unsuccessfully to ban the sale of electricity generated within its boundaries to other states.[27] Although most of these rivalries are settled by the Supreme Court, the time and money wasted, the inconvenience suffered by citizens, and the frustration of sensible and fair nationwide policies surely violate the effectiveness and efficiency principles; and they call into question whether reasoned decision making is being served by the consequences of federalism.

Other Consequences. Federalism's impact extends more broadly. The Electoral College system of electing presidents, like the Senate, is built on the federal foundation. Allocations of delegates to the Democratic and Republican national conventions every four years are based on state population and measures of states' loyalties to the parties. Federal law providing funding for presidential primary election campaigns reflects state-by-state allocations; indeed, American political parties have always been for the most part state parties, not national ones. The way Americans vote—ballot form, type of voting machine, procedures for nominating candidates, registration— and the ways in which ballots are or are not counted are determined by state and local laws and administration, not by a national authority. Thus election results can differ solely because of the state's electoral mechanics. The judiciary is forced to spend a good deal of its limited and valuable time refereeing jurisdictional squabbles among states and between the states and Washington.

It is easy to dismiss the above arguments. They hardly counter the reality that a continental nation as complex as the United States cannot be governed from one city on the East Coast. Of course it cannot! That does not mean, however, that a federal system, or at least one that runs like the current system, is the ideal arrangement. What might abolition of the existing federal system mean?

Can Federalism Be Fixed?

Truly *local* government is essential, but it is possible to have both a strong central government and strong local governments without granting sovereignty to those local units and without current borders. Sovereign intermediary government, states, are not necessary, as seen in the way most countries arrange their governmental systems. Localities can be and are granted measures of home rule for truly local matters, allowing them considerable taxing and spending authority. The national government undoubtedly needs some regional pattern of *administration*; the upper Midwest is different from the coasts, just as the Gulf south differs from the Rocky Mountains. There must be some flexibility in how national laws are applied to different geographical areas (forests and deserts, land and lakes, terrain that facilitates and inhibits rail lines and highways, producing and consuming regions of energy, and so on). Indeed, that already is the case; federal government regional administration offices are found across the land, and administrators do take into consideration regional needs and differences. Such regional administrative units, however, just like local governments, need not be sovereign; they easily could function with a *measure* of independence while being subject to national policy directives.

It is tempting, in summary, to imagine that combining central policy making with regional administrative flexibility and local self-government, perhaps held together and led by a parliamentary form of government, would in many ways make American government more effective, efficient, accountable, representative, responsive, reasonably and appropriately deliberative, and participatory while guarding rights and liberties. The Senate could be abolished. Nebraska, after all, has a one-house legislature, and the state survives quite well. In many parliamentary democracies, the upper house has no substantial legislative power. If a bicameral legislature were desired, it could be fashioned as is now done in the states, with each upper-chamber district consisting of three or four contiguous lower-chamber districts. Without states, there would be no Electoral College, so another means of electing presidents would be needed—unless, of course, there were a parliamentary rather than the presidential separation-of-powers system. There would be other consequences as well, but they are hard to predict.[28]

2.3 IMPLICATIONS

It does not take a genius to realize that neither of these changes, switching to parliamentary government or abolishing federalism, is remotely possible under the U.S. Constitution. Nonetheless, reformers have been inspired by the ideas and turned to other means of linking Congress and the presidency and of improving federal–state interactions. Many of the first group will be discussed in later chapters, but for now consider several alterations to the way American federalism is conducted. A serious one, almost as significant as abolition of federalism, would be to reverse the allocation of powers, as is the case in Canada: specify in the Constitution the powers of the states, reserving the remainder to the central government. This would give Washington much greater authority to impose national laws, rules, and norms on the country and avoid many of the roadblocks that states throw up against the federal government. Another, seen, for example, in the Basque country and Catalonia of Spain, the Aceh territory in Indonesia, and in other lands, is the combination of strong central government with considerable nonsovereign regional autonomy. Catalonia is not sovereign but it does enjoy measures of independence from Madrid on certain matters—a sort of hybrid of the unitary and federal systems.

One scholar suggested a novel way to impose national standards on the entire country, obliterating many state policies and rules. The argument is that Congress possesses the authority to enforce the Fourteenth Amendment provisions guaranteeing the equal protection of the laws and ensuring "due process of law" for any taking of life, liberty, or property. Accordingly, Congress could impose the Federal Rules of Civil Procedure, and other provisions of law, on state judicial systems and perhaps on legislatures to ensure such equality and due process.[29] Thus far, few reformers have jumped on this bandwagon; more importantly, the Supreme Court trimmed back congressional authority to enforce the Fourteenth Amendment in a 1997 case, rendering this scheme inoperable.[30]

At a lower and more likely level of reform, more could be done to facilitate and encourage interstate compacts that foster cooperation and standardization across state borders by means of generous federal funding to support them. Tunneling under the Hudson River, building bridges across the Mississippi or Delaware River, merging water or sewage systems, and the like require funds that states often do not have. Revenue sharing—if only the federal government had excess revenue to share!—could be enhanced, always with serious strings attached to coax states into cooperative compliance with national policies and standards. Improved central government mechanisms for sharing information and policy ideas with and among the states, over and above what the National Conference of State Legislatures and the National Governors Association do, might help the spread of innovation and combat the proliferation of different, sometimes contradictory, programs and policies. All would be costly.

Fundamental reform is a pipe dream. Short of enacting a new constitution, the states will not disappear; the constitutional provisions giving states a veto on their demise prevents that. There will be no merger of the presidency with Congress to form a parliamentary system. Nonetheless, a radical look at what is too often blindly accepted highlights issues and provides context and a guiding star for less radical but serious reform proposals that follow in subsequent chapters, many of which will remind the reader of this chapter.

QUESTIONS TO CONSIDER

1. Given your priorities among the seven criteria for good democratic government, which system of government—parliamentary fusion of powers or the U.S. separation of powers—would be preferable?
2. Short of amending the Constitution, what reforms might move the current American system of government closer to the parliamentary model?
3. Should the states be abolished, creating a unitary sovereign government? Why or why not?

NOTES

1. Sanford Levinson, "Our Imbecilic Constitution," *New York Times*, May 29, 2012: A21. See his *Our Undemocratic Constitution: Where the Constitution Goes Wrong (and How We the People Can Correct It)* (Oxford: Oxford University Press, 2006).
2. Elijah Ben-Zion Kaminsky, "On the Comparison of Presidential and Parliamentary Governments," *Presidential Studies Quarterly* 27 (1997): 221–28.
3. See Joy E. Esberey, "What If There Were a Parliamentary System?" In Herbert M. Levine et al., *What If the American Political System Were Different?* (Armonk, NY: Sharpe, 1992), chap. 5.
4. "Growing Gap in Favorable Views of Federal, State Governments," Pew Research Center (April 26, 2012), http://pewresearch.org/pubs/2252/federal-state-local-government/.
5. Eventually the U.S. Supreme Court intervened. *Sporhase v. Nebraska*, 458 U.S. 941 (1982).
6. Michael A. Bailey, "Welfare Migration and the Multifaceted Decision to Move," *American Political Science Review* 99 (2005): 125–35.
7. Jonathan Rodden and Erik Wibbels, "Fiscal Decentralization and the Business Cycle: An Empirical Study of Seven Federations," *Economics & Politics* 22 (2010): 37–67.
8. Shantae Goodloe, "HUD Awards $1.8 Billion to Improve, Preserve Nation's Public Housing," U.S. Department of Housing and Urban Development No. 15-017, http://portal.hud.gov/hudportal/HUD?src=/press/press_releases_media_advisories/2015/HUDNo_15-017
9. U.S. Department of Education, *Fact Sheet on Title I, Part A*, August 2002, http://www.ed.gov/rschstat/eval/disadv/title1-factsheet.doc/.
10. Matthew Bandyk, "The Stimulus: States Getting the Most Money So Far," *US News and World Report*, February 22, 2010, http://money.usnews.com/money/business-economy/articles/2010/02/22/the-stimulus-states-getting-the-most-money-so-far/.
11. Matthew L. Wald, "3 States Challenge Federal Policy on Storing Nuclear Waste," *New York Times*, February 16, 2011: A26.
12. Thomas J. Knudson, "Bullfrog County, Nev., (Pop. 0) Fights Growth," *New York Times*, August 30, 1987: 30.
13. *Romer v. Carlucci*, 18 ELR 21092.

14. Bruce Finley, "Colorado Coal Miners Fear Losing Jobs If Access to Federal Lands Curbed," *Denver Post*, January 17, 2010, http://www.denverpost.com/ci_14208902/.

15. Matthew L. Wald, "Japan Nuclear Crisis Revives Long U.S. Fight on Spent Fuel," *New York Times*, March 24, 2011: A1.

16. "Business Digest: Friday December 18, 1987," *New York Times*, December 18, 1987: D1.

17. *Alaska Dept. of Environmental Conserv. v. Environmental Protection Agency et al.*, 540 U.S. 461 (2004).

18. Julio V. Cano, "Block Grant Angers Briggs Workers, Local Groups," *Milwaukee Sentinel*, April 10, 1994: 3.

19. John Eligon, "Governor Calls for End to Contest of Incentives," *New York Times*, November 13, 2013: A21.

20. *New York Times*, December 11, 2013: A14.

21. Linda Greenhouse, "Supreme Court Roundup; Border Dispute Will Get a Hearing," *New York Times*, June 30, 2000, http://www.nytimes.com/2000/06/30/us/supreme-court-roundup-border-dispute-will-get-a-hearing.html/.

22. "S.C.–Georgia Border Dispute Continues," *The Times-News* (Hendersonville, North Carolina), May 11, 1977: 3.

23. Linda Greenhouse, "Supreme Court Awards Island to Mississippi," *New York Times*, November 1, 1995, http://www.nytimes.com/1995/11/01/us/supreme-court-awards-island-to-mississippi.html/.

24. Charles Duhigg, "Clean Water Laws Are Neglected, at a Cost in Suffering," *New York Times*, September 12, 2009: A1.

25. Linda Loyd, "Pennsylvania Officials Celebrate Continued Delaware Dredging," *Philadelphia Inquirer*, August 9, 2012, http://articles.philly.com/2012-08-09/business/33101383_1_delaware-river-river-channel-corbett/.

26. Arian Campo-Flores, "Florida Sues Georgia over Water Use," *Wall Street Journal*, October 2, 2013: A2.

27. *New England Power Co. v. New Hampshire*, The Oyez Project at IIT Chicago–Kent College of Law, August 24, 2012, http://www.oyez.org/cases/1980-1989/1981/1981_80_1208/.

28. For speculations, see Thomas H. Ferrell, "What If There Were a Unitary Rather Than a Federal System?" in Levine, *What If the American Political System Were Different?*, chap. 2.

29. George Richard Poehner, "Fourteenth Amendment Enforcement and Congressional Power to Abolish the States," *California Law Review* 55 (1967): 293–317.

30. *City of Boerne v. Flores*, 521 U.S. 507 (1997).

CHAPTER 3

✌

The People's Role

A dependence on the people is, no doubt, the primary control on the government.

—JAMES MADISON, *The Federalist No. 51*

The people should have as little to do as may be about the government. They lack information and are constantly liable to be misled.

—ROGER SHERMAN,
Madison's Notes of Debates in the Federal Convention

The heart of the political system is the citizen, whose acquiescence, demonstrated especially in the electoral process, constitutes the "consent of the governed" that gives legitimacy to government. Participation in elections is essential for accountability, responsiveness, and representation. It follows that the electoral process should be inclusive of adult citizens; fairly, efficiently, and honestly run; free from unreasonable restrictions; and competitive. Votes should be counted accurately; they should determine representation in the elected branches of the government; and those elected should govern in reasonable correspondence with the wishes of the voters who selected them. Reality does not always square with these traits. As Richard L. Hasen characterized it, the United States has a "convoluted, contradictory, partisan, decentralized mess" of an election system.[1] This chapter explores these issues with an eye to the reforms that would advance participation, responsiveness, accountability, and representation.

3.1 THE PROBLEM: LOW TURNOUT AND PARTICIPATION

The record of voting turnout has not been sterling, with about 60 percent of eligible voters casting ballots in recent presidential elections and 40 percent in midterm congressional balloting. Turnout for special elections and primaries is miserable, often in the teens. Such was not always the case; in the latter half of the nineteenth century, turnout for presidential elections was in the 70 to 80 percent range. Interestingly, that period preceded universal suffrage and the Progressive Era reforms such as the Australian secret ballot (on which the names of all candidates were arrayed on a government-produced document), primary elections, and voting registration. It seems that whenever the franchise expanded, turnout rates dropped. Measuring turnout, however, is far from a precise exercise. The numerator of the fraction, those actually voting, varies according to whether all ballots are properly cast and counted. The denominator usually is the number of age-eligible people, but of course not all age-eligible residents may participate. One must be a citizen; and in many states felons may not vote, at least those still incarcerated. Turnout in the late 1800s was boosted by political machines that were not above cheating to boost the numerator; the suffrage (denominator) was more limited; and perhaps politics meant more to people. Turnout as a percentage of *registered* voters is notably higher than the numbers commonly reported, perhaps as much as 80 percent.[2] Three questions are worth asking: (1) Why don't more people vote? (2) What difference does it make? (3) Assuming that something should be done about it, what is that "something"?

Why Don't They Vote?

For the first question, the Census Bureau's Current Population Surveys provide answers, as shown in Table 3.1, but one must read these data with a skeptical eye, given the tendency of people to rationalize their behavior. Roughly half of those surveyed claimed that they failed to vote because of barriers or circumstances, whereas at least a third point fingers at themselves (refusals to answer and "don't know" responses probably fall into that category as well). Not surprisingly, the elderly are far more likely to cite disabilities, whereas younger, better-educated, and wealthier people are more likely to be out of town or to report scheduling conflicts, presumably because of business or school commitments.

Does It Matter?

This second question is more consequential. First, low turnout may signal a threat to the system's legitimacy. Bumper stickers that proclaim "Don't blame me; I voted for [whichever candidate lost]" are familiar. If many said "Don't blame me; I didn't vote," it would speak volumes. Low participation, it is asserted, rips the civic fabric, leading citizens to question the efficacy of the ballot box; and low rates in several sequential elections can be insidious because voting and political participation seem to be acquired habits: the more one does, the more one is likely to do.[3]

Second, nonvoting creates a potential for bias in representativeness, responsiveness, and accountability. Turnout has an upper- and middle-class bias; marginalized groups—the homeless, the disabled, language minorities—tend not to vote and thus are less well represented in Washington. There are implications. Strong turnout signals to legislators that constituents are watching; higher rates of voting among particular constituency groups send messages to members of Congress, leading to enhanced responsiveness to them on policy issues and to more federal funding in those districts and states.[4] According to a Task Force on Inequality and American Democracy of the American Political Science Association in 2004,

> The privileged participate more than others and are increasingly well organized to press their demands on government. Public officials, in turn, are much more responsive to the privileged than to average citizens and the least affluent. Citizens

Table 3.1 Reasons for Not Voting among Registered Voters (percentage giving answer): 2000–2012

	ELIGIBILITY	SITUATIONAL REASONS: CIRCUMSTANCES LARGELY BEYOND ONE'S CONTROL						PERSONAL REASONS			
YEAR	REGISTRATION PROBLEMS	TOO BUSY, CONFLICTING SCHEDULE	ILLNESS OR DISABILITY	OUT OF TOWN	TRANSPORTATION PROBLEM	BAD WEATHER	INCONVENIENT POLLING PLACE	NOT INTERESTED	DID NOT LIKE CANDIDATES OR CAMPAIGN ISSUES	FORGOT TO VOTE	OTHER, DON'T KNOW, REFUSED
2012	6	19	14	9	3	1	1	16	13	4	14
2010	3	27	11	9	3	*	2	16	9	8	12
2008	6	18	15	9	3	*	3	13	13	3	18
2006	4	27	12	11	2	1	3	12	7	6	16
2004	7	20	15	9	2	1	3	11	10	3	9
2000	7	21	15	10	2	1	3	12	8	4	18

REASONS GIVEN

* Less than 0.5%.

Note: Row totals may not equal 100 percent because of rounding.

Source: U.S. Census, Current Population Survey, "Voting and Registration": http://www.census.gov/hhes/www/socdemo/voting/publications/p20/index.html/.

with lower or moderate incomes speak with a whisper that is lost on the ears of inattentive government officials, while the advantaged roar with a clarity and consistency that policymakers readily hear and routinely follow.[5]

The obvious conclusion is that turnout must be enhanced. Voting is a right that should not face roadblocks; reforms are in order.

Not so fast, skeptics reply; low turnout really does not matter much, if at all; and it certainly does not call for major reforms.[6] Don't people have a right to abstain from periodic treks to the polling places? And why, after all, should someone vote? Voting involves effort and time; there may be a dozen more interesting or rewarding things to do on election days. Does it make sense to take time off from jobs, from school, or from whatever else citizens deem important to travel to the polls to cast a ballot that is almost certain not to make a difference? Few elections turn on margins narrow enough that higher turnout would matter; more importantly, when surveyed, nonvoters frequently report that they would have voted for the winner.[7] Of course there are "close call" exceptions, such as the 2000 presidential election results in Florida, when George W. Bush and Al Gore battled to a virtual tie; the 2008 Coleman–Franken senatorial race in Minnesota; the 1985 four-vote margin in the Indiana congressional election that caused the U.S. House of Representatives to determine which candidate to seat; and the 167 vote margin in the second congressional district in Arizona in 2014. None of these results depended on any single vote. In some state and several local elections (e.g., for a town's sheriff), razor-thin margins or tie votes are a bit more common, often featuring humorous accounts such as the spouse of a candidate who forgot to vote, costing the candidate the election. But these examples truly are rare.

Not voting might be a form of tacit approval of current policies and politicians, in effect constituting a low-turnout vote for the status quo that, paradoxically, could give the forces of change a better shot at winning. The important question is whether greater turnout elects different candidates. Although nonvoters lately tend more in liberal and Democratic directions and generally favor a more activist government, on many policy preferences they resemble voters. Depending on the election year there are or are not significant differences in terms of candidate preference.[8] Short-term electoral forces such as issues and candidates drive turnout. "The candidate who benefits from turnout will be the one favored by the electoral mood, whether the candidate is a Democrat or a Republican. The effect is strongest on the most uninvolved and marginally interested voters."[9] Voters and nonvoters do differ in terms of intensity of their interest in elections and government, but that difference is more likely to matter in extremely low-turnout contests.

Encouraging more voters to participate necessitates more poll workers, ballots, and voting machines. It could be dangerous and destabilizing if some current short-term issue or crisis stimulated huge numbers of disinterested and ill-informed citizens who perhaps could more easily be swayed by misleading campaign ads, superficial candidate attractiveness, or emotional appeals to vote.[10] Increasing the voting population might encourage congressional candidates to "dumb down" and oversimplify their messages even further. Can smaller be as good, or better? After all, the U.S. governmental system was not designed as a democracy but rather as a representative republic, with limited suffrage.

3.2 ENHANCING PARTICIPATION: PROBLEMS AND REFORMS

Assuming that nonvoting is a problem and that higher participation rates are desirable, what can be done? Reforms must address three categories of causes: (1) registration issues that can prevent one from voting; (2) situational factors that make voting difficult; and (3) personal decisions not to vote.

Registration Limits Participation

Registration is the gateway to voting. It helps to prevent fraud; it structures the election process, making sure people know in which ward or precinct to vote; and it facilitates party efforts to identify and mobilize voters. One cannot vote if not registered. The Pew Center on the States reported that at least 51 million eligible citizens remained unregistered in 2012, almost a quarter of the eligible population.[11] According to the Census Bureau, roughly half of them said they failed to register because they were not interested; 15 percent failed to meet deadlines; 12 percent said they were not eligible; and 4 percent believed that voting makes no difference. Skeptics wonder whether they would vote even if registered. There are two problems: difficulty in registering and accurate registration lists.

Problems in Registering. Traditionally, one registered in person, well in advance of an election. Under a 1972 Supreme Court ruling, states cannot set final registration dates more than 30 days before an election. Because county or municipal registration offices sometimes are inconveniently located and tend to work on standard business hours, registration requirements hit some groups harder than others: low-income, low-education, and low-interest citizens. Moreover, changing residences from one jurisdiction to another requires new registration, and even the most political of citizens get sidetracked with the relocation.

States can make registration difficult in a variety of ways, such as requiring various types of identification or putting restrictions on groups involved in registration outreach. How these affect voting participation is unclear. Florida, for example, in 2011 enacted legislation, subsequently overturned by a federal judge, requiring groups that undertake voter registration drives to submit completed registration forms within 48 hours of sign-ups—similar to new Illinois rules. This reportedly caused the League of Women Voters and other organizations to stop their efforts and dissuaded still others, such as Rock the Vote, from its efforts. Although causality is hard to prove because of other factors affecting decisions to register, in 2012 registrations fell.

Faulty Registration Lists. It often happens that a registered voter walks into a polling place only to learn that her name is not on the list. Perhaps she missed voting in several successive elections and her name was purged; maybe she failed to complete the registration process or did it incorrectly; or there might have been an error in the paper-based registration systems still used in most locations. According to the Caltech/MIT Voting Technology Project Report in 2001, as many as 3 million voters in 2000 were ruled ineligible because of registration mishaps and snafus. Keeping registration records is not an exact science—there are more than 130 million registrations spread over almost 9,000 voting jurisdictions—and errors are common. The Pew Research Center reported that more than 1.8 million deceased individuals were listed as voters in 2011; roughly 2.75 million people were registered to vote in more than one state; and about 12 million records have incorrect addresses.[12] A more recent estimate puts invalid registrations at 8 percent (16 million) of all registrations; in some states the figure rises to 15 percent.[13]

Tearing Down Registration Barriers

Accurate Registration Lists. The 1993 National Voter Registration Act (NVRA) required states to maintain current lists and issued standards for doing so. The 2002 Help America Vote Act (HAVA) went further, requiring that each state implement a single, centralized, interactive computerized voter registration list. As with other HAVA mandates, such as requiring first-time voters who registered by mail to show identification when voting, this one has not worked to perfection. The 2014 report of the Presidential Commission on Election Administration noted that one weakness has been a lack of coordination of state lists. Currently there are at least two possibilities. The Interstate Voter Registration Crosscheck Program helps 29 states to exchange voting data to cull duplicative registrations and enables law enforcement to pursue people engaged in double voting. The Electronic Registration Information Center, involving 7 states, allows voter registration lists to be checked against other government lists (e.g., Social Security or Postal Service) to account for moves, deaths, and name changes. Both have been successful in cleaning up registration lists, preventing errors, and eliminating fraud possibilities.[14] For example, North Carolina searched 27 state databases and found more than 700 of its voters had the same names, birth dates, and last four social security number digits as individuals who voted in other states. Some 81 deceased citizens were recorded as having voted.[15]

States have sought to "purge" their lists to remove deceased and incarcerated citizens, those who have left their election jurisdictions, and others who have not demonstrated eligibility. Doing so can be complex and potentially unfair, as Florida learned in 2000 when the state hired an outside firm to eliminate felons from registration lists. The firm made numerous errors, stripping from registration lists many perfectly eligible voters. Again in 2012, Florida launched an effort to remove suspected noncitizens, but it quickly discovered that the lists of such ineligible voters themselves were inaccurate. The state obtained a database of noncitizen residents from the U.S. Department of Homeland Security, the Systematic Alien Verification for Entitlements—a far more authoritative list than drivers' license records that Florida had been using. By the time Florida was ready to move, federal courts stopped it, ruling that the purge would have fallen within the 90-day "no change" period preceding an election. Ohio in 2008 witnessed purge-related legal battles trying to get the secretary of state to reveal mismatches between voting lists and motor vehicle records. It is safe to anticipate similar incidents in the future.

Provisional Ballots. HAVA allowed voters who thought they were registered but did not appear on voting lists to cast provisional ballots that are not counted till the voters' eligibility had been subsequently established. The reform's effectiveness has been uneven. Provisional ballots, like absentee mail ballots, are often tossed out if they could not have any bearing on the outcome; and verification of eligibility to vote can create a headache for election administrators. In addition, many voters simply do not follow up to prove that they were in fact eligible. Rejection of provisional ballots varied greatly in 2008, ranging from 2 to 3 percent in Arizona and Montana to 84 percent in Delaware. Not surprisingly, states that are generous in giving out provisional ballots are least likely to reject them. To facilitate registration and voting, the U.S. Election Assistance Commission was established, and a number of private organizations, such as Common Cause, are active as well.

Registering Felons. One reform already adopted by more than 20 states is to restore voting rights to convicted felons who have completed their debt to society and are out of prison. The Democracy Restoration Act has been introduced in Congress and has been endorsed by the Attorney General. Supporters see it as a way to strengthen democracy, advance civil rights of minorities (the majority of prisoners), give former convicts a stake in their society, simplify the maintenance of accurate registration lists, and add about 4 percentage points to the total of registered voters—if all of them registered. Opponents claim that there is no constitutional authority for Congress to overturn state laws unless restrictions on voting are judged to violate the Fourteenth or Fifteenth Amendments, which does not seem to be the case. They also argue that loss of the franchise is an appropriate punishment.

Easier Registration Procedures. Other possibilities are to lengthen the period for registration, keep election offices open longer and at more convenient times—although that would incur costs—and reduce the negative effects of residential mobility. The latter can be addressed, as Minnesota mandated in 2008, by automatically updating voter registration lists with data from the U.S. Postal Service whenever people change addresses—much as the military has done when its members are transferred from one base to another. The numbers in Minnesota, of course, are much smaller than what the Postal Service might face on a national basis. Colleges and universities could increase existing cooperative efforts with local election commissions to register students as local voters or to help them secure absentee ballots to vote in their home jurisdictions.

Past reforms could be extended. The National Voter Registration Act of 1993 (NVRA), known as the "Motor Voter" law, sought to implement a mandatory federally designed registration form for use in various government offices, especially state Departments of Motor Vehicles (DMV) that issue drivers' licenses and official state identification cards. The idea was that when any person comes into contact with a state DMV, state or federal public assistance office, or military recruiting center, he or she would be provided with registration materials and given an opportunity to register. The record of DMV compliance is mixed, according to the 2014 Presidential Commission report; some have failed to implement the law aggressively or experienced glitches in transferring data to local election commissions. Opponents of Motor Voter see dangers in this approach and would have a field day if such efforts produced inconsistencies, faulty records, partisan intimidation, or fraud. Oregon, in March 2014, went a step farther. A new law provides that citizens who dealt with the state's Driver and Motor Vehicle Services Division since 2013 will automatically receive a ballot at least three weeks before the next election, potentially adding 300,000 voters to the rolls.

Some commentators, concerned that young Americans fail to register, have suggested the implementation of a "preregistration" for teenagers, probably best linked to obtaining a driver's permit. On their 18th birthdays they would receive a registration card in the mail or some other reminder via social media. California, Hawaii,

Louisiana, Maine, Massachusetts, and Oregon offer some version of this service or have recently enacted legislation to do so.

Mail and Online Registration. Registration by mail was another reform contained in the 1993 NVRA law; and by 1997 the Federal Election Commission reported that 45 states had some form of mail registration. It has been extended to online Internet registration, used fully or partly by 20 states and enacted in 4 others as of late 2014.[16] These are potentially more efficacious and efficient than facilitating in-person registration, but there are negatives: costs that many localities cannot afford, issues of certification to verify eligibility, uneven access to computers, and the problem of fraud—ensuring that the person making the application is who he or she claims to be.

Election-Day Registration. The least burdensome and potentially most effective reform is election-day (EDR) or same-day registration, a practice used or enacted, permanently or on a pilot basis, in Idaho, Wyoming, Wisconsin, Minnesota, Maine, Montana, New Hampshire, Iowa, California, Connecticut, Colorado, Hawaii, Illinois, Utah, and the District of Columbia. Interestingly, these states had high levels of voter registration and turnout before adopting EDR.[17] Eight others enable voters who have changed addresses within the state to *switch* registration at the polling places. North Dakota tops all these schemes: voters are not required to register at all!

On the negative side, a crush of new registrants could lead to longer waiting times and lines and carries with it the potential for cheating. Such dangers are minimized by requiring identification that links the potential registrant to the state or electoral district, but even that can be problematic; having a utility bill with a name and address on it does not necessarily prove one's permanent residency. Segregating questionable EDR registrations until they can be verified takes time and effort, potentially delaying the final balloting results. Finally, there is the remote possibility that making EDR available could spur last-minute voting by citizens who know and care little about the election itself.[18]

Universal Registration. The United States could follow the lead of other democracies and adopt automatic permanent universal registration. Instead of citizens having to register, the responsibility would shift to states or possibly the federal government. With registration good for a lifetime, at least for federal elections, and assuming that registration could be certified whenever people move or change names, something like 50 million people become eligible voters. Generating registration lists from census data, social security data, drivers' license data, postal records, and income tax returns would do the trick, although it raises privacy and security concerns; and the cost and especially the complexities involved are not trivial.

Will Registration Reforms Increase Turnout?

Easing registration *should* produce more voters. A classic study of the late 1970s suggested that if all states had the registration systems of the most accommodating states, turnout would have increased by perhaps 8 to 10 percentage points.[19] One might be skeptical. It is possible that those who must exert themselves to register are more likely to take voting seriously and go to the polls. Indeed, registration is dramatically easier than it was then, yet turnout over time barely seems to budge.

The effects of the 1993 NVRA and earlier state Motor Voter–type laws have not been impressive. The Federal Election Commission estimated that *registration* in 1996 increased only 2 percent over 1992, with the DMV portion of NVRA apparently accounting for about a third of that gain. *Turnout* in 1996, however, actually *fell* from that of 1992, and the effects of Motor Voter were scarcely visible.[20] In Kentucky, for example, only 7 percent of nonvoters registering when obtaining a driver's license turned out to vote versus 25 percent who registered in conventional fashion. The most sophisticated study of the topic indicates typically small—although in a few states moderate—increases in registration, but mixed and generally low *turnout* effects, on the order of 0 to 3 percentage points, depending on whether Motor Voter was enacted before or after the federal NVRA mandate and on the state's historical voting turnout.[21]

Testimony before the Presidential Commission on Election Administration in 2013 was positive about the benefits of online registration, which helped younger citizens between 18 and 24 to increase their registration rates from 29 to 53 percent. However, with the exception of voters under 34 years of age—who increased registration in Arizona by 20 percentage points, for example—online registration has not moved the actual *turnout* needle much at all. At the same time, online registration may have other benefits; registrations can be checked quickly and electronically against existing data to minimize errors; polling place congestion attributable to registration errors can be reduced; and, to date, it seems to be cost-effective. For example, Arizona's Maricopa County has saved 80 cents per registration compared to paper, and Washington State saved 18 cents. Delaware saved $100,000 over four years.[22]

In the six states that had on-site EDR prior to 2006, turnout traditionally ran as much as 8 percentage points higher than the national average. EDR boosted their turnout by about 3 percentage points over 1972, compared to a 1.5-point gain in non-EDR states.[23] Was the bump in turnout the result of EDR, or might it be the result of a spurious correlation attributable to the historical eagerness of people in these states to vote and embrace new mechanisms for doing so? One study concluded that the latter is more likely the case, finding important effects in the early-adopting states but not in those subsequently doing so. Other studies find moderately positive turnout effects of EDR in general, with great variation across states.[24] EDR has one drawback. Having registration lists well ahead of polling day allows local party officials to engage in voter mobilization, encouraging people to vote; that doesn't work for same-day registration.

The consensus seems to be that EDR and NVRA effects are most efficacious for younger voters, those with less than high school education, and in states with "high registration bias," that is, where fewer people in low socioeconomic or minority groups are registered. There is evidence that *highly educated* citizens, however, take advantage of EDR. The implication is that a more widespread use of EDR will slightly increase turnout among those who typically do not register and vote.[25] If eased registration systems increase turnout, that might be good news for Democrats. However, a study of Wisconsin's early EDR experience found that it was the Republican candidate for president who received the boost. The reason is that the people most likely to take advantage of the new opportunity were those unregistered voters attracted to the most appealing candidate who, in that year, happened to be the Republican.[26]

Situational Factors Cause Low Participation
As seen in Table 3.1, the most common reasons given for not voting among those registered were situational: (a) being too busy or having conflicting schedules and

(b) illness, disability, or family emergency. Convenient and timely access to polling places affects turnout,[27] and simply getting to the polls during normal voting hours of 7 a.m. to 7 or 8 p.m. on a Tuesday, when federal elections are held, can present a real hardship. People have to work; they go to school; many have child-care concerns; emergencies occur; and others simply don't have transportation.

Three other situations matter. (1) Turnout may be adversely affected by language barriers faced by citizens who are not fluent in English. (2) Weather is a minor factor, but in tight races it could be decisive: an inch of rain or five inches of snow can reduce turnout in presidential elections by 1 percent.[28] Folklore decrees that bad weather helps Republicans, but political scientists have not come to any consensus on the matter; turnout paradoxically is highest in the harsher weather states of the upper Midwest.[29] (3) Voting mechanics such as inadequate numbers of printed ballots or voting machines, machine breakdowns and errors, and rude or incompetent election administrators—often leading to long lines and waits—frustrate voters and can depress turnout. In 2008, Ohioans were exposed to these problems; estimates are that some 200,000 voters in Florida's 2012 elections gave up in frustration and left polling sites without voting.[30] The danger is that, having once or twice faced these difficulties, people would be turned off and skip the next election.

Overcoming Situational Barriers

Polling Times. Polling hours could be extended, perhaps to 24 or even 48 hours, as is done in a handful of nations, but doing so would prove expensive for cash-strapped localities. Election day could be changed from Tuesday, a day selected for the benefit of rural voters in the nineteenth century, to weekends; or perhaps election Tuesday could be made a national holiday, as often suggested.[31] Holding elections on weekends, a popular reform proposal, could run afoul of some religions' dictates, not to mention conflicts with autumn football mania. Adding another national holiday to set aside a weekday for voting has nontrivial economic implications; besides, one wonders whether people would use the day off to vote or spend the time on household chores, shopping, or recreation. A similar financial concern argues against a government mandate that employers give workers time off at the beginning or end of the day to do their civic duty. In some states, such laws are on the books, but it is uncertain whether they actually bolster turnout.

Absentee Voting. For decades, voters living or traveling abroad or away from their residences, those who were ill, and those with unavoidable conflicts on voting day took advantage of mail-in absentee ballots. Doing so took planning. One had to know that she or he would be gone on election Tuesday; file an application in person or by mail that provided a reason for one's absence; receive the ballot and instructions; and then complete and mail it in. Most of these burdens have been alleviated because 30 states allow people to request mail ballots on a "no excuse/minimal excuse" basis. Oregon and Washington use mail balloting for virtually all statewide and national elections; Colorado has a mixed system allowing mail voting in most elections; and 7 states and the District of Columbia allow permanent mail-in voting to those who sign up for it. The share of votes cast by mail depends on the type of system in place, ranging from low single digits in strict absentee ballot states to nearly 100 percent in Oregon.[32] Mail voting avoids problems of crowded polling sites; may reduce the numbers of poll workers; accommodates travelers, military personnel, and those with disabilities; saves time and money; and gives voters time to think and to fill out their ballots. The picture, however, is not all rosy.

One negative concerns the dependability of voting by mail. Many voters do not return the ballots (some of them vote in person, some forget, and some don't care to vote), and a few mail them in too late or forget properly to sign or mark their ballots. In 2008, a fifth of all requests for absentee ballots failed to produce recorded votes for president because the ballots never reached the appropriate election offices or were improperly filled out and thus rejected.[33] Although the Uniformed and Overseas Citizens Absentee Voting Act and the Military and Overseas Voter Empowerment Act have helped members of the armed forces to vote when away from home, a number of states have exhibited inconsistencies, process breakdowns, and administrative sloppiness.

Absentee voting tends to be used more by the elderly, frequent travelers, those living away from home, and members of the armed forces; these tend to be Republican supporters. Thus partisan considerations probably explain the many battles fought in the states over absentee voter drives, the times and means by which voters can request absentee ballots, the requisite documentation of eligibility to vote, the time periods after the election during which ballots may be accepted, and the counting of such votes. Worse, voters sometimes cast absentee mail ballots and then show up at polling places to vote, filing provisional ballots that occasionally differ from their absentee versions. In addition to delaying vote counts, and recounts if necessary, this situation forces administrators to judge which ballots were the real McCoy. No wonder that absentee-ballot voters are less confident that their votes will be counted correctly than are those casting ballots in person.[34]

Early Voting. To avoid election Tuesday problems and stimulate turnout, 21 states have added early on-site voting to mail balloting to avoid election Tuesday crowding, and others are considering it; altogether, two-thirds of the states allow some type of voting outside of election day.[35] In 2004, 20 percent of votes were cast in early voting of all sorts, mail and in-person. Four years later, the number rose to almost 30 percent; and in so-called "battleground" states, the percentage of early votes approached half of the total votes cast.[36] For 2012, the percentage inched up to slightly more than 31 percent. In a number of states, election day has become "election month"—or longer. In 2014, balloting in several states began in mid-September. Some state and federal courts have blocked state efforts to trim back (yet retain) early voting in Ohio and North Carolina, arguing that doing so discriminates against the poor and minorities, thus elevating early voting, once enacted, to something like a controversial constitutional right. In September 2014, the Supreme Court in effect upheld Ohio and allowed it to reduce the early voting period. Appeals of other cases are ongoing. Not surprisingly, the biggest group to take advantage of early voting is the elderly.[37]

Early voting has drawbacks. Voting well before the scheduled election day can mean that early voters miss important late-breaking news. For example, in the 2010 Florida primaries, Rick Scott won the Republican gubernatorial nomination by locking up early votes. Late in the campaign, negative stories about Scott emerged, causing a swing to Bill McCollum, but it was too late to matter because so many ballots had already been cast. In an era where presidential elections sometimes feature an

"October surprise" and all sorts of groups scurry to uncover and report scandals and bombard voters with ads just before balloting day, early voting could skew results in a fashion that differs from what would happen if everyone voted on that crucial Tuesday. Counterintuitively, early voting seems to produce longer waits in line to cast ballots, mostly because of delays in the check-in process and limited numbers of voting sites.[38] Early voting also complicates and frustrates campaign strategy. Efficiently targeting last-minute advertising requires that candidates, parties, and political action committees know when ballots are going to be cast. Waiting till the last week of a campaign to capture the attention of regular voters could miss everyone who voted weeks earlier.[39] Similar consequences hold for on-the-ground voter mobilization efforts.

High-Tech Voting. An alternative or supplement to these schemes is the use of electronic technology and the Internet. Colorado launched one reform initiative, picked up by Texas and Indiana, that distributes voting centers throughout the state where citizens could cast their votes electronically. Wherever they may find a polling station, citizens simply punch in their identification codes to validate eligibility and then vote; the system allocates their votes to their local electoral jurisdictions. As of mid-2011, nine states have undertaken pilot Internet voting projects of various sorts, usually in primary elections; and Congress has called for explorations of this technique, particularly for military members serving abroad.[40] The advantages are obvious, and if it worked well, a New Yorker traveling to Louisiana for business, a college student from Montana studying in Texas, and vacationers in the U.S. Virgin Islands could go to authorized Internet polling stations and cast their votes in their home state elections. As always, there are complications. One is the loss of the traditional civic experience of voting with neighbors at a local polling place, affirming identification with and concerns about the community. Another is the cost of setting up and operating the system, educating voters, and maintaining records and backups. Moreover, all voting machines would have to carry ballots for all elections in the state and, if used for absentee voting, for the entire country.[41]

It is only a small step from voting centers to voting over the Internet from one's home computer, laptop, or smartphone. Nothing could beat it for convenience, and turnout almost certainly would increase. The same objections can be lodged against this form of voting as against off-site distributed voting.[42] The biggest concern is technology itself. Possibilities of electronic breakdowns, software glitches, and hacking explain why there has been no rush to implement Internet voting. Even systems that require voters to download ballots, print, sign, scan, and then email them in are susceptible to hackers. There were problems in 2006 in Sarasota, Florida, when the presence of a computer worm caused havoc with voting. In a 2010 test of online voting for local elections in Washington, D.C., the city invited computer enthusiasts to try to hack into the system. A University of Michigan team did so, altering all the ballots and leaving their calling card: the lyrics to "Hail to the Victors," the University's fight song. The plans for online voting were scuttled.[43] Hackers could employ malware that changes votes; denial of service attacks like the one that hit the San Diego County Registrar of Voters' website in 2012; "spoofing" of election websites to send votes to the wrong locations; and viruses that could lock up computers or change votes. The incidence of such troublemaking has been low, but there is no guarantee that it will continue that way into the future. In many cases, unless there is some paper or preserved electronic trail, recounts will be difficult or impossible. Moreover, to the extent that easy access to computers is not universal, there could be conflicts with the 1965 Voting Rights Act (VRA), which frowns on any voting scheme that adversely affects minorities.

Other Fixes. For the most part, reforms already have overcome the language barriers. The federal government in 2011, relying on the 1965 VRA, required 248 counties and other jurisdictions to provide bilingual ballots to Hispanics and other minorities. Nearly 5 percent of electoral jurisdictions are required to provide foreign-language assistance in pre-election publicity, voter registration, early voting, absentee applications, and election-day balloting. The evidence suggests that such efforts have increased Hispanic turnout in California.[44] Implementation, however, has been far from perfect, and not all eligible voters receive this help; one occasionally recommended reform is to ensure that bilingual poll workers are available.

The only practical way to address the weather issue, outside of prayer, is to extend the time period for voting from one day to two or utilize some form of "convenience" voting, as explained above. Some East Coast states did precisely that during Super Storm Sandy. Using such measures solely to avoid or cope with weather problems, however, is hardly worthwhile, given the reliability of weather forecasts. Dealing with the discouraging effect of long lines—defined by the 2014 Presidential Commission as having to wait more than 30 minutes—depends on the causes, which are multiple and often unpredictable. For most cases, the solution is simply to plan better and spend more money on voting machines, facilities, and administrative staffing. A radical reform is to hold election officials personally responsible by means of fines and lawsuits. In cases where illegal activity is the cause—the problem always is proving it—rigorous enforcement of existing law should suffice. That, too, entails allocation of resources to observe, investigate, and prosecute. Such remedies may have some long-term benefits, but they are unlikely to affect citizens' short-term voting behavior.

Will These Reforms Work?

The rather mixed scholarly evidence suggests that these convenience reforms, especially mail balloting, have led to marginal increases in turnout—1 or 2 percentage points more than states that did not adopt these reforms—especially when first implemented. Results depend on which reform, which elections, and which states are examined and on how recently the reform occurred. An early study of the Larimer County, Colorado, experiment with voting centers, for example, found an increase in turnout, especially among infrequent voters.[45] Despite increasing the volume of election news coverage, early in-person voting seems to have had little or no lasting effect, merely shifting the times when people vote.[46] Apparently, when the novelty of new modes of voting wears off, turnout regresses toward its previous levels. Indeed, several scholars have concluded that early in person voting, when implemented by itself, correlates with *lower* turnout; they speculate that it reduces the importance of elections and reduces parties' and groups' incentives for voter mobilization.[47]

Perhaps more important than the turnout numbers is the question of who would be affected. Most reformers are interested in spurring turnout among groups that tend to participate less: the disadvantaged, poor, young adults, minorities, and the poorly educated. The evidence to date, however, suggests that convenience voting increases participation among those who are *already* inclined to vote much more than it enhances turnout among these targeted groups and other perennial nonvoters.[48] Most measures to ease voting will not have much effect on nonvoters' propensity to vote. After reviewing the scholarly findings on voting by mail, early voting, and absentee voting, one scholar concluded,

> Across both aggregate and individual-level datasets, using both panel and cross-sectional designs, and employing exit polls, validated vote records, and telephone surveys, the results are consistent. Individuals who utilize easy voting procedures tend to be more politically engaged and interested than those who do not take advantage of the opportunity. . . . Moreover, individuals who make use of less restrictive voting procedures are better educated (in the case of [voting by mail] and absentee voting) and have higher incomes (for all reforms). Thus, voting reforms do not correct the biases inherent in the electorate, and in some cases, reforms may even worsen these biases.[49]

According to another expert, "the effects of these reforms have been modest both in terms of increasing the size of the participating electorate and in altering its demographic and attitudinal characteristics."[50]

One implication is that convenience voting reforms are unlikely to make much of a difference, if any, for the political parties. Neither party seems to have benefited from reforms, but that has not stopped the parties from engaging in some monumental battles over early voting.[51] Republicans in particular, fearing a flood of low-socioeconomic-status pro-Democratic voters, have sought to limit early voting—as in Florida and Ohio in 2012 and 2013—touching off a series of messy court cases. In Congress, Democrats have introduced legislation to curtail such limits.

Virtually all convenience reforms carry costs. Early voting requires that polling stations must be open and manned for four or six weeks, increasing administrative complexities. In some states, early voting dates vary according to location, raising problems of inconsistency and potentially unfair advantage. Ostensibly to limit these effects, legislatures in several states, such as Florida, North Carolina, Ohio, and Wisconsin, recently undertook efforts to cut back on early voting (and to enhance scrutiny of absentee voting and provisional ballots). Easing registration carries similar costs; Oregon is near the top in the number of problems its easy registration system created.[52] It is not unreasonable to raise a question about whether the reforms and their results are worth the costs.

It's Me, Not the System, That Causes Low Participation

Net of eligibility and situational roadblocks, citizens bear the ultimate responsibility for voting. Why don't more people participate? For the 1 in 10 nonvoters claiming to be conflicted about the candidates, electoral reforms will not affect their calculus. Nor can they do much for the politically disinterested, disaffected, and disconnected.[53] Public opinion polls document demoralization, a low sense of political efficacy, a tanked trust in government, and political cynicism among many citizens. Elections simply are not meaningful enough, let alone sufficiently exciting, to motivate marginal voters. William Flanigan and Nancy Zingale point to five factors that account for differences in levels of interest and stimulus:[54]

1. The significance attached by voters to the office under contention;
2. The level of competitiveness in the contest;
3. The attractiveness of the candidates;
4. The importance of the issues raised in the campaign; and
5. The degree of media coverage relative to the election.

First, not all elections are comparable in importance. Presidential elections entice more people to the polls than any others, and general elections draw more voters than primaries. Pity the poor dog catcher in any town who needs a heavy turnout to win office. The sheer number of elections can turn off voters.[55] With some 89,000 units of government, Americans have more electing to do than any other democracies. In 2008, to cite an extreme case, many Georgians were asked to go to the polls five times. Voting can become too common, too boring, and too costly in terms of time and effort. Moreover, for all but a few people, politics is not the focus of their lives; they have limited time and emotional energy. Attention spans are limited, and politics is confusing.

Second, competition affects turnout by exciting voters and inducing activists to work harder to mobilize voters. Intense ideological polarization between competitors, however, seems to dampen turnout among the politically less sophisticated.[56] The problem is that many electoral contests lack real competition. For example, from 1986 to 2010, an average of 59 House incumbents faced no major party opposition in the general election, although in 2012 that number dropped to 38. Competition in primaries is much weaker; in 2010, a year generally characterized as intense, 56 percent of all representatives and 12 percent of senators seeking re-election faced no primary challenge.[57] The House figure dropped a bit to 49 percent in 2012. More than 90 percent of House and more than 80 percent of Senate incumbents seeking re-election win, usually by significant margins.[58] Not many more than 60 to 80 districts are competitive in any real sense.

National election turnout since 1900 has saw-toothed up and down. Unusually challenging times, serious policy differences between contenders on salient issues, and candidate attractiveness all seem to explain variation in turnout.[59] If so, why did turnout not skyrocket during the 1960s, with Vietnam, civil rights, and the war on poverty in the news? Franklin Roosevelt in the 1930s, Dwight Eisenhower (1952), John Kennedy (1960), Bill Clinton and Ross Perot (1992), and Barack Obama (2008) brought out higher than normal crowds of voters. Why not Ronald Reagan in 1980 and 1984 or Jimmy Carter in 1976? Why not Clinton in 1996? Sorting through these traits is a fool's errand, unlikely to provide a definitive answer.

Finally, media coverage stimulates turnout.[60] With a few exceptions, the level and type of elections determine the amount of "news" and advertising, with volume and intensity declining as one moves from presidential to senatorial to congressional to state and local contests.

Getting Them to Vote

Election Importance. If elections lack significance, one "fix" is to reduce the number of elected offices and the number of elections, or at least to consolidate election dates—both to focus attention and to save money. In other nations with fewer elections, turnout rates are higher; each election matters more. So why not cut back or consolidate? Electing all sorts of government officials and holding lots of elections somehow resonate with Americans' democratic instincts, and eliminating some may violate notions of accountability. Never mind that turnout often is abysmally low and many elected positions could be filled better by appointments of highly qualified individuals to enhance effectiveness and efficiency. Another concern is that by lumping together at the same time a number of elections at different levels, campaign contributions and media time will be gobbled up by candidates for the major federal offices, denying some funding and attention to those at the bottom of the ticket. Holding presidential elections simultaneously with lesser state and local elections could attract voters interested in the next occupant of the White House but who care little for local or state affairs. This risks having uninformed and uninterested voters determine local electoral results, undermining the concept of responsible citizen participation and accountability. This problem is acute in localities that include concentrations of out-of-the-area college students unconcerned with matters that affect long-term residents or who might have an interest in candidates or referendum issues that provide short-term benefits to them but lead to the discomfort of permanent residents. Furthermore, electing the same number of officials at fewer elections implies that ballots must grow in length and complexity, adding to the frustration and delays. In short, fixing aggregate turnout problems by means of reducing the number of elections or offices brings consequences that some, at least, are unwilling to chance.

Competition. Competitiveness depends on multiple factors—the partisanship of the state or district (for congressional races), the particular issues, and the slate of candidates. District partisanship can be adjusted (see chapter 9), and stronger parties might affect the slate of candidates. There is a popular belief that the presence of a strong and viable third party will engage citizens and increase turnout, but that proposition cannot be tested until that party appears. Some things that can be done to alter the competitive landscape and perk up voters' interests, such as multimember districts and proportional voting, are discussed in the next chapter.

Media Influence. The role of the media in spurring interest and turnout might be susceptible to reform. Proposals for free or much less costly media coverage, as found in most other democracies, are common. "Free," of course, is misleading because someone has to pay: taxpayers directly, media consumers indirectly, advertisers, or owners. Given the dispersion of Internet news coverage and the growing number of news outlets, urging a greater media role in elections seems redundant. Anyone claiming ignorance about a presidential, Senate, or House election because of lack of media coverage is on the wrong side of the digital divide, a hermit, or disingenuous. Media coverage follows electoral politics, taking its cues and giving space and airtime to interesting races, rarely creating them. The effectiveness of free time depends on the audience; it would do little good if only those already interested in elections were watching and listening, which is likely. At any rate, given the first amendment's guarantees of media freedom, there may be little the government can do to foster more coverage. Perhaps, however, volume is not what is important.

It has been argued that negative campaign advertising and attack ads turn off potential voters who find such ads distasteful and demeaning, but there is little or no evidence that critical ads reduce turnout; to the contrary, some studies suggest that they stimulate interest.[61] As negative advertising has risen to an art form in recent elections, turnout has been a bit healthier than in the previous 20 or 30 years. Two types of detrimental effects have been documented. Negative advertising may have a depressing effect on voters whose favorite candidates become targets of negative advertising,[62] and "mudslinging" ads focusing on personal rather than political characteristics seem to discourage participation among the least interested.[63]

Media can have other effects. Because early network "calls" of presidential election results, based on exit polls in the eastern half of the country, seemed to depress later-in-the-day turnout in the west, television networks several decades ago agreed to delay announcing projections and to avoid predicting election results on the basis of sparse data. In 2000, an early call on Florida had to be revoked as later results poured in, muddying earlier exit poll implications. Some experimental studies suggest that when polls show that an upcoming race is going to be close, turnout rises; if polls show a lopsided victory, turnout drops. Whether such reduction in turnout will bias results, however, is less clear. An election that is a foregone conclusion could discourage supporters of both candidates.

Other Reforms. A classic belief is that more education, mandatory civics classes in high school and college, and mass mailings or Internet availability of information on candidates and issues might help, but there is little hard evidence to support it. One possible exception concerns students' college experiences. Taking more social science courses and experiencing politically relevant instruction at least correlate with participation and turnout while in school and in later life, but causality is hard to prove and the linkage could be spurious.[64]

Ground-level efforts to mobilize voters have real, albeit limited, impacts on turnout rates. Door-to-door canvassing works surprisingly well, particularly in prominent elections, when done by neighbors, and when followed up by phone contacts, but the effectiveness of phone soliciting alone is a matter of debate.[65] Aggressive text messaging could boost turnout by several points.[66] A clever experiment found that a special Facebook message informing Facebook users that their best friends had voted stimulated them to vote at a slightly higher rate than those not receiving the message.[67] Sending letters to habitual nonvoters indicating that their failure to vote was a matter of public record and that their neighbors might find out led to a 27-point boost in turnout for a local Detroit election, but it stretches credulity to think that there can be anything approaching this magnitude of effect for a congressional or presidential election.[68] Even saying "thank you for voting" in a given election seems to encourage turnout in the next one.[69] At best, these tactics can increase turnout by 1 or 2 percentage points.[70] States could enhance their current efforts to employ social media to remind citizens to vote. Tweets or email reminders on one's cell phone, perhaps with easy "app" access to information, might help. By definition, these techniques get to a limited group of people, involve costs, might be resented, and probably will not have much effect. Perhaps more surprising, mobilization efforts are more likely to stimulate turnout among those with greater propensity to vote (probably higher socioeconomic status individuals) than they are to inspire low-propensity individuals to vote.[71] Some of these activities are essentially nongovernmental actions immune to official reform efforts.

There is an "iron law" of social science that everything matters a little to explain a phenomenon, but nothing matters all that much. Perhaps the same is true concerning efforts to expand voting turnout. Many factors inhibit participation; many things can be done to increase turnout a little bit, at least in the short run, here and there. The bottom line seems to be that barriers should be removed *and* incentives should be devised. Political scientists Thomas Mann and Norman Ornstein and former congressman Mickey Edwards, among others, have suggested that in federal elections Uncle Sam offer people a tax credit for voting. A less expensive alternative might be a lottery, what Mann and Ornstein refer to as "Election PowerBall."[72] Whatever the incentive, it would have to be significant to matter.[73] One is reminded of the days of urban machine politics, when ward healers could turn out the vote with a five-dollar bill or the promise of a Christmas turkey. Today, of course, such activity is illegal.

The ultimate turnout reform bomb is compulsory voting, practiced in some 30 countries. Subjecting nonvoters to a fine while giving those who do show up to cast ballots the option to vote "present" or "none of the above" will surely improve participation. The downside, beyond the potential embarrassment of too many "none of the above" votes, could be to engender more irresponsible and uninformed voting, not to mention its effect on personal liberty. Setting the right level of penalty will stir a debate: how much is enough to entice someone to go to the polls without being oppressively expensive? Enforcing such a scheme could cost more than the revenue it takes in, especially when the enforcement mechanism has to cope with a wide range of perfectly legitimate excuses. Mix-ups, improper fines, bureaucratic inefficiency, a dab or two of corruption, and a glut of messed up ballots are likely. How does such a system make government officials more accountable?

Conclusion—The Real Question about Turnout

Reforms may add a few percentage points to turnout. Research, however, seems to indicate that most reforms have marginal effects that may not match, let alone outweigh, their costs and less salubrious consequences. A concern for efficiency is always relevant in considering changes. A number of proposals lie beyond the purview of public policy or invite clashes with First Amendment rights and with the states' authority over elections. Outside of mandatory voting, probably the reforms that offer the best cost–benefit efficiency ratio are universal registration and weekend voting or at least significantly extending voting hours on election day itself. These work well in other lands. Beside considerations of cost, however, pure partisan politics and institutional processes of legislating and amending constitutions present hurdles.

Suppose, however, that the hurdles can be surmounted. There is a more profound question to be asked: is it in fact desirable to exert great effort to stimulate a slight increase in turnout if the increase will come from low-interest, low-information voters, if the costs of so doing are significant, and if the results will be little different from what now occurs? Advocates focus on the importance of citizenship and community, arguing that democratic values of participation and representation are primary, whereas opponents focus on effectiveness and efficiency and worry about the reasoned quality of voting choices. Members of a democratic society who work, pay taxes, serve in the military, help their neighbors, and so on have, as fundamental to the notion of a political community, both a right and an obligation to vote; and the government's job is to enable and entice them to do so. On the other hand, many citizens recoil from compulsion, doubt the efficacy of incentives, and worry about abuse. Some of them challenge the wisdom of universal suffrage on the grounds that citizens who do not pay federal or state taxes—the group often labeled the "takers," as opposed to the "makers" of wealth—should not have the right to choose the officials who have power and the electoral incentive to redistribute money and benefits from the latter to the former, especially if many in the takers group do not want to vote and/or are neither interested in nor informed about government and politics. To such critics, participation and representation, along with their effects on accountability and the responsiveness of elected officials, are trumped by the other criteria for good government: effectiveness, efficiency, and reasoned judgment.

3.3 SECURING THE VOTE

The Problems

Removing roadblocks is important; so is making sure that voting is appropriately conducted and that votes are accurately counted. Scholars have long been fascinated with how ballot types, ballot order of candidates, and election administration affect elections. For example, unintentionally voting for the wrong candidates is greater when ballots are of the "straight party" type (voters vote for all candidates of a party by making one "X," pulling one lever, or punching one button) than the "office-bloc" type (candidates are listed for each office, and the voter must vote for each office). To the extent that the order in which candidates are listed affects results, one remedy is to randomize the placement of candidates' names on ballots. At the same time, ballot design affects which races a voter might miss or skip.[74] Polls document the public's fear that their votes may not be properly counted and often don't matter. All such concerns paled in comparison to the veritable panic that set in after the 2000 presidential election in Florida, where ballot design issues and inconsistent election and recount administration may have cost Al Gore the election.[75] Voters trying to do exactly what they were supposed to do had their ballots miscounted or ruled invalid.

Fixing the Problems

Voting Machines. After the 2000 Florida fiasco, scholars, pundits, and the federal government jumped in, eager to prevent such events from reoccurring. Although the debacle was in good part a statutory and ultimately a constitutional issue—the Supreme Court resolved it by stopping the complex recount—one of the first places reformers looked for a solution was election administration and technology. The race was on to invent a better ballot "mousetrap" to minimize lost or erroneous votes, discouraged voters, and fraud. The National Commission on Federal Election Reform in 2000 recommended that the federal government propose voting equipment standards and that each state establish standards for defining a "vote" on each type of voting equipment. More than 150 bills were introduced in Congress. The definition of the problem—flaws in voting mechanisms and machines—determined what followed, the Help America Vote Act. HAVA provided more than $3 billion in federal funding, mostly for new voting equipment and the development of centralized voter files. It also included other long-standing items that were on reform agendas, such as mandatory use of provisional ballots, voter education, poll worker training, access for disabled citizens, and identification requirements for new voters.

Americans continue to utilize a variety of mechanisms to vote. Which is best, and can it be widely implemented? "Best" may be the wrong word, since all voting machines (lever, punch card, optical scan, electronic) as well as paper ballots have well-documented liabilities.[76] Some or all counties of 16 states use paperless machines that leave no record of the vote, and 22 states employ paper-based balloting. Twenty require that marked ballots be returned by precinct administrators to election officials in case of a recount; typically these states forbid the use of the Internet to report results.[77] As of 2012, more than 95 percent of all counties used optical scan or other electronic systems.[78] With any voting system there will be glitches, some of which are the fault of the voters, some of the system. Undervoting—when voters fail to indicate for whom they want to vote for a given office—is attributable to deliberate decisions not to vote for a given office, to voter carelessness, to confusing ballots, and to machine flaws. Especially on paper ballots and punch-out systems, there also can be overvoting, when people vote for more than the allowed one candidate for each office. Electronic machines, which can be programmed to prevent double voting or remind voters that they have missed some contests, can solve some of these problems. Finally, there can be misvoting, when voters do not properly mark or cast their ballots.

The Caltech/MIT analysis of the 2000 Florida vote and subsequent elections revealed that paper ballots, lever machines, and optical scanned ballots had the lowest error rate; punch card and electronic systems performed less well. Punch cards are tricky; the 2000 Florida "hanging chads" (the punch-outs that were not cleanly removed) have become an election icon. Faulty ballot design can cause voters to overlook certain races or make errors, and software problems can frazzle electronic systems. In 2009, for example, a software problem in a South Dakota county added thousands of nonexistent votes to the actual results. In 2012, software glitches in Palm Beach, Florida, assigned votes to the wrong candidate and wrong election contest; and in the 2008 GOP primary in one South Carolina county, there was a temporary failure in 80 percent of precincts, making it impossible for voters to cast ballots in those locales.[79]

Other factors complicate the choice of the best system. Counting paper ballots, rather rare these days, takes time and often requires discretion on the part of election officials. Optical scan systems, the best choice for minimizing errors, share some of the problems of paper ballots when voters fail to fill in the ovals properly. Electronic machines are costly, causing voting jurisdictions to purchase fewer than are needed. Scarcity of machines, coupled with the "learning curve" in using electronic gadgets, probably means that casting ballots will require more time, building up long lines that frustrate voters and could cause some to give up or vote with careless haste. Moreover, electronic machines utilizing wireless technology have been shown to be vulnerable to cyberattacks. Cities and counties have responded in different ways; in spring 2013, for example, after spending $95 million on new high-tech machines, New York City dumped them to return to the old lever-style mechanical devices bought in 1962 and kept in storage. Other jurisdictions, having purchased new voting machines with HAVA money, find that they have worn out, and there is no new federal money to purchase new ones. Perhaps some "off the shelf" technology (tablets, laptops, etc.) will prove to be the solution.

Despite difficulties, there is progress. Residual vote rates, the difference between the number of all ballots cast in a location and the number of votes cast for the presidency, dropped in 2004 and 2008 compared to 2000.[80] Most experts want to make sure that, whatever the system, there is some form of documented (preferably paper) backup for recounts and for postelection audits aimed at discovering errors and differences among types of voting systems. National standards for dealing with absentee and provisional ballots make sense if they can be enforced, and more money would help on that score. Some observers, however, worry that the focus on the technology fix may distract reformers from other issues such as ballot design, election administration, and election personnel.[81]

Election Administration. Conducting elections is a local function subject to inconsistency and unfairness—as when, for example, one set of vote counters takes a harder line on the mismarking of ballots than does another or when time pressures cause errors. Poll workers have considerable discretion in accepting or rejecting voters whose registration status is unclear; and workers vary in their ability to handle voting machines. Sometimes ballots are lost or misallocated. In a Minnesota legislative race in 2012 in which one vote determined the outcome, dozens of ballots were given to and erroneously cast by voters from a different legislative district.[82] Election officials have erroneously tabulated ballots or accidentally misplaced results—as when, in a 2011 Wisconsin judicial election, a local official stored election results in a personal laptop and forgot to report them to the state. When she did, the results provided the victory margin for one of the candidates. In the 2012 election in Florida, lines at the polls were excessively long (because of a lengthy ballot, new voting machines, inadequate number of machines, and sometimes ill-trained workers), and ballots went missing. Broward county officials found a thousand ballots in a warehouse a week after the election. How well elections are administered and how poll workers perform can affect voters' confidence in the electoral process.

As the 2014 Presidential Commission indicated, more can be done, such as additional staffing, better recruitment and training of poll workers, multilingual poll workers, easier access for the disabled, electronic poll books (listing registered voters) instead of paper books, clear and rigid standards at all balloting locations, or the hiring of professional staff to replace volunteers at the polls.[83] All would improve matters, but many are prohibitively costly for local governments; and eliminating volunteers somehow feels "undemocratic" and does little to foster broader citizen involvement in the democratic process. Under any reform, problems will persist.

Fraud

The Problem. Voting errors are inevitable. Voting fraud is another matter. On the one hand, there is precious little evidence documenting anything other than rare and minor instances of cheating in recent years; and the extent of the fraud typically was too small to matter.[84] This is true even in states with EDR, which presumably is susceptible to mischief. On the other hand, there are numerous, mostly unproven but occasionally persuasive, anecdotes and allegations of attempted and actual fraud. One recent and controversial study found substantial voting by non-citizens that probably affected Electoral College votes and congressional elections.[85] Establishing fraud's nature, extent, and consequences is almost impossible and always controversial.[86]

The Pew Center's report, above, of millions of errors on registration lists could include some deliberate hanky-panky. Dismissing the issue of fraud is dangerous, not because in-person voter fraud is common—it is anything but that—but because if it were shown to have affected election results, it could undermine the legitimacy and integrity of elections and diminish the value of voting. So far, however, people's perceptions of the presence of voter fraud and their views on antifraud policies do not seem to affect the likelihood of their voting.[87]

Although polling place cheating seems rare and inconsequential, experts spot some threat of voter fraud in convenience voting systems: mail ballots, online registration and voting, and electronic voting. For many aged and invalid voters, casting an independent mail ballot opens doors to fraud, especially when, for instance, "get out the vote" organizations arrive to help residents of senior centers and assisted-living establishments exercise the franchise. Can election officials be sure that the people to whom they send ballots are in fact the registered voters they claim to be? A version of this problem occurred in 2012 in Florida's Miami–Dade county, courtesy of a cyberattack on the state's online election system, when more than 2,500 "phantom requests" for absentee ballots for the August primary election apparently were sent from computer IP addresses in the United States and overseas—apparently the first documented straightforward attempt to cheat the system. Because the attempt lacked sophistication, it was caught with no consequences for the election.[88]

What to Do. The most controversial but popular antifraud reform measure is the state requirement that voters provide proof that they are who they say they are. Interestingly, HAVA encouraged such laws by its requirement that states enact implementing legislation for HAVA's various provisions. Under current federal law, people certify their citizenship and eligibility by checking a box on a federally mandated form, acknowledging that doing so falsely makes them liable to prosecution.

As of mid-2014, 34 states have gone further, requiring voters to present some form of official identification at the time of voting; several others are considering doing so. In 8 states, the identification must be a government-issued photo ID card, such as a driver's license or similar document.[89] The ostensible purposes are to prevent ineligible people from casting ballots, prevent double voting, and prevent voting by cemetery occupants. The general population seems to share some of these concerns; as many as 7 of 10 Americans believed voter fraud to be at least a somewhat serious problem and do not think that requiring people to show a photo ID is unreasonable.[90]

The judiciary is heavily engaged with this issue. The Supreme Court upheld a mandatory identification law in Indiana, but subsequently ruled against Arizona's ID law requiring proof of citizenship on the grounds that federal immigration laws took precedence over state action.[91] Throughout 2013 and 2014 state and federal courts issued inconsistent decisions, rejecting some voter ID laws—in Pennsylvania, Texas, and Arkansas, for example—and upholding one in North Carolina. Appeals courts have come down on both sides of the issue. The Supreme Court in late 2014 and early 2015 allowed Wisconsin and Texas to implement new restrictions. A 2013 Supreme Court decision voiding sections of the 1965 VRA that called for federal reviews of changes in election laws in many southern states seemed to open the gates. Texas and North Carolina quickly moved to institute photo ID requirements and change other laws, such as election day registration. Relying on a remaining section of the VRA, the

Justice Department has sued them with partial success. The Supreme Court, however, upheld North Carolina's ending of same-day registration. Other cases are ongoing. In retaliation, Kansas and Arizona in late 2013 decided to forego government photo IDs for federal elections but mandate them—in addition to the standard federally approved form declaring one's citizenship eligibility—for state and local ones. The plan was upheld in federal district court but overturned by an appellate court in November 2014. Missouri and Illinois had previously tried that tactic but were rebuffed by the courts.[92] This is an issue to watch.

Other versions of official identification have been proposed. One is a digital photo available to poll watchers, who would exercise their judgment: is this balding, white-haired person wearing glasses the same as the dark-haired guy with the beard in the photo? Another idea is to require the voter to present an official and unique voter identification number—perhaps the first three and last four digits of one's social security number—to be matched against a master list of registered voters.

Reformers seeking to impose state government–issued photo ID cards face strenuous objections. First, there is the suspicion that such efforts are in fact politically motivated and targeted against the poor, elderly, minorities, women who change their names when they get married, and college students—which many translate as "against Democrats." Three recent book titles clearly demonstrate one side's claim: *The Politics of Voter Suppression, The Politics of Disenfranchisement,* and *Stealing Democracy: The New Politics of Voter Suppression.*[93] Second, since fairness and efficiency depend on consistency across election jurisdictions, states should not be free to require identification beyond the standard federal format.

Third, the tighter the rules governing registration and voting, the lower will be voter turnout—and representation, accountability, and responsiveness. The Government Accountability Office, after reviewing studies that showed mixed results, undertook an analysis of the 2012 election, comparing Kansas and Tennessee, which had toughened their voter ID laws, to four others. It concluded that imposition of these new requirements decreased turnout by about 2 to 3 percent.[94] The report came under considerable criticism from those two states. The debate pits encouraging turnout by making electoral access easy against claims that the integrity of the electoral system is at risk. Conversely, to the extent that convenience voting can be made fraud- and mistake-proof, and as voters get used to new ways of voting, turnout might rise. Thus far, however, the effect on turnout where such laws are in place is less than certain. It seems to vary and probably does not exceed 2 or 3 percentage points; possibly it is nil. In some states turnout rose despite such laws.[95]

Fourth, what is the cost–benefit ratio of spending taxpayer funds to reduce mistakes and prevent fraud when such problems cannot be shown to affect election results? Where will money have the greatest effect in protecting the integrity of elections? In some locales, purchasing high-tech voting systems causes officials to reduce the number of machines they can buy and/or consolidate polling places—both of which make voting more inconvenient and quite possibly reduce turnout.

Since the greatest likelihood of fraud comes with online or mail voting and since these are the easiest ways to cast one's ballot, new means of voter verification and anti-hacking protection would be needed; but the only certain means to those ends is excessively intrusive, burdensome, and costly. Can anyone be sure that grandma's absentee ballot was filled out by her or that the person casting a vote online is in fact the authorized voter?

Perhaps the most telling questions are who will be most affected by reforms and what difference will it make? No one knows for certain, and much depends on the type of identification needed. Upper socioeconomic groups are unlikely to be discouraged from voting regardless of the nature of the proof of identity. Requiring a *government-issued photo ID*, even if free, supposedly hits those in the lowest socioeconomic classes the hardest, but since many currently are not registered and since this population does not vote now at high rates, the *drop* in voting by that group would be small and unlikely to make a difference in most elections. Time will tell as various requirements are implemented. Partisan effects, as well, are hard to predict. Not too many years ago one might reasonably have assumed that marginal voters—the types who could easily be discouraged from voting—are overwhelmingly Democratic. That may not be as much the case today because of the party realignments that have flip-flopped many of the traditional voter blocs. Consequences there will be; what they look like remains to be seen.

3.4 CONCLUSION

Even if many of these reforms, summarized in Table 3.2, come to pass, one must be cautious in expectations. Even knowing what the problems are, increasing turnout

Table 3.2 Summary and Assessment of Reforms to Increase Voting Turnout

ASSESSMENT OF REFORM		
Probable positive effects on turnout that outweigh costs and other negative consequences	Uncertain, neutral, or mixed effects on turnout and/or possible serious adverse costs and consequences	Probable negative effects on turnout that outweigh benefits; likely costs and negative consequences that outweigh positives
Universal registration Online registration Cross-state coordination of registration lists Longer poll hours Weekend voting Fewer elections and elected offices Stimulating competition (e.g., by redrawing congressional district boundaries)	More convenient registration office locations; longer office hours More aggressive local and college registration drives Pre-registration at age 16 Allowing ex-felons to vote Election-day registration Purging registration lists to eliminate ineligible voters Strengthen parties to facilitate mobilization Stimulate competition (e.g., by multimember districts) Voter education Mail-in balloting Early voting Distributed electronic voting centers Antifraud measures such as government-issued photo ID	Compulsory voting Financial incentives to vote Free media Make voting day a holiday Mandatory time off work to vote Internet voting

and assuring the accuracy of the vote are harder to address than most reformers think. Participation is not likely to increase much—although the mix of voters surely will change as minorities grow in population—and that means only slow and incremental change in the representational nature of government. Lethargy explains some of the failure; politics surely explains at least as much. Responsiveness of elected officials to a slowly changing electorate and the sense of accountability they evince are both likely to evolve, but slowly. Two things are certain: pressures for and efforts to impose and implement reforms will continue, and the judiciary will become more involved.

QUESTIONS TO CONSIDER

1. How important is turnout? Does it really matter? Do you see any dangers in encouraging greater voting participation?
2. If you were to conduct a study to determine the effects of higher turnout, how would you proceed? What would you be looking for, and how would you measure it?
3. If you could pick three reforms to increase turnout, what would they be? Why pick those three? Would there be any negative consequences to weigh against the positive ones?
4. How much of a danger is voting fraud? Is it worth taking additional precautions to prevent?
5. Do you favor or oppose mandatory photo identification to vote? Why?

NOTES

1. Richard L. Hasen, *The Voting Wars* (New Haven, CT: Yale University Press, 2012), p. 111.
2. Michael P. McDonald and Samuel Popkin, "The Myth of the Vanishing Voter," *American Political Science Review* 95 (2001): 963–74.
3. Eric Plutzer, "Becoming a Habitual Voter: Inertia, Resources, and Growth in Young Adulthood," *American Political Science Review* 96 (2002): 41–56; John H. Aldrich, Jacob M. Montgomery, and Wendy Wood, "Turnout as a Habit," *Public Behavior* 33 (2011): 535–63.
4. Paul S. Martin and Michele P. Claibourn, "Citizen Participation and Congressional Responsiveness: New Evidence That Participation Matters," *Legislative Studies Quarterly* 38 (2013): 59–81; John D. Griffin and Brian Newman, "Voting Power, Policy Representation, and Disparities in Voting Rewards," *Journal of Politics* 75 (2013): 52–64; Paul S. Martin, "Voting's Rewards: Voter Turnout, Attentive Publics, and Congressional Allocation of Federal Money," *American Journal of Political Science* 47 (2003): 110–27; Larry Bartels, *Unequal Democracy: The Political Economy of the New Gilded Age* (Princeton, NJ: Princeton University Press, 2008).
5. "American Democracy in an Age of Rising Inequality," http://www.apsanet.org/Files/Task%20Force%20Reports/taskforcereport.pdf.
6. Austin Ranney, "Nonvoting Is Not a Social Disease," *Public Opinion* 6 (1983): 16–19.
7. In postelection surveys, respondents also usually indicate a higher level of turnout than actually occurred.
8. Jan E. Leighley and Jonathan Nagler, *Who Votes Now?: Demographics, Issues, Inequality, and Turnout in the United States* (Princeton, NJ, and Oxford: Princeton University Press, 2014), chap. 6; William H. Flanigan, Nancy H. Zingale, Elizabeth A. Theiss-Morse, and

Michael W. Wagner, *Political Behavior of the American Electorate*, 13th ed. (Los Angeles, London, New Delhi, Singapore, and Washington, D.C.: CQ Press, 2014): 85; Pew Research Center, "The Party of Nonvoters," (October 29, 2010), http://pewresearch.org/pubs/1786/who-are-nonvoters-less-republican-educated-younger/; Pew Research Center for the People & the Press, "Nonvoters: Who They Are, What They Think" (November 1, 2012), http://www.people-press.org/2012/11/01/nonvoters-who-they-are-what-they-think/.

9. Karen M. Kaufmann, John R. Petrocik, and Daron R. Shaw, *Unconventional Wisdom: Facts and Myths about American Voters* (Oxford and New York: Oxford University Press, 2008): 152.

10. Danny Hayes, "Trait Voting in U.S. Senate Elections," *American Politics Research* 38 (2010): 1102–29; Bryan Caplan, *The Myth of the Rational Voter: Why Democracies Choose Bad Policies* (Princeton, NJ: Princeton University Press, 2007); Ilya Somin, *Democracy and Political Ignorance: Why Small Government Is Smarter* (Stanford, CA: Stanford University Press, 2013).

11. "Inaccurate, Costly, and Inefficient: Evidence That America's Voter Registration System Needs an Upgrade," *The Pew Charitable Trusts State and Consumer Initiatives* (February 14, 2012), http://www.pewtrusts.org/en/research-and-analysis/reports/2012/02/14/inaccurate-costly-and-inefficient-evidence-that-americas-voter-registration-system-needs-an-upgrade. See the Caltech/MIT Voting Project studies at http://www.vote.caltech.edu/.

12. *Ibid.*

13. *The American Voting Experience: Report and Recommendations of the Presidential Commission on Election Administration*, January 2014: 23.

14. *Ibid.*, 26–29.

15. Andrew Johnson, "N.C. State Board Finds More Than 35K Incidents of 'Double Voting' in 2012," *National Review Online,* April 2, 2014, http://www.nationalreview.com/corner/374882/nc-state-board-finds-more-35k-incidents-double-voting-2012-andrew-johnson/.

16. National Conference of State Legislatures, "Electronic (or Online) Voter Registration," http://www.ncsl.org/research/elections-and-campaigns/electronic-or-online-voter-registration.aspx/.

17. "Same-Day Voter Registration," http://www.ncsl.org/research/elections-and-campaigns/same-day-registration.aspx#links/; "States That Expanded Voting in 2013 and 2014," Brennan Center for Justice, http://www.brennancenter.org/states-expanded-voting-2013-and-2014/. North Carolina, Maryland, and Ohio allow residents to register and vote in an early voting period, but not on the official voting day.

18. Matthew J. Streb, *Rethinking American Electoral Democracy*, 2nd ed. (New York and London: Routledge, 2011): 19.

19. Raymond E. Wolfinger and Steven J. Rosenstone, *Who Votes?* (New Haven, CT: Yale University Press, 1980); Rosenstone and Wolfinger, "The Effects of Registration Laws on Voter Turnout," *American Political Science Review* 72 (1978): 22–45.

20. "Executive Summary of the Federal Election Commission Report to the Congress on the Impact of the National Voter Registration Act of 1993 on the Administration of Federal Elections, June, 1997," http://www.fec.gov/votregis/nvrasum.htm/.

21. Michael J. Hanmer, *Discount Voting: Voter Registration Reforms and Their Effects* (Cambridge, UK: Cambridge University Press, 2009). Hanmer shows why studies of the effects of reforms are so difficult to perform with certainty and precision.

22. *American Voting Experience*: 22–27.

23. Leighley and Nagler, *Who Votes Now?*, chap. 4.

24. Hanmer, *Discount Voting*, 104. See also Michael P. McDonald, "Portable Voter Registration," *Political Behavior* 30 (2008): 491–50; Roger Larocca and John S. Klemanski, "U.S. State Election Reform and Turnout in Presidential Elections," *State Politics & Policy Quarterly* 11 (2011): 76–101; Barry C. Burden, David T. Canon, Kenneth R. Mayer, and Donald P. Moynihan. "Election Laws, Mobilization, and Turnout: The Unanticipated Consequences of Election Reform," *American Journal of Political Science* 58 (2014): 95–109; Thad E. Hall, "US Voter Registration Reform," *Electoral Studies* 32 (2013): 589–96.

25. Hanmer, *Discount Voting*, chap. 6; Leighley and Nagler, *Who Votes Now?*, chap. 4; Elizabeth Rigby and Melanie J. Springer, "Does Electoral Reform Increase (or Decrease) Political Equality?," *Political Research Quarterly* 64 (2011): 420–34.

26. Jacob R. Neiheisel and Barry C. Burden, "The Impact of Election Day Registration on Voter Turnout and Election Outcomes," *American Politics Research* 40 (2012): 636–64.

27. Henry E. Brady and John E. McNulty, "Turning out to Vote: The Costs of Finding and Getting to the Polling Place," *American Political Science Review* 105 (2011): 115–34; J. G. Gimpel and J. E. Schuknecht, "Political Participation and the Accessibility of the Ballot Box," *Political Geography* 22 (2003): 471–88; Moshe Haspel and H. Gibbs Knotts, "Location, Location, Location: Precinct Placement and the Costs of Voting," *Journal of Politics* 67 (2005): 560–73.

28. Brad T. Gomez, Thomas G. Hansford, and George A. Krause, "The Republicans Should Pray for Rain: Weather, Turnout, and Voting in U.S. Presidential Elections," *Journal of Politics* 69 (2007): 649–63.

29. A. Wuffle, Craig Leonard Brians, and Kristine Coulter, "Taking the Temperature: Implications for Adoption of Election Day Registration, State-Level Voter Turnout, and Life Expectancy," *PS: Political Science and Politics* 45 (2012): 78–82.

30. Scott Powers and David Damron, "Analysis: 201,000 in Florida Didn't Vote because of Long Lines," *Orlando Sentinel*, January 29, 2013: 1–2.

31. National Commission on Federal Election Reform in 2000, http://web1.millercenter.org/commissions/comm_2001.pdf/.

32. Christopher B. Mann, "Mail Ballots in the United States: Policy Choice and Administrative Challenges," in Barry C. Burden and Charles Stewart III, *The Measure of American Elections* (New York: Cambridge University Press, 2014), chap. 5.

33. Charles Stewart III, "Losing Votes by Mail," *Journal of Legislation and Public Policy* 13 (2010): 573–602.

34. Thad Hall and Lucy Williams Smoot, Voting Machines: The Question of Equal Protection," in Matthew J. Streb, *Law and Election Politics*, 2nd ed (New York and London: Routledge, 2013): 85.

35. "Absentee and Early Voting," http://www.ncsl.org/research/elections-and-campaigns/absentee-and-early-voting.aspx#early/.

36. Andrew Grossman, "Early Voters Gain Influence in Races," *Wall Street Journal*, August 8, 2012: A4.

37. Lydia Saad, "In U.S., 15% of Registered Voters Have Already Cast Ballots—Early Voting Highest in the West and among Seniors; Similar by Party ID," *Gallup* (October 29, 2012), http://www.gallup.com/poll/158420/registered-voters-already-cast-ballots.aspx/.

38. Robert M. Stein and Greg Vonnahame, "Polling Place Practices and the Voting Experience," in Burden and Stewart, *Measure of American Elections*, chap. 7.

39. Kevin A. Pirch, "When Did the Campaign End? An Examination of the Timing of Vote Returns in the 2008 General Election in Washington State," *PS: Political Science and Politics* 45 (2012): 711–15.

40. U.S. Election Assistance Commission, "Testing and Certification Technical Paper#2: A Survey of Internet Voting," September 14, 2011, http://www.eac.gov/assets/1/Documents/SIV-FINAL.pdf/.

41. http://www.ncsl.org/legislatures-elections/elections/vote-centers.aspx/. See also Streb: 98–99.

42. Douglas W. Jones and Barbara Simons, *Broken Ballots? Will Your Vote Count?* (Stanford, CA: Center for the Study of Language and Information, 2012), chap. 11.

43. Mike DeBonis, "Hacker Infiltration Ends D.C. Online Voting Trial," *The Washington Post*, http://voices.washingtonpost.com/debonis/2010/10/hacker_infiltration_ends_dc_on.html/.

44. Daniel J. Hopkins, "Translating into Votes: The Electoral Impacts of Spanish-Language Ballots," *American Journal of Political Science* 55 (October 2011): 814–30; Michael Jones-Correa, "Language Provisions under the Voting Rights Act: How Effective Are They?" *Social Science Quarterly* 86 (2005): 549–64.

45. NCSL, "Vote Centers," http://www.ncsl.org/legislatures-elections/elections/vote-centers.aspx/.

46. Paul Gronke, Eva Galanes-Rosenbaum, and Peter A. Miller, "Early Voting and Turnout," *PS: Political Science and Politics* 40 (2007): 639–45; Robert M. Stein and Patricia A. Garcia-Monet, "Voting Early but Not Often," *Social Science Quarterly* 78 (1997): 657–71; Paul Gronke and Peter Miller, "Voting by Mail and Turnout in Oregon: Revisiting Southwell and Burchett," *American Politics Research* 40 (2012): 976–97; Joseph D. Giammo and Brian J. Brox, "Reducing the Costs of Participation: Are States Getting a Return on Early Voting?," *Political Research Quarterly* 63 (2010): 295–303; Leighley and Nagler, *Who Votes Now?*, chap. 4; Johanna Dunaway and Robert M. Stein, "Early Voting and Campaign News Coverage," *Political Communication* 30 (2013): 278–96; Common Cause: "Getting It Straight for 2008: What We Know about Vote by Mail Elections and How to Conduct Them Well," 2008, http://www.commoncause.org/research-reports/National_Getting_It_Straight_In_2008_Voting_By_Mail.html/.

47. Burden, Canon, Mayer, and Moynihan, "Election Laws, Mobilization, and Turnout"; Roger Larocca and John S. Klemanski, "Reform and Turnout in Presidential Elections," *State Politics & Policy Quarterly* 11 (2011): 76–101.

48. Gronke, Galanes-Rosenbaum, and Miller, "Early Voting and Turnout"; Hanmer, *Discount Voting*; Elizabeth Rigby and Melanie J. Springer, "Does Electoral Reform Increase (or Decrease) Political Equality?" *Political Research Quarterly* 64 (2011): 420–34.

49. Adam J. Berinsky, "The Perverse Consequences of Electoral Reform in the United States," *American Politics Research* 33 (2005): 471–81.

50. Michael W. Traugott, "Why Electoral Reform Has Failed: If You Build It, Will They Come?" in Ann N. Crigler, Marion R. Just, and Edward J. McCaffery, *Rethinking the Vote: The Politics and Prospects of American Election Reform* (New York and London: Oxford University Press, 2004): 167–84.

51. R. Michael Alvarez, Ines Levin, and Andrew J. Sinclair, "Making Voting Easier: Convenience Voting in the 2008 Presidential Election," *Political Research Quarterly* 65 (2012): 248–62.

52. Charles Stewart III, "What Hath HAVA Wrought? Consequences, Intended and Not, of the Post-Bush v. Gore Reforms," VTP Working Paper No. 102: 28. MIT Political Science Department Research Paper, http://papers.ssrn.com/sol3/papers.cfm?abstract_id=1843583/.

53. Ruy A. Teixeira, *The Disappearing American Voter* (Washington, D.C.: Brookings, 1992).

54. *Political Behavior*: 49.

55. Streb, *Rethinking American Electoral Democracy*: 11–15.
56. Jon C. Rogowski, "Electoral Choice, Ideological Conflict, and Political Participation," *American Journal of Political Science* 58 (2014): 479–94.
57. Paul S. Herrnson, *Congressional Elections: Campaigning at Home and in Washington*, 6th ed. (Los Angeles, London, New Delhi, Singapore, and Washington, D.C.: CQ Press, 2012): 35, 55.
58. Gary C. Jacobson, *The Politics of Congressional Elections*, 8th ed. (Boston: Pearson Education, 2012): 34–36. Jacobson warns, however, that large margins do not automatically translate into secure seats.
59. Leighley and Nagel, *Who Votes Now?*, chap. 5.
60. Michael M. Franz, Paul B. Freedman, Kenneth M. Goldstein, and Travis N. Ridout, *Campaign Advertising and American Democracy* (Philadelphia: Temple University Press, 2008).
61. Richard R. Lau and Gerald M. Pomper, *Negative Campaigning: An Analysis of U.S. Senate Elections* (Lanham, MD: Rowman & Littlefield, 2004); Deborah Jordan Brooks and John G. Geer, "Beyond Negativity: The Effects of Incivility on the Electorate," *American Journal of Political Science* 51 (2007): 1–16.
62. Yanna Krupnikov, "When Does Negativity Demobolize? Tracing the Conditional Effect of Negative Campaigning on Voter Turnout," *American Journal of Political Science* 55 (2011): 797–813.
63. Bryce Corrigan and Ted Brader, "Campaign Advertising: Reassessing the Impact of Campaign Ads on Political Behavior," in Stephen K. Medvic, *New Directions in Campaigns and Elections* (New York and London: Routledge, 2011), chap. 5.
64. D. Sunshine Hillygus, "The Missing Link: Exploring the Relationship between Higher Education and Political Engagement," *Political Behavior* 27 (2005): 25–47; James R. Simmons and Bryan Lilly, "The University and Student Political Engagement," *PS, Political Science and Politics* 43 (2010): 347–49.
65. Donald P. Green and Alan S. Gerber, *Get Out the Vote*, 2nd ed. (Washington, D.C.: Brookings, 2008); Melissa R. Michelson, Margaret A. McConnell, and Lisa García Bedolla, "Heeding the Call: The Effect of Targeted Two-Round Phone Banks on Voter Turnout," *Journal of Politics* 71 (2009): 1549–63; Kevin Arceneaux, Thad Kousser, and Megan Mullin, "Get out the Vote-by-Mail? A Randomized Field Experiment Testing the Effect of Mobilization in Traditional and Vote-by-Mail Precincts," *Political Research Quarterly* 65 (2012): 882–94; David W. Nickerson, "Volunteer Phone Calls Can Increase Turnout: Evidence from Eight Field Experiments," *American Politics Research* 34 (2006): 271–92; Betsy Sinclair, Margaret McConnell, and Melissa Michelson, "Local Canvassing: The Efficacy of Grassroots Voter Mobilization," *Political Communication* 30 (2013): 42–57.
66. Allison Dale and Aaron Strauss, "Don't Forget to Vote: Text Message Reminders as a Mobilization Tool," *American Journal of Political Science* 53 (2009): 787–804; Diana Burgess, Beth Haney, Mark Snyder, John L. Sullivan, and John E. Transue, "Rocking the Vote: Using Personalized Messages to Motivate Voting among Young Adults," *Public Opinion Quarterly* 63 (2000): 29–52; Neil Malhotra, Melissa R. Michelson, Todd Rogers, and Ali Adam Valenzuela, "Habitual Voting and Election Salience: Text Messages as Mobilization Tools: The Conditional Effect of Habitual Voting and Election Salience," *American Politics Research* 39 (2011): 664–81.
67. Zoe Corbyn, "Facebook Experiment Boosts US Voter Turnout; Mass Social-Network Study Shows That Influence of Close Friends Raises Participation," *Nature* (September 12, 2012): http://www.nature.com/news/facebook-experiment-boosts-us-voter-turnout-1.11401#/ref-link-1/.

68. Alan S. Gerber, Donald P. Green, and Christopher W. Larimer, "Social Pressure and Voter Turnout: Evidence from a Large-Scale Field Experiment," *American Political Science Review* 102 (2008): 33–48.

69. Costas Panagopoulos, "Thank You for Voting: Gratitude Expression and Voter Mobilization," *Journal of Politics* 73 (2011): 707–17.

70. Gary C. Jacobson "How Do Campaigns Matter?" *Annual Review of Political Science* 18 (2015): 1.1–1.17

71. Ryan D. Enos, Anthony Fowler, and Lynn Vavreck." Increasing Inequality: The Effect of GOTV Mobilization on the Composition of the Electorate," *Journal of Politics* 76 (2014): 273–88.

72. Thomas E. Mann and Norman J. Ornstein, *It's Even Worse Than It Looks: How the American Constitutional System Collided with the New Politics of Extremism* (New York: Basic Books, 2012): 143; Mickey Edwards, *The Parties versus the People: How to Turn Republicans and Democrats into Americans* (New Haven, CT, and London: Yale University Press, 2013).

73. Costas Panagopoulos, "Extrinsic Rewards, Intrinsic Motivation and Voting," *Journal of Politics* 75 (2013): 266–80.

74. Paul S. Herrnson, Michael J. Hanmer, and Richard G. Niemi, "The Impact of Ballot Type on Voter Errors," *American Journal of Political Science* 56 (2012): 716–30; John A. Krosnick, Joanne M. Miller, and Michael P. Tichey, "An Unrecognized Need for Ballot Reform: The Effects of Candidate Name Order on Election Outcomes," in Crigler, Just, and McCaffery, *Rethinking the Vote*: 51–74; Streb, *Rethinking American Electoral Democracy*, chap. 5.

75. The problem stemmed from the "butterfly" ballot that had two columns of names but one column of punch-outs ("chads"). Some voters punched out the wrong chads; some punched two; others failed to punch the chad cleanly, leading to the famous "hanging chads." Ballots with such problems were inconsistently counted. E. J. Dionne and William Kristol, eds., *Bush v. Gore: The Court Cases and the Commentary* (Washington, D.C.: Brookings, 2001), and Richard A. Posner, *Breaking the Deadlock: The 2000 Election, the Constitution, and the Courts* (Princeton, NJ: Princeton University Press, 2001).

76. Roy G. Saltman, *The History and Politics of Voting Technology in the United States* (New York: Palgrave Macmillan, 2006); Martha Kropf and David C. Kimball, *Helping America Vote: The Limits of Election Reform* (New York and London: Routledge, 2012); Frederic Charles Schaffer, *The Hidden Costs of Clean Election Reform* (Ithaca, NY, and London: Cornell University Press, 2008), chap. 6.

77. Common Cause, "Counting Votes 2012: A State by State Look at Election Preparedness," http://www.countingvotes.org/; Streb, *Rethinking*, chap. 6; Kropf and Kimball, *Helping America Vote*, chap. 1.

78. Harold W. Stanley and Richard G. Neimi, *Vital Statistics on American Politics, 2013–2014* (Washington, D.C.: CQ Press, 2014), table 1-34.

79. Common Cause, http://www.countingvotes.org/.

80. Kropf and Kimball, *Helping America Vote*, 37.

81. Kropf and Kimball, *Helping America Vote*, 114 and chap. 5; Jones and Simons, *Broken Ballots*, chaps. 13–14.

82. Lonna Rae Atkeson and Kyle L. Saunders, "The Effect of Election Administration on Voter Confidence: A Local Matter?" *PS: Political Science and Politics* 40 (2007): 655–60; Thad Hall, J. Quin Monson, and Kelly D. Patterson, "Poll Workers and the Vitality of Democracy: An Early Assessment," *ibid.*: 647–54.

83. Presidential Commission, *American Voting Experience*: 31–53.

84. Natasha Kahn and Corbin Carson, "Analysis: In-Person Vote Fraud near Zero," *Philadelphia Inquirer,* August 12, 2012: A1; Ivan Moreno, "GOP Search for Voter Fraud Turns Up Little," Philadelphia *Inquirer,* September 25, 2012: A4; Hasen, *Voting Wars;* Lorraine C. Minnite "Voter Identification Laws: The Controversy over Voter Fraud," in Matthew J. Streb, *Law and Election Politics: The Rules of the Game,* 2nd ed. (New York and London: Routledge, 2014), chap. 5; Minnite, *The Myth of Voter Fraud* (Ithaca, NY: Cornell University Press, 2010).

85. Jesse T. Richman, Gulshan A. Chattha, and David C. Earnest, "Do non-citizens vote in U.S. elections?" *Electoral Studies* 36 (2014): 149–57.

86. John Fund and Hans von Spakovsky, *Who's Counting* (City: Encounter, 2012); Hasen, *The Voting Wars;* Chandler Davidson, "The Historical Context of Voter Photo-ID Laws," *PS: Political Science and Politics* 42 (2009): 93–96.

87. Stephen Ansolabehere and Nathaniel Persily, "Vote Fraud in the Eye of the Beholder: The Role of Public Opinion in the Challenge to Voter Identification Requirements," *Harvard Law Review* 121 (2008): 1737–77; Hans von Spakovsky, "Voter Photo Identification: Protecting the Security of Elections," The Heritage Foundation, http://www.heritage.org/research/reports/2011/07/voter-photo-identification-protecting-the-security-of-elections/.

88. Gil Aegerter, "Cyberattack on Florida Election Is First Known Case in US, Experts Say," NBC News, http://openchannel.nbcnews.com/_news/2013/03/18/17314818-cyberattack-on-florida-election-is-first-known-case-in-us-experts-say?lite?ocid=twitter/.

89. NCSL, "Voter Identification Requirements," http://www.ncsl.org/research/elections-and-campaigns/voter-id.aspx/.

90. Rasmussen Reports, "71% Favor Proof of Citizenship before Allowing Voter Registration," March 20, 2013.

91. *Arizona et al. v. Intertribal Council of Arizona, Inc., et al.*

92. The National Council of State Legislatures and the New York University Brennan Center for Justice provide current data: "Voter Identification Requirements/Voter ID Laws," http://www.ncsl.org/research/elections-and-campaigns/voter-id.aspx/; "States That Expanded Voting in 2013 and 2014," http://www.brennancenter.org/new-voting-restrictions-2010-election/; and "States with New Voting Restrictions since 2010 Election," http://www.brennancenter.org/new-voting-restrictions-2010-election/.

93. Tova Andrea Wang, *The Politics of Voter Suppression: Defending and Expanding Americans' Right to Vote* (Ithaca, NY, and London: Cornell University Press, 2012); Richard K. Scher, *The Politics of Disenfranchisement: Why Is It So Hard to Vote in America?* (Armonk, NY, and London: Sharpe, 2011); Spencer Overton, *Stealing Democracy: The New Politics of Voter Suppression* (New York and London: Norton, 2006). See also Minnite, *Myth of Voter Fraud.* See, however, Rene R. Rocha, and Tetsuya Matsu Bayashi, "The Politics of Race and Voter ID Laws in the States: The Return of Jim Crow?" *Political Research Quarterly* 67 (2014): 666–79.

94. U.S. Government Accountability Office, "Elections: Issues Related to State Voter Identification Laws," GAO-14-634, September, 2014.

95. Minnite, "Voter Identification Laws"; U.S Government Accountability Office, "Elections: Issues Related to State Voter Identification Laws"; Von Spakovsky, "Voter ID Was a Success in November: Turnout Was Higher in States That Took a Simple Step to Prevent Fraud," The Heritage Foundation, January, 31, 2009, http://www.heritage.org/research/commentary/2009/01/voter-id-was-a-success-in-november-turnout-was-higher-in-states-that-took-a-simple-step-to-prevent-fraud/; "Requiring Identification by Voters," testimony before the Texas Senate, March 10, 2009. The Heritage Foundation, http://www.heritage.org/research/testimony/requiring-identification-by-voters/; a Robert D. Popper, "The Voter Suppression Myth Takes Another Hit," *Wall Street Journal,* December 29, 2014, A-13.

CHAPTER 4

⊁

Election Processes and Systems

A pure democracy . . . can admit of no cure for the mischiefs of faction. . . . [A republic can] refine and enlarge the public views by passing them through the medium of a chosen body of citizens, whose wisdom may best discern the true interest of their country. . . . Under such a regulation it may well happen that the public voice, pronounced by the representatives of the people, will be more consonant to the public good than if pronounced by the people themselves.

—James Madison, *The Federalist No. 10*

The rules governing elections influence turnout, candidate behavior and strategy, results, and the way citizens' votes translate into legislative seats and public policy.[1] An electoral system should: (a) promote citizen participation; (b) give voters genuine choices that make representation and accountability real and promote government responsiveness; (c) be structured so that voters can understand it and exercise their franchise reasonably and rationally; (d) produce decisive results; and (e) be efficient in time and cost. Does the American election system meet these standards?

4.1 BASIC ELECTORAL RULES

Elections for the United States follow three general rules. The first is that only one candidate per office is elected from an electoral district. This single-member district contrasts with multimember district systems in which more than one representative is elected from a given district. Multimember district systems are found around the globe, once were rather common in the U.S. state legislatures, and in varying forms still are used or constitutionally allowed in about 10 states.[2]

The second rule, the "single nontransferable vote," limits voters to one vote per office, regardless of how many candidates there are for that position. Third is the decision rule used to determine the victors. With some exceptions, whoever gets the most votes, majority or not, wins. This is a plurality-winner or "first past the post" system. Reformers must pay attention to all three rules.

Single-Member, Single Nontransferable Vote
Plurality System: Pros and Cons

A Good System. The single-member district, single nontransferable vote, plurality-winner system used in the United States has consequences. On the positive side, election contests focus on candidates as much as or more than on parties, forging a linkage between one legislator and a fixed number of citizens she or he represents. Simplicity and decisiveness reign: voters need concern themselves with only two or three candidates per office, choosing the one they like best, with the winner determined by who has the most votes. This system is a bulwark of, and works best in, a two-party system for a couple of reasons. First, individuals who might prefer to vote for a third or fourth party but who nonetheless want a final result that comes close to their preferences are likely to cast their lot with one of the two major parties, rather than "waste" a vote for a party that would almost inevitably lose. Second, groups that might be tempted to form a third party are inclined to join one of the major parties to influence policy. These tendencies were long ago described in "Duverger's law."[3] Two-party systems, by producing instant and enduring majorities, usually make for more effective government that can easily be held accountable by throwing the "ins" out.

A Bad System. One can find a plethora of criticisms of the American electoral system.[4] If multiple candidates contest a given race, it is relatively common for one to emerge victorious with less than a majority of the votes cast. In 1998 the former professional wrestler Jesse "The Body" Ventura won the Minnesota governorship with 37 percent of the vote; House and Senate victories with 47 or 48 percent of the vote are common. At the presidential level, because of Electoral College arithmetic, candidates can win all of a state's electoral votes by securing only a plurality of its popular votes, as Bill Clinton did in 1992, winning Maine's four electoral votes by capturing only 38.7 percent of voters' ballots. In 2000, George Bush won Florida with under 48.9 percent of the popular vote. Winning with less than a majority, some argue, weakens one's authority to govern.

Plurality elections make third-party and minority-group candidacies difficult because it is almost impossible to beat both of the major parties' candidates. Thus, supporters of the losing parties are left essentially unrepresented by their senators or representatives. Minorities that together might constitute a significant bloc could still, if they are broadly scattered, end up with absolutely no legislative seats because they did not constitute a plurality in any one district. For example, presidential candidate Ross Perot in 1992 picked up 19 percent of the popular vote across the nation but won no electoral votes because he failed to place first in any state. Plurality vote systems can lead to somewhat perverse results, as when a bloc of voters vote for the candidate of a minority party who has no chance of winning, in effect denying votes to their second most preferred candidate and throwing the election to their least favored one. This apparently happened in Florida in 2000, when enough people voted for Ralph Nader to deny Al Gore a majority and give Florida's electors to George Bush—although it is most likely that they preferred Gore.

The fashion in which voters are concentrated in a given geographical area reinforces the effects of a plurality vote system. There always is a difference between the percentage of votes cast for one party's members of the U.S. House nationwide and the percentage of House seats that party wins. Imagine that in a state of 20 districts,

10 members of party A win their contests by 1 or 2 percent each, even if their total falls below a majority, whereas in each of the 10 other districts, party B's candidates win by a 30 percent margin. The latter would have dominated the statewide vote comfortably but won the same number of seats as the former. So-called red or blue states, in which one party holds most of a state's House and state legislative seats, usually really are purple; one party may win the lion's share of seats but constitute only a slim majority overall—a function not of people's policy or party preferences but rather of the electoral rules and residential patterns. In every U.S. election from 1946 through 2010, the party that won the most popular votes won an even greater share of seats in the House, with the difference exceeding 10 percentage points in the Democratic victories of 1976 and 1978. In 2012, conversely, Republicans captured only 48 percent of the national two-party vote for the House, yet they won 54 percent of the seats in the House.[5] In 2014, winning 55 per cent of the vote earned them 57 per cent of the seats.

4.2 REFORMING ELECTORAL RULES

Majority versus Plurality Vote: How to Decide the Winner?

One Shot or Two—Runoffs. In congressional elections, exceptions to the plurality vote system are few, but reformers show an interest in some of them. Majority vote systems are much more common around the world, with most using runoffs between the top two first-round finishers. In the United States, Georgia has long required a straight majority; failing that, there is a runoff between the top two. Louisiana for years has used a dual election system wherein if no one wins a majority in the first round, there is a runoff in November. Some countries allow the top three or even four vote getters to advance to the runoff, using a plurality-winner system at that point. The typical U.S. runoff between two candidates provides clarity and definitiveness to the final result.

There are drawbacks. Runoff systems incentivize more candidates and parties to enter the fray, hoping to "bump" one of the major parties or candidates and end up in the finale. This leads to higher costs in terms of total campaign expenditures, state resources, and, perhaps most importantly, voters' eagerness to participate in two elections. Voter turnout almost always drops in a runoff, potentially distorting voters' original preferences. Whether a problem that makes effectiveness and accountability more difficult or a benefit that enhances representation, it is possible, albeit unlikely, for third-party candidates to win in such contests. That could be dangerous. With multiple candidates, voters might exercise their passion or anger, voting for an extremist to "send a message" in the first election, although they do not actually want to elect that person. If too many electors do that, the moderate candidates could come in third or fourth, leaving the runoff to be contested between extremists. It turns out, however, both in the United States and around the globe, that majority systems favor the two largest parties, in effect usually freezing out minorities. To ensure that winners have a clear majority of the votes while avoiding the runoff problem, some reformers have called for alternate systems.

Preferential Voting. One alternative is preferential voting, sometimes called the instant runoff vote or alternative vote system. Voters rank the candidates by preference. If a candidate garners a majority of first-preference votes, she wins; if there is no majority, the candidate who placed last is eliminated, and his votes are reallocated to the remaining candidates based on the second preferences of his supporters. If that fails to produce a majority vote for one of the candidates, the next lowest vote getter is dropped, with the votes of his supporters being distributed based on their second choices. This process repeats until one candidate has a majority. The advantages of this system are that it allows voters to support more than one candidate, with grada-tions of preference, and potentially forces candidates to appeal to a broader base of voters in case they need those second- or third-preference votes. That might weaken polarization in the electorate. In the United States, San Francisco, San Jose, Aspen, and Minneapolis, for example, have used preference voting; and several states have employed it for voters living or traveling overseas.

All is not positive, however. Counting second- or third-round votes takes time and adds cost. Furthermore, there is the potential for error in marking ballots and for con-fusion as people struggle to figure out why a candidate who came in second or third in the original election emerged as the winner.[6] The problems would be greater in higher-level elections that attract huge numbers of voters. Moreover, the more complicated the rules, the more opportunities there are for manipulation and fraud in the counting.

Approval Voting. Another option is "approval voting," whereby voters cast as many votes as they choose, up to the number of candidates in the race, voting their "approval" of all candidates they like. The candidate with the greatest approval wins. This system gives voters options to vote for their favorite only or for several candidates they like. Some believe that approval voting might increase voter turnout because people can simultaneously express their preference for some minor candidate and vote for a major candidate who is more likely to emerge victorious. The need to garner widespread approval might force candidates to appeal to the broadest possible seg-ment of the voting populace, thus moderating polarization. Approval voting avoids the possibility, in instant runoff vote systems, that someone who came in second or third in "first-place preference" votes might ultimately win. Approval voting encour-ages many candidates to run and allows voters the ability to express themselves better.

Approval voting's weaknesses are real. It does not allow any ranking of candi-dates; it could lead to virtual deadlocks among two or more candidates; it could invite such a multiplicity of candidates that voters would easily be confused. If implemented widely, and if the major parties did not advance their strongest candidates, approval voting might tend to undermine the two-party system.

Changing from plurality to majority election rules, especially with instant runoff or approval voting, could cause candidates to appeal more broadly and moderate some of their ideological appeals. On the other hand, the complexity of these systems probably would make for less efficient elections. What would happen to participation is anybody's guess, but surely it would be affected by how the systems worked in practice.

Multimember versus Single-Member Districts

The major alternative to the single-member district, single nontransferable vote, plurality-winner system employed in congressional elections is a multimember dis-trict system. The goal of multimember districts is to increase representation and participation by ensuring that each political party or group has a chance to elect its own representatives to the legislature and that the number of seats it wins is closely proportional to its support in the electorate. The degree to which a multimember proportional representation system is accurately proportional depends on the number of legislators elected per district and how the votes are cast and counted.

Multimember Districts: Voting for Parties. There are basically two approaches. In the first, citizens simply cast ballots for their favorite parties. The number of winning candidates of each contending party is proportional to the popular votes cast for it. If a party wins 60 percent of the vote in a district having 10 legislators, it puts its top 6 candidates into the legislature. Because of the need to adjust popular vote percentages to a limited whole number of seats in a district, the more seats there are, the more precise is the proportionality and the greater the chance that any block of voters can elect at least one candidate from their favorite party. Apply popular vote percentages of, say, 37, 23, and 9 percent to districts electing 3, 8, and 15 members from among five or six parties, and the results and the proportionality of the representation thereby produced are quite different. Countries around the globe have districts ranging from 2 seats to 100 or more.

The party list system makes the voting easier and focuses accountability on the parties, but the mechanics of calculating voting results are complicated.[7] The "largest remainder" or "quota" system sets a quota for the number of votes required to elect a party's candidate. For example, in a district that elects five legislators and has 100,000 voters, one way to set the quota is to divide the number of voters by 5 so that any party winning 20,000 votes puts one of its candidates into office. A party winning 40,000 votes it gets two seats, and so on. The remaining votes above 20,000 (or 40,000) won by that party are compared to the quota remainders for other parties and to the totals for any party that failed to achieve the quota, and the party with the largest remainder (or "unused" votes) gets the next seat. This "Hare" system, named for its inventor, makes it easier for smaller parties to garner seats. Variations of this quota system are found in some countries that divide the total vote by the number of seats plus one (the "Droop" system) or plus two (the "Imperiali" system) to lower the quota number.

The other party list method is the "highest average system," in which each party's votes are divided by a number to produce an "average" number. These averages are compared, and seats are allocated within the multimember district based on a rank ordering of the averages. The divisors used vary across countries and lead to different results. Both of these counting systems, largest remainder and highest average, usually help minor parties, but neither of them nor any of their many variations produces a perfectly and fairly proportional result because the number of seats is limited. As David Farrell points out, "the best way to maximize proportionality is to have the entire country as one vast constituency,"[8] as is done in Israel. The more seats available in a district, the fewer will be the wasted votes.

Multimember Districts: Voting for Individual Candidates. The alternative to party list systems is to cast ballots for specific candidates, rather than for parties. Variations of this system, used in Japan, Ireland, Malta, and Australia, are several. The most common in the American state experience is the "single-vote" type in which a voter gets as many votes as there are seats up for election in the district but may cast only one vote for any particular candidate. In "cumulative" voting, the voter may cast all of her votes for one candidate or divide them among several contenders. The systems in New Zealand and Germany combine party list and candidate-based voting in each electoral district.

In multimember systems that provide for voting for candidates rather than party lists, cumulative voting can enhance the proportionality of results and elect candidates of more parties.[9] If majority-party voters spread their votes rather evenly, giving one to each of the party's candidates (for example, five candidates from party A seek to fill the five seats in the district, each getting one vote from that party's supporters), but members of a sizeable minority party target all five of their ballots on a single candidate, that candidate stands a good chance of beating the vote total of one or more of the majority-party candidates. Such a result in support of representation by means of multiple parties could be almost guaranteed if voters could cast fewer votes than the number of seats being filled.

Which Reform Would Be Better? The big questions, then, are: (a) which would be better to improve American politics, single or multimember districts, and (b) which of the voting schemes is preferable? The answers depend on which of the criteria for good government one prefers, on the likelihood that one or the other options will produce results that favor those criteria, and on the degree of complexity or simplicity that one thinks is appropriate. Unfortunately, the work of social scientists has not been able to give certain guidance, in large part because of the avalanche of factors that affect elections. Moreover, even if there were convincing proof that any one system best met the criteria in a given country or locality, it is wise to heed the words of Mark Rush, who warned that "different electoral systems work differently in different countries."[10] Each has it its own history, political culture, party system, and constitutional structure. The systems discussed above are mostly found in parliamentary governments, where the legislature tends to be much weaker than the executive and focuses on representation, service responsiveness, discussion, and criticism of the "government" (the executive), rather than serious policy making as found in the U.S. Congress. At the same time, it remains true that manipulating the election system can generate different electoral and political results yielding advantages or disadvantages for any given group or party. Cumulative voting, for example, appears to render incumbents more vulnerable to defeat than single nontransferable vote plurality schemes.[11] Multiple goals, motives, incentives, and disincentives characterize proposals to change electoral rules. In examining other systems, there is food for thought, if not specific models to consider.

Possible Consequences. Table 4.1 summarizes some of the consequences of these reforms. Some are clearly positive. In principle, switching to a multimember district with a proportional voting system should facilitate the competitiveness of one or more "third" parties, giving voters more choices. That would bolster participation and representation. Voters choosing a third or fourth party would be less likely to face the "spoiler" effect under which a vote for one's favorite candidate A instead of an acceptable but less favored candidate B actually helps the least favorite candidate C win the election. It also should eliminate the "wasted vote" syndrome wherein the supporter of a third-party candidate knows that her vote won't matter because that candidate cannot possibly win. Reformers hope that these positives will lead to greater satisfaction and increased interest in elections and thus to higher voter turnout and political participation. Recent surveys of the scholarly literature on multimember districts, however, throw some cold water on such hopes.[12] It is likely, however, that a multimember system would reduce the incentives to gerrymander district lines to

Table 4.1 Summary of Election System Reform Effects

REFORM	CONSEQUENCES
Majority rather than plurality election using runoff	Participation probably harmed; lower turnout in runoff Reasoned judgment possibly enhanced: voters have wide choice at first, then must make clear choice Efficiency diminished; increased cost and time Representation probably unaffected, but could lead to a third-party victory Accountability slightly more difficult because of greater number of "outs" to replace "ins"
Majority rather than plurality election using instant runoff	Participation probably unaffected Reasoned judgment enhanced; voters must think about second and third candidate preferences Efficiency better than runoff but less than plurality vote because of complexity; additional time needed to count Representation unaffected or slightly enhanced because of possible third-party victory Accountability slightly more difficult because of greater number of "outs" to replace "ins"
Multimember or multiparty districts with proportional representation	Participation enhanced because of more choices Reasoned judgment enhanced; voters have multiple parties and candidates to choose from; could confuse Efficiency unaffected or slightly diminished because of need to determine proportions and allocate seats Representation enhanced because voters can select a more narrowly defined party fitting their preferences Effectiveness of government diminished; harder to form majority coalitions Accountability more difficult; who is in charge if different parties control different branches of government? Responsiveness possibly enhanced as parties work hard to fill needs and expectations of their supporters
Direct democracy: initiative and referendum	Participation in governance enhanced; turnout always is a problem Reasoned judgment hard for voters; referendums denigrate elected officials' deliberative judgment Government efficiency diminished by frequent referendums; judicial complications; costly and time-consuming Representation eliminated on referendum items; citizens decide issues Accountability irrelevant; voters creditor blame themselves
Deliberative assemblies	Participation possibly enhanced for some, but no effect on election turnout Reasoned judgment encouraged for participants; could assist voters

ensure the re-electability of a given incumbent or the maximum number of a party's winners in a state. The more seats there are in a given district, the less incentive there would be to rig the boundaries.

Other consequences could be negative or positive. Because it is hard for one party to capture a majority of legislative seats, multimember proportional representation systems tend to produce coalition governments, rendering them less stable, effective, and efficient. How would the presence of three, four, or five parties affect congressional effectiveness and efficiency? Such electoral systems and the resulting multiple parties can make it hard for voters to discern before an election what the winning side's policies are likely to be; and they can confound accountability because it is hard to tell which party or group of legislators is responsible for government output. Furthermore, there is the danger of weakening the tie between a representative and his constituents that occurs in single-member districts, perhaps diminishing responsiveness and personal accountability to one's constituents. In the American case, single-member districts do produce a two-party system that, were it not for separation of powers, would concentrate power, render it more effective and accountable, and maintain the sort of personal responsiveness members of Congress exhibit.

Multimember proportional representation systems using party lists are likely to focus elections more on policy issues and partisan differences than is the case in single-member plurality-winner systems where the focus is more on candidates. The latter often emphasize the attractiveness of individual legislators and their faithfulness to their constituents. Legislatures in proportional representation systems are more operationally partisan, and the parties themselves more unified, than those functioning under a single-member plurality-winner system.[13] Most European parties, for example, traditionally are ideologically more distinct than Democrats and Republicans in the United States, although recently American parties have taken on the European ideological tone. When Illinois used multimember districts for its House, the lower chamber witnessed more ideological parties and less effectiveness than the single-member district Senate.[14]

In state legislatures, multimember districts seem to reduce the electoral advantage held by incumbent legislators in single-member districts.[15] If used for the House of Representatives, they might increase competition and turnover. In other countries, proportional representation systems tend to produce center-left governments favoring more redistributive social welfare and economic ("tax and spend") and liberal trade policies; majoritarian systems seem to yield center-right governments.[16] This could be a result of the tendency of proportional representation systems to elect parties that emphasize policies reflecting their narrower ideological or perhaps class-based constituencies, as opposed to American parties that until recently resembled decentralized and broadly based umbrella-type coalitions.[17]

Those favoring greater ethnic and gender representation in Congress might want to support proportional representation multimember systems because minority groups or those favoring women candidates could more easily capture one or more seats. All would depend on how the election system were set up. In the experience of some American local governments using single-vote voting and running all candidates simultaneously in "at-large" districts, it often is hard for minority groups to capture legislative seats because of the propensity of majority-group voters to cast all their ballots for one party's or one ethnic group's candidates. Cumulative voting might work better, but the evidence is not clear.[18]

4.3 DIRECT DEMOCRACY

Regardless of how votes translate into seats in legislatures, there is a reformist strain that argues that the republican form of government is out of date and even corruptive of democratic values; no representative system can adequately reflect citizens' views on policy and produce good government. Given education levels, the broadening of political awareness, and modern technology, they argue, the United States can achieve genuine democracy and near-universal participation by injecting the citizenry directly into the decision-making process rather than passing the public's views through representatives.

There seem to be three assumptions underlying the direct democracy movement. One is that representative democracy, as preached by the founders, is untrustworthy and basically undermines citizenship.[19] Elected politicians—the "political class"—cannot be trusted to do the people's business. A second assumption is that if democracy and citizen participation are good, more democracy and more participation are better. The third assumption is that the majoritarian principle trumps all else. A majority or perhaps plurality of votes, however informed or intense, should carry the day and determine policy—not some form of indirect representation that may favor minorities or factions. In terms of reform, there are two approaches to the problem. The first advocates the introduction at the federal level of the initiative and referendum. The second seeks to establish a deliberative citizen's forum to inform or, in extreme versions, determine, policy.

Let Me Decide: The Initiative and Referendum

Begun in 1897–1899 as part of the Populist and Progressive movements in South Dakota and Nebraska, the initiative movement to allow citizens to force legislatures to take up certain issues, or to enact laws themselves, spread quickly to Utah, Oregon, Montana, Oklahoma, Maine, Michigan, California, and beyond.[20] Currently some two dozen states and a majority of localities encompassing more than 70 percent of all Americans employ some form of the initiative.

Rules governing initiatives vary. Generally, constitutions and laws specify a predetermined number of signatures for citizen petitions, which include the text of the proposed law, that start the initiative process. In some states, signatures must be distributed across counties or other electoral districts. States with low signature requirements and no distribution restrictions lead in the use of the initiative; those with strict distribution requirements and high signature requirements have the least activity. Once a state's secretary of state, attorney general, elections board, or county clerk certifies a petition, the measure is scheduled for the next election, where a positive vote turns the proposition into law—or, in one version, nullifies a law passed by the legislature. Unlike acts of state legislatures, most governors may not veto laws passed through the initiative and referendum process.

The referendum comes in two basic versions. A "popular referendum" allows voters in some 24 states, after a successful petition drive, to hold a vote to accept or reject measures enacted by the state legislature. Under the much more common "legislative referendum," the legislature solicits the approval, or sometimes just the opinion, of the voters for some action. Some referendums are binding; others are merely advisory.

The initiative and referendum processes are used for a wide variety of constitutional amendments, statutes, regulatory matters, or advisory questions. In 2012 and 2013, for example, Maine and Maryland referendums legalized gay marriage; Minnesota voters rejected a constitutional amendment banning it; Colorado and Washington legalized marijuana use; Californians backed a $6 billion tax increase; Georgia and Washington addressed charter school issues; and North Dakotans adopted stringent antiabortion laws—to name only a few examples. Unlike the initiative, referendums are common around the world, led far and away by Switzerland, which has accounted for about half of all the worldwide national-level referendums. Only five major countries—India, Israel, Japan, Netherlands, and the United States—have never had a national referendum.[21] Referendums unified Italy, split Norway from Sweden, and dissolved the USSR. Often national leaders use referendums to retain or expand their power. Needless to say, governments seldom lose referendums.[22]

Initiative and Referendum—The Positive Side

The case for instituting the initiative and especially the referendum at the national level is straightforward.

1. People want them, and by solid—two-thirds—margins, perhaps because of a distrust of government institutions, processes, and personnel.[23] Support for and participation in initiatives and referendums are greatest among the better educated and more interested.[24]

2. Direct democracy stimulates popular interest in politics, educates and engages voters, enhances their sense of political efficacy and trust in the political system, and thus encourages participation and voter turnout. Election turnout in states having initiatives or referendums on the ballots is slightly higher than elsewhere, but that could be caused by other factors. There is not much evidence that direct democracy has lasting effects on political engagement or efficacy.[25]

3. Initiatives and referendums have institutional consequences. They tend to force officeholders to consider issues that they would prefer to duck, sometimes to avoid what they consider worse consequences flowing from initiatives. Referendums can lift interest group pressures off the shoulders of legislators. They can substitute for or reduce some of the machinations of the normal legislative process, such as logrolling, pork barrel spending, and reliance on messy omnibus (large, multifaceted) bills designed to force legislators to support specific issues they would otherwise oppose if given the chance in a separate bill. Referendums can clarify policy issues by focusing attention on the substance of an issue rather than on its politics. Ultimately, they have the potential to bring public policy into closer alignment with popular wishes. In more formal terms, direct democracy mitigates the "principal-agent" problem in which the agent (legislators) can ignore or modify the wishes of the principals (the electorate). There is some evidence, for example, that the mere existence of the initiative procedure changes the way state legislators behave, bringing policy into alignment with public opinion, particularly on tough issues like abortion, the death penalty, civil rights, and electoral reform. Based on a survey of referendums worldwide, Mads Qvortrup concluded that they "induce the elected representatives to govern with due regard [to] the prevailing sentiments of the community," compensating a bit for a lack of robust electoral competition, especially when there is an ideological gap between citizens and legislators.[26] Another scholar observed that increased use of initiatives seemed to lead to more conservative fiscal and social policies and lower taxation,

concluding that "allowing the general public to participate in lawmaking often seems to improve the performance of government, pushing public policy toward the preferences of the median voter."[27] Others, however, have disagreed;[28] a review of recent ballot measures on social issues found both conservative (antiabortion) and liberal (marijuana use) effects.

4. The direct democracy process, especially initiatives, seems to encourage the formation of new interest groups, especially citizen interest groups. Such groups apparently utilize outside lobbying tactics such as campaigning and protests more than the traditional inside lobbying efforts (testifying, contacting legislators, and the like).[29]

Initiative and Referendum—Problems and Objections

Arguments on behalf of direct democracy are powerful, but there is another side to the coin. Specifically:

1. The processes of direct democracy are difficult, complicated, and confusing, potentially leading to bad laws. One estimate is that only a quarter to a third of the people who sign petitions actually read the initiative measure and talk to the petition circulators; many sign because they believe it is the "fair thing" to do.[30] The wording of ballot measures can be tricky; how can complex issues be framed clearly? They usually are "all or nothing," "yes or no," propositions, with no provision for dealing with the trade-offs involved (how to pay for some initiative or how to deal with adverse consequences) or for expressing preferences among policy options. Strange results may emerge. A Colorado initiative in 2006, for example, banned gifts valued at more than $50 to state officials and employees; little did voters realize that the language might forbid a university scientist from accepting Nobel Prize money![31] There are questions, as well, about whether a legislature is permitted to "fix" a law enacted via initiative or referendum that has flaws deriving from the language of the measure.[32] Reasoned deliberative judgment, compromise, and even old-fashioned horse-trading—characteristics of a legislative process—give way to a one-shot plebiscite, with no accounting for intensity of preferences. James Madison would recoil at the thought.

2. Referendums and especially initiatives place a huge burden on voters. When legislators, policy analysts, and scholars do not or cannot master the details of policy or of legislation, how can one expect the average citizen to do so? Faced with a complex decision, a common tendency seems to be to vote "no," which may explain why the success rate on initiatives runs in the neighborhood of 40 percent.[33] Favorable votes on referendums placed before voters by state governments are approved at a much higher rate, perhaps because voters can take the legislature's approval as a safe voting cue. One scholar argues that because of the tendency to vote against ballot propositions, good laws may fail to pass, whereas bad policies are hard to overturn via direct democracy. David Haskell asks, would the Marshall Plan, emancipation of slaves, or integration of public schools have been approved?[34]

Others defend voters' capabilities, depending on the nature of the issue and how much information voters have.[35] Voters look for shortcuts such as recommendations by prominent officials they identify with, new media endorsements, or (on spending measures) their perception of the health of the economy.[36] It is likely as well that voters facing complex issues and difficult choices they are unable to resolve simply abstain. As Thomas Cronin has noted, "How competent, informed, and rational are ballot issue voters? Not as competent as we would like them to be, yet not as ill-informed or irrational as critics often insist."[37]

3. Although "hot" referendums bring out crowds, participation rates are not impressive, especially if not coincident with a general election.[38] Turnout matters. A study of Swiss referendums, for example, found that about 35 percent of ballot measures would have had different results if all citizens had voted. Interestingly, greater turnout tended to work in favor of right-wing parties' issues.[39] Some countries require a minimum turnout for a measure to pass.

4. Legislators use referendums to sidestep votes on tough issues, especially those that might split their parties.[40] Officials might slice off one controversial issue from a bigger matter, lest the former threaten passage of the latter. For example, in 1992 the Irish population was asked to vote separately on abortion, a matter likely to be part of the Maastricht Treaty that the Irish leaders thought might be jeopardized by inclusion of the abortion question.[41]

5. Many initiatives are promoted or opposed by high-spending special interests, rather than by citizen groups representing the "voice of the people," and the preponderance of the evidence does suggest that when opponents seriously outspend proponents, the propositions tend to fail.[42] The record, however, is hardly crystal clear. Elisabeth Gerber found that when a citizen's group advocates but an economic interest group opposes an initiative proposition, the proposal passes twice as often as when the reverse is the case.[43]

Money is essential in the initial stages of the initiative process. Collecting signatures can be costly, especially when the signature threshold for qualifying a petition is high and when the jurisdiction is extensive (a state). For anything approaching a national measure, it would be necessary to engage armies of paid circulators and expensive political consultants.[44] In fact, it may be that one reason there are more initiatives of late is the rise of a veritable "initiative–industrial complex" of political consultants. These businesses make a lot of money and have a stake in promoting initiatives.[45] A series of judicial rulings over time makes it clear that states cannot limit the amount of money spent on ballot initiatives.

6. Initiatives allow a "tyranny of the majority" to trample on or take away minority interests that often are protected in the normal legislative process. According to Haskell, "There is not a single such group—representing homosexuals, African Americans, or immigrant groups—that would take its chances with a plebiscite."[46] Again, the evidence is mixed. California minorities have fared as well as white majorities, and a variety of recent state ballot measures have supported gay marriage and marijuana use while banning affirmative action, restricting abortion, and even demonstrating the desire of several counties to secede from a state.[47] Defenders of direct democracy say that the courts will rescue bad ballot decisions, implying paradoxically that an undemocratic institution is needed to save the direct democracy process. In fact, one of the biggest enemies of the initiative and referendum process seems to be the judiciary, which is forced to weigh its constitutional views not against the views of an often narrowly split legislature but against the decisions of a local or state population. The implication is either that courts defer to the wishes of the citizenry or that they should be particularly suspicious of such measures that bypass normal legislative procedures.[48] Courts have routinely struck down initiative results on term limits, campaign finance schemes, primary nominating systems, the rights of illegal immigrants, abortion restrictions, gay marriage, and criminal penalties. By one count, as of 2000, courts had voided more than half of the initiatives in the Pacific states.[49] The very processes involved in initiatives, especially collecting and certifying signatures on petitions and drafting appropriate language, encourage litigation.[50]

Would Direct Democracy Work at the National Level?

Whether the United States should adopt, at the national level, the initiative and referendum depends on how the pros and cons discussed above play out in a much wider arena with a much more diverse set of voters and higher stakes. The problems seem almost insurmountable. Can voters in 50 states with conflicting views and interests render judgment on complex matters? Some have proposed resorting to a referendum only on those highly specific issues on which Congress and the president are deadlocked or on nonbudgetary and nonregulatory matters. Could citizens decide issues of foreign and defense policy, energy, and environment? Perhaps a lesson can be learned from Mississippi, whose rules prevent initiatives from negating laws passed by the legislature and mandate that spending measures must include provision for corresponding revenues.[51]

Setting rules to guide the processes would be crucial, but the possibilities are almost endless. Could national referendums be placed on the ballot only by an act of Congress, or would there be some initiative process? In terms of an initiative, is it even possible for a petition drive to occur within a reasonable period of time at a reasonable cost? Could signatures for an initiative be gathered by mail or via the Internet? How many signatures would be required? A proposal decades ago by Senator James Abourezk of South Dakota called for 3 percent of the votes in the last presidential election—about 4 million signatures—including 3 percent in each state. Would initiatives enact statutes or merely force issues onto the congressional agenda? If placed before Congress, may the legislature amend the proposition? Must it act? What if it doesn't? In Switzerland, the world's heaviest user of the referendum process, the government can accept an initiative and pass a law, reject it and send it to the voters in referendum, or reject it and offer the voters an alternative proposal along with the original initiative. To pass, a referendum must receive a majority of all votes, and it must win in a majority of cantons. It may be worth noting that only about one-tenth of Swiss national initiatives have been approved.[52] A provision requiring that some fixed percentage of eligible voters participate in the referendum would make sense, as might a requirement that the measure receive approval in two-thirds or more of the states to ensure broad approval. Perhaps no more than one or two measures should be allowed per election to focus voters' attention.

How senators and representatives would respond to these questions is unclear, but state legislatures have not been overly friendly toward initiatives and referendums, imposing all sorts of barriers—limiting where and when petition signatures may be collected, imposing time limits, and setting standards for documenting the validity of those collecting signatures.[53] What happens to the presidential function of approving or vetoing bills? Would or should the judiciary give special deference to laws passed, or even proposed, through the initiative and referendum techniques?

4.4 ALTERNATIVES

There are other ways to tap the wisdom of the citizenry and engage people in governance at the national level. Congress can use polls to ascertain public opinion, but they carry at least as many complications and flaws as do referendums. Interestingly, in 2011 the White House launched a Web site called "We the People" in which citizens could write online petitions. If a petition garners 25,000 signatures within 30 days, the White House will respond. To date, some responses have been issued, and, as expected, some of the petitions have been a bit strange, such as the one from Texans seeking secession from the Union.

A sophisticated twist on opinion polling is the notion of "deliberative democracy," best associated with Professor James S. Fishkin.[54] His intention is to overcome the weaknesses of direct democracy (too many participants at the mercies of purveyors of information, with no deliberative give-and-take among voters who must make "one-shot" snap decisions) while solving the problems of competitive electoral democracy (little chance to confront candidates and no assurances of their compliance with voters' preferences). Fishkin proposes an assemblage of one or more absolutely representative groups of citizens who would be provided with ample and accurate information, have candidates and advocates appear before them for questioning, and then deliberate for several days—a sort of selective populist parliament. The results would be made widely known to all citizens before elections, and both elected and high-level appointed government officials would take their "instructions" from the deliberations of these gatherings. This system assumes total political equality wherein each participant's views count as much as any other's; there is no external interference with or pressure on the participants; and they get to hear all the same arguments and see the same relevant information.

Others have proposed a national Web-based "town hall" meeting or a series of randomly chosen citizen policy panels on various topics. Fishkin and his colleague, Bruce Ackerman, suggested a national holiday on which all citizens would be incentivized (by a $150 grant) to take part in a series of deliberative exercises—what they call Deliberation Day.[55] One purpose would be to inject widespread reasoned deliberation into political life, thereby improving policy decisions and offering the public a means to correct past political mistakes.[56] When concentrating on a single well-defined issue, such citizen deliberation presumably could prove valuable to participants and observers alike; elected legislators would show more than a passing interest in the conclusions that emerge from such a process.

These ideas have met skepticism and resistance[57] because citizen deliberation:

- Is costly and unwieldy, little more than political "chitchat" that might pressure Congress to delay much needed action or, worse, focus on the wrong issues;
- Focuses on individuals, bypassing legitimate group and institutional interests;
- Cannot possibly address the myriad issues facing American government daily;

- Takes politics (political interaction and conflict by elected officials) out of politics and gives legislators an excuse to shift the blame for enacting bad policies;
- Would be susceptible to the influence of participants who exhibit special rhetorical or bargaining skills; and
- Does not automatically mean that the results of the deliberation group would meet the approval of a majority of citizens.

4.5 CONCLUSION

One can make a case that direct democracy or deliberative assemblies could contribute to governmental effectiveness, responsiveness, and certainly participation, but the case rests on shaky ground and is challenged by substantial scholarship. With referendums and initiatives, reasoned deliberative judgment and efficiency could take it on the chin. Would the people's ability to hold elected officials accountable for policy be threatened when, by definition, some policies had been taken out of their hands? As John Haskell put it, "It is my belief that more direct democracy promises irresponsible and unaccountable government and constitutes a threat to some of the most basic American ideals."[58]

Representative institutions are needed for deliberation, compromise, flexibility, and ability to reverse course—the very characteristics of effective and responsive government. A national initiative process seems out of the question unless it were limited to only recommendations—in which case it would likely have little consequence. Probably the best case to be made would be for a limited form of referendum wherein Congress could put certain narrowly defined issues before the public for approval. That, of course, requires a constitutional amendment on which few bookmakers would wager in the affirmative.

Evidence on the benefits of electoral reforms—multimember districts, proportional results, new forms of voting, initiative, and referendum—is at best mixed. The search for the ideal means to implement the founders' goal of a democratic republic is likely to be futile—not to say difficult to enact via constitutional change. Perhaps what would be worse is blindly to import systems that may work well elsewhere on the assumption that political procedures are transferable. Differences in size and culture matter enormously, so merely comparing what happens elsewhere to what might be desirable in the United States is a risky business. Jumping to conclusions about cause and effect can mislead. The reason is spurious correlation, the existence of third factors such as political culture or historical events that might explain both a switch to a different electoral scheme *and* higher turnout or more parties.

The conclusion seems inevitable: no voting system and no mechanism for injecting popular views and/or deliberation will solve political problems easily or come even close to doing so. None will maximize all or even some of the criteria for good government, and some might undermine them.

QUESTIONS TO CONSIDER

1. Which is better, a plurality-winner election system or a runoff system? Why?
2. Would instant runoff preference voting or approval voting be better than current runoff schemes? Why?

3. Given a choice, would you prefer the existing single-member district plurality-winner system or a multimember district proportional representation system? Why?
4. Would some form of direct democracy, say a representative deliberative assembly that could make recommendations to Congress, be feasible? Would you participate?

NOTES

1. Douglas W. Rae, *The Political Consequences of Electoral Laws* (New Haven, CT: Yale University Press, 1967); David M. Farrell, *Electoral Systems: A Comparative Introduction*, 2nd ed. (New York: Palgrave–Macmillan, 2011); Giovanni Sartori, *Comparative Constitutional Engineering: An Inquiry into Structures, Incentives, and Outcomes*, 2nd ed. (Washington Square, NY: New York University Press, 1997); G. Bingham Powell Jr., *Elections as Instruments of Democracy: Majoritarian and Proportional Visions* (New Haven, CT: Yale University Press, 2000); Gary W. Cox, *Making Votes Count: Strategic Coordination in the World's Electoral Systems* (Cambridge, UK: Cambridge University Press, 1997); Bernard Grofman and Arend Lijphart, *Electoral Laws and Their Political Consequences* (New York: Agathon, 1986).
2. Karl Kurtz, "Changes in Legislatures Using Multimember Districts after Redistricting," *The Thicket at State Legislatures* (National Council of State Legislatures), September 11, 2011, http://ncsl.typepad.com/the_thicket/2012/09/a-slight-decline-in-legislatures-using-multimember-districts-after-redistricting.html/. Until 1842, when Congress required single-member districts, several states elected their congressmen in an at-large fashion.
3. Maurice Duverger, *Political Parties: Their Organization and Activity in the Modern State*, trans, Barbara North and Robert North (New York: Wiley, 1954). Single-member districts do not always produce two-party systems because of regional or ideological third parties. Matthew M. Singer, "Was Duverger Correct? Single-Member District Election Outcomes in Fifty-Three Countries," *British Journal of Political Science* 43 (2013): 201–20.
4. Douglas J. Amy, *Real Choices/New Voices: The Case for Proportional Representation Elections in the United States* (New York: Columbia University Press, 1994); Mark E. Rush, "The Hidden Costs of Electoral Reform," in Mark E. Rush and Richard L. Engstrom, *Fair and Effective Representation? Debating Electoral Reform and Minority Rights* (Lanham, MD, New York, Boulder, CO, and Oxford: Rowman & Littlefield, 2001): 69–120.
5. Norman J. Ornstein, Thomas E. Mann, Michael J. Malbin, and Andrew Rugg, *Vital Statistics on Congress* (Washington, D.C.: Brookings, 2013), table 2.2.
6. Craig M. Burnett and Vladimir Kogan, "Ballot (and voter) 'exhaustion' under Instant Runoff Voting: An examination of four ranked-choice elections," *Electoral Studies* 37 (2015): 41–49.
7. Farrell, *Electoral Systems*, chap. 4; Arend Lijphart, *Electoral Systems and Party Systems: A Study of Twenty-Seven Democracies, 1945–1990* (Oxford: Oxford University Press, 1994).
8. Farrell, *Electoral Systems*: 74.
9. Elisabeth R. Gerber, Rebecca B. Morton, and Thomas A. Rietz, "Minority Representation in Multimember Districts," *American Political Science Review* 92 (1998): 127–44.
10. Rush, "Hidden Costs": 72.
11. Philip D. Habel, "The Consequences of Electoral Institutions for Careerism," *Legislative Studies Quarterly* 33 (2008).
12. Shaun Bowler and Todd Donovan, *The Limits of Electoral Reform* (Oxford: Oxford University Press, 2013), chap. 4; Christopher J. Anderson and Christine A. Guillory, "Political Institutions and Satisfaction with Democracy," *American Political Science Review* 91

(1997): 66–81; Andre Blais and R. K. Carty, "The Psychological Impact of Electoral Laws: Measuring Duverger's Elusive Factor," *British Journal of Political Science* 21 (1991): 79–93.

13. Giovanni Sartori, *Parties and Party Systems: A Framework for Analysis* (Cambridge, UK, and New York: Cambridge University Press, 1976); Anthony Downs, *An Economic Theory of Democracy* (New York: Harper, 1957).

14. Greg D. Adams, "Legislative Effects of Single-Member vs. Multi-Member Districts," *American Journal of Political Science* 40 (1996): 129–44.

15. Gary W. Cox and Scott Morgenstern, "The Incumbency Advantage in Multimember Districts: Evidence from the U.S. States," *Legislative Studies Quarterly* 20 (1995): 329–49.

16. Torben Ivesen and David Soskice, "Electoral Institutions and the Politics of Coalitions: Why Some Democracies Redistribute More Than Others," *American Political Science Review* 100 (2006): 165–81; Sean D. Ehrlich, *Access Points: An Institutional Theory of Policy Bias and Policy Complexity* (New York: Oxford University Press, 2011).

17. Carl H. Knutsen, "Which Democracies Prosper? Electoral Rules, Form of Government and Economic Growth," *Electoral Studies* 30 (2011): 83–90.

18. Farrell, *Electoral Systems*, 163–65, 225–26; Lilliard E. Richardson Jr. and Christopher A. Cooper, "The Mismeasure of MMD: Reassessing the Impact of Multi Member Districts on Descriptive Representation in U.S. State Legislatures," http://0-paws.wcu.edu.wncln .wncln.org/ccooper/mismeasure.pdf/.

19. Benjamin Barber, *Strong Democracy* (Berkeley: University of California Press, 1984); Barber, *A Passion for Democracy* (Princeton, NJ: Princeton University Press, 1998).

20. M. Dane Waters, *Initiative and Referendum Almanac* (Durham, NC: Carolina Academic Press, 2003): 4–12; Dennis Polhill, "Democracy's Journey," in M. Dane Waters, *The Battle over Citizen Lawmaking* (Durham, NC: Carolina Academic Press, 2001): 5–15.

21. David Butler and Austin Ranney, *Referendums around the World* (Washington, D.C.: AEI, 1994): 258.

22. Dennis Polhill, "The Issue of a National Initiative Process," in Waters, *Battle over Citizen Lawmaking*: 521–23.

23. Jeffrey M. Jones, "Americans in Favor of National Referenda on Key Issues; Majority also Backs Shorter Presidential Campaigns and National Primary," *Gallup Politics* (July 10, 2013), http://www.gallup.com/poll/163433/americans-favor-national-referenda-key-is-sues.aspx?utm_source=alert&utm_medium=email&utm_campaign=syndication& utm_content=morelink&utm_term=All%20Gallup%20Headlines%20-%20Politics%20 -%20Social%20Issues; Todd Donovan and Shaun Bowler, *Reforming the Republic: Democratic Institutions for the New America* (Upper Saddle River, NJ; Pearson/Prentice Hall, 2004): 134–36.

24. Todd Donovan and Jeffery Karp, "Popular Support for Direct Democracy," *Party Politics* 12 (2006): 672–73.

25. Todd Donovan and Shaun Bowler, "Election Reform: What Is Expected, and What Results," in Stephen K. Medvic, *New Directions in Campaigns and Elections* (New York and London: Routledge, 2011): 251–53; Bowler and Donovan, *Limits of Electoral Reform*, chap. 7.

26. Mads Qvortrup, *A Comparative Study of Referendums: Government by the People* (Manchester: Manchester University Press, 2002): 153; Robert J. McGrath, "Electoral Competition and the Frequency of Initiative Use in the U.S. States," *American Politics Research* 39 (2011): 611–38.

27. John G. Matsusaka, "Direct Democracy Works," *Journal of Economic Perspectives* 19 (2005): 185–206; Matsusaka, "Fiscal Effects of the Voter Initiative: Evidence from the Last Thirty Years," *Journal of Political Economy* 103 (1995): 587–623; and Joshua J. Dyck,

"Political Distrust and Conservative Voting in Ballot Measure Elections," *Political Research Quarterly* 63 (2010): 612–26.

28. Edward L. Lascher Jr., Michael G. Hagen, and Steven A. Rochlin, "Gun behind the Door? Ballot Initiatives, State Policies, and Public Opinion," *Journal of Politics* 58 (1996): 760–75; John F. Camobreco, "Preferences, Fiscal Policies, and the Initiative Process," *Journal of Politics* 60 (1998): 819–29; Todd Donovan and Jeffery Karp, "Popular Support for Direct Democracy," *Party Politics* 12 (2006): 672–73.

29. Frederick J. Boehmke, *The Indirect Effect of Direct Legislation: How Institutions Shape Interest Group Systems* (Columbus: The Ohio State University Press, 2005); Boehmke and Daniel C. Bowen, "Direct Democracy and Individual Interest Group Membership," *Journal of Politics* 72 (2010): 659–71.

30. Thomas Cronin, Direct Democracy: *The Politics of Initiative, Referendum, and Recall* (Cambridge. MA: Harvard University Press, 1989): 64.

31. John A. Straayer, "Direct Democracy's Disaster," *State Legislatures* 33 (2007): 30–31.

32. "Judicial Approaches to Direct Democracy," *Harvard Law Review* 118 (2005): 2748–69.

33. According to the National Conference of State Legislatures, from 2010 through 2013, 43 percent of initiatives were approved, compared to 74 percent of legislative-proposed referendums; http://www.ncsl.org/research/elections-and-campaigns/ballot-measures-database.aspx/.

34. John Haskell, *Direct Democracy or Representative Government: Dispelling the Populist Myth* (Boulder, CO: Westview Press, 2001): 8.

35. Rich Braunstein, *Initiative and Referendum Voting: Governing through Direct Democracy in the Unites States* (New York: LFB Scholarly Publishing, 2004): 96; Elisabeth R. Gerber, "The Logic of Reform: Assessing Initiative Reform Strategies," in Larry J. Sabato, Howard R. Ernst, and Bruce A Larson, eds., *Dangerous Democracy? The Battle over Ballot Initiatives in America* (Lanham, MD, Boulder, CO, New York, and Oxford: Rowman & Littlefield, 2001): 143–72.

36. Jeffrey A. Karp, "The Influence of Elite Endorsements in Initiative Campaigns," in Shaun Bowler, Todd Donovan, and Caroline J. Tolbert, eds., *Citizens as Legislators: Direct Democracy in the United States* (Columbus: The Ohio State University Press, 1998), chap. 7; Bowler and Dononvan, *Demanding Choices: Opinion, Voting, and Direct Democracy* (Ann Arbor: University of Michigan Press, 1998).

37. Cronin, *Direct Democracy*: 87.

38. Cronin, *Direct Democracy*: 66; Caroline J. Tolbert, John A. Grummel, and Daniel A. Smith, "The Effects of Ballot Initiatives on Voter Turnout in the American States," *American Politics Research* 29 (2001): 625–48.

39. George Lutz, "Low Turnout in Direct Democracy," *Electoral Studies* 26 (2007): 624–32.

40. Mark Clarence Walker, *The Strategic Use of Referendums: Power, Legitimacy, and Democracy* (New York: Palgrave–MacMillan, 2003): 3.

41. Lawrence LeDuc, *The Politics of Direct Democracy* (Peterborough, Ontario: Broadview Press, 2003): 167–69.

42. Charles Price, "Initiative Campaigns: Afloat on a Sea of Cash," *California Journal* 19 (1988): 481–86; Cronin, *Direct Democracy*: 113–16, 123; *Waters, Initiative and Referendum Almanac*, 456–57; Rich Braunstein, *Initiative and Referendum Voting: Governing through Direct Democracy in the United States* (New York: LFB Scholarly Publishing, 2004): 96.

43. Elisabeth Gerber, *Interest Group Influence in the California Initiative Process* (Berkeley: Public Policy Institute of California, 1998); Gerber, *The Populist Paradox: Interest Group Influence*

and the Promise of Direct Legislation (Princeton, NJ: Princeton University Press, 1999); Daniel Smith, "Campaign Financing of Ballot Initiatives in the American States," *ibid*.: 71–90.

44. Elizabeth Garrett and Elisabeth R. Gerber, "Money in the Initiative and Referendum Process: Evidence of Its Effects and Prospects for Reform," in Waters, *Battle over Citizen Lawmaking*: 73–96.

45. Smith, "Campaign Financing;" Todd Donovan, Shaun Bowler, and David McCuan, "Political Consultants and the Initiative Industrial Complex," in Sabato, Ernst, and Larson, *Dangerous Democracy?*: 101–34.

46. Haskell, *Direct Democracy*, 111; Daniel C. Lewis, *Direct Democracy and Minority Rights: A Critical Assessment of the Tyranny of the Majority in the American States* (New York and London: Routledge, 2014). In Switzerland, minorities tend to lose at the level of the cantons but often win nationally, perhaps suggesting that the broader the constituency, the less there is to fear. Qvortrup, *Comparative Study*: 158.

47. Todd Donovan and Shaun Bowler, "Direct Democracy and Minority Rights," *American Journal of Political Science* 43 (1998): 1020–25; Zoltan Hajnal, Elisabeth Gerber, and Hough Louch, "Minorities and Direct Legislation: Evidence from California Ballot Propositions," *Journal of Politics* 64 (2002): 154–77.

48. Philip P. Frickey, "Interpretation on the Borderline: Constitution, Canons, Direct Democracy," *1996 Annual Survey American Law* (1996): 477–534; and "Judicial Approaches to Direct Democracy," *Harvard Law Review* 118 (2005): 2748–69.

49. Mads Qvortrup, "The Courts v. the People: An Essay on Judicial Review of Initiatives," in Waters, *Battle over Citizen Lawmaking*, chap. 12.

50. Waters, "The Courts and the Initiative Process," in Waters, *Initiative and Referendum Almanac*, chap. 6.

51. Matthew J. Streb, *Rethinking American Electoral Democracy*, 2nd ed. (New York and London: Routledge, 2011): 65.

52. Donovan and Bowler, *Reforming the Republic*: 145.

53. Angelo Paparella, "The Barriers to Participation: The Consequences of Regulation," in Waters, *Battle over Citizen Lawmaking*, 121–30; and Waters, *Initiative and Referendum Almanac*, chap. 7; Gregory M. Randolph, "Measuring the Indirect Effect: Voter Initiatives and Legislative Production in the American States," *Public Finance Review* 38 (2010): 762–86.

54. *Democracy and Deliberation: New Directions for Democratic Reform* (New Haven, CT, and London: Yale University Press, 1991).

55. Bruce Ackerman and James S. Fishkin, *Deliberation Day* (New Haven, CT, and London: Yale University Press, 2004); Fishkin, *When the People Speak: Deliberative Democracy and Public Consultation* (Oxford: Oxford University Press, 2009).

56. Amy Gutmann and Dennis Thompson, *Democracy and Disagreement* (Cambridge, MA: Harvard University Press, 1996).

57. Macedo, ed., *Deliberative Politics: Essays on Democracy and Disagreement* (New York and Oxford: Oxford University Press, 1999).

58. Haskell, *Direct Democracy*: x.

CHAPTER 5

∿

Political Parties

There is nothing which I dread so much as a division of the republic into two great parties, each arranged under its leader, and concerting measures in opposition to each other. This, in my humble apprehension, is to be dreaded as the greatest political evil under our Constitution.

—JOHN ADAMS, *letter to Jonathan Jackson*

If I could not go to Heaven but with a party, I would not go there at all.

—THOMAS JEFFERSON, *letter to Francis Hopkinson*

Functioning as organizations, as candidates seeking to win elections and capture control of government, as policy makers in legislatures and executive mansions, and as voters and activists in the electorate, parties from the earliest years have organized around elections and the governing process. As explained below, they have the potential to advance the criteria of chapter 1. The questions are do they, why or why not, and, if not, what can and should be done about it?

5.1 WHAT PARTIES CAN DO

Parties contribute to the goal of public participation primarily by providing an opportunity for people to "get involved." They facilitate representation and responsiveness by aggregating many of society's interests and groups under broad party umbrellas and programs; by presenting citizens' needs and wants to presidents, congresses, and bureaucracies; and by exerting electoral pressure on those officials to respond. Parties are crucial for accountability. They recruit and nominate candidates for office, often assembling and presenting to the electorate broadly representative slates of candidates who stand for a common set of policies. Parties raise money, provide campaign support, and stimulate turnout on behalf of their nominees. Electorally, parties orient voters and make the voting choice much easier by offering a shortcut to voting decisions. The losing party remains active, criticizing the governing group and offering alternatives, thus educating and sharpening the choices for voters.

Political parties contribute to effective and efficient government. For example, in Congress, parties organize each chamber, select the leadership, and assign members to committees. Party leaders schedule the business of the legislature, promote the policies for which they campaigned, and try to accommodate their members' need for action on their favorite bills and for time to debate others. A common party agenda and party loyalty can provide the linkage between the president and Congress, between House and Senate, and, ideally, between the federal government and the states.

Reasoned, fair, and deliberative judgment can be fostered to the extent that party platforms, proposals, and strategies receive scrutiny among leaders and others before, during, and after elections. Party leaders can focus and guide discussion and debate; through criticizing government performance or providing alternatives, the "out" party can enrich the debates over policy. Knowing that the majority party could tomorrow be the minority tends to support the deliberative nature of policy making; running roughshod over the minority can lead to "payback" after the next election. Finally, through all these means and others, parties can help put the brakes on government excesses. Pulling together disparate and often passionate interest groups under a party banner both requires and enforces moderation, compromise, and reasoned judgment, transforming what might be religious, economic, social, or ethnic tensions into partisan political battles that can be fought, and lost, without fundamental damage being done to the country or the participants. Party leaders "police" their members, seeking to keep them under control, avoid scandals, or— as when senior Republican leaders urged President Nixon to resign in 1973 after Watergate—leave office lest there be electoral backlash in the future. In the extreme, party can shelter legislators from some of the pressures of special interests, elites, and even the media. In light of all these functions, it is little wonder that E. E. Schattschneider proclaimed many decades ago that "modern democracy is unthinkable save in terms of the parties."[1]

How well the parties perform these tasks is open to much debate. The American experience in the past 40 or 50 years casts doubt on many of these claims. Parties can fail or, worse, do damage. They can undermine sound government by substituting short-term electoral interests for longer-term public policy improvement, by focusing on the politics rather than the substance of policy, by ducking the hard issues that might cost them electoral victories, by dividing the public, by blocking enactment of the other parties' policies, and by forcing voters to choose between two unpalatable candidates. To the extent parties fail to accomplish their tasks or, worse, actually harm the polity, reforms are called for. But which reforms? The answer may be found in three interrelated questions. First, what *should* American political parties look like, and how should they function to advance the seven criteria? Second, should efforts be made to continue the conditions that make for a two-party system, or is it time to encourage multiple parties? Third, what sorts of reforms are needed to bring these conditions about?

5.2 WHAT KIND OF PARTIES?

What *should* American parties look like and how should they function? The answers can be arrayed along a continuum of models, depending on which values one wishes to advance. Anchoring one end are the traditional parties: decentralized, overlapping, and sometimes fragmented *coalitions* of groups, interests, and individuals— sometimes well organized and sometimes not—that every four years constitute a national party to nominate and elect presidential candidates. The model is the parties formed by the realignment of the 1930s that left two national coalitions that survived until roughly 1970. Democrats were urban, Jewish, Catholic, southern, working class, and ethnic (especially black and, outside of southern Florida, Latino); Republicans tended to be rural or suburban, wealthier, Protestant, and white. Voters aligned themselves with one or the other party, but there was movement back and forth when the parties failed to please the voters.

As organizations, this type of party is heavily rooted in local and state politics where, until the twentieth century, most government and politics occurred. With the New Deal social welfare and regulatory systems in place, however, and on U.S. entry into World War II, Washington became the focus of popular expectations for public policy. In Washington, congressmen and senators of a given party generally shared the same views, but bipartisanship worked; there was room for outliers, dissenters, and mavericks, as long as they supported their leadership on procedural and organizational matters to protect their parties' interests. For a good many years, until the 1980s, this model described the state of the parties; and for many today, it is the goal to be sought.

Responsible Versus Coalitional Parties: Pros and Cons

Given the loose structure of political parties in Washington at the time, and in light of the conservative coalition of Republicans and southern Democrats, many activists, scholars, and journalists became frustrated by the divisions within the parties and the needlessly slow pace of government, bemoaning the "deadlock of democracy."[2] By the 1950s, political scientists through their national association called for a change, seeking to establish a far more structured, organized, and disciplined "responsible" party system modeled after the British system[3]—the model described in chapter 2 that anchors the other end of the party continuum. That type of party seeks to elect presidents and members of Congress on the basis of national party platforms and to implement those policy preferences by directing the governing process in Washington and reinforcing linkages between House and Senate, between Congress and the president, and between the national and state government leaders. Voters choose one or the other party to control Congress and the presidency, and they then hold that party responsible for delivering on its promises. The losing party serves as the "loyal opposition," to use a parliamentary term, less involved with policy making and more oriented toward criticizing the governing party and offering alternatives to the voters, in hopes of winning the next election.

Which of these two models might better serve the country? The coalition or pluralist party structure has advantages. It is consistent with the decentralized federal system insofar as parties are based in the states and localities. It provides easy access for citizens seeking to participate in government and to assume positions of influence locally, where aspiring politicians and party leaders can get their feet wet, testing their abilities and proving their mettle before trying to capture higher offices. It is permeable, open to the many interest groups.

Parties of this type enhance *dyadic* representation, responsiveness, and accountability by linking senators and representatives to their local or state supporters and constituents—rather than pressuring them to subject their own preferences and those of their constituents to the wishes of national party leaders who are more attuned to a national electorate. Policy is made not by presenting a coherent platform of policies and then pushing it through Congress, but rather by bringing together more or less independent-minded representatives of diverse constituencies who generally share the same broad views but whose primary orientation and loyalty are to their local parties and voters. Thus a premium is placed on deliberation, compromise, and the possibility of bipartisan action in Congress. How this plays out in reality depends, naturally, on how and by whom those legislators are chosen to run for office (the nomination process). There are big differences among being nominated and supported (a) by a broadly representative group of voters back home who share many common views under the party umbrella, (b) by a more focused ideological group of party activists and leaders, or (c) by a tightly controlled patronage-oriented party elite. Finally, a coalitional party system supports the notion of a limited national government, making it difficult for party leaders to enact comprehensive policies that fail to win support across the country.

But wait! This kind of party has disadvantages, just as the responsible party system has advantages. If the loose coalitional party system fosters an *individualistic* type of representation, responsiveness, and accountability, the stronger "responsible" party system yields *collective* versions of these values. Instead of electing one's preferred candidate, uncertain of what his party leaders will demand of him once he arrives on Capitol Hill—as in the coalitional party—under the responsible party system voters know that if party A rather than party B wins a majority of seats, its members will push through policies on which it campaigned. Under the coalitional system, one can help elect her party's nominee, thus giving that party majority control in Washington, only to see the party enact policies quite different from what she wanted and her preferred candidate campaigned on. Accountability in the responsible party system is thus collective rather than individualistic.

Parties leaning toward the responsible party category typically would possess internal means of disciplining wayward members, keeping them aligned in support of the party's platform. The party's control over nominations and its assistance with reelection, along with the congressional party's ability to hand out choice (or not so choice) committee appointments, funding or not funding members' local projects, and various other perquisites traditionally helped keep members of Congress in line. Responsible parties are more effective and efficient, able to act decisively and be responsive to national needs, especially if the same party controlled Congress and the White House. To the extent that a strong and centralized national party controlled nominations, it could ensure a diverse and representative slate of candidates. Reasoned deliberation across party lines in Congress might well suffer, as has been apparent for a decade or more, but it might be strengthened *within* the party caucuses and at national party meetings because putting together a party platform requires leadership, negotiating skills, compromise, and discussion. Strong parties are especially vigilant with respect to members who could cause embarrassment by pursuing dangerous policies or through scandals or ill-timed utterances of the sort that hurt Republican hopes to capture the Senate in 2010 and 2012. On the negative side, however, is the fact, brutally brought home to Americans over the past 20 years, that strong unified parties, backed by ideological voters, can create total gridlock when each party controls one chamber of Congress and neither is willing to bend and compromise. Which party system would better fit the American character and culture? Which would enhance the values one deems most important?

5.3 REFORMS

Beyond issues of shared ideology, parties try to exercise influence over their members through their ability to nominate candidates for office, support their campaigns, and turn out the vote. In government, presidents and congressional leaders use a range of techniques to encourage loyalty and faithfulness. Efforts to steer American parties toward either end of the continuum depend on changing these techniques and incentives.

Today, most candidates for Congress, and indeed most political offices, are self-starters; but state and national parties have become much more involved in recruiting and supporting candidates.[4] To affect the nature of the parties, the rules governing these activities and laws regulating political party organization and authority would have to change. For example, to bring about more disciplined parties, the national party leaders would have to exercise much greater control over nominations for president and Congress. At the extreme, the national party committee might have a veto over a candidate's ability to run under the party label. State party committees, or even the national party organizations, might actually do the nominating or have the ability to steer it. That implies the elimination or modification of primary elections, as explained in chapter 6. Federal election laws would need to give parties far more influence over the raising and spending of campaign funds, as detailed in chapter 7. The matter of patronage would have to be revisited to allow elected officials more control over appointments of government employees. These changes would invoke a storm of objections, but they are the logical steps to stronger parties. Reformers must have a clear goal in mind before thinking about the particular means.

Within Congress, party leaders could be given greater authority over their members than the considerable influence they now wield, controlling not only committee and subcommittee assignments and chairmanships, but also members' staffs, office budgets, and other perquisites of office. Their ability to punish wayward party members would have to increase. Is the American public prepared for or sympathetic to such moves?

On the other hand, to support a loose, coalitional form of party, existing rules and national party controls would have to be relaxed and the current means of influence of congressional leaders over their members reduced. The Republican and Democratic National Committees and the two parties' House and Senate campaign committees would have to be constrained from raising and spending money for their candidates and from running independent campaigns on their behalf. State and local parties, on the other hand, might be given an easier hand in financing campaigns and in the nomination process. If weakening the parties were the goal, legal restrictions on party fundraising and spending could be tightened in favor of private sources of campaign donations. Political action committees, divorced from party linkages, would take on more influence. Congressional leaders' powers would need to be trimmed.

5.4 ALTERNATIVES AND PROSPECTS

They Got What They Wanted!

Over the past four decades or so, American parties have veered from the coalitional type toward the responsible party model, although it would appear that the American public is not enamored of that approach.[5] The two national party committees and the four congressional campaign committees have grown in skill, organization, resources, and activity—usually with an eye toward "nationalizing" congressional elections. This evolution coincided with and exacerbated the polarization of the electorate, reflecting what two scholars have called "conditional party government." That is, as the country divides more cleanly over issues, the parties in Washington become more internally homogeneous and distant from each other. In turn, senators and especially representatives grant more authority to their leaders to maintain control of one or the other chamber.[6]

Parties today raise money, recruit and support candidates, run media ads, and provide all sorts of support services for their candidates. Voters support their parties on election day with great consistency and enthusiasm. At the government level, on Capitol Hill, the parties are stronger now than in the past hundred years, with party leadership having taken over many of the functions and powers that traditionally lay in the purview of the committee system and with members lining up to cast party-line votes at a rate not seen in a century. Many longstanding affiliations between the parties and ethnic, regional, religious, or economic groups have come under pressure or even flip-flopped, as social issues like abortion and gay rights cut across traditional lines of cleavage, as the church-going population has become heavily Republican, as Protestants have split into the evangelicals and the "mainline" churches, and as the South changed dramatically into a bastion of Republicanism whereas the northeast has become strongly Democratic. At the same time, the number of independents has grown more numerous than either party's identifiers. Advocates of strong responsible parties should be jumping for joy, but often that is not the case for a couple of reasons.[7]

First, the constitutional separation of president from Congress, and that of House from Senate, wreaks havoc with any notion of linkage when the various branches are in the hands of different parties or when internal legislative rules such as the filibuster provide unusual power to minority parties. Divided government frequently produces gridlock and slows down the policy process.[8] For the past several decades, it has meant bitter rivalry, obstructionism, and perhaps sundering of the congressional system. President Obama in 2011–2014 faced a strong and unified Republican majority in the House of Representatives (except when Tea Party renegades refused to cooperate with their own party leaders) that frustrated his initiatives. Meanwhile, in the Senate, Democrats held a slim majority, but the filibuster and other procedural rules, practices, and traditions gave the minority Republicans the ability to block any proposals from the majority, just as Democrats did when the GOP held the majority. In 2015–2016, Republicans controlled both House and Senate. Under these circumstances, strong unified and semidisciplined parties undercut the effectiveness and efficiency for which they are supposedly well suited.

Second, American parties have become extremely polarized. Whether it was caused by a polarization among the American public, was the result of massive demographic shifts, or was a consequence of an increasingly divided "political class" and a provocative media, as some contended,[9] the reality is that the United States has experienced two deeply divided and obstinate national parties. Bitterness and rancor now characterize the governing process, with ideologues on both extremes seemingly more content to make political points (in hopes of winning more seats at the next election or to curry favor with their ideologically extreme supporters) than to make public policy. Thus the paradox: supporters in the 1950s, 1960s, and 1970s of more responsible parties have seen their wishes come true and now lament the fact, suggesting that a return to the "old-time" system that they bemoaned back then might be preferable. The country now faces a *fundamental incompatibility* between the nature of the party system and the political institutions described in the Constitution.

Anti-Party Reforms

There are alternatives to ponder. One extreme strain suggests eliminating or drastically weakening political parties, returning to the George Washington era before parties developed or to the "Era of Good Feelings" (one might cynically say the era of no feelings) circa 1816–1824. The rise of self-described independents, now approaching 40 percent of the electorate, speaks volumes. Reforms mentioned above and elaborated on in some of the following chapters to weaken parties—reducing parties' roles in election processes and slashing internal congressional leadership powers—could take the country in this direction. Banning party labels on ballots, forbidding party funding of campaigns, and the like would clinch the deal. Citizen participation might be increased; responsiveness and accountability would be local and personalized, with each representative tied closely to his or her electoral supporters. "I vote the man, not the party" would take on new meaning. More real deliberation, debate, and compromise might ensue, breaking today's gridlock and thus leading to greater policy-making effectiveness. On the other hand, organizing and running Congress would prove more difficult; candidates for office probably would have to spend even more of their own time and energy fundraising and campaigning; and the influence of interest groups and the media would grow because party leaders could not provide political "cover" and protection for members.

Why Not More Parties?

The Record. Rather than abandon the parties, a number of commentators,[10] three-fifths of the public,[11] and such notables as ex-GOP presidential candidate John Huntsman think that the country needs a viable third party. Historically, third parties—more than 80 of them have competed in national elections[12]—have been of an ideological, splinter, regional, or single-issue type; only once, in the 1850s, did a third party, the Republicans, replace one of the two major parties, the Whigs. In a few presidential elections, third parties or independent candidates garnered significant numbers of popular votes: the Free Soil Party in 1848, Southern Democrats and the Union Party in 1860, the Progressives in 1912 and 1924, George Wallace of the American Independent Party in 1968, and Independent candidate Ross Perot in 1992 and 1996. Of late, however, there has been no sign of a vibrant third-party movement other than the so-called

Tea Party faction of the GOP. In 2012, Libertarian Party nominee Gary Johnson placed third with nearly 1.3 million votes; Green Party nominee Jill Stein placed fourth with a mere 469,000 votes; and Virgil Goode, the Constitution Party nominee, was next with a whopping 122,000 votes.

Because of the single-member district, winner-take-all nature of the Electoral College, it is impossible for a third-party or independent candidate to win many electoral votes. Theodore Roosevelt's 27 percent of the popular vote garnered 88 electoral votes (16.6 percent of the total) in 1912. George Wallace in 1968 picked up 46 southern electoral votes (8.5 percent) from 13.5 percent of the popular vote. In 1980, Congressman John Anderson of Illinois ran as an independent, winning about 6.6 percent of the popular vote but no electoral votes. Ross Perot's 19 percent of the popular vote in 1992 likewise failed to pick up a single electoral vote. At the congressional and state levels, tough ballot access laws in some states make it difficult for third-party candidates to emerge.[13] Congressional and state legislative candidates thinking of a third-party bid face the triple whammy of the plurality vote electoral system (recall Duverger's law from the previous chapter), voters' disdain for "wasting" votes by supporting a party that is unlikely to win, and difficulties in raising campaign money. Thus relatively few third parties succeed in races for Congress, governorships, and other state offices, although scores of third-party candidates and independents make the attempt. Winning is not impossible; on a couple of occasions in the late nineteenth century, 7 or 8 percent of the members of the House were from third parties.[14] More recently, in 1990 two third-party governors were elected in Alaska and Connecticut; in 1998 Maine and Minnesota chose third-party governors; and for a while recently, Connecticut and Vermont had one independent senator each. Such situations are rare. For 150 years, the existing two parties have shown a remarkable resemblance to giant sponges—absorbing hot issues being raised by third parties and soaking up most of their advocates.

In today's highly polarized and divided system that seems to lack a political middle, some reformers see an opportunity to create not a fringe or splinter party, but a centrist, moderate, and accommodating party. The argument is simple. If the distribution of the mass public's views resembles a normal curve, but party leaders and their hard-core activist supporters who turn out for primary elections line up in a bimodal distribution, the time is ripe for a party to form and capture that vast middle ground where most voters reside. For more than 20 years, one-third to two-fifths of Americans classified themselves as moderates, furnishing fertile ground for a centrist party.[15] Even if the bulk of voters are themselves at the extremes, if they want governance rather than political rhetoric and ideological rigidity, they might favor a more centrist party that could effectively govern by winning over the moderates of each party. Moreover, if they did not get all or most of what they want, they would get some of it—rather than getting none, which is what they get today because of the polarized, unified, oppositional, and often obstructionist nature of the Democrats and Republicans. What would it take?

A Third Party? There are three scenarios, none of which is likely. One features a popular, centrist, and independent presidential candidate who attracts professional political activists, raises hundreds of millions of campaign dollars, and advocates policies and take positions that appeal to huge numbers of voters of all stripes. The public demonstrably wants political leaders and parties that are open to compromise, so it is likely to be receptive to such an appeal.[16] In turn, this candidate, having won, needs to build a party almost from scratch. That is a tall order. It is far from clear, or even plausible, that congressional candidates or incumbents would risk moving to join such a party. In recent years, no independent or third-party presidential candidate has won even a fifth of the popular vote. The candidate would need the resources and organization to get on the presidential ballots in all 50 states—but that is what parties help to do. Interestingly, an Internet-driven movement sprang up in 2012 to allow the mass public to nominate a presidential candidate independent of the two parties. By May of that year, however, the effort fizzled. No "name" candidates made themselves available; one of the top vote getters was Ron Paul, who formally competed for the Republican nomination from a Libertarian, not centrist, perspective. Reforms to make this scenario plausible include easing ballot access in all 50 states and changing the presidential campaign-funding law from reimbursing third-party candidates after the election to funding them up front, as is done with the two major parties in the general election. Beyond the organizational and financial hurdles, there remains the challenge of Electoral College arithmetic: one must win a plurality of votes in a good number of large states (see chapter 10).

A second scenario involves the growth of centrist third parties at the state level, either in the state legislatures or in states' congressional delegations. Although there are a few examples of third-party successes in the states, such as the Farmer–Labor Party in Minnesota, the old LaFollette Progressives in Wisconsin, and New York's Liberal and Conservative parties, although independents occasionally do pick up seats, and although many congressional and state legislative elections include candidates from a half dozen parties, the rise of a group of popular and well-funded centrist independent-party candidates in any one state, let alone a slate of candidates throughout a large number of states, simply is unlikely and may be impossible. America's political party culture and the roadblocks mentioned above make it too difficult.

A final scenario is reminiscent of the pre–Civil War era, when two existing parties primarily defined by one set of substantive issues (primarily rural–urban tensions) and one set of political matters (an intense rivalry to control the political spoils of electoral victory) were split by a new issue, slavery, that pulled together antislavery factions from both parties.[17] Is there a looming crisis and a new issue comparable to slavery that would break up both parties and split off these centrists? One might be social issues like homosexuality and abortion; there are pro-life and pro-choice, and pro- and anti-gay marriage, activists in both parties. Are there enough to create a split? It is hardly imaginable that a new party system would emerge based on marriage or abortion. To compete, a party must cover a range of issues. For an economic disaster to cause both parties to fracture, the matter would somehow have to be such that the ideological wings of each party remained intransigent and prevented action to solve the crisis, alienating the citizenry, driving moderates and problem-solvers into a single camp, and thus creating that third-party movement. If what happened in 2008 and 2009 is any indication, that is not going to happen; crises have a way of pulling together even bitter rivals. Neither party exhibits a death wish.

Nothing today is quite like the slavery dispute. At any rate, reform of electoral and campaign finance rules would be a pre- or at least co-requisite of such a revolution, and they are not in the offing, as the next chapters will discuss.

Third Parties—So What?

What might be the consequences if somehow a viable third party would emerge?[18] Much depends on the nature of that party, which most likely would be based on a limited number of issues. Suppose, however, that there were such a party, large enough to attract a quarter or a third of voters. One implication might be enhanced citizen interest in politics, leading to an increase in voting turnout and perhaps more participation in party activities. A more diverse three- or four-party system would provide improved representation insofar as people devoted to those issues would have a political home and institutional mouthpiece. Under the right conditions, they might have a better chance to put into Congress someone who represented those issues. If that occurred, government's symbolic and service responsiveness to that party's members would be enriched, but since it is unlikely that that party could carry the day on its issues without the support of other parties, policy and pork barrel responsiveness probably would not be any better.

The effect of a third or fourth party on government effectiveness and efficiency is worth considering. If genuinely a centrist party, it would command substantial leverage and bargaining clout, enticing or possibly forcing one or both of the other parties to negotiate. Conversely, if it were an ideological or one-issue party and commanded a significant number of seats in Congress, and if to retain its electoral supporters it refused to compromise, the three-way way split could stymie the policy-making process and lead to deadlock. Majorities would be hard to fashion. One positive is that, as has been true historically, such a party could force new issues onto the agenda.

A crucial issue is accountability. With three or more parties in government, electoral confusion increases: who gets the blame or praise for government actions? Imagine the situation of one party controlling the House, a second party the Senate, and a third party the presidency—or, perhaps worse, the House and Senate about equally divided among the three or four parties. For which party does one vote? Pondering the next election, a third-party candidate for Congress would have to do some rather careful calculating in terms of how to pitch his or her campaign to garner a plurality of votes.

Arguably, a system of multiple parties would make hasty or extreme government action even more unlikely than if one party controls everything, protecting against the dangers of enacting bad policies. If multiple parties were to present moderate and well-thought-out policy views in the legislative halls, more reasoned and deliberative judgment might ensue. An alternate result might simply be more intense rhetorical dueling by members of Congress as they play to their more narrowly focused base of supporters. One rather scary research result, based on a study of 70 democratic and semidemocratic countries from 1987 to 2005, found that multiparty systems in countries using single-member districts were associated with higher levels of corruption.[19] One hesitates to impute that linkage to the United States.

Theodore Lowi points to another interesting possibility: a strong third party, if competitive at the presidential level, could prevent any presidential candidate from winning a majority in the Electoral College, thus throwing the election into the House of Representatives, "immediately making Congress the primary constituency of the presidency" and forcing closer presidential–congressional relations.[20] Such a development could lead to greater cooperation and a smoother policy-making process. For supporters of a strong presidency, however, the likely result disappoints; if anything, Congress would become stronger relative to the White House. Chapters 8 through 11 address these matters.

If It's Broke, Fix It: Tweak the Existing Parties

What about repairing the existing parties? Can their ideological extremism and incessant feuding be broken in favor of more reasonable and compromising stances? Can there be strong parties that differ on almost all key issues but that, nonetheless, are able to work together, find common ground, and govern? In short, there may be nothing wrong with two divided and polarized parties *provided* they are composed of members (a) who see governance as more important than partisanship and winning elections and (b) who are led by sensible professionals exercising a degree of control over the members. Such professionals might drive their parties toward the middle, at least on some key issues, to capture moderate and independent voters. When, however, the ability to decide which candidates will represent their parties at the next general election is in the hands of those who are focused on certain wedge issues and/ or absolute adherence to certain principles regardless of the consequences, the likelihood of nominating a presidential candidate who can lead the party toward the middle is slim. Choosing moderate senators and representatives to follow reasonable party leaders, likewise, is extremely difficult. Changing the rules governing the nomination process, as discussed in the next chapter, is a goal of many reformers. Leaders of the Republican establishment and traditional "business-type" Republicans, shocked by the string of 2010 and 2012 election losses attributable to extremely conservative GOP candidates, spent late 2013 and much of 2014 planning and implementing ways to counter the Tea Party extremists. The 2014 congressional primary results suggest that they may have succeeded.

5.5 CONCLUSION

Those who are dissatisfied with political parties and wish to reform them ultimately must make choices on two dimensions: (1) a two-party versus a multiparty system and (2) the type of parties: loose and somewhat overlapping coalitions versus more tightly organized and more ideologically focused disciplined and responsible parties. Each option has advantages and disadvantages, few of which are absolutely clear or unerringly predictable. Table 5.1 presents a shorthand summary of possible consequences. Party reform, clearly, is interrelated with a number of other dimensions of government and the political system. Subsequent chapters will explore those relationships in depth.

Table 5.1 Summary of Party Reform Effects

CRITERIA	REFORMS			
	DISCIPLINED RESPONSIBLE PARTIES	COALITIONAL AND OVERLAPPING PARTIES	TWO-PARTY SYSTEM	MULTIPLE-PARTY SYSTEM
Participation and voter turnout	Uncertain; limited participation within party; turnout effect depends on attractiveness to voters	Neutral to positive, especially if access and opportunities for advancement are easy	Neutral	Positive; more choices and opportunities
Reasoned deliberative governmental decision making	Neutral; major decision making limited to party leaders	Neutral to positive; decisions made across party lines	Neutral; policies set inside each party; voters choose	Neutral to positive, depending on party ideological breadth and the need to compromise
Effectiveness	Positive, but potentially dangerous	Neutral; could overcome gridlock but would yield compromised policies	Positive	Neutral to negative; harder to form majority coalitions
Efficiency	Positive	Negative to neutral; takes time and negotiating to reach decision across parties	Positive	Neutral to negative; harder to form majority coalitions
Accountability	Positive for collective accountability; negative for dyadic accountability	Neutral to positive at dyadic level; negative at collective level	Positive: "ins" and "outs" are clear	Negative: who is in charge?
Representation	Neutral to negative; collective rather than dyadic	Probably positive; stronger dyadic representation	Positive collectively; negative dyadic representation	Positive; groups can have their "own" parties
Responsiveness	Positive responsiveness to national majorities; neutral for individual responsiveness	Neutral, varying according to legislators' skills and focus	Neutral and mixed; collective but less individual dyadic responsiveness	Neutral; stronger symbolic responsiveness; weaker policy and pork barrel responsiveness

QUESTIONS TO CONSIDER

1. Are the existing Democratic and Republican parties up to the task of governing? Why or why not? What could be done to fix them?
2. Would strong, disciplined, and responsible parties be preferable to loose coalition-type parties or would the latter be better? Why?
3. Should there be more than two viable and active parties? What might the consequences be for participation, representation, responsiveness, effectiveness, efficiency, accountability, and reasonable deliberative judgment in Washington?

NOTES

1. E. E. Schattschneider, *Party Government* (New York: Holt, Rinehart, & Winston, 1942): 1.
2. James MacGregor Burns, *The Deadlock of Democracy: Four Party Politics in America* (Englewood Cliffs, NJ: Prentice Hall, 1963).
3. American Political Science Association, Committee on Political Parties, "Toward a More Responsible Two-Party System," *American Political Science Review* 64, Part 2, Supplement, 1950: 1–96.
4. L. Sandy Maisel, "American Political Parties: Still Central to a Functioning Democracy?," in Jeffrey E. Cohen, Richard Fleisher, and Paul Kantor, eds., *American Political Parties: Decline or Resurgence?* (Washington, D.C.: CQ Press, 2011), chap. 5.
5. Marc J. Hetherington and Bruce A. Larson, *Parties, Politics, and Public Policy in America*, 11th ed. (Washington, D.C.: CQ Press, 2010): 13–15.
6. John Aldrich and David Rohde, "The Consequences of Party Organization in the House: The Role of the Majority and Minority Parties in Conditional Party Government," in Jon R. Bond and Richard Fleisher, *Polarized Politics: Congress and the President in a Partisan Era* (Washington, D.C.: CQ Press, 2000), chap. 3.
7. Morris P. Fiorina, "Parties as Problem Solvers," in Alan S. Gerber and Eric M. Patashnik, eds., *Promoting the General Welfare: New Perspectives on Government Performance* (Washington, D.C.: Brookings, 2006): 237–53.
8. Sarah A. Binder, "The Dynamics of Legislative Gridlock, 1947–1996," *American Political Science Review* 93 (1999): 519–33; David R. Mayhew, *Divided We Govern: Party Control, Lawmaking, and Investigations, 1946–1990* (New Haven, CT: Yale University Press, 1991); James A. Thurber, ed., *Divided Democracy: Cooperation and Conflict between the President and Congress* (Washington, D.C.: Congressional Quarterly Press, 1991); Morris P. Fiorina, *Divided Government* (New York: MacMillan, 1992).
9. Morris P. Fiorina, with Samuel J. Abrams and Jeremy C. Pope, *Culture War? The Myth of a Polarized America*, 2nd ed. (New York: Pearson/Longman, 1996). For an opposing view, see Alan I. Abramowitz and Kyle L. Saunders, "Is Polarization a Myth?" *Journal of Politics* 70 (2008): 542–55; and Abramowitz, *The Polarized Public? Why American Government Is So Dysfunctional* (Boston: Pearson, 2013).
10. Theodore J. Lowi and Joseph Romance, *A Republic of Parties: Debating; The Two-Party System* (Lanham, MD: Rowman & Littlefield, 1998); Kay Lawson, "The Case for a Multiparty System," in Paul S. Herrnson and John C. Green, eds., *Multiparty Politics in America*, 2nd ed. (Lanham, MD: Rowman & Littlefield, 2002): 31–44.
11. Jeffrey M. Jones, "Americans Continue to Say a Third Political Party Is Needed," *Gallup Politics* (September 24, 2014), http://www.gallup.com/poll/177284/americans-continue-say-third-political-party-needed.aspx?utm_source=alert&utm_medium=email&utm_content=morelink&utm_campaign=syndication/.

12. Earl R. Kruschke, *Encyclopedia of Third Parties in the United States* (Santa Barbara, CA, Denver, and Oxford: ABC-CLIO, 1991).

13. Scot Schraufnagel, *Third Party Blues: The Truth and Consequences of Two-Party Dominance* (New York and London: Routledge, 2011), chap. 2.; Barry C. Burden, "Ballot Regulations and Multiparty Politics in the States," *PS: Political Science and Politics* 40 (2007): 669–73; Daniel J. Lee, "Take the Good with the Bad: Cross-Cutting Effects of Ballot Access Requirements on Third-Party Electoral Success," *American Politics Research* 40 (2012): 267–92.

14. Schraufnagel, *Third Party Blues,* chap. 2.

15. Lydia Saad, "U.S. Political Ideology Stable with Conservatives Leading, Most Republicans Are Conservative, but One in Five Is 'Very Conservative,'" *Gallup Politics* (August 1, 2011), http://www.gallup.com/poll/148745/Political-Ideology-Stable-Conservatives-Leading.aspx/.

16. Jeffrey M. Jones, "Democrats, Republicans Differ in Views of Compromise in D.C.," *Gallup Politics* (November 10, 2010), http://www.gallup.com/poll/144359/Democrats-Republicans-Differ-Views-Compromise.aspx/; Frank Newport, "Americans Again Call for Compromise in Washington," *Gallup Politics* (September 26, 2011), http://www.gallup.com/poll/149699/Americans-Again-Call-for-Compromise-Washington.aspx/; Lydia Saad, "Americans' Top Critique of GOP: 'Unwilling to Compromise,'" *Gallup Politics* (April 1, 2013), http://www.gallup.com/poll/161573/americans-top-critique-gop-unwilling-compromise.aspx/.

17. James L Sundquist, *Dynamics of the Party System: Alignment and Realignment of Political Parties in the United States,* rev. ed. (Washington, D.C.: Brookings, 1983).

18. John J. Pitney Jr., "What If There Were Three Major Parties?" in Herbert M. Levine, Neil B. Cohen, Joy E. Esberey, Thomas H. Ferrell, Judith F. Gentry, Glen Jeansonne, and John J. Pitney Jr., *What If the American Political System Were Different?* (Armonk, NY: Sharpe, 1992): 45–72.

19. Nicholas Charron, "Party Systems, Electoral Systems and Constraints on Corruption," *Electoral Studies* 30 (2011): 595–606.

20. Lowi, "Toward a Responsible Three-Party System: Prospects and Obstacles," in Lowi and Romance, *A Republic of Parties,* 11.

CHAPTER 6

※

Choosing the Candidates: Nominations

I don't care who does the electing, just so I do the nominating.

—BOSS TWEED *of Tammany Hall*

The quote from Tweed may be an exaggeration, but it captures a lot of political wisdom. A party's nominees either are chosen in primary elections or are selected by party members in conventions or caucuses. Critics charge that these processes are flawed and undermine the characteristics of good democratic government:

- They are *ineffective* in producing the best candidates, thereby denying the voting population good choices in the November general elections and probably *discouraging turnout*. If elected, they are insufficiently able to contribute to effective policy making and implementation.
- Nominating practices are *inefficient* in terms of time and money.
- They involve a limited number of participants who are *not representative* of or *accountable* to the voting public or of the general population.
- They are infrequently characterized by *careful deliberation and reasoned judgment*.

6.1 CAUCUSES AND CONVENTIONS: CONGRESS

State and congressional district conventions and the less formal caucuses are for the most part assemblies of party activists. Depending on the state and locality, conventions and caucuses were open and participatory, at least for those with established party credentials. As tightly controlled party "machines" evolved in the late nineteenth century, the party elites—"bosses" in many locations—dictated nominations, often amid a good deal of seedy and money-laced shenanigans. Almost inevitably, resistance arose in the form of the Progressive movement, leading to the establishment of the direct primary election to give rank-and-file party members control over who would run for office under the party label.

Today, some states still use state party conventions, directly or indirectly in conjunction with primaries, to nominate governors, U.S senators, and other statewide offices; and a few use variations on the convention/caucus theme for congressional and state legislative nominations. These party gatherings are open and participation is easy, although limited to party members. Candidates make their cases for nominations, often devoting months or years of formal and informal campaigning to the goal.

6.2 PRIMARY ELECTIONS

Parties introduced direct popular primaries for a couple of reasons. One was to "clean up" politics and shift nominating power from party leaders to the broader party membership. The other was to inject competition into the politics of the South, where the only real electoral contests occurred within the dominant Democratic Party. In most states, primaries replaced or supplemented the traditional convention and caucus systems. Local party organizations have not lost all influence, however. They can recruit, endorse, support, finance, and work for their favorite candidates; and in some states running in a primary depends on having some success at state conventions.

Primaries come in several flavors. Eleven states operate "purely" closed primary elections, in which only registered members of a party may vote to choose its candidates.[1] At the other end of the spectrum, 11 states use open primaries, in which any registered voter may participate, regardless of his or her political affiliation or lack thereof. A third form of primary, the "semiclosed" or "semiopen" hybrid, splits the difference between open and closed in a variety of ways. In some states independents but not members of the other party may vote in a party's primaries. In others, one must register as a partisan but can do so as late as the date of the primary, even if it means changing one's party membership. Even within a given state, the parties may employ different approaches. In 2008 and 2010, Alaskan Democrats ran an open primary, whereas Republicans chose the closed option.

Primaries usually employ the plurality vote principle to determine winners, but 11 states use some form of runoff to ensure a majority winner. Runoff primaries have come under fire, most notably by Jesse Jackson, the civil rights leader and former presidential candidate, for making it difficult for black candidates to emerge victorious, even if they led in the first rounds.

Perhaps the most intriguing version is the "top-two" or "jungle" system used in Louisiana, California, and Washington congressional primaries. All candidates of any parties are listed on the ballot for a given office. Each voter marks the ballot for his or her preferred candidate, and the two candidates with the most votes become the finalists in the general election. In Louisiana, the "primary" *is* the general election and ends the process if one of the candidates wins a majority of the votes. If not, there is a runoff.

6.3 WHICH ARE BETTER: CONVENTIONS OR PRIMARIES?

Conventions and Caucuses

In only a few states do conventions and caucuses play a decisive role in nominating candidates for the U.S. Senate, House, or major statewide offices. Should they?

One advantage presumably is the promotion of deliberative judgment and peer review in the nominating process. When candidates are chosen by knowledgeable activists and officeholders with whom they will need to work once elected, and when would-be candidates have to encounter face to face those who hold the candidates' electoral future in their hands, one expects robust deliberation, interrogation, truthtelling, caution, and reasoned bargaining, along with a careful weighing of strengths and weaknesses. The results should be more rational than when nominations are made by primary voters who probably have never personally encountered the candidates or studied their records. The process would seemingly be more efficient in terms of time and costs. Party professionals hesitate to place bets on risky candidates who could damage the party's reputation. They want to present to the general voting public candidates who embody the party's principles. Furthermore, a convention's ability to deny renomination to renegade senators and representatives ought to induce caution and perhaps a tendency toward moderation among incumbent officeholders. Conventions allow those doing the nominating to enforce a degree of policy consistency among the candidates and—in the old New York tradition of including the sons and daughters of Italy, Ireland, and Israel—to factor in ethnic backgrounds as a way to strengthen the party's appeal. The party's collective responsiveness and accountability to the voters would be the likely result.

This picture of a rational, cautious, responsive, effective, efficient, accountable, and deliberative nomination enterprise is seductive but simplistic. Depending on how delegates to caucuses and conventions are chosen—and history provides numerous models, some more appointive and some more elective—there are potential flaws. First, participation is limited; parties are lucky if 1 percent of their members attend. Second, selective participation threatens the value of representation. Nonattenders and those who had no say in choosing the delegates can find themselves unrepresented by, essentially, unaccountable convention delegates. Perhaps worse, as the proportion of partisans in the electorate has shrunk, the danger is that disproportionate numbers of "hard-core" partisans—very liberal Democrats or very conservative Republicans—are left to dominate the proceedings.

In some states, one need not be a registered party member, certainly not a proven loyalist, to attend the local party meetings and caucuses. This opens the possibility that outsiders or party renegades could "crash" local caucuses and influence the selection of delegates to state or district conventions. If parties nominated their candidates for the House of Representatives in district caucuses, such "raiders" could select the nominees. A simple reform is to make sure that attendees at conventions and caucuses are in fact registered members of the party, maybe long-standing members, and conceivably even "proven" loyalists. Party rules and state laws could ensure that the first condition is fulfilled and possibly the second. The third (proven loyalists) is impossible, likely leading to all sorts of litigation and bad press.

Any of these scenarios—partisans becoming more extreme, policy activists infiltrating the nominating conventions, or a caucus or convention tightly controlled by "establishment" party members who exclude dissident newcomers—can result in slates of nominees who may be quite unrepresentative of some significant faction, or even a majority, of the party's supporters. If extremists control the nominating process in both parties, the moderate center is lost, and voters in November face unpalatable choices. When the winners go to Washington, the consequence can be ideologically partisan warfare and legislative gridlock. The values of representation and accountability, not to mention effective governance, are at risk. No wonder Progressive reformers instituted primaries across the land.

Primary Elections—A Better Approach?
Primaries invite broader participation and give candidates a chance to get their messages out to voters. They foster responsiveness and accountability of the winner to

party voters; and winners would be less beholden to party professionals. Not all, however, is positive. First, restrictive ballot access laws that place burdensome requirements for nomination petitions can discourage some potential candidates. Second, primaries are more costly than caucuses or conventions, both to the localities running the election and to the candidates—an especially challenging issue for relatively unknown challengers.[2] Money and the advertising it buys matter more in primaries than in general elections where visibility of candidates is greater, money is easier to attract, and voters know more and have the benefit of the party labels to guide their decisions. Third, although the "retail" person-to-person politics of caucus and convention nominations is time-consuming, the "wholesale" politics of running in primaries is more so. Candidate exhaustion can be a problem, as is the need for media coverage.

Fourth, primaries can be divisive, revealing candidate weaknesses, alienating voters, chewing through campaign funds, and giving the opposition ammunition to use in the general election campaign. Scholars, however, find little consistent or strong evidence that intensely fought primaries do lasting harm.[3] Indeed, they can help candidates in the general election by attracting supporters, sparking voter interest, highlighting candidate strengths, and increasing turnout[4]

Fifth, the hopes that primaries will nominate better challengers who provide stiffer general election competition have not played out. From 1946 through 2012, only 6 percent of incumbent members of the House seeking re-election lost in general elections, an average of just over 24 per year; and roughly 70 percent captured 60 or more percent of the vote.[5] On the Senate side, 16 percent of incumbents seeking re-election lost. Likewise, intraparty primary competition has been weak. It is not uncommon for as many as half of House incumbents to have no primary challengers, and when they do, they win. From 1946 to 2012, only 224 incumbent representatives lost primary contests, an average of about 6.5. Only 13 lost in 2012 and 4 in 2014. On the Senate side there were 44 primary nomination casualties in that period, an average of 1.3 per election cycle. No incumbent lost in 2014. Primary competitiveness peaks when the seat being sought is open. Nor, as a rule, have party primaries succeeded in encouraging greater voter participation. Turnout typically runs no higher than about 20 percent of the eligible electorate, about half of what occurs in general elections.

Such election statistics do not comfort incumbents. A candidate's core supporters are crucial, but that base can become a threat if angered. Moderate members of Congress live in mortal fear of primary challenges from their parties' extremes. These attacks sometimes come from political amateurs with nothing to lose, rather than from experienced politicians who wait for seats to come open or for situations that render incumbents vulnerable. Although being "primaried" is a worry for all incumbents, it seems to affect Republicans the most, as Tea Party and libertarian-oriented political action committees eagerly pounce on members who stray from the straight and narrow ideological path.[6] For example, in the 2010 and 2012 Republican senatorial primaries in Nevada, Delaware, Indiana, and Missouri, primary voters selected ideologically extreme candidates (Sharron Angle, Christine O'Donnell, Richard Mourdock, Todd Akin) who lost the November contests their party should have won. How much fear of primary attacks induces paralysis in the committee rooms and floor of the Capitol is unclear, but conventional wisdom assumes that the impact is significant. Candidates move toward the ends of the ideological spectrum, snuggling up to their base electorates.[7] When they play to the extremes, they establish expectations; then, if in the general election they need to move back toward the center, trouble can brew, as their primary supporters see inconsistency and even treachery while opponents gloat over "flip-flopping."[8]

To the extent that congressional candidates depend on voters rather than on party leaders for their nominations, to the extent that their base has become more ideological, and to the extent that probably 80 percent of congressional districts are secure for one or the other party, newly elected representatives arrive in Washington with little inclination to follow their leaders in the House. Speaker John Boehner (R-OH) learned as much trying to corral support his fellow Republicans in 2013 and 2014. Reasoned decision making can be a casualty.

Sixth, there is the representativeness of primaries. Primary voters are in various degrees demographically different from their fellow partisans or from the general electorate—older, better educated, more interested in politics, more intensely partisan; but there is little hard evidence about how different they are in terms of policy preferences and ideology. Scholarship in the 1980s suggested that primary participants were rather similar in political attitudes and policy preferences to nonprimary voters in the same party (but *not* to the general electorate), at least in presidential primaries.[9] Today, it looks as though Democratic primary voters are more liberal, and Republicans more conservative, than their fellow party identifiers. The differences have grown in the past decade, leading to the nervousness on the part of incumbents discussed above. There is a real danger that someone not representative of or loyal to the party could capture a nomination for a congressional seat, putting party leaders in the awkward position of occasionally wanting to repudiate their own candidates.

A seventh concern, focusing on voters' behavior, is that voters in primaries are more prone than voters in general elections to "incorrect," perhaps uninformed, voting in which they cast votes for candidates who do not agree with them on important issues.[10] Finally, primaries do little for the strength of the parties by depriving party leaders of the opportunities to reward loyalists by nominating some of them for office and by opening possibilities for intraparty insurgencies.

Open or Closed?

The differences between open and closed primary elections could affect one's thinking about reforming the nominating system. Closed primaries encourage people to join and participate in parties, ensure that each party offers the general electorate reasonably clear and distinct choices of candidates and policies (furthering the cause of accountability), and foster strong party organizations. The negative is that closed primaries disenfranchise the nearly 40 percent of the voting public who call themselves independents, leaving the selection of a party's congressional candidates in the hands of strong partisans and risking the nomination of rather extreme candidates.[11]

Open primaries allow for broader and more representative citizen participation. The inclusion of independents and members of the other parties *should* have a moderating effect on the type of candidate selected. Open primary campaigns might force candidates to speak to a broader segment of voters that more closely resembles the electorate that they will face in November. In turn that should foster better dialogue and deliberation once the candidates arrive in Washington, and it should encourage elected representatives to take a broader view of their responsiveness obligations. Whether open primaries have this moderating effect, however, is a subject of scholarly dispute. There is some evidence that open primaries and hybrids that allow unaffiliated voters to declare partisanship at the polling places encourage younger voters to participate and bring about better representation and "ideological convergence" toward moderation than do closed primaries.[12] Other scholars, however, have provided evidence to challenge the moderation thesis.[13] The track record of recent years points to a limited but growing number of extremists who are competitive in open as well as closed primaries.

The problem is that allowing independents and especially members of another party into a party's nomination contest dilutes the party's ability to choose candidates who best reflect its philosophy, denying its control over its own destiny.[14] Simple campaign chores like developing targeted mailing and contact lists are made more difficult by open primaries; who knows in which party a given Democrat, Republican, or independent will cast his or her ballot next time? There also is the possibility of sabotage—crossing over into the other party's primaries to vote for the weakest candidate. There is little scholarly documentation of such behavior, but the ability of voters to cross over into the other party's contest in an open primary is intriguing.

The Newcomer: Top-Two Primaries

The "top-two" primary offers possibilities for bolstering competition and giving moderates a better chance. The now obsolete blanket primaries that allowed people to vote for any party's candidate for any office on the ballot—probably more analogous to the top-two primaries than purely open or closed primaries—tended to produce more moderate and well networked candidates.[15] Minor parties oppose jungle primaries because, since the top two finishers typically are one Republican and one Democrat, their candidates have no chance to contest the general election. The major parties are skeptical of the top-two system because of its costs and the possibility that two of their own would be fighting each other twice, splitting the party into factions. A remote danger is that several centrist candidates might beat each other up and split the moderate voters, allowing one or two extremists to end up in the general election. That is exactly what happened in the 1991 Louisiana gubernatorial primary, when Ku Klux Klan leader David Duke slipped into the general election runoff.

If the experiences so far are indicative, the system is popular with voters, but it is too soon to know the long-term effects. In 2012, in 7 of 53 U.S. House races in California, the top two finishers were of the same party—as was true of 22 of 100 state legislative contests. In Louisiana, it was 2 of 6. Most races retained their relatively noncompetitive nature, with the first-place primary finisher gathering a majority of votes, but in a number of traditionally noncompetitive districts, competition did arise in the dominant party.[16] A good number of votes were cast for marginal candidates, but in most cases the leaders were mainstream party contenders. Still, there were some strange results. California congressional district 31 had a 41 to 36 percent Democratic advantage in voter registration and its population was nearly majority Latino. Yet two white Republican candidates emerged from the primary to compete in November because four Democrats split their party's vote. In conservative District 8, six Republicans divided the vote such that the top qualified for the November election by picking up about 15 percent of the vote each. And in the strongly Democratic 51st Congressional District in San Diego, "the lead candidate, a Democratic state senator, spent nearly $50,000 in support of a penniless Republican opponent to prevent his strongest rival, a fellow Democrat, from making the November election."[17] The generous Democrat won the general election with about 70 percent of the vote. The 2014 California primaries resembled those of 2012. In 5 congressional races, two Democrats emerged to contest the November election; in 2, the top two finishers were Republicans. In 1, an independent finished among the top two. Turnout was low. In Washington, in 1 of 10 districts, the finalists were both Republicans.

Blended Systems?

Conventions and primaries can be blended such that conventions filter the candidates eligible to run in the primaries, thus injecting a measure of "peer review," reasoned deliberation, and a blend of party *and* voter participation and accountability into the nomination system. A mild version of this occurs when state party conventions or district caucuses endorse preferred candidates before the primary election, as is done in Wisconsin, Illinois, and Minnesota, for example. This "blessing" of the candidates can bring excitement and publicity, sometimes along with financial and personnel assistance from the party organization. The research on the efficacy of endorsements, although mixed, points to some real effects that depend on circumstances, location, form and type of endorsement, and candidates' situations.[18]

A more potent approach is to allow or require a party's convention to select the primary competitors. In Iowa's Republican congressional primaries, if no candidate wins 35 percent of the vote, a nominating convention makes the call. That occurred in 2014 for only the second time in 50 years. More common is the system employed in New York, Colorado, New Mexico, Rhode Island, Delaware, Utah, Massachusetts, and North Dakota. Gaining convention approval or winning a fixed percentage (15 percent in Massachusetts, for example) of the convention votes assures one a primary ballot position; other contenders access the ballot only via petition. Connecticut uses the "challenge" primary in which the convention's choice is the nominee unless someone challenges him or her in the subsequent primary. In fewer than 10 percent of cases did U.S. House candidates endorsed by district conventions face a primary challenge.[19]

This mixed system can be a curse as much as a blessing. When the convention is full of staunch ideological partisans, it can deny a spot on the primary ballot to someone who may be the best or most popular candidate. That happened in 2010 in Utah, when veteran Republican senator Bob Bennett failed to win one of the top two endorsements, denying him the chance to run in the primary. Most observers thought that he would have easily won re-election in November had he been on the ballot. He was not, and the Republicans lost the seat. Still, despite these problems, blended nominating systems appeal because they support many of the key values. Voter participation, accountability, and representation are present in the primaries; the deliberative peer review process in the convention is likely to filter out renegade candidates and reward those who likely to be competent public officials, thus contributing to the effectiveness that should characterize government. Nominated and then elected candidates would

Table 6.1 Summary of Nominating System Effects: Congress

NOMINATING MECHANISM	ADVANTAGES AND DISADVANTAGES
Convention or caucus	Limited participation; enhanced deliberative judgment and peer review
	Can be unrepresentative of broader party members and subject to "capture" by unrepresentative activists
	Efficient in time and cost
	Could encourage linkages among candidates and incumbents of various offices
	Allows the party to present to voters a slate of candidates who would be collectively responsive to voter concerns
Open primaries	Enhanced participation compared to conventions, caucuses, and open primaries
	More representative of electorate
	Might produce more moderate candidates
	Little deliberative judgment and peer review
	Less efficient than caucuses or closed primaries
	Greater media and money influence than caucuses and conventions
Closed primaries	More participation than caucuses but less than open primaries
	More representative of party loyalists but less of general electorate
	Subject to "flooding" by ideologically motivated partisans
	Little deliberative judgment and peer review
	Greater media and money influence than caucuses and conventions
Top-two primaries	More participative than regular primaries, conventions, or caucuses
	Representative of general electorate
	Little deliberative judgment and peer review
	Can hurt parties by pitting two fellow partisans against each other
	Could allow third-party candidates to win but more likely freezes them out
	Could cost more with multiple candidates
Hybrid: convention plus primary	Blends party involvement with public participation
	Provides peer review
	More representative than conventions or caucuses alone; slightly more limiting than pure primary systems
	More cost efficient than a pure primary system

surely have no less incentive to be responsive to voters, but they also would want to be responsive to their national party. Efficiency would be enhanced by eliminating the need for primaries whenever the choice of the logical nominee is obvious and by eliminating marginal candidates from the primaries. Table 6.1 summarizes these nominating systems.

6.4 PRESIDENTIAL NOMINATIONS

Every four years, the parties' national conventions nominate candidates for the presidency. The vast majority of delegates at the conventions are chosen by state primaries and caucus-convention systems and are bound to cast their votes at the national convention according to the results of those state selection processes. This system is complex: the rules are different in each party and in each state, yielding 112 different nominating schemes (50 states, D.C., and 5 territories, each with two parties).

Many of the framers of the Constitution thought that the Electoral College would become the *de facto* instrument for nominating presidents because no candidate would earn a majority of electoral votes, pushing the final decision on the presidency to the House of Representatives. In the first years of the new nation, leaders of congressional factions (Federalists and Anti-Federalists, the latter subsequently morphing into the Democratic Republican or Jefferson Republican party) gathered together and easily chose their parties' nominees for 1796 and 1800: John Adams and Thomas Jefferson. After 1800, when the House of Representatives was forced to break the electoral vote tie between Jefferson and his running mate, Aaron Burr, the Federalist Party expired, leaving presidential nominations to the Democratic Republican Party caucus. When it failed to control matters in 1824, a three-way battle for the presidency among John Quincy Adams, William Crawford, and Andrew Jackson broke out, splitting the electoral votes and again throwing the election into the House, where a "corrupt bargain" between Henry Clay and Adams put the latter into the White House. Four years later, Adams (representing the "National Republicans") lost decisively to Jackson, whose populist policies spawned a new party, the Whigs. That name replicated that of the British party opposed to the monarchy. In the United States, their target was "King Andrew." By 1832, a new and more democratic reform emerged, the national party convention that assembled each party's leaders from around the country to nominate its presidential candidate. That system stood for the remainder of the century, although the Lincoln-led Republicans replaced the Whigs, and Democratic Republicans changed their names simply to "Democrats."

Over time, the system settled into a pattern. At their convention, delegations, following their party leaders (often governors), voted as a bloc for a given candidate who in the early rounds of balloting often was a "favorite son" of that state. The goal was to maximize their leaders' bargaining power on the convention floor or in the proverbial smoke-filled rooms. Delegations sought candidates whose winning margins would help sweep into office their parties' other candidates on the state tickets; who would pursue policies that would attract broad voter approval; and who would remember which states provided the support needed to capture the nomination, so that there would be political payoffs down the road. A quarter to a third of the states in the first half of the twentieth century held primaries, only a minority of which actually chose delegates to the national convention. Most were popularity polls, providing signals that candidates had the ability to garner citizens' votes—as when John F. Kennedy in 1960 had to prove, in West Virginia, that a Catholic could win support from Protestant voters. Candidate strategies before and during the conventions focused on convincing state party leaders that they could and would meet the leaders' expectations. That meant lots of schmoozing, promising, and negotiating. Candidates carefully chose which primaries to enter, avoiding those in which they could not do well. The system had mixed results, producing strong and weak, highly and marginally talented, candidates, but it worked. It contained, however, the seeds of its own destruction.

As popular expectations for participatory democracy grew after World War II, the existing system appeared fossilized, out of touch, and unfair. State delegations, often chosen in undemocratic ways, were not representative of the party's supporters; sometimes they had been selected by processes begun long before the nomination season began. The formulas for allocating delegates seemed unrepresentative, favoring small and medium-size one-party states rather than the larger competitive states that would be crucial for winning the Electoral College vote.

The 1968 Democratic convention and the months leading up to it were one huge nightmare. President Johnson barely defeated Senator Eugene McCarthy of Minnesota in the New Hampshire primary in February, sending a shock wave through the party. At the end of March, Johnson declared that he would not seek re-election, leaving Vice President Hubert Humphrey as the heir apparent. Then New York senator Robert Kennedy jumped into the race. His assassination just after winning the California primary persuaded Senator George McGovern (SD) to pick up the Kennedy standard, becoming the third major contender. The problem was that Humphrey had not competed in any of the primaries, relying instead on the party faithful for the nomination. The forces met at the Chicago convention. With protests from the McCarthy and McGovern supporters resounding through the hall, and college student anti–Vietnam War and pro–McCarthy/McGovern protesters being arrested and often beaten bloody by Chicago police outside—all well covered by television—the convention was a disaster. Humphrey won the nomination but lost to Richard Nixon in November.

The party reacted with a reform effort, adopting the recommendations of the McGovern–Fraser Commission.[20] The major ones included the following:

- Enhanced demographic representativeness at the convention in terms of race, age, and gender;
- Rules governing how state caucuses and conventions had to operate more openly;
- Timely selection of delegates in the year of the presidential election, with requirements that delegates specify the candidates to whom they were pledged; and
- A new formula for allocating delegates to the national convention.

The complexity of the new rules led many state Democratic parties to opt for simplicity by adopting binding primary elections to select delegates to the national convention. That changed the landscape forever, and its effects reverberated through the parties. Senator McGovern won the nomination in 1972 but was thrashed by President Nixon in November, causing Democratic officials to take some of the reforms back to the drawing board. There followed a succession of commissions whose recommendations were adopted, leading to current Democratic Party rules that, with exceptions and variations:

- Specify that three-quarters of a state's delegates must be chosen from congressional districts and require that the number of delegates for any given candidate be proportional to the votes the candidate won in the primary or caucus/convention contest, subject to a minimum threshold;
- Mandate that primaries be closed;
- Ban the unit rule under which a state's delegates would vote as a single bloc on the convention floor (delegates must vote for the candidates to whom they were pledged at the time of their selection); and
- Include in the convention "superdelegates"—unpledged senators, representatives, governors, and party leaders, whose task is to balance the influence of "rank-and-file" and/or "amateur" delegates like whose who helped chose McGovern in 1972.

Some of the reform commissions had a not-so-secret agenda to influence subsequent nominations by, for example, making it harder for fringe candidates to win delegates. The problem was that each time the party changed its rules, some states would object and find ways around the rules, or ignore them, which in turn led to another round of changes. Eventually, Republicans picked up some of the Democratic reforms. Thus, current practices are the product of dozens of efforts to reform the nominating system, adding and subtracting, moving this way and that.[21] As seen in Table 6.2, primaries account for about two-thirds of Democratic and four-fifths of Republican convention delegates.

The rules governing primaries, caucuses, and conventions have consequences. For instance, if a party in a state chooses to follow the unit ("winner-take-all") rule to pick its delegates, that state will have more influence at the convention and likely will attract more of the candidates' campaign time than a neighboring state that follows the proportional model. The rules often change from one election season to the next, leading to strange machinations and affecting candidates' prospects. An example of the confusion occurred in Iowa in 2012, where Mitt Romney apparently won a majority in the

Table 6.2 Presidential Primaries

YEAR	DEMOCRATS		REPUBLICANS	
------	NUMBER OF PRIMARIES	PERCENTAGE OF DELEGATES SELECTED IN PRIMARIES	NUMBER OF PRIMARIES	PERCENTAGE OF DELEGATES SELECTED IN PRIMARIES
1960	16	38	15	39
1964	16	46	16	46
1968	15	40	15	38
1972	21	65	20	57
1976	27	76	26	71
1980	34	72	34	76
1984	29	52	25	71
1988	36	67	36	77
1992	39	67	38	84
1996	35	65	42	85
2000	40	65	43	84
2004	37	68	27	56
2008	38	69	39	80
2012	26	47	36	71

Source: Harold W. Stanley and Richard G. Neimi, *Vital Statistics on American Politics, 2013–2014* (Washington, D.C.: CQ Press, 2014), table 1–23.

Note: Some states cancel primaries if there is only one candidate; some hold nonbinding "beauty contest" primaries but select delegates in caucuses and conventions (not shown in chart)

local caucuses, only to learn, several days later, that some caucus votes were discovered that put Rick Santorum ahead. Another example occurred in Michigan, where Santorum and Romney essentially tied at 41 to 38 percent, but Michigan Republican leaders decided to allocate two at-large delegates supposedly chosen in proportion to the statewide primary vote to Romney, providing him a 16–14 delegate edge. Nevada's Republican process varied by county, causing delays in determining the final results; and in Maine, caucus activities lasted more than a week, with results from at least one county "lost" for a while. Early results had to be recalculated and reported well after the "official" caucus date, and even then, there remained uncertainty over the final numbers.

The System Is Flawed

Defenders of the presidential nomination system praise the primary/caucus mix and the lengthy process that gives voters a chance to learn about the candidates and tests the endurance of those who would be president. Nonetheless, the process is rife with problems crying out for reform. Briefly stated, the major criticisms include the following:

- The wrong people, using the wrong processes that vary from state to state, determine the nomination. Does the process involve people competent to make such decisions, and is there the opportunity for reasoned deliberation about candidates?
- The process stretches on for too long, with states jockeying to position themselves at the front of the line.
- The cost is excessive, often leaving defeated candidates with millions of dollars in debt.
- The system gives too much power to the media.
- The system affects the operations and health of the political parties, and it can have a negative effect on governance.

Participation. Who should nominate presidential candidates? At least four groups come to mind:

1. *All interested citizens*, regardless of political party affiliation, participating in a process that is no less democratic than that used in the final election of a president;
2. *Partisans*, with Democrats choosing their candidate and Republicans choosing theirs;
3. *Party loyalists and "regulars"* who do the work of the party, are engaged consistently, and best represent the parties' enduring principles; and
4. *Other elected officials* of the candidate's party with whom the president must work to govern.

If one's answer is (1), then some form of open primary with broad participation seems best. If (2) is the choice, then a closed primary is ideal; but if one prefers (3), the caucus/convention approach makes the most sense. Finally, selecting (4) puts the nomination in the hands of the party's members of Congress and governors. The public prefers a system that is broadly participatory, and it is suspicious of any system that empowers party leaders or other elite groups; but it does not seem upset with the way nominations work.[22]

If participation is desirable, neither primaries nor caucuses do the job very well, nor are they, especially primaries, conducive to deliberative judgment. Presidential primary turnout in both parties combined has dropped from just over 30 percent of eligible voters in 1972 to the high teens recently. It jumped back in 2008 to about that 30 percent level, thanks to the intense race between Barack Obama and Hillary Clinton and a much shorter but vigorous contest on the Republican side, but it slid in 2012 because there was no serious Democratic contest.[23] In only 9 states in 2012 did the turnout exceed 20 percent of eligible voters; in 7 states turnout fell below 10 percent.[24] In 2012, in 12 of the 13 states for which data are available, caucus participation rates fell below, and usually much below, 5 percent. Iowa's caucuses, the first nominating event, pulled in 6.5 percent of eligible voters; Wyoming's Republican caucus garnered 0.3 percent. The norm is between 1 and 3 percent.

Representation. Demographically, both caucuses and primaries exhibit a bias toward older, better educated, higher socioeconomic status participants relative to fellow partisans and to the average voter.[25] There are differences. Blacks, for example, attracted by Obama's candidacy, were overrepresented on the Democratic side but underrepresented in GOP contests.

Conventional wisdom assumes that there are significant ideological differences among caucus attenders, primary voters, and partisans who only vote in November's general elections. Something distinguishes the hearty group that attends local caucuses that choose delegates to district or state conventions from those who merely pull levers, punch buttons, or touch screens. Thirty years of scholarly studies, however, have failed to find significant and consistent ideological or policy differences nationally between caucus-goers and primary voters.[26] There is not much difference in terms of levels of passion or ideological commitment. What may spur people to participate in caucuses is a community orientation and commitment to community engagement.[27] Surprisingly as well, most studies do not find that primary voters in general are ideologically out of touch with fellow partisans who vote in November. Many observers think that the situation changed in the past decade, but until scholars dig deeper, the question of representativeness remains somewhat open.

Strange Results. Primaries and caucuses can produce inconsistent results. In 1996 Patrick Buchanan dominated the Republican caucuses, but the eventual nominee, Senator Robert Dole, fared better in the primaries; in 2008, Hillary Clinton garnered a higher percentage of votes in the primaries, but Obama edged her out in the caucuses. On the GOP side, Mitt Romney was the overall caucus winner, whereas Senator John McCain (R-AZ) dominated the primaries and captured the nomination.

Primaries and especially caucuses are susceptible to surges of participants, often those who are passionately committed to particular candidates. One thinks of the McGovern supporters in 1972 and Reagan backers in 1976 and 1980; the Reverend Pat Robertson's loyal followers who flooded the Iowa and Michigan caucuses in 1988; and Jesse Jackson's enthusiasts that same year in the Michigan Democratic caucuses. More recently there were the Obama and Clinton loyalists in 2008 and the Michele Bachmann and Rick Santorum "true believers" in 2012. The Republican winner-take-all system in many states leverages the influence of such participants. At times it appears that these groups are more interested in being "right" or "pure" in their stances than in winning.

Delegates. To confuse matters just a bit, it is worth recalling three issues. One concerns the rules of the game. Not all primaries, and very few, if any, first-round caucuses, actually *choose* national convention delegates. In most states, those who win at local party caucuses go, directly or after another selection process at district-level meetings, to the state conventions that name the delegates to the national convention. Delegates are bound to support the candidates they backed in the caucuses, but there are exceptions and anomalies. The North Dakota caucus, for example, is a beauty contest; delegates who win locally remain unbound until formally selected at the state convention. In Missouri, the primary is a popularity contest; the state convention actually decides who goes to the national convention. In Iowa, despite losing narrowly to Santorum and Romney in the much-publicized first round in 2012, Ron Paul and his loyalists triumphed at the state convention, securing 23 of Iowa's 28 delegates to the national convention. Both parties include delegates who are not formally bound. Democrats have their superdelegates, whereas Republicans include unpledged state party leaders and delegations from several states that do not bind their delegates. Rules in several caucus states (Maine, Minnesota, Montana, and North Dakota) yield other unpledged delegates; and if candidates drop out of the race before the end, they frequently release their pledged delegates.

Rules Matter. Second, differences between the winner-take-all and the proportionality systems matter. Recall how Senator McCain in 2008 took advantage of the unit rule in many states to knock out his challengers early on. He won 47 percent of caucus and primary votes but got 75 percent of the delegates in those states. In the events of February 5, 2008, for instance, under a straight winner-take-all system, McCain would have won 664 delegates, Romney 313, and Huckabee 252; under a purely proportional system, Romney would have won 425 delegates, McCain 422, and Huckabee 238.[28] The winner-take-all system can hasten the end of the nomination process when someone quickly dominates three or four big state events, but it can prolong the process as well by helping an underdog explode into contender status for several months before fading. The proportional rule is commonly understood to have elongated and intensified the Democratic race in 2008; had it been run under Republican rules, Obama would most likely still have bested Clinton, but by a thinner margin.[29] Norrander's calculation shows that under winner-take-all rules in *every* state, Clinton would have won the nomination. In 1988, Democratic governor Michael Dukakis would have won about 13 percent fewer delegates under a purely proportional system than under a winner-take-all scheme; Jesse Jackson would have won almost three times as many as he did.

The parties set a 15 percent threshold that candidates must cross to win any delegates at all in a congressional district or statewide. The purpose is to screen out marginal candidates who, under an absolute proportional system, might gather enough delegates to deny a major contender a majority or at least delay the process.[30] The rule influences candidates' choices of which primaries they should contest and which they should ignore.

Crossover Voting. If independents are counted, crossover voting in open or semiopen primaries can be significant, and it raises the possibility that a party's winner might not represent the preferences of that party's members.[31] At least in the 1960s through the 1980s, as many as 30 to 40 percent of voters in Wisconsin primaries were independents or members of the other party; in 1964 and 1972, "visiting" Republican partisans voted for candidates other than the ones preferred by Democratic identifiers. Democrats returned the favor by helping to swing Michigan to John McCain over George W. Bush in 2000. Four years later, Democrats Howard Dean and John Edwards got a boost from Republican voters. In the 2012 Michigan GOP primary, 9 percent of voters self-identified as Democrats, and they favored Rick Santorum over Mitt Romney three to one. In March of that year, Santorum fared well in a number of Republican "Super Tuesday" open primaries, picking up 41 percent of Democrat crossovers, whereas Mitt Romney won 23 percent.

Crossover voting seldom is attributable to "sabotage raiding." Studies reveal that crossover voters tend to support candidates they like and think would be good presidents. Sometimes, assured that their own party's nomination is settled, they might participate in the other party's primary to vote for the person they think is next best—just in case their party's candidate should lose in November. When there is a real contest in the voters' own party primary, odds are that they would stay home to influence their own party's result. Real crossover voting is quite limited, no more than 10 percent of voters, and the amount of sabotage raiding constitutes a fraction of such activity.[32] Still, the temptation to "mess around" in the other party remains. Talk-show host Rush Limbaugh, in what he called "Operation Chaos," urged Republicans to vote in the 2008 Democratic primary for Hillary Clinton. Liberal activist Michael Moore did the same in 2012, urging Michigan Democrats to vote in the GOP primary for Rick Santorum. There is no conclusive evidence on how effective this stratagem was, but probably very little if at all; if anything, crossovers likely hurt Clinton in 2008.[33]

Voting Decisions. Absent party labels to distinguish one candidate from another, primary voters must spend time and effort to learn about the candidates, seek alternative voting cues, or rely on instinctive judgments. That may explain why, early in the 2012 Republican nomination process, no fewer than five different candidates led in the polls—a sort of "flavor of the week" exhibition. Massive media advertising and news coverage eases that burden, but given voters' relative inattention to political issues early in a presidential year (they do seem to learn as the campaigns develop), the problem remains. More importantly, the media tends to focus on the "horse-race" aspect of the nomination, so it is likely that voters know more about who is ahead in the polls and delegate count and who is spending how much money than they know about the issue positions of the candidates. A focus on the race fuels the bandwagon effect in which winning often begets winning. When an incumbent president or vice president is running, retrospective voting comes into play, as citizens ask: "How have things been going?"[34] Among sophisticated voters, of course, there is a good dose of ideological and issue voting; for candidates, taking strong stances on such matters can hurt the nominee and his party in November when a broader appeal is needed.

There is considerable evidence, at the same time, that voters are quite concerned about the electability of the candidates for whom they cast their primary ballots.[35] In 2012, one of Mitt Romney's primary appeals was to his electability. Voting decisions are amalgams of a host of matters, and much depends on the cues being emitted from the candidates and the sorts of traits they stress, whether it be experience, "outside of

Washington" status, or new policies. Clearly, however, voting cannot rest on the powerful voting cues furnished by party labels when all candidates wear the same labels; nor are the voters looking at candidates through the lenses of those who will eventually have to work with the nominee if he or she is elected.

Divisiveness. Long and bitterly fought presidential primaries can hurt candidates. One review of the extensive literature concludes that "being challenged for the presidential nomination is rarely considered helpful in the long term" because supporters whose preferred candidate loses the nomination are more likely to abstain or cross over to vote for the other party's candidate in November than are those whose favorite contender won the nomination.[36] Examples of costly nomination wars include Ted Kennedy's efforts to unseat President Carter as the Democratic candidate in 1980 and efforts by Gary Hart and Jesse Jackson to tumble Walter Mondale from frontrunner status in 1984. The most recent example occurred in 2008 when Hillary Clinton and Barack Obama fought bitterly for the Democratic nomination. Scholars have, alas, reached quite different conclusions about the effects.[37] There is some polling evidence that the rough-and-tumble 2012 Republican nominating battle may have hurt Mitt Romney and weakened Republicans' opinion of their own party.[38]

The Problem of Sequencing—Front-Loading

The dramatic shift to primaries after 1968 triggered a race to see which states would be first (or second or third) in the nominating events. The earliest states draw more attention from candidates and the media, giving them more influence; and they enjoy a short-term economic boom as candidates, their supporters, and media personnel pour in, spending rather freely. By long-standing tradition and state laws, Iowa and New Hampshire have held the early honors. Competition to be next in line after New Hampshire has been ferocious, leading in 2008 to Florida's and Michigan's willingness to risk having their delegates denied seating at the national conventions as punishment for breaking the approved sequence. Jockeying for early positions is especially contentious because of Super Tuesday, a day on which multiple states hold primaries. Super Tuesday's influence has meant that the winner is usually all but determined before April. Whereas in 1968 only 12 percent of the primaries occurred by the end of April, 31 states held primaries on or before February 5 in 2008. By February 10, 60 percent of Democratic delegates had been chosen. By the start of March, it was more than 80 percent. In 2012, Republicans in Iowa, New Hampshire, South Carolina, and Florida held their events in January, quickly followed in early February by Nevada, Colorado, Minnesota, and, with a nonbinding primary, Missouri. Arizona, Michigan, and Wyoming followed later that month. All of this happened despite the national parties' insistence that, except for the four early states, the window for nominating events should be March, April, and May.

Does It Matter? Front-loading has consequences.[39] Candidates understand that they must win, come in second, or significantly beat the media's predictions in the four early states. Failure is fatal: losers drop out of the media spotlight; supporters and campaign volunteers shift loyalties or at least lose enthusiasm; and campaign contributions dry up. In the last 14 competitive nomination contests, the eventual party nominee won the Iowa caucuses or the New Hampshire primary or both. Given opinion poll data and the need to raise a lot of money early enough to contest the early contests, some candidates typically throw in the towel before these four events or shortly thereafter. In 2012, the Republican "race" was limited to four candidates as early as January 19 (after Iowa and New Hampshire) when Texas governor Rick Perry bailed. Representative Michele Bachmann, Ambassador John Huntsman, business-man Herman Cain, and Minnesota governor Tim Pawlenty had left the race before then. In 2008, would-be contenders Senators Joe Biden and Christopher Dodd, former senator Mike Gravel, Representative Dennis Kucinich, and former new Mexico gover-nor Bill Richardson had all but disappeared from the Democratic contest by February, essentially leaving a two-candidate field. On the GOP side, former senator Fred Thompson, former governor Tommy Thompson, and Representative Duncan Hunter did not last long; three other candidates withdrew even before the first of the year. Former New York mayor Rudy Giuliani, leader in many of the early polls, opted not to contest either Iowa or New Hampshire, putting all his eggs in the Florida basket, the seventh event of the season. By then, it was too late; and shortly after his weak showing, he withdrew. There is another matter: lesser-known candidates may have to spend too much time and money on Iowa and New Hampshire, as Howard Dean did in 2004, leaving them short of the resources needed in the next several states.

Front-loading tends to advantage well-known candidates, although recently that seems less important, given the easy access to the media and money. The early knock-out of good candidates can mean that the nominee is not the same person who would have been nominated had the nominating process been allowed to play out over the five- or six-month period. The questions of representativeness and effectiveness leap out. There also is a smidgeon of evidence that candidates promise more benefits and pork to those early states, at least when the races are very competitive. Delivery of the goods follows if the nominee is elected president.[40]

Iowa and New Hampshire exemplify "retail" politics that requires organizational skills and a strong "ground game," as Obama showed in the 2008 Iowa race. An un-tested unknown compared to Hillary Clinton and Senator John Edwards, Obama built a superb organization that pulled Iowans to the caucuses. A perennial complaint about these early states is that they are small and rural, and their citizens—especially those who participate in nomination events—are unrepresentative of the broader base of voters in each party.[41] The reality is more complex. Concerning social and eco-nomic traits, Iowa is "at least reasonably" representative of the country; and where it isn't, it seems superior socially (education) or politically (turnout, lack of corrup-tion.)[42] As for ideology, the political scientist Gerald C. Wright showed that Iowa Democrats on the whole are ideologically similar to, but New Hampshire Democrats are a bit more liberal than, the average Democrat nationwide.[43] When South Carolina and Nevada—the next two states to hold nominating events—are included in the mix, the difference disappears. Republicans in Iowa and New Hampshire are essentially identical ideologically to the national GOP averages, but when southern states are included in the "early" contests, the resulting bias tilts conservative.

The story is a bit different for Democratic *participants* in Iowa caucuses and New Hampshire primaries. They are somewhat more liberal than other states' participants and slightly more liberal than fellow Democrats in their own states. In 2008, for ex-ample, likely caucus attendees claimed to be more oriented to Edwards than were statewide registered Democrats, who preferred Clinton.[44] Wright showed that Iowa's

Republican caucus attendees were more conservative than Republican primary voters elsewhere, but not more than other Iowa Republicans. He concluded that there is a modest, but potentially important, exaggeration of ideological tendencies in these early states relative to what one would find nationwide among party identifiers and among caucus and primary participants.[45]

The Invisible Primary. A second front-loading consequence is the "invisible primary." Organizing volunteers for the Iowa and Nevada caucuses and ginning up turnout in New Hampshire and South Carolina primaries take time and money. Would-be presidents set up "exploratory committees" or their own political action committees and then begin visiting those states aggressively in the year—or two or three— preceding election year. Increasingly sophisticated use of the Internet has become almost the *sine qua non* of these early tactics, along with heavy reliance on party insiders and political elites.[46] Given their primary responsibilities and demands on their time, officeholders may find themselves slightly disadvantaged in these early efforts, although their status and name recognition may compensate. Candidates with deep pockets have a leg up on the competition. Everyone competes for media attention, including making much of various "straw polls," the most famous of which occurs in Iowa in late summer of the year preceding the presidential election. These at times have been so hotly contested that, in 1999, a poor showing forced Lamar Alexander out of the GOP race. Candidates go through considerable contortions to lure potential supporters to the Iowa State Fair, offering transportation, lunches, and other freebies. The invisible primary has become a *de facto* preprimary in that failure to attract money, media attention, and good poll numbers by January 1 of election year leads candidates to drop out.

Participation. Third, front-loading inhibits voter participation because the nominees almost always are determined relatively quickly. For example, between 1980 and 2008, the average number of primaries remaining *after* the Democratic candidate had locked up the nomination was almost 16. Only in 1984 and 2008 did the races go down to the wire. For Republicans over that time span, the number was 20. In 2012, there was no competition for Democrats, and Mitt Romney secured the nomination in early April with 18 primaries left to go.[47] When nominations are wrapped up early, voters in states that have not yet held caucuses or primaries have little incentive to show up. Turnout typically drops in the later events—into the neighborhood of 3.5 to 7 percent. That translates into tens of thousands of voters per state who have no influence over the nomination. In the 2012 Republican nomination contests, about 2 million fewer people participated than in 2008, when there was a more prolonged contest.

The Media. The media's influence is exaggerated because of its role as gatekeeper, handicapper, scorekeeper, and judge.[48] When the media pronounces a candidate "strong," "weak," or "viable," electoral odds and fundraising potential shift. When the media decides to focus on a scandal (Gary Hart, Bill Clinton), verbal miscue (George Romney, Joe Biden, Jimmy Carter, Rick Perry), or emotional breakdown (Edmund Muskie), the results can be devastating. Emotional outbursts and tears, on rare occasion, can be turned in one's favor as was the case for Hillary Clinton in 2008 in New Hampshire. When a candidate fares better or worse than predicted by the media, his or her stock soars or plummets. Media treatment of Senator Edmund Muskie in 1972 helped spur his downfall; a friendly media in 1976 clearly helped Jimmy Carter; four years later, media coverage helped Ronald Reagan balance an Iowa loss with a New Hampshire victory. The media see-sawed in 1992, at first battering Bill Clinton because of alleged marital infidelity and his avoidance of Vietnam War service, then helping resurrect his candidacy after his second-place finish in New Hampshire. Meanwhile, the media was not kind to Senator Bob Dole. In 2000 the media seemed to fall in love with Senator John McCain because of his "straight talk" on issues and the easy access he accorded the press. Howard Dean's front-runner status in the 2004 Democratic contest against John Kerry crashed amid what could be termed "mocking" media coverage after placing third in the Iowa caucuses. During the 2012 Republican contest, media coverage explained much of the rise and decline of the five different front-runners.[49]

Pros and Cons. A fifth consequence of front-loading is ambiguous in that, by ending the process early, it can help or hinder candidates. On the positive side, candidates can relax, plot strategy, rethink what they said and did during the primary season, and spend more time raising money for the fall battle. On the other hand, wrapping up the nomination early can hurt. If candidates go into hibernation or spend time at small gatherings raising money, there is a risk of being "out of sight and out of mind." For a challenger to an incumbent president, to be invisible is to concede the arena to the chief executive. Since voters have relatively short memories and attention spans, early winners can suffer, especially if capturing the nomination early depleted their campaign treasuries. This problem may have hurt Mitt Romney in 2012. After spending almost all his money battling other Republican hopefuls, once the requisite number of delegates was in the bag, Romney had little left to counter the flurry of ads put out by the Obama campaign and pro-Obama committees. The president, of course, had no competition and could spend his money on efforts to "define" Romney for the voters. Romney was all but helpless to reply.

Front-loading is a serious problem, but 2008 was the exception that proved the rule. Both parties scrambled for early primaries and caucuses on the assumption—by then almost gospel truth—that the game could be over quickly. But the script had to be torn up. Obama won the Iowa caucus with 38 percent of the delegate vote; Edwards won 30 percent and Clinton 29. Clinton then won in New Hampshire, 39 percent to Obama's 37, with Edwards picking up 17 percent. The war was on, not ending until June. States that failed to position themselves early ended up playing key roles and getting national attention. States such as Montana, South Dakota, Oregon, and Kentucky, normally all but ignored, surpassed the 17 Super Tuesday states in importance, reminding veteran observers of the "good old days."

That's Not All—Other Issues and Problems

Peer Review. When voters rather than officeholders and party elites decide the nominee, just about any semblance of "peer review" is lost. Effective government is important, depending on cooperation between a president and his fellow partisans in Congress. That might be facilitated if the latter had a greater say in the former's nomination. Who better knows, and who has a greater stake in, the qualifications of presidential candidates? One wonders whether George McGovern, Jimmy Carter, Michael Dukakis, or George W. Bush would have won the support of fellow partisans on the Hill. Democratic superdelegates were supposed to furnish peer expertise, but they have been irrelevant because the game is over before they have to cast their ballots. At best, Mondale's claim that he had the superdelegate vote locked up in 1984 may have influenced caucus or primary activity, but that is the strongest case that can be made for superdelegate impact.[50] In 2008, hopes that Democratic superdelegates would support Hillary Clinton were dashed by a successful Obama argument that they dare not violate the "decision" reached by the voters in the primaries and caucuses. The near total separation of presidential and congressional concerns in the spring of an election year does nothing for a new president's pleas for cooperation a year later. Senators, representatives, and governors can endorse, raise money, and campaign for a presidential candidate, but they have to calculate carefully the consequences of such actions on their future roles and influence.

New Participants. The post-1972 reforms have opened the conventions to a much larger range of attendees than previously. Women, minorities, and young people show up in greater numbers, especially among Democrats. Some come as *de facto* representatives of special interests, such as teachers. Some are "amateurs" or "zealots," many of whom are committed to unlikely candidates (Ron Paul in 2012) or to ideological issues that, if pressed hard, can hurt their party's nominee in November.

The Convention. Because the identities of the parties' nominees are known well in advance, conventions have become little more than pep rallies to unify and energize the parties, serving as kickoffs to the fall campaigns. They can be a little bit raucous and divisive if ideologues clash over elements or even words in the party platforms—none of which is either binding or very influential on the nominees—but conventions now are scripted, ordered, organized, and rather dull. What once was a forum for bargaining and serious politicking now is a stage that affords the speakers a chance to shine (Obama in 2004), embarrass themselves (Clint Eastwood's dialogue with an empty chair at the 2012 Republican gathering), or bore their audiences (too many examples to mention). One clear result is that Republican convention attenders are very conservative relative to their own party's voters, and Democratic delegates are more liberal than their rank and file.

Money. Finally, there is the gold. Primaries cost the states and localities a packet in election administration, totaling into the double-digit millions; and rounding up volunteers to work at the polls sometimes is a challenge. Scheduling dictates that fundraising commence three years before the first primary, and a candidate's ability to raise money sends a message to potential supporters, the media, and potential competitors. With only a few exceptions since 1980, the candidates who raised the most money by the end of the year preceding election year ended up winning the nomination.

The Federal Election Campaign Act of 1971, amended in 1974, provided matching funds for candidates who raise $5,000 in each of 20 states in small donations of $250 or less. The government matches subsequent donations of the same amount, up to an annually adjusted limit—provided the candidates abide by the rules. Those rules limit candidate contributions to their own campaigns, spending in the prenomination period, and spending in each state. Given the radically uneven importance of different states, candidates tend to max out their spending in the early primary and caucus states and set up shop in neighboring states, often spending those states' quotas to influence the target states. Boston television reaches New Hampshire, so candidates spend in Beantown. Because of these limits, no major candidates agree to them anymore, preferring to raise and spend their own money. Steve Forbes began the trend in 1996, opting to use some of his vast fortune. George W. Bush followed suit in 2000 and 2004; in 2004, Democratic candidates Howard Dean (who raised surprising amounts of money in small donations) and multimillionaire John Kerry did the same. Four years later, all major candidates except John Edwards passed on federal funds. Obama and Clinton that year alone spent $500 million fighting for the nomination until June. McCain and Romney spent $231 million.[51] In 2012, Mitt Romney's campaign spent $78 million by the end of March, when he mathematically locked up the nomination; his official Federal Election Campaign report as of September was about $298 million.[52]

In sum, the nominating system constitutes a blessing and a curse. On the positive side, it tests a candidate's planning and organizational skills, stamina, consistency, fundraising abilities, and, as needed, recuperative or "bounce-back" capabilities. It challenges both their retail and their wholesale political skills, and it showcases their abilities to stand up under pressure in debates. For voters, it can be educational, allowing for gradual learning about candidates' competence and attractiveness. It allows for participation and activism. Nonetheless, it remains fraught with negatives. The process seems to take forever; the caucus and primary schedules are questionable with respect to effectiveness and efficiency; and the events involve small numbers of voters who can be rather unrepresentative of the general public, if not of their fellow partisans. The campaigns frequently feature simplistic and nasty rhetoric hardly designed to endear the eventual winner to his rivals, whose support he may need in November. The system is costly and exacts a toll on the candidates. Recently, at least, the contests seem to drive candidates toward the extremes, and they lack significant "peer review" by other public officials who have a huge stake in the outcome. Is there a better way?

6.5 REFORMS

More or Better Participation

Reforms should follow the criteria outlined in chapter 1. A common proposal is to broaden participation and representativeness by replacing caucuses with primaries and stimulating turnout. Switching to primaries could quadruple participation rates in today's caucus states. That decision is up to state political parties; the national parties cannot force them to do so, although they could bring pressure to bear. States would have to decide whether the primaries would be open, closed, or hybrid; whether they would be stand-alone events or held in conjunction with elections for other offices; and when the primaries would occur. The consequences of changing, at least in some states, alter the nature of state politics.

Broadening primary turnout could be accomplished by switching from closed to open primaries, by replacing winner-take-all primary rules with proportionality, and by arranging primary dates so that no candidate could amass a majority of delegates until late in the season (when the determination of a party's candidate lingers into late spring, turnout in later primaries is greater).[53] The addition of independents would alter the audiences for candidates' appeals, perhaps requiring them to tone down the rhetoric and potentially producing more centrist nominees. That, in turn, could affect the governing process and policies for the next four years.[54] It might also, however, have the effect of denying to general election voters as sharp a choice as they might want. Is the country better off with two moderate candidates or with two distinctive ones? Would opening the primaries reduce peoples' incentives to join and work for political parties? If so, could the parties do the jobs for which they are intended?

Allocation and Binding of Delegates

A related reform concerns the relative merits of the winner-take-all versus the proportional rule for allocating delegates. The former usually accelerates the accumulation of committed delegates for one or two candidates, favors big states, and exacerbates the jockeying for early slots in the nomination schedule. It violates the representation criterion and might discourage participation by supporters of all but the leading candidates. Proportionality would advance those values, provided there remains some threshold to prevent marginal candidates from gumming up the works. Democrats require proportionality. For 2016, Republicans mandate proportionality for any state primary before mid-March and limit the number of convention delegates for states holding events before March 1—except for Iowa, New Hampshire, Nevada, and South Carolina. Proportionality is a two-edge sword: it enhances representation, but it lengthens the nominating season, and that can eat up a candidate's finances. Efficiency suffers. Streamlining procedures for 2016, Republicans moved the convention date earlier; mandated that all delegates must be chosen at least 45 days before the convention; took greater control over the candidate debates; and required that to be nominated at the convention, a candidate must have the backing of a majority of delegates in eight or more states.

Parties wrestle with whether and when delegates should be bound. Recall that the attention-getting Iowa caucuses do not actually choose delegates to the national convention; rather, they select delegates to a state convention where the final allocation and binding of delegates is done. Missouri holds a preference primary, but the parties choose delegates later on. In 2008, Texas went the Show Me state one better, holding a primary during the day (won by Clinton) and a caucus at night to allocate delegates (won by Obama)—the now famous "Texas Two-Step." Colorado and Maine also hold early events but make delegate selection later. Looking to 2016, reflecting on some misbehavior in 2012 and seeking more accountability and responsiveness to participants, Republicans mandated that the first event in a state's nomination system must be binding on delegates chosen there. State parties are not happy with this rule.

Back-Load the Front-Load

Proposals to address front-loading are of two sorts: (a) shorten the nomination season or at least manage it better; and (b) switch to a single one-shot event, such as a national primary. A lengthy nomination period forces candidates to campaign in a range of states, facilitates voter learning, and allows less well known (and often less experienced) candidates to emerge—not always a positive development. Most commentators think the ideal would be to begin with a heavy dose of "retail" politics in small but representative states, with a primary or caucus about every other week, allowing the biggest and most competitive states to seal the deal at the end. Three months of activity should be sufficient: March through May with a late June convention, as Republicans want to do in 2016, or April through June, with the convention in August or early September, as now.[55]

Both parties tried to condense the nominating season, allowing four states to begin early. That effort worked somewhat in 2012, but neither party has been able to lock it in because state laws, not national party decisions, ultimately determine the calendar. State legislatures and governors are as much concerned about garnering national attention (and dollars) and about the intangible impact of holding their events early as they are in the actual power of their party delegations at the conventions. The only enforcement tool the national parties have is to deny seats at the national convention to delegations chosen out of sequence. Both parties did this in 2008 to no avail. The rule-violating Florida and Michigan delegations eventually were seated. A few states seek to get the best of both worlds by playing the primary–caucus game, holding an early nonbinding primary to attract attention and then selecting delegates later, during the permissible delegate selection period. When Republicans in 2012 mandated proportional delegate selection for states holding events before April, Arizona and Florida thumbed their noses, held their primaries early, and allocated delegates on the winner-take-all basis.

The parties need to charter a joint commission to work out a solution, hoping for state cooperation. One approach is to reward states with the highest voting turnout in the previous presidential election by letting them lead off the primary and caucus season.[56] That means that such states as Minnesota, Wisconsin, Maine, and Oregon would join New Hampshire and Iowa, creating an incentive for broader voter participation. At least it would provide a clear rationale for being first.

Group the Nominating Events

A popular alternative is to clump primaries into groups, by size or region. The so-called Delaware Plan, which seemed to appeal to the Republican National Committee but not to candidate George W. Bush, would create four pods determined by state population. The smallest 13 states would conduct primaries or caucuses in February or March, followed by the next smallest 13 in April, then 12 medium-size states in May, concluding with the dozen biggest states in early June. Loading the tail end of the schedule should encourage turnout, keep everyone in suspense, and potentially deliver a mélange of delegates to the national convention where—if no one held a majority—the final bargaining and negotiating would occur. Some large states feared that most candidates would be knocked out early, leaving them with little real choice or influence at the end. Any fixed schedule plays favorites. In 2008 the Republicans dallied with the Ohio Plan, which would have the least populous states start the process on the same day. Then would come three groups, each with fixed membership. Every fourth year a different group would follow the lead-off small states. Senator McCain objected, and the plan died.

The American or California Plan would establish 10 two-week intervals. In the first interval, any state or group of states with a combined total of 8 congressional districts (roughly equal to the size of Iowa plus New Hampshire) could hold events. Two weeks later, the second round would include any state or group of states totaling 16 congressional districts. Every two weeks thereafter, the eligibility total would increase, to 16, 24, and 32 districts. Finally, the remaining states would hold their primaries and caucuses in the last period. In addition to its complexity, the system would vary from election to election, and one could imagine all sorts of strange combinations of states scattered widely across the nation, forcing candidates to chase from one region of the country to another. It would be costly and inefficient, as would the so-called Interregional Primary Plan that called for six groups, each of which would include a mixture of states from different regions. In 2000, the National Association of Secretaries of State recommended the Rotating Presidential Primary Plan. The idea was to divide the country into four regions of equal Electoral College size, and all states in each region would hold their nominating contests on the same day—in effect establishing four Super Tuesdays. The timing would be well spaced to enable candidates more efficiently to concentrate efforts in one region at a time, allowing them to get to know the problems and issues better and facilitating the work of campaign staffs. The most popular version would systematically rotate the regions every fourth year, but no matter how that is done, one region, along with Iowa and New Hampshire, gets the advantage of being first in line in a given year.

Finally, the political scientist Larry Sabato has advocated a regional lottery scheme established via constitutional amendment.[57] He proposes four regions composed of contiguous states, except Alaska and Hawaii. All states in a region hold nominating events in succession from April through July. States within the region could hold their events any time within their month, with some rushing to the beginning of that month's calendar and others opting for a later day when there is no competition for media attention. A national lottery determines which region is first, preventing candidates from focusing too far in advance on any one state or region and robbing Iowa and New Hampshire of their preferred positions. All states in the first region would have an incentive to go first, creating a bit of a traffic jam. To give "retail" politics a role, Sabato adds a separate lottery for all small states and the District of Columbia, with the winners allowed to hold their primaries in mid-March, ahead of the first region. Whether his scheme passes the test of efficiency and representativeness, let alone the deliberative criterion, is less than clear. It is full of uncertainties for the candidates and states, and extending campaigning into July surely will conflict with Americans' vacation schedules.

After the 2012 election, the Republican National Committee charged a five-member panel of GOP notables to evaluate Mitt Romney's defeat and make proposals to improve the party's competitive stance. Its report, "The Growth and Opportunity Project," proposed (a) creating a regional primary cluster to follow the four traditional early states; (b) shortening the nominating process; and (c) replacing caucuses and conventions with primaries. The goal was to end the internecine warfare among GOP candidates and reduce campaign spending during the nominating process to save money for the fall campaign. Reaction was swift and strong, particularly from members of the party's right wing. "It looks like a system of the establishment, by the establishment, and for the establishment," said conservative public relations executive Greg Mueller.[58] The major complaint was that these reforms would bias the nomination in favor of familiar and well-heeled candidates, undermining those outside the party "establishment." Nor did they like the emphasis on expensive media-intensive primaries, preferring the more grass-roots caucuses that outsiders can capture. Mike Huckabee's and Rick Santorum's Iowa victories in 2008 and 2012 and Ron Paul's 2012 efforts are, they claimed, proof positive. How these proposals will play out will be decided over the next couple of years.

Just Do It—A Single National Primary

The oldest and most popular reform proposal is to establish a one-shot national primary in each party.[59] The arguments are enticing:

- Participation will rise. If independents could participate, candidates would need to appeal broadly, enhancing representation and accountability, possibly leading to the selection of more centrist nominees.
- The campaign season will be shorter, reducing wear and tear on the candidates, possibly saving millions of dollars, and providing relief to weary citizens.
- National contests will force candidates to focus on national issues and constrain them to preach the same message everywhere and always.
- Problems of sequencing will disappear, reducing the influence of the early caucus and primary states and reinforcing the "one person, one vote" equality principle.
- Voters will simultaneously evaluate all candidates against each other, avoiding the bandwagon effect that forces out some candidates before they can make their cases.

Simple solutions have problems. Will a national primary directly select the parties' nominees, or will it choose delegates to the party's national convention? If the former, how and when is the vice presidential candidate chosen—appointed by the presidential candidate after the primary or selected beforehand so as to run as a team? If there is to be a team approach, potential candidates must decide early on whether to seek the presidency themselves or to sign on with other candidates as their vice presidential partner. A national primary that selects delegates to the national convention opens a Pandora's box of the same problems found in the current system, such as apportionment of delegates (by states or by congressional districts?), the winner-take-all versus proportional question, and the matter of binding delegates.

Almost surely, a national primary will advantage well-known candidates. It probably also favors those with effective money-raising skills and those particularly skilled in media relations. If the results of a national primary are measured by the national vote, what constitutes victory—a majority of all votes, a simple plurality, or a plurality that passes some threshold—say 40 percent? If a majority is needed, what happens if there is no majority? Runoffs have their own problems (chapter 4). If an absolute majority were needed, would that attract a large number of candidates, each hoping to garner enough votes to prevent any candidate from winning, thus enhancing his or her subsequent bargaining power at the convention? Or, if there were no convention, losing candidates' endorsements of one of the leading candidates would be important in a runoff. Similarly, if only a plurality were needed to win, it is likely that third- and fourth-party candidates would split up the votes so that the winner might pick up only 30 or 35 percent of the votes. That is hardly a ringing endorsement, and it could undermine somewhat the legitimacy of the first-place finisher, weakening prospects in November. A plurality system might invite a boatload of candidates.

The usual questions and arguments over open, closed, or semiopen/semiclosed hybrid primaries remain, as does the matter of cost and coordination, especially if the presidential primaries were held separately from primary elections for state and local candidates. Candidates would be forced to conduct "tarmac campaigns," flying here and there several times a day to indicate concern for all regions of the country and to capture local news coverage. National primaries are likely to do nothing but enhance the influence of the media and the importance of money. With all the eggs in one basket, campaigns could become nastier, raising the specter of the divisive primary.

Better Ideas?

Several scholars have proposed a series of early small state primaries and caucuses that would be followed by a national primary, seeking to blend the benefits of "retail" with "wholesale" politics.[60] Another possibility is a form of the top-two primary, advanced by those who see excessive partisanship ruining the current system.[61] Let all candidates of whatever party who can afford it run in a single national primary (or, under other highly complicated versions, in each state), and then have the top two run it off several weeks later. Other than registration, there would be no barrier to voting and certainly no partisan barrier. Although it is likely that the top two finishers would be one Democrat and one Republican, there is no guarantee if one party had two popular candidates and the other was found wanting.

A hybrid convention–primary system, reversing the current sequencing, is worth consideration. Each party's national convention, composed of state party delegates, would select two candidates who would compete in a one-shot national primary. This would incorporate deliberative peer review, but in the end leave the final decision to the voters. All the issues relating to primaries, of course, must be negotiated. A related idea, proposed by Lloyd Cutler, is a bicameral convention for each party, with one chamber consisting of delegates chosen as they now are and a second chamber composed of the party's nominees for House and Senate seats. Each would pick a presidential candidate. If both selected the same person, fine. If not, each chamber would hold a runoff between the top choices of each chamber, and the winner—the party's presidential nominee—would be the one with the highest combined total of votes. The idea is messy at best. If there were a runoff, even the winner could be branded by the opposition as a loser because she or he was rejected by one of the two bodies.[62] Another novel idea was launched in 2011 by an organization called "Americans Elect." Using the Internet, it solicited presidential nominations from the mass public with the expectation that the organization would work to put on state primary ballots whichever candidate "won" the national poll. Leaving other considerations aside, making such a scheme work would require a strong organizational capability to achieve those ballot positions. In the end, the effort fizzled.

Surely the least popular reform proposal would be one that may be most intriguing: a return to the congressional caucus system of the early nineteenth century. The scheme and justification are simple. Each party would hold a caucus composed of its U.S. senators and representatives, governors, state party chairs, and perhaps a sampling of mayors, and that caucus would nominate the party's presidential and vice presidential candidates. Although this is far from being directly democratic and participatory, it is so indirectly, since all these people except the state party chairs were themselves elected and because, in the end, the voters still pick the president. The advantages are clear: intense peer review by elected representatives; reasoned deliberation guiding the selection; efficiency in terms of minimizing cost and candidate wear-and-tear; and, arguably, effectiveness in picking the candidates who, in the minds of those who have to govern with them, would be the best leaders for country. Who, after all, is best able to know the character and abilities of the candidates than their colleagues and peers? The influence of money, special interests, and the media would largely vanish at this stage of the electoral cycle; competence, experience, and negotiating skills would be the important variables in the equation. The fears of "back room corruption" could be set aside; politics today is in the spotlight, and any shenanigans would be immediately made public.

This plan is not directly participatory; the public probably would deem it illegitimate; and it is likely to make the president beholden to his or her party on the Hill. The latter concern, on reflection, might not be so bad after all, since it would induce cooperation because legislators and governors would have a real stake in the president's success. If this arrangement were combined with giving the president some measure of control over his party's support for its congressional candidates, a balance might be achieved. Moreover, unless the members of the caucuses were of an extreme sort—rather doubtful, especially in the case of governors—they would be more likely to nominate reasonable and more centrist presidential candidates. Their decisions, of course, would be subject to the review of their constituents when next they faced elections, but that is what democratic politics is all about.

6.6 CONCLUSION

Large numbers of Americans want to see the presidential nominating system reformed, but the old political truism, where you stand depends on where you sit, applies, with citizens from smaller states differing from those in larger ones and those in the more influential early states differing from those in the states that caucus or vote later.[63] In the end, there is no perfect nominating system. The constraints and complications of a federal system, along with the constitutionally protected privileges and powers of the private political parties, render any system complex. As Barbara Norrander remarked, "All election systems are biased."[64] Any formula will favor one group over another. Nor is there any necessary connection between the skills needed to secure a nomination—or win an election, for that matter—and those needed to govern wisely and well. The presidential nominating system perhaps is the best example of how a focus on some of the seven criteria—participation and representation—can conflict with others and potentially influence the nature and effectiveness of the presidency and of presidential–congressional relations. Reforms in one area always affect other areas, although it may not always be obvious.

QUESTIONS TO CONSIDER

1. Which of the approaches to congressional nominations—caucuses and conventions versus primaries or open versus closed versus top-two primaries—best comports with your preferred criteria for good government? Why?

2. Is there a case to be made for giving up on broad-based participation in the nominating process?

3. Which of the reforms would you support to replace the existing presidential nominating system? Why?

NOTES

1. Closed primaries are run in Delaware, Florida, Kansas, Kentucky, Maine, Nevada, New Jersey, New Mexico, New York, Pennsylvania, and Wyoming; open primary states include Alabama, Arkansas, Georgia, Hawaii, Michigan, Minnesota, Missouri, Montana, North Dakota, Vermont, and Wisconsin. For what follows, see the National Conference of State Legislatures Web site, http://www.ncsl.org/research/elections-and-campaigns/primary-types.aspx/; L. Sandy Maisel and Mark D. Brewer, *Parties and Elections in America: The Electoral Process*, 6th ed. (Lanham, MD, Boulder, New York, Toronto, and Plymouth, UK: Rowman & Littlefield, 2012), chaps. 6 and 8; and Marc J. Hetherington and Bruce A. Larson, *Parties, Politics, and Public Policy in America*, 11th ed. (Washington, D.C.: CQ Press, 2010), chap. 3.

2. Marni Ezra, 'The Benefits and Burdens of Congressional Primary elections," in Peter F. Galderisi, Marni Ezra, and Michael Lyons, eds., *Congressional Primaries and the Politics of Representation* (Lanham, MD, Boulder, CO, New York, and Oxford: Rowman & Littlefield, 2001), chap. 4.

3. David W. Romero, "Divisive Primaries and the House District Vote," *American Politics Research* 31 (2003): 178–90; Gregg B. Johnson, Meredith-Joy Petersheim, and Jesse T. Wasson, "Divisive Primaries and Incumbent General Election Performance: Prospects and Costs in U.S. House Races," *American Politics Research* 38 (2010): 931–55; and James M. Snyder Jr. and Michael M. Ting, "Electoral Selection with Parties and Primaries," *American Journal of Political Science* 55 (2011): 782–96.

4. Robert E. Hogan, "The Effects of Primary Divisiveness on General Election Outcomes in State Legislative Elections," *American Politics Research* 31 (2003): 27–47; Caitlin E. Jewitt and Sarah A. Treul, "Competitive Primaries and Party Division in Congressional Elections," *Electoral Studies* 35 (2014): 140–49.

5. Gary C. Jacobson, *The Politics of Congressional Elections*, 8th ed. (Upper Saddle River, NJ: Pearson, 2013): 30–38; Norman J. Ornstein, Thomas E. Mann, Michael J. Malbin, and Andrew Rugg, *Vital Statistics on Congress* (Washington, D.C.: Brookings, 2013), table 2.8; Stephen Ansolabehere, John Mark Hansen, Shigeo Hirano, and James M. Snyder Jr., "More Democracy: The Direct Primary and Competition in U.S. Elections," *Studies in American Political Development* 24 (2010): 190–205.

6. Robert G. Boatright, *Getting Primaried: The Changing Politics of Congressional Primary Challenges* (Ann Arbor: University of Michigan Press, 2013).

7. David W. Brady, Hahrie Han, and Jeremy C. Pope, "Elections and Candidate Ideology: Out of Step with the Primary Electorate?," *Legislative Studies Quarterly* 32 (2007), 79–105; Shigeo Hirano, James M. Snyder Jr., and Michael M. Ting, "Distributive Politics with Primaries," *Journal of Politics* 71 (2009): 1467–80.

8. Barry C. Burden, "The Polarizing Effects of Congressional Primaries," in Galderisi, Ezra, and Lyons, *Congressional Primaries*, chap. 7.

9. John G. Geer, *Nominating Presidents: An Evaluation of Voters and Primaries* (New York: Greenwood Press, 1989); Barbara Norrander, "Ideological Representativeness of Presidential Primary Voters," *American Journal of Political Science* 33 (1989): 570–87.

10. Richard R. Lau, "Correct Voting in the 2008 U.S. Presidential Nominating Elections," *Political Behavior* 35 (2013): 331–55.
11. Karen M. Kaufmann, James G. Gimpel, and Adam Hoffman, "A Promise Fulfilled? Open Primaries and Representation," *Journal of Politics* 65 (2003): 457–76.
12. *Ibid.*; Elisabeth R. Gerber and Rebecca B. Morton, "Primary Election Systems," *Journal of Law, Economics, & Organization* 14 (1998): 304–24; Todd L. Cherry and Stephen Kroll, "Crashing the Party: An Experimental Investigation of Strategic Voting in Primary Elections," *Public Choice* 114 (2003): 387–420; Kristin Kanthak and Rebecca Morton, "The Effects of Electoral Rules on Congressional Primaries," in Galderisi, Ezra, and Lyons, *Congressional Primaries*, chap. 8.
13. Eric McGhee, Seth Masket, Boris Shor, Steven Rogers, and Nolan McCarty, "A Primary Cause of Partisanship? Nomination Systems and Legislator Ideology," *American Journal of Political Science* 58 (2014): 337–51. See the debate between Masket and Mark A. Siegel, "Resolved, States Should Require Open Primaries," in Richard J. Ellis and Michael Nelson, eds., *Debating Reform: Conflicting Perspectives on How to Fix the American Political System*, 2nd ed. (Los Angeles, London, Dew Delhi, Singapore, and Washington, D.C.: CQ Press, 2014), chap. 9.
14. The Supreme Court has sided with the parties. *Tashjian v. Republican Party of Connecticut*, 479 US 208 (1986), and *California Democratic Party v. Jones*, 530 U.S. 567 (2000).
15. Will Bullock and Joshua D. Clinton, "More a Molehill Than a Mountain: The Effects of the Blanket Primary on Elected Officials' Behavior from California," *Journal of Politics* 73 (2011): 915–30; R. Michael Alvarez and Betsy Sinclair, "Electoral Institutions and Legislative Behavior: The Effects of Primary Processes," *Political Research Quarterly* 65 (2012): 544–57.
16. J. Andrew Sinclair, "Results and Implications: The June 'Top-Two' Primary & California's 2012 Legislative Races," VTP Working Paper No. 107, Caltech/MIT voting Technology Project (October 2, 2012), http://www.vote.caltech.edu/sites/default/files/WP_107.pdf/. Campaign spending may also have risen. Eric McGhee and Daniel Krimm, "California's New Electoral Reforms: The Fall Election," Public Policy Institute of California (November 2012), http://www.ppic.org/main/publication_show.asp?i=1039/.
17. Steven Hill, "Viewpoints: Top-Two Primary Hurt Competition in the Golden State," *Sacramento Bee*, August 4, 2012: A9, http://www.sacbee.com/site-services/archives/#navlink=subnav.
18. Casey B. Dominguez, "Does the Party Matter? Endorsements in Congressional Primaries," *Political Research Quarterly* 64 (2011): 534–44.
19. See Maisel and. Brewer, *Parties and Elections*, 177–78.
20. William J. Crotty, *Decision for the Democrats: Reforming the Party Structure* (Baltimore: Johns Hopkins University Press, 1978).
21. Barbara Norrander, *The Imperfect Primary: Oddities, Biases, and Strengths of U.S. Presidential Nomination Politics* (New York and London: Routledge, 2010): 21. Other good treatments of nominations include Steven S. Smith and Melanie J. Springer, eds., *Reforming the Presidential Nomination Process* (Washington, D.C.: Brookings, 2009); James Caesar, *Reforming the Reform: A Critical Analysis of the Presidential Selection Process* (Cambridge, UK: Ballinger, 1982); Robert Loevy, *The Flawed Path to the Presidency, 1992: Unfairness and Equality in the Presidential Selection Process* (Albany: State University of New York Press, 1995); and William G. Mayer, ed., *In Pursuit of the White House: How We Choose Our Presidential Nominees* (Chatham, NJ: Chatham House, 1996).

22. Melanie J. Springer and James L. Gibson, "Public Opinion and Systems for Nominating Presidential Candidates," in Smith and Springer, *Reforming the Presidential Nomination Process*, chap. 6.

23. Thomas E. Paterson, "Voter Participation: Records Galore This Time, but What about Next Time?," in Smith and Springer, *Reforming the Presidential Nomination Process*, chap. 3.

24. U.S. Elections Project, George Mason University, http://www.electproject.org/2012p.

25. David Redlawsk, Daniel Bowen, and Caroline Tolbert, "Comparing Caucus and Registered Voter Support for the 2008 Presidential Candidates in Iowa," *PS: Political Science and Politics* 41 (2008): 129–38.

26. *Ibid.*; Costas Panagopoulos, "Are Caucuses Bad for Democracy?, *Political Science Quarterly* 125 (2010): 425–42; John G. Geer, "Assessing the Representativeness of Electorates in Presidential Primaries," *American Journal of Political* Science 32 (1988): 929–45; William G. Mayer, "Caucuses: How They Work, What Difference They Make," in Mayer, *Pursuit of the White House*, 105–57. For Iowa and New Hampshire, however, there are some differences. See the discussion below.

27. Eitan Hersh, "Primary Voters versus Caucus Goers and the Peripheral Motivations of Political Participation," *Political Behavior* 34 (2012), 689–718.

28. Norrander, *Imperfect Primary*, 85.

29. Brian Arbour, "Even Closer, Even Longer: What If the 2008 Democratic Primary Used Republican Rules?" *The Forum* 7 (2009), ISSN (Online) 1540–8884, doi:10.2202/1540-8884.1301.

30. Priscilla L. Southwell, "Rules as 'Unseen Participants': The Democratic Presidential Nominating Process," *American Politics Quarterly* 20 (1992): 54–68.

31. Gerald C. Wright, "Rules and the Ideological Character of Primary Elections," in Smith and Springer, *Reforming the Presidential Nomination Process*, chap. 4.

32. Gary D. Wekkin, "Why Crossover Voters Are Not 'Mischievous Voters': The Segmented Partisanship Hypothesis," *American Politics Quarterly* 19 (1991): 229–57.

33. For conflicting reports, see Gerald C. Wright, "Rules and the Ideological Character," chap. 4, and Frank Stephensen, "Strategic Voting in Open Primaries: Evidence from Rush Limbaugh's 'Operation chaos,'" *Public Choice* 148 (2011): 445–57; D. Sunshine Hillygus and Sarah A. Treul, "Assessing strategic voting in the 2008 US presidential primaries: the role of electoral context, institutional rules, and negative votes," *Public Choice* 161 (2014): 517–36.

34. William G. Mayer, "Retrospective Voting in Presidential Primaries," *Presidential Studies Quarterly* 40 (2010): 660–85.

35. Karen M. Kaufmann, John. R. Petrocik, and Daron R. Shaw, *Unconventional Wisdom: Facts and Myths about American Voters* (Oxford and New York: Oxford University Press, 2008): 196–98.

36. Marni Ezra, 'The Benefits and Burdens," 50; James L. Lengle, Diane Owen, and Molly W. Sonner, "Divisive Nominating Mechanisms and Democratic Party Electoral Prospects," *Journal of Politics* 57 (1995): 370–83.

37. Todd Makse and Anand E. Sokhey, "Revisiting the Divisive Primary Hypothesis: 2008 and the Clinton–Obama Nomination Battle," *American Politics Research* 38 (2010): 233–65. Apparently, a number of Clinton and Edwards supporters did defect in November. Pricilla L. Southwell, "The Effect of Nomination Divisiveness on the 2008 Presidential Election," *PS: Political Science and Politics* (2010): 255–58. The other view is from Amber Wichowsky and Sarah E. Niebler, "Narrow Victories and Hard Games: Revisiting the Primary Divisiveness Hypothesis," *American Politics Research* 38 (2010): 1052–71, and Michael Henderson, D. Sunshine Hillygus, and Trevor Tompson, "'Sour Grapes' or

Rational Voting? Voter Decision Making among Thwarted Primary Voters in 2008," *Public Opinion Quarterly* 74 (2010): 499–529.

38. Mark Murray, "Primary Season Takes Corrosive Toll on GOP and Its Candidates," *NBC/WSJ Poll* (March 4, 2012), http://firstread.nbcnews.com/_news/2012/03/04/10578249-nbcwsj-poll-primary-season-takes-corrosive-toll-on-gop-and-its-candidates?lite/.

39. William G. Mayer and Andrew E. Busch, *The Front-Loading Problem in Presidential Nominations* (Washington, D.C.: Brookings, 2004).

40. Andrew J. Taylor, "Does Presidential Primary and Caucus Order Affect Policy? Evidence from Federal Procurement Spending," *Political Research Quarterly* 63 (2010): 398–409.

41. Hugh Winebrenner, *The Iowa Precinct Caucuses: The Making of a Media Event*, 2nd ed. (Ames: Iowa State University Press, 1998); Peverill Squire, ed., *The Iowa Caucuses and the Presidential Nominating Process* (Boulder, CO: Westview, 1989); Redlawsk, Bowen, and Tolbert, "Comparing Caucus and Registered Voter Support."

42. Michael S. Lewis-Beck and Peverill Squire, "Iowa" The Most Representative State?," *PS: Political Science and Politics* 42 (2009): 39–43.

43. Wright, "Rules and the Ideological Character of Primary Electorates."

44. Redlawsk, Bowen, and Tolbert, "Comparing Caucus and Registered Voter Support," 137.

45. Wright, "Rules and the Ideological Character of Primary Electorates," 36.

46. John Aldrich, "The Invisible Primary and Its Effects on Democratic Choice," *PS: Political Science and Politics* 42 (2009): 33–38.

47. Lonna Rae Atkeson and Chaerie D. Maestas, "Meaningful Participation and the Evolution of the Reformed Presidential Nominating System, *PS: Political Science and Politics* 42 (2009): 59–64.

48. Nelson W. Polsby, Aaron Wildavsky, Steven E. Schier, and David A. Hopkins, *Presidential Elections: Strategies and Structures of American Politics*, 13th ed. (Lanham, MD, Boulder, CO, New York, Toronto, and Plymouth, UK: Rowman & Littlefield, 2012), chap. 4.

49. John Sides and Lynn Vavreck, *The Gamble: Choice and Chance in the 2012 Presidential Elections* (Princeton, NJ, and Oxford: Princeton University Press, 2013), chap. 3.

50. William G. Mayer, "Superdelegates: Reforming the Reforms Revisited," in Smith and Springer, *Reforming the Presidential Nominating Process*, chap. 5.

51. Federal Election Commission, "Presidential Campaign Disbursements through June 30, 2008, http://www.fec.gov/press/summaries/2008/tables/presidential/Pres2_2008_18m.pdf/.

52. Federal Election Commission, Presidential Campaign Finance Summaries, "Presidential Pre-Nomination Campaign Disbursements September 30, 2012," http://www.fec.gov/press/summaries/2012/ElectionCycle/21m_PresCand.shtml/.

53. Caitlin E. Jewitt, "Packed primaries and empty caucuses: voter turnout in presidential nominations," *Public Choice* 160 (2014): 295–312.

54. Such need not be the case. For example, in 2012, Rick Santorum, considered the more conservative, won five states with open and six states with closed primaries; Mitt Romney, arguably more moderate, fared equally well in closed, open, and hybrid states.

55. Mayer and Busch, *The Front-Loading Problem*; and "An Incremental Approach to Presidential Nomination Reform," *PS: Political Science and Politics* 42 (2009): 65–69.

56. Heather Frederick, "Reforming the Presidential Primary System: The Voter Turnout Initiative," *PS: Political Science and Politics* 45 (2012): 51–56.

57. Larry J. Sabato, *A More Perfect Constitution: 23 Proposals to Revitalize Our Constitution and Make America a Fairer Country* (New York: Walker, 2007): 131–34.

58. Jonathan Martin and Maggie Haberman, "Right Blasts RNC 'Autopsy' as Power Grab," *Politico* (March 18, 2013), http://dyn.politico.com/printstory.cfm?uuid=8E184271-A2A9-4810-9CC2-DAEA87F2CD9D/.

59. Jeffrey M. Jones, "Americans in Favor of National Referenda on Key Issues; Majority Also Backs Shorter Presidential Campaigns and National Primary," *Gallup Politics* (July 10, 2013), http://www.gallup.com/poll/163433/americans-favor-national-referenda-key-issues .aspx?utm_source=alert&utm_medium=email&utm_campaign=syndication&utm_ content=morelink&utm_term=All%20Gallup%20Headlines%20-%20Politics%20-%20 Social%20Issues/.

60. CarolineTolbert, Amanda Keller, and Todd Donovan," A Modified National Primary: State Losers and Support for Changing the Presidential Nominating Process," *Political Science Quarterly* 125 (2010): 393–424.

61. Phil Keisling, "To Reduce Partisanship, Get Rid of Partisans," *New York Times*, March 22, 2010: A27.

62. James L. Sundquist, *Constitutional Reform and Effective Government*, rev. ed. (Washington, D.C.: Brookings, 1992): 256–58.

63. Caroline J. Tolbert, David P. Redlawsk, and Daniel C. Bowen, 'Reforming Presidential Nominations: Rotating State Primaries or a National Primary," *PS: Political Science and Politics* 42 (2009): 71–78.

64. Norrander, *Imperfect Primary*: 122.

CHAPTER 7

⌇

Campaigns and Campaign Finance

A national political campaign is better than the best circus ever
heard of, with a mass baptism and a couple of hangings thrown in.
—H. L. MENCKEN

Money is the mother's milk of politics.
—JESSE UNRUH

Once nominated, candidates for federal offices face grueling campaigns leading
up to the November elections. For voters, understanding where candidates and
parties stand on issues and what they might do if elected is essential to hold government accountable. Campaign effectiveness and efficiency are traits candidates worry
about concretely in terms of getting out their messages successfully and allocating
resources. Campaigns are about strategy, organization, messaging, media, and money,
and for presidential candidates, there is the Electoral College math. Although strategy
and organization lie beyond the reach of reform efforts, they have consequences for
the competition needed for accountability, the electoral participation essential for
representation and responsiveness, the integrity of the election process, and—in the
long run—the effectiveness of government.

7.1 THE PROBLEM: CAMPAIGN MESSAGES

To paraphrase Thomas Hobbes's description of life, campaigns are nasty and brutish.
They are not, however, short, and limiting them seems impossible. Since television
burst onto the scene in the 1950s, campaigns have depended on it to stimulate interest, transmit information, and influence voting preferences.[1] Both free "news" coverage and paid advertising are important. Candidates seek to control news coverage,
issuing streams of statements, staging media events, and trying to appear on radio
and television shows of all sorts. The impact of some 428 cable TV stations, 1,986
broadcast TV stations, and 15,358 over-the-air radio stations (as of December 31,
2013) has done nothing but multiply opportunities for and pressure on candidates to
gain as much exposure as possible.[2] Shameless they may be in pursuing such attention, but necessary it is, especially for unknowns challenging incumbents.

    To call candidate advertising a growth industry might be the understatement of
the century. Spending to produce and place ads in the 2012 presidential election ran
more than $1 billion, with huge amounts focused on 10 or so "battleground" states.[3]

124

More than 1 million campaign ads flew across the airways between June 1 and election day—39 percent more than four years earlier. Candidates and reporters have become masters of the Internet and especially outlets such as Facebook, Twitter, and YouTube, to name only three. For a decade, candidates and their campaigns used Web sites and other Internet tools to raise funds, lay out policy positions, blast their opponents, and defend against the opposition's ads. Micro targeting caught on. Campaign committees and their hired guns comb the Internet for all sorts of information about people, merging it with polling data to identify hot issues and likely voting preferences (it is said that Pandora Radio can predict with 75 percent accuracy how listeners will vote based on their location and musical tastes). They then drive appropriate ads to, and contact with, those targeted individuals. The one drawback of this tactic can occur when "mistargeted" voters resent the messages they accidentally receive and penalize candidates for it.[4]

Negative Ads

It makes for great entertainment to look at old TV campaign ads from the 1950s and early 1960s. One finds slogans, cartoon-like videos, and jingles ("You like—I like Ike," played to accompany an Uncle Sam–like character leading a marching band). It didn't take long for more serious messages to fill the airwaves, followed quickly by negative ads, perhaps the most famous of which was the anti-Goldwater ad in 1964 showing a little girl counting as she plucked petals off a daisy. When she got to 10, a sonorous voice began counting back to zero; then came the explosion of a nuclear bomb, followed by President Johnson's message about taking risks and loving one another! It has been downhill from there, as attack ads have proliferated. In 1988, for example, the Bush campaign attacked Michael Dukakis for allowing weekend passes to prison inmates like the infamous Willie Horton, a convicted murderer who raped a woman while on a weekend furlough. By 2008, according to Darrell M. West, 61 percent of Democratic and 43 percent of Republican ads were negative, exceeding the 31 and 36 percent averages over the 1972–2008 period. Conversely, he classified only 13 percent of Democratic and 18 percent of GOP ads as "policy specific." The imperatives to simplify, attract, and stimulate voters are powerful, often leading to "dumbing down" the message so as not to offend supporters while enticing undecided voters. Claiming that the other candidate will cut Social Security and Medicare is a standard tactic.[5]

Complicating the landscape is the emergence of political action committees (PACs) and advocacy groups such as the 527 and 501(c) organizations, named after the sections of the tax code under which they operate. The former collect unlimited funds from individuals, groups, corporations, and unions, using them to promote their issues. The 501(c)(3) groups are mostly charitable organizations. Forbidden to engage in overt political campaign activities, they are allowed to engage in voter education and "get out the vote" efforts, to run ads to promote or oppose specific issues (but not candidates), and to engage in limited forms of lobbying. The 501(c)(4) groups are civic and other local associations operating "exclusively" to promote "social welfare." They may engage in political advertising that does not directly support or oppose specific candidates, but the majority of their spending must be on their nonpolitical goals. Contributions to 501(c) organizations are tax deductible up to normal limits, and contributors' identities are not reported.

These organizations run their own ads on television, radio, and other media sites independent of the candidates, in theory rendering them impervious to candidates' campaign strategies and control. Their advertising emphasizes attack ads, such as those of the "Swift Boat Veterans for Truth" group that hammered Senator Kerry in 2004 for his Vietnam War record. Attack ads come in two varieties: those criticizing a candidate for his or her record or proposals and "mudslinging" attacks against one's character.

Reformers have concerns, some of which may be ill-founded. As shown in chapter 3, negative ads do not seem to turn off voters, and they may actually stimulate them. Nor do they seem to confuse voters any more than positive ads. They probably are more memorable, often present information that might otherwise go unmentioned, and may stimulate knowledge about the campaign. Several scholars have concluded that, on balance, they make a positive contribution.[6]

The effects of negative ads seem to depend on the situation and type of negativity. People distinguish the negative tone of ads from their informational content, disdaining the former. Politically sophisticated listeners and viewers probably learn from negative ads, whereas the less sophisticated are less likely to do so.[7] An attack ad's relevance to governing and the sensitivity of its viewers matters.[8] Attack ads from unknown sources seem to carry more weight with voters than those sponsored by candidates.[9] Naturally, such ads sometimes backfire on the perpetrators, questioning their decency and generating sympathy for the attacker's target.[10] Chances are that negative ads are more useful to challengers than to incumbents, although in 2012 pro-Obama ads successfully helped pin a label of "job destroyer" on Mitt Romney. The evidence suggests that the duration of any effect such ads have is short lived. Maybe that is why they are growing in frequency and repetition.

Cleaning Up the Negative Ads

There have been efforts to institute codes of conduct, such as proposed by the Pew Charitable Trusts in the late 1990s. Although popular with voters, they are voluntary and violated with impunity—if not by the candidates themselves, then by the many outside groups acting on their behalf. Ramping up the media's fact-checking activities to highlight falsehoods in negative ads should improve matters by influencing how people understand and learn from negative ads, although there is no guarantee.[11] Fact-checking is subject to some subjectivity, can lead to "he lied"–"she lied about his lying" battles, and can boomerang, as demonstrated by the "ad-watch" phenomenon in the 1990s, when original attack ads were repeated in videos seeking to debunk them. Sometimes efforts to show falsehoods in ads merely serve to convince voters that all politics is nasty. Given federal regulatory commission interpretations and court decisions on free speech, there is not much that can be done about negative ads—or advertising of any sort. The lesson seems to be that negative advertising is not worth worrying about all that much, if only because there is no realistic way to stop or control it.[12]

The behavior of the 527 and 501(c) groups is particularly troublesome, and many observers think that candidates should be able to control their advertising. It is easy to think of solutions, but none is either practical or legally feasible. It is one thing to require that candidates identify themselves and "approve" messages sent by their own campaigns, as is currently required. It is quite another to empower candidates to approve or veto the speech of private groups. As tempting as the idea maybe, reformers are bound to be frustrated.

7.2 DEBATES

Televised debates are established rituals that have generated a rich folklore. The best scholarship, however, indicates that although they may give a flutter to candidates' poll numbers, they have little lasting effect and change few minds. If anything, they probably help challengers a bit more than incumbents.[13] Richard Nixon's performance against John F. Kennedy in 1960 should have warned incumbents and leading candidates to avoid debates. Presidents Lyndon Johnson in 1964 and Nixon in 1972 heeded that warning, but President Gerald Ford agreed to debate Jimmy Carter in 1976. Carter apparently didn't learn the lesson because he suffered at Ronald Reagan's hands in 1980. Reagan successfully bucked the trend in 1984 against Walter Mondale. Mitt Romney's performance in the first debate with President Obama on October 3, 2012, watched by 70 million viewers, boosted his poll numbers among undecided voters and seemed to turn his campaign around for a while.[14] It may be that two or three presidential debates and one vice presidential debate now are so well established that candidates cannot avoid them. If 2012 was any indicator, debates also have taken over the nomination process. Republican candidates held 20 debates between May 2011, and February 2012, providing grist for the media's mills and seemingly affecting opinion poll results. The Republican National Committee has moved to reduce the number and to exercise greater control over GOP debates in 2016.

Critics argue that the debates are little more than shows in which candidates, having spent hours in predebate "boot camps," mouth platitudes, unleash their best one-line zingers, and duck tough questions.[15] Every four years, candidates and their representatives joust over the number and style of the debates, each candidate seeking to position himself as the underdog to make his performance look better than it actually might be. Said former president George H. W. Bush, "I think it's too much show business and too much prompting, too much artificiality, and not really debates. They're rehearsed appearances." Media expert Newton Minow's response is instructive: "the choice is not between ideal debates and less ideal debates but between debates and no debates."[16] He defended the debates on three grounds: "the debates are the *only* time during presidential campaigns when the major candidates appear together side by side under conditions that they do not control," they highlight differences between the candidates, and they present a range of issues that voters must consider.[17] Debates potentially are important because voters so easily limit their information sources to those with which they already agree. Scholarly analyses show that debates feature more positive claims and position taking than attacks, that policy issues dominate over issues of character, and that debates affect voters' evaluations of the candidates and their interest in the election. However, they do little to enhance knowledge of candidates' *issue* stances or change voting intentions.[18] Reinforcement, rather than conversion, seems to be the result. Debates also affect the candidates. Claimed President Bill Clinton, "You're forced to learn the things that you ought to know anyway about issues that you may not be all that interested in, or you didn't have time to deal with [and] they force you to come to terms with what you really believe in."[19]

Can They Talk to Each Other?—Debate Problems and Reforms

Objections to debates focus on format, frequency, number of debaters, and media coverage. Since the late 1980s, the Bipartisan Commission on Presidential Debates has had responsibility for managing the debates. Formats threaten to be deal breakers because of the advantages that might accrue to one or the other candidate from a particular setup. Does standing behind a lectern help the taller candidate? Experienced showman-type candidates love to roam the stage. Who should ask the questions—a panel of television news personalities, a single one, political scientists, the audience, or viewers calling, texting, or emailing? How much time should there be for answers and rebuttals? All sorts of variations have been tried, and there is no perfectly neutral format. One popular suggestion is to reduce the formality and to stifle the canned responses that resemble stump speeches, perhaps by having the candidates question each other. At the least, the moderator needs to push, probe, and challenge to keep the candidates focused and stymie their efforts to evade tough questions or to answer the questions they *want* to address. It is unlikely that the Commission can *impose* a format on the candidates against their wishes. But, given the inevitability of debates, the Commission has more leverage than its predecessors.

At least since 1980, when President Carter refused to participate in any debate with Independent John Anderson, the issue of who shows up on stage has been controversial. Ross Perot and his running mate, Admiral James Stockdale, participated in 1992, but in 1996 the major candidates and the Commission vetoed Perot because he did not have a "realistic chance" of winning. That standard has been the rule ever since. Operationally, the Commission uses a five-poll average to determine a candidate's viability, with 15 percent needed to qualify. Accordingly, in 2000 the Commission ruled out Pat Buchanan of the Reform Party and Ralph Nader of the Green Party. The 15 percent threshold strikes many as too high, especially given the volatility of polls. Some reformers argue for a 5 percent cutoff coupled with a national poll asking the public which candidates they want to see in the debates. Whether the presence of less known or less popular candidates matters is unclear. Other reformers urge more debates, but candidates, especially the frontrunners, are not enthusiastic; and voters have limited attention spans and probably would lose interest.

Media coverage of debates could stand improvement. Pre-event coverage should focus more on policy issues and less on speculating who will "win." When the debates are finished, the press could serve the public well by foregoing judgments about who won and who lost, instead concentrating on the accuracy of the claims, on the policy implications, and on the differences between the candidates. Voters need useful information, not an ESPN-like report on "the game." Of course, none of these is subject to any legal or regulatory control; the ball is squarely in the courts of the media.

Roughly 9 of 10 congressional races include at least one debate, and the issues of concern resemble those at the presidential level. Few studies have examined the effects of congressional debates, but it is certain that the effect on voters derives not from the debates (which are watched by relatively few) but from subsequent media treatment. Incumbents shy away from debates when they can, rather than help showcase less well known challengers. There probably are few reforms that could contribute more to enhancing congressional elections than face-to-face interactions, well and fairly covered by the press.

7.3 THE MEDIA SOMETIMES IS THE MESSAGE

Problems with Political Media

The media's political functions are extensive, including its roles as

- "Great Mentioner" (identifying potential candidates);
- "Image Creator" (portraying candidate traits);
- "Expectation Setter" (setting the odds on victory, predicting results);
- "Issue Identifier" (deciding what issues are important);
- "Field Narrower" (judging who has survived the early rounds);
- "Campaign Critic" (evaluating candidate performance); and
- "Purveyor of Results" (reporting results and interpreting exit polls).[20]

One might add "political cheerleader" or "attack dog," in recognition of how some TV and radio stations have taken on a strong partisan tilt.

At least four aspects beg for reform. The first concerns *what* and *whom* the media covers. For decades newspapers, television, and radio have focused on the horse-race aspect of campaigns, with daily stories about surges and declines in popular approval, demographic differences in polling results, and campaign strategies and tactics. As commercial enterprises in the entertainment business, traditional media must report on the newsmakers, especially candidates who are most likely to succeed. Commentators and bloggers love to stir the pot with coverage of even the most outrageous allegations, scandals, maneuvers, gaffes, and pratfalls. How much did Sarah Palin spend on her campaign wardrobe, and who paid for it? Why didn't Obama wear an American flag lapel pin? What are the implications of Mitt Romney's comments about the 47 percent of Americans who pay no taxes? Did Al Gore really have a wardrobe consultant? Many of the talking heads on TV and the "talk radio" hosts have a stake in pandering to particular viewers and stirring up trouble. There is no way to curtail the media, and a return to the days of three major TV broadcasters and neutral radio is a fantasy. The good news is that once presidential finalists are chosen, both usually receive ample attention; in many congressional races, however, challengers scramble to get the coverage they need.

A second problem is the negative tone of much media coverage. Certainly that was true in 2012 for both candidates most of the time; in 2008, Obama benefited from a more positive coverage than is typical. Negativity is a product of the need to report "news," and news has come to be perceived and defined in terms of errors candidates make, attacks and charges against candidates, and just about anything that will catch a viewer's eye. The degree of negativity varies across the duration of campaigns and with the source, and different media provide differing perspectives and tonal coverage.[21]

Third, media bias is a concern. Journalists tend to be liberals and Democrats, and owners and publishers tend to be Republicans and conservatives. Editorials reflect these realities. Evidence of bias in news coverage is harder to come by—unless one focuses on radio and television stations that seek to line up one way or another, or unless one digs to find the use of ideologically tinted terms such as "radical," "extreme," or "uninformed" that creep into more than a few media accounts.[22] MSNBC and Fox are the classic examples of media with a message, as are local talk radio stations. What often passes for bias is a tendency of reporters to be intrigued by front-runners, new faces, dark-horse candidates, "interesting characters," and "nice guys," not to mention surprise events and scandals. Smart candidates understand this and, with help from their media experts, know how to play to the reporters. Pack journalism—the same horde of journalists following the same candidate and reporting the same things— fuels the fire, often leading to unbalanced coverage at least during portions of campaigns. Howard Dean was the darling of the media in 2003 and 2004; John McCain was popular during the 2000 primary season; and Barack Obama attracted a great deal of positive, and Sarah Palin negative, attention in 2008. The bloom soon comes off the rose, however, and matters tend to settle into more routine coverage.

A fourth criticism derives from sensitivity to being criticized for bias. It may be that reporters, understanding their own political orientations, deliberately lean in the opposite direction at times, producing "wrong-way" unbalanced coverage. Alternatively, reporters engage in what Marjorie Randon Hershey called "two-handed journalism," referring to their tendency to get both sides of a story, especially after one candidate has fired off a charge against the other.[23] Reporting often is uncritical, based on the notion that each side must be equally guilty or equally innocent or that their positions are equally reasonable and meritorious. Reporters provide each side a chance to voice its version of the story but do little to inquire as to the actual truthfulness or completeness of the claims. Should reporters merely report what candidates say, or do they have a deeper obligation to their viewers, readers, and listeners? The recent appearance of "fact-checking" may begin to balance out harm done by blind reporting; but even that activity can be skewed, overdone, or misapplied. Given the growing reliance on ideological and partisan-oriented media, one wonders whether the "real" stories have much hope of being assimilated.

Campaign coverage can be too much, too selective, too irrelevant, and occasionally too biased. People pick and choose their sources of information, and there is a natural tendency to seek news from sources one trusts and agrees with.[24] Combine these problems of media coverage with the penchant for selective perception and selective retention, and it is not hard to see how charges of "distortion" or "favoritism" emerge or how the media can feed political polarization.

Can Campaign Media Be Fixed? Reforms
Scholars such as Larry Bartels, Lynn Vavreck, and Bruce Buchanan want serious coverage of campaigns focused on substance rather than the horse race or candidates' peculiarities. They urge reporters to add "perspective" to the campaign, wishing they would spend less time with the candidates and campaign advisors and more time reporting on broader issues. Thus they suggest that reporters traveling with the candidates rotate assignments to bring "fresh insights to routine campaign coverage, avoiding the jaded, know-it-all tone that infects too much political news."[25] Some critics think reporters should spend less time voicing their own views and give more airtime to the candidates' own statements; that, of course, runs the risk of two-handed journalism and frees journalists of their responsibilities to dig out the truth. Because most readers, viewers, and listeners are not well informed on the basics, critics propose repetition of key facts and concepts, such as which parties control which branches of government and which candidates favor more or less government activity. The bottom line is that journalists should be less concerned with impressing their professional

peers and more concerned with serving their clientele. Individuals unhappy with media coverage have dozens of Web-based sources for news.

Some have suggested that one way to limit the media's influence is to create a public forum or "public square" for straightforward, honest, unbiased information. Thomas E. Mann and Norman J. Ornstein argue on behalf of public media like the PBS *News Hour*, Charlie Rose, and Diane Rehm shows, all of which need substantial funding to do their jobs. The proposal resembles efforts to require newspapers to run side-by-side columns comparing the stances of candidates—something private groups like the League of Women Voters have done for years. To fund these neutral media outlets, Mann and Ornstein, noting that the airwaves are public property and are licensed by the government, propose charging broadcasters a rental fee.[26] The trick, of course, is to get people to take advantage of them.

7.4 COMPETITION

The Decks Are Stacked

Incumbents hold immense advantages. That is not to say that incumbency guarantees victory. Presidents lose trying for a second term: Gerald Ford in 1976 lost to challenger Jimmy Carter who, as an incumbent, lost to Ronald Reagan; and George H. W. Bush lost to Bill Clinton in 1992. Virtually every presidential decision offends and alienates some group, and offenses accumulate. The burdens of the job limit campaigning, and an improper remark or false statement, however inadvertent, will go viral. If the economy is sliding, blame falls on the president.

In their favor, incumbents have the Rose Garden and Air Force One. They command the spotlight and bask in the glory of good new. They travel across the country, ostensibly for "official" purposes but often in reality to campaign at taxpayers' expense. Presidents make decisions and allocate public resources strategically, often to their electoral benefit.[27] In a crisis, the public usually rallies around the flag in his support.

At the congressional level, incumbents seldom lose. Some, however, do; others, reading the tea leaves, retire. As Gary Jacobson has noted, the benefits of incumbency "are neither automatic, nor certain, nor constant across electoral contexts."[28] Interest groups track and "score" the voting records of senators and representatives, and at election time these become campaign fodder. Votes often have to be explained or defended; worse, when single-minded voters focus on their pet issues (guns, abortion, or whatever), incumbents willing to take tough positions can amass a coalition of opponents. Nothing is certain. That said, incumbency brings advantages that offend any principle of fairness. Senators and representatives raise money easily. Their ability to travel home just about every week, along with the attention received back home, reinforces the high recognition factor that they enjoy. Assiduous attention to constituents, the efforts of congressional staffs, relatively easy access to the media, the skills that veteran legislators build up over the years, the establishment of a comfortable "home styles,"[29] and the franking privilege all contribute to the incumbency advantage and to a sense of imbalance. As David Mayhew noted, members of Congress advertise, take credit, and take popular positions.[30] No wonder senators running for reelection win about 80 percent of the time and members of the lower chamber are successful more than 9 times of 10.[31]

Reforms

To give challengers a decent shot, commentators want to give them free or inexpensive television and radio time. Since free time does not displace paid advertising, it probably means much more TV exposure. For the media, the proposal involves costs; nothing is free, and someone will pay the piper. Proponents respond that the airways are public property, that the Communications Act of 1934 requires that broadcasters "serve the public interest," and therefore that television outlets should give up a little bit of commercial advertising to foster electoral competition. A version of free air time was tried in the 1996 presidential elections with mixed results and varied evaluations.[32] Besides cost, there are complications. Does free media time extend to third-, fourth-, and fifth-party candidates? How much free time is enough? Should challengers who cannot raise as much money as incumbents get additional free time to even the playing field? Interestingly, the United States may be the only industrialized nation that does not provide free media time during elections; and so one can anticipate continued pressure for this reform, especially in congressional elections.

7.5 LET'S BUY AN ELECTION—CAMPAIGN FINANCE

Pleas for reforming campaign finance are hardly novel. They focus on five concerns that bear on efficiency and accountability: the cost of elections, the imbalance of campaign finance resources that favors incumbents, improper influence from campaign contributors, the time and energy that go into fundraising and the negative consequences for effective and responsible governance, and independent expenditures made by interest groups.

It Costs a Lot

Table 7.1 reports overall spending on all federal elections by candidates, parties, and outside groups. The data undoubtedly understate actual spending.

Table 7.1 Total Election Spending, 1998–2012

YEAR	TOTAL COST OF ELECTION	CONGRESSIONAL RACES	PRESIDENTIAL RACES
2014	$3,769,652,999	$3,769,652,999	N/A
2012	$6,285,557,223	$3,664,141,430	$2,621,415,792
2010	$3,643,942,915	$3,438,675,910	N/A
2008	$5,285,680,883	$2,485,952,737	$2,799,728,146
2006	$2,852,658,140	$2,852,658,140	N/A
2004	$4,147,304,003	$2,237,073,141	$1,910,230,862
2002	$2,181,682,066	$2,181,682,066	N/A
2000	$3,082,340,937	$1,669,224,553	$1,413,116,384
1998	$1,618,936,265	$1,618,936,265	N/A

Source: Center for Responsive Politics, "The Money behind the Elections," http://www.opensecrets.org/bigpicture/; "Total Cost of Election 2014," http://www.opensecrets.org/overview/cost.php

The numbers are staggering, but do they constitute a problem? Election spending is less than what Americans spend on potato chips or greeting cards and less than the advertising budgets of major U.S. retailers. Spending in the 2012 federal elections was less than the cost of candy and costumes at Halloween, half of what is spent on cosmetic enhancements, and one-fifth of what Americans spend on beauty products, or roughly equal to what Google was prepared to spend to purchase Groupon in 2010.[33] Still, the sums are far from trivial. Costs rise for multiple reasons, the greatest of which is media advertising, which in the 2012 presidential races ran to $765 million—not counting independent spending by outside groups.[34] Although media spending can be efficient for presidential races, where candidate messages must be spread widely, it can be horribly wasteful when congressional candidates need to buy into major media markets that are much larger than their target constituencies. Campaign staffs, travel, polling, consultants, compliance with federal and state finance laws, technology, building and employing contact lists, and fundraising itself all have driven up costs. Fueling it all is competition. Close elections make the cash registers sing.[35] In 2012, the Massachusetts Senate race featured spending of more than $77 million; Connecticut's ran a tab of nearly $60 million, followed by $43 million in Ohio and more than $35 million in Pennsylvania. On the House side, five races burned through more than $10 million apiece.[36] In 2014, 6 Senate races spent over $33 million each, while 7 House contests exceeded $9.5 million. If one includes outside spending, at least 10 Senate races cost $50 million or more; in the House, 9 ran over $16 million.[37]

Money has a "rhetorical impact."[38] Lots of money, especially early in a race, brings attention. A scarcity of cash is a double curse, depriving candidates of the ability to get their messages out and undermining their standing in the media and with the attentive public. Raising money is a sort of "pre-primary" in which candidates must persuade donors of their viability.

Election after election, millionaires run for office on their own nickel. In 2010, for example, 33 House and (mostly) Senate candidates spent at least $1 million of their own money on their campaigns, including $50 million by Linda McMahon in a failed effort to capture the Connecticut Senate seat and nearly $24 million by Jeff Greene in Florida. In 2012, McMahon coughed up another $49 million. David Dewhurst spent nearly $20 million of his own seeking the Texas Senate seat, and Tom Smith parted with more than $16 million in a losing Pennsylvania effort. Two years later, the top self-funder was David Alameel, who dropped $5.68 million in a losing effort in Texas. House races were not exempt; no fewer than 10 candidates in 2012 spent $2 million or more of their personal funds; in 2014 7 did so.[39] So what? Jennifer A. Steen provides answers.[40] First, that kind of money affects the candidate field. But for their own fortunes, most of these candidates would not run. Self-financed candidates have a depressing effect on the number of other candidates competing in primary elections. Second, millionaires do not fare well at all. From 2002 to 2010, 68 House candidates laid out $1 million or more, but only 11 won, all but 1 in open seat races; in the Senate, 7 of 18 million-dollar spenders won, but 4 were incumbents.[41] In 2012, of the top 12 self-funders in House contest, only 4 won; in the Senate, 1 of 12 won. In 2014, 3 of the top 10 self-funded House candidates and 2 of the top 10 self-funded Senate candidates won.[42] Millionaires who do win boast that they owe nothing to anyone except the voters who elected them.

Imbalance in Funding

A second concern is the imbalance in campaign money. Incumbents routinely raise and spend much more than challengers, although it is true that the more incumbents spend, the worse they fare—because they are spending in response to heavy outlays by serious challengers. Politicians are risk averse, so they spend what they can ("I know that half of what I spend is a waste; I just don't know which half"). Precisely because incumbents are likely to win, interest groups that must deal with them after the election feel compelled to donate, lest they alienate them.[43] They do not want to be seen supporting the incumbents' opponents.

For presidential *general elections* the differences in spending are not great and present few worries; both major candidates spend ample amounts of money and receive plenty of media coverage—a condition that rarely applies to third-party candidates or independents. The 2008 election, for example, cost President Obama and his supporters more than $700 million, more than doubling John McCain's $300 million. Nonetheless, McCain ran a respectable campaign but probably would not have won had he doubled Obama's spending. For 2012, Obama spent $737 million and Romney $483 million—not including another billion provided by the parties, PACs, and other organizations that heavily favored Romney.[44] Naturally, whatever the amounts, they never are enough; the loser's supporters always gripe about being outspent. How, when, and where campaign treasure chests are emptied matters; wasting money on states that are safe for one or the other candidate, or spending too much or too little early, can hurt a candidate—as it did in 2012 when the nominating contest forced Romney to exhaust his coffers. Although spending more is unlikely to make a difference, it certainty will not curtail future funding races.

The same logic does not apply to the nomination stage, where money matters a lot, especially in the pre-primary period and in the first half dozen or so primary and caucus events. Candidates require ample funds to build political organizations and project themselves into voters' consciousness. That need has driven them to abjure the limited federal matching money in the nominating contests. Less well known candidates have problems raising money. In 2008, for example, 12 of the 20 presidential hopefuls failed to hit the $25 million mark; only 5 qualified for federal matching money.[45] For all but Clinton, Obama, Edwards, McCain, Romney, and Rudy Giuliani, the game was over after a handful of primaries and caucuses.[46]

In 2012, for the primary season, the imbalance was significant. By the end of January, five candidates raised a good deal of money: Mitt Romney ($62 million), Ron Paul ($31 million), Rick Perry ($20 million), Newt Gingrich ($18 million), and Herman Cain ($17 million). Others, who dropped out early, raised less: Michele Bachmann ($10 million), John Huntsman ($6 million), and Tim Pawlenty ($5 million). Three minor candidates, Gary Johnson, Buddy Roemer, and Thaddeus McCotter, *together* raised $1.6 million. Rick Santorum had $7 million but raised a lot more as his campaign developed.[47]

At the congressional level, the problem of inequities is more serious. Incumbents need not outspend challengers, but they almost always do. The imbalance is striking, perhaps best illustrated by the fact that in 2008, House incumbents had almost as much money left over after the election ($184 million) as challengers raised ($218 million).[48] Table 7.2 provides the data on fund raising for the past four elections.

Table 7.2 Congressional Campaign Funds

TYPE OF CANDIDATE	NUMBER OF CANDIDATES	AVERAGE AMOUNT RAISED ($)
Senate		
2008 Incumbent	36	8,741,224
2008 Challenger	104	1,152,146
2010 Incumbent	30	11,244,157
2010 Challenger	153	962,994
2012 Incumbent	25	11,847,275
2012 Challenger	129	1,380,844
2014 Incumbent	29	12,144,397
2014 Challenger	138	1,220,978
House		
2008 Incumbent	435	$1,356,510
2008 Challenger	653	335,101
2010 Incumbent	420	1,513,308
2010 Challenger	1,115	265,338
2012 Incumbent	418	1,606,154
2012 Challenger	830	267,375
2014 Incumbent	425	1,557,526
2014 Challenger	669	258,198

Source: Center for Responsive Politics, Open Secrets.org, http://www.opensecrets.org/bigpicture/incumbs.php?cycle=2008/; http://www.opensecrets.org/bigpicture/incumbs.php?cycle=2010/; http://www.opensecrets.org/overview/incumbs.php/.

Why Is Money Important?

The most pressing question—whether spending affects results—has spawned a cottage industry within political science. However, clear answers are elusive because so many intertwined factors affect elections: candidate quality and skills of the candidates, voter familiarity with and evaluation of them, voters' reactions to heavy campaign spending, candidates' party and ideology, the status of the national economy, and nationwide partisan swings.

Truly strong challengers are likely to be current or former state officeholders who are highly strategic and won't run unless they think they have a good enough chance to warrant risking their current positions.[49] Accordingly, incumbent senators and representatives strive to build up campaign treasure chests to ward off challengers. The effectiveness of so doing is far from clear.[50] To the extent that it succeeds, it undermines the accountability principle by denying voters a realistic chance to replace incumbents with serious alternative contenders.

Money buys all sorts of things that challengers have less of than do incumbents: advertising, research, polling, staff, travel, media time, and so on. The more money challengers spend or is spent on their behalf, the better are their chances. Donors and

PACs also behave strategically, supporting strong challengers they like when the situation seems ripe for victory and taking a powder when favorable conditions do not obtain. Because most incumbents are deemed unbeatable, strong challengers are scarce, as are funds to support them. Money sometimes makes a difference in vote margins and, in exceptional cases of close elections, it might help elect a challenger. Conversely, sometimes spending helps incumbents more than challengers.[51] As a general rule, however, except in cases of major incumbent scandals, economic disaster, or a terribly unpopular president (for his party's incumbents), and given a competent challenger, money is the only thing that can make for a fair contest.[52] In open seat races, with no incumbents, in both primaries and general elections, money matters.

Corruption and Donor Influence

Background. The fear of undue donor influence and corruption led to a series of campaign finance laws, beginning with the Tillman Act in 1910 and leading up to the 1971 Federal Election Campaign Act (FECA) and related Revenue Act. Those two laws limited the amount of money candidates and their families could spend on their elections, capped the amounts candidates could spend on media advertising, and mandated disclosure. FECA also provided funding for presidential elections via a check-off on annual tax returns and permitted tax deductions for small contributions to federal election campaigns. In 1974 Congress removed the limits on media spending; imposed a $1,000 cap per election cycle on individual contributions to any one campaign; limited one's total contributions to $25,000 for all campaigns; tightened reporting and disclosure requirements; and created the Federal Election Commission (FEC) to enforce the laws. In *Buckley v. Valeo*,[53] the Supreme Court declared that the limits on self-funding and the cap on independent expenditures unconstitutionally violated the guarantee of free speech and allowed presidential spending limits only in connection with acceptance of public funding.

Consequences followed. Labor, corporate, professional, and issue-oriented groups rushed to form PACs, organizations whose administrative expenses are underwritten by their sponsors but which collect donations that the PACs' leaders spend on campaigns. In 2008 PACs contributed $386 million directly to congressional candidates, almost a third of total campaign receipts. PACs also donate to parties and spend freely on an independent basis for and against candidates. In the 2010 electoral cycle, 5,486 PACs spent $1.35 billion, mostly on House races and mostly on behalf of incumbents. In 2012 they raised and spent $1.26 billion, donating about half of it to congressional candidates.[54] PACs in 2014 raised $1.7 billion and donated $467.9 million to candidates.[55]

A subsequent amendment to FECA permitted *state and local* parties to solicit unlimited "soft money" contributions for grass-roots "party building" activities and to issue "issue advocacy" ads. Such funds could not be used to advocate for or against someone's election, but there is precious little distinction between ads that say "Senator X fights for the little guy" and one that says "vote for Senator X." In 1996 the Supreme Court removed the limits on what parties could independently spend on behalf of their candidates, provided only that such spending was not coordinated with candidates.[56] Soft money spending by parties skyrocketed, from $100 million in 1992 to five times that amount 10 years later, exceeding the money spent by the candidates themselves.[57] PACs and other organizations plunged headlong into issue-advocacy ads, careful not to endorse or oppose specific candidates. The cost of elections went through the roof, accompanied by a raft of scandals and near scandals that built a fire under reformers' efforts.

Reform Efforts. During this time, campaign finance reform efforts floundered. Eventually, senators John McCain (R-AZ) and Russ Feingold (D-WI) teamed with representatives Chris Shays (R-CT) and Marty Meehan (D-MA) to win passage of the Bipartisan Campaign Reform Act of 2002 (BCRA). The law forbade national party organizations from raising and spending soft money, and it prohibited state and local parties from using their soft money for federal election activities. To compensate, BCRA roughly doubled the old FECA limits on "hard money" contributions that are overseen by the FEC, indexing them for inflation. McCain–Feingold prohibited spending soft money on "electioneering communications," defined as ads and other communications that referred to specific candidates and were broadcast within 30 days of a primary or 60 days of a general election. Such ads appear in volume just before elections, offering little opportunity for rebuttal. The law raised limits on contributions to candidates whose opponents' spending of their own money on their campaigns exceeded a threshold—the so-called "millionaires" provision designed to level the playing field. Reformers rejoiced. The law, however, did nothing to stop individuals, businesses, or other groups from contributing to single-issue 527 organizations for issue-advocacy advertising. Spending by such groups and by the political parties exploded into the hundreds of millions.

Following the 2004 election, the FEC tightened regulations on 527 groups, causing their spending to drop. Illustrating the "hydraulic" principle that campaign money flows like water to any available outlet, campaign dollars found a home in the tax-exempt 501(c) organizations described above. Together the 527 and 501(c) groups now account for a large portion of campaign spending. In 2008, for example, the Service Employees International Union spent $25 million from its 527 Committee; America's Agenda: Healthcare for Kids, a 501(c)(4) committee, spent more than $13 million a month before the election.[58] In 2012, at least 16 such organizations spent a million dollars or more on campaign advertising.[59] In the 2014 election, 1,340 Super PACs claimed to have raised $695,958,131 and made independent expenditures of $348,545,054.[60] The question was and remains: who is behind these groups, and what are they after?

Again, the judiciary entered the fray. In late 2003, the Supreme Court upheld the ban on soft money but overturned a couple of lesser provisions.[61] In *FEC v. Wisconsin Right to Life,*[62] the Court ruled that political communications can be regulated only if they are "susceptible of no reasonable interpretation other than as an appeal to vote for or against a specific candidate." A year later the Court struck down the millionaires amendment because it imposed "an unprecedented penalty on any candidate who robustly exercises that First Amendment right."[63] The floodgates opened in two other cases. In *Citizens United v. Federal Election Commission,* in 2010, the Court ruled that corporations and unions not only may engage in issue advocacy but also may spend and advertise in support of or in opposition to federal candidates.[64] The BCRA limitations were judged to violate First Amendment rights. Corporations and unions could not, however, contribute directly to campaign war chests; spending must be independent.

Shortly thereafter, the U.S Court of Appeals for the District of Columbia ruled that limiting anyone's donations to PACs that raise and spend money only for independent expenditures for or against candidates was unconstitutional.[65] This ruling established the so-called Super PACs. These are *political* committees that may raise and spend as much money as they can from any source for or against candidates, provided that they may not coordinate with the candidates' campaigns. Their donations and spending must be reported to the FEC. However, as Marian Currinder has noted, the "lines that separate candidate campaigns from the Super PACS that support them can be extremely fuzzy," with both types of organizations sharing consultants, sometimes being located in the same buildings, and often owing their founding to the same persons.[66] In July 2014, the Second Circuit Appeals Court ruled that a Vermont Super PAC that made independent expenditures was not, in reality, distinct from a related PAC that contributed to candidate campaigns.[67]

For donors who do not want their identities made public, the 501(c)(4) social welfare organizations are ideal. Some such organizations, despite their ostensible purposes, are primarily political instruments heavily involved in campaign advertising. To cite only one example, former Bush assistant Karl Rove established Crossroads Grassroots Policy Strategies GPS that collected fortunes from a handful of anonymous wealthy donors, spent a lot of money on its own, and also gave large amounts to the Super PAC American Crossroads, also a Rove organization. Only the latter must report its donations and expenditures. Pro-Obama organizations behaved similarly. By Election Day 2012, there were well over 1,000 Super PACs registered with the FEC; their spending on the presidential election was slightly more than $240 million.[68]

In early 2014, the Supreme Court put what may be the final nail in the coffin when it ruled, in *McCutcheon v. FEC*,[69] that the *overall* limit on how much an individual may donate in an election cycle violates the first amendment. Limits on donations to a specific candidate or party remain in place. Someone can "max out" her donations to every House and Senate candidate, to one's political party nationally and in each state, and to PACs with no total limit. That could mean millions of dollars in contributions, not the $123,200 that was the maximum. It is not hard to indicate to these recipients the donor's expectations that they would redirect some of their (i.e., her) money to her favorite candidates. One might also anticipate the rise of joint fundraising committees that could amass as much as $3.5 million from such schemes.

The campaign finance picture is anything but simple. Money comes from a variety of sources, flows to a number of organizations, and is spent in numerous ways, some with and others without FEC supervision. Spending ultimately is unconstrained although certain contributions are limited. The complexity and obfuscation make understanding, let alone reforming, the situation difficult.

Presidential Races. Consider 2012. Presidential candidate campaign organizations raised about half of the money spent. The Democratic Party disbursed more than $292 million and the Republican Party $386 million. PACs, Super PACs, and 501(c) groups independently spent some $653 million.[70] Candidates and PACs rely on heavy hitters. In 2008 Barack Obama raised almost half, and John McCain about 60 percent, of their general election war chests from gifts of more than $1,000. In 2012, $233 million of the Obama campaign funds came from small donors and $490 million from large donors. For Romney, it was $80 million and $366 million, respectively.

Among major donors were such notables as Sheldon Adelson (casinos), Robert Perry (real estate), Harold Simmons (business), and the Koch brothers (diversified Koch Industries). Small donors do play a role. The availability of the Internet has opened the door for more and more effective solicitations from donors of modest means. Howard Dean pioneered the Internet technique that President Obama mastered.

Congress. In congressional elections, individual contributions are prominent, accounting for about 60 percent of fundraising for Senate races and more than half for the House.[71] PACs made between 12 and 20 percent of Senate and about 30 percent of House contributions. Loans from candidates to themselves constituted the third largest source in both House and Senate races.[72] In 2012, 56 percent of the $1,136,539,473 raised by House candidates and 63 percent of $742,281,898 raised by Senate contenders came from individuals; PACs donated 31 percent of House and 11 percent of Senate candidate receipts. Candidates themselves accounted for 10 percent of House and 22 percent of Senate contributions.[73] Direct party funding of congressional campaigns amounts to small change, relatively speaking, largely because of federal limits. Parties, however, make "coordinated expenditures" to support ancillary activities of campaigns.

Like presidential candidates, congressional contenders rely heavily on large contributions to their committees, but the real problem of big money concerns independent expenditures by Super PACs and 527 and 501(c) committees. The fact that a handful of huge donations fund many of these groups bothers many observers. Adelson, Perry, and Simmons gave millions to support independent spending, most of which was targeted at tight Senate races in Wisconsin, Florida, Ohio, Massachusetts, Nevada, and Missouri. Much the same was true of House races.

So What? Some critics conclude that all this is unfair and undermines political equality: no person should have more influence on elections than another. Such equality is impossible and perhaps unwise. Pundits, TV personalities, respected politicians, and perhaps even political science professors have more sway than the average citizen. As Matthew J. Streb noted, the criterion for democratic government is "one person, one vote"—not "one person, one dollar."[74] Many commentators worry that hefty donations buy influence, undermining the participation criterion and ultimately skewing the deliberative process in Congress. In the words of Brooks Jackson's book on the subject, fundraising sometimes resembles *Honest Graft.*[75] Although political scientists have concluded that campaign contributions do not "buy" votes on the House and Senate floors, let alone determine presidential decisions on major matters, and although the bulk of campaign money is given to keep friendly members in their seats and to ingratiate donors with them, there is little doubt that money matters.[76] It is not a sense of good citizenship that leads special interests to donate to members of Congress who can influence decisions. That does not mean that such contributions achieve their purpose, although undoubtedly sometimes they do, as many former senators and representatives have claimed. (They personally, of course, were immune to such blandishments.) On issues that may not be of importance to most members, are largely invisible to voters, and are decided at low levels of subcommittee deliberations, the relationships campaign donations make possible have potential for influence. There is no doubt that money buys access.

One long-standing donor tactic is "bundling," wherein lobbyists gather checks from dozens or more individual donors and deliver them as a package "on behalf of" a given interest as a campaign contribution. There is no ambiguity as to where the money is coming from. In 2008, some 200 bundlers each gathered $70,000 or more; one "mega-bundler" in Texas put together a package of $285,000 for the Obama campaign.[77] The *McCutcheon* decision, above, will expand this practice. Since 2009, the names of bundlers must be reported to the FEC. Occasionally blatantly illegal contributions make the news, such as those made in 2005 by Jack Abramoff, who collected money from Native American groups and channeled it to campaign organizations with the expectation that it would affect the behavior and votes of senators and representatives on issues of concern to the tribes. Some commentators have expressed concern that foreign money can seep into the American election system, with consequences for U.S. foreign policy. Muckrakers have had a field day describing such activities over the years.

Fundraising, however, is a two-way street, initiated by candidates who woo and solicit donors. Sometimes fundraising efforts come close to "shaking the money tree," pressuring interest groups to cough up donations with an implicit threat of noncooperation or even retaliation. Presidents reward major donors in a variety of ways: ambassadorships, appointments to executive positions, honorary positions, invitations to State dinners, coffee with the president or key staffers, and even overnight stays in the White House (the Lincoln bedroom achieved particular notoriety during the Clinton presidency as a coveted resting place). On the Hill, members can and do thank contributors with their actions, both symbolic and substantive, such as earmarks in defense bills to steer contracts and other payouts to loyal contributors.[78]

Effects on Governance—Maybe the Biggest Problem

Incumbents spend countless hours working the phones, meeting with potential donors, and attending fundraising events in Washington and back home. Estimates run as high as one-third of members' time; indeed, Democratic leaders in January 2013 suggested to incoming freshmen that they spend as many as five hours per day on the phone, mostly seeking contributions, with only three to four hours for legislative and constituent work.[79] According to one calculation, former senator Rick Santorum (R-PA) would have needed to bring in $11,800 per day over his six-year Senate term to cover what he spent in his 2006 Senate campaign. Matters have gotten worse since then. Said the late senator Robert C. Byrd (D-WV),

> We are too busy out there engaging in the money chase. We cannot be here in the committees, we cannot be here on the floor doing our work. . . . We are kept so busy out there knocking on doors all over the country, seeking money, asking for money, begging for money, getting on hour hands and knees for money, we do not have time to give thought to new ideas and to be putting them into creative legislation.[80]

Announcing his retirement in March 2012, veteran Michigan senator Carl Levin complained about the time it takes to do fundraising. Virtually every book or magazine article written by a retiring member of Congress makes the same point. Fundraising is tedious, humiliating, embarrassing, and a diversion from governance. It is never-ending. No wonder congressional productivity declined dramatically over the years. With increasing regularity, the cost of campaigns and the nationalization of congressional races have led members to seek funding from outside their states and districts. PACs and donors across the country, moved by partisan or ideological interests, are eager to pour money into races deemed to be important.

Congressional party leaders long ago shared their surplus campaign funds with their parties and with colleagues. Because limits on PAC contributions are less restrictive, they established "leadership PACs" to do so. The practice dates back to the House reforms of the 1970s that undermined the seniority rule and made key committee leadership positions subject to the votes of colleagues. Ambitious backbenchers seeking such positions followed the example of their leaders. Today, at least 90 percent of senators and two-thirds of representatives have PACs, sending cash to their House and Senate campaign committees and directly to the campaigns of less well-off colleagues and challengers. Indeed, a veritable "dues structure" exists on the Hill; all members are expected to contribute to their parties' campaign committees. The dollars being transferred are significant. In 2012, six House leaders each passed along more than $1 million. Altogether, congressional leadership PACs contributed about $46 million to fellow party candidates and to their House and Senate party campaign committees; members' own campaign committees tossed in another $100 million.[81] Numbers were similar in 2014. The danger of these developments is that more members become indebted to their colleagues or to the interest groups that provide the money, rather than to their constituents, threatening the principles of responsiveness, representation, and reasoned deliberate judgment.

Leadership PACs have a shady side as well. Some incumbents use their PAC funds to hire family and relatives for their campaigns, paying them generously. Some have made personal loans to their campaigns to be reimbursed, at high rates of interest, by their leadership PACs. Still others tap into their PAC money to fund all sorts of trips for themselves and their families under the guise of "political travel."

Independent Spending

Probably the most controversial issue of campaign finance concerns independent spending by, especially, 527 and 501(c) groups. In 2012, total independent spending by 816 organizations, excluding the parties, exceeded $1 billion, led by American Crossroads and American Crossroads GPS at $176 million and Restore Our Future at $142 million. In 2014, outsiders spent $565 million.[82] This development threatens to overtake traditional candidate- and party-centered (and FEC-regulated) funding. In 2012, in 11 of the 25 closest House races, candidates' own campaign funds accounted for less than half of total spending.

Independent spending presents problems. One is that, if actually beyond the control of the candidates, it can skew or distort their images and messages. Second is the suspicion that the spending is not really independent of the candidates. Third is the simple matter of fairness when outside spending heavily favors one contender over the other. Another concern is that most of the spending buys media communications that are heavily negative and can explode in the last few days of a campaign, denying the target candidate a chance to respond—and thus denying voters a balanced view. The need for last-minute money to counter those independent media blasts is one reason incumbents accumulate funds. Fifth, at the congressional level, much and probably most of this spending comes from outside the candidates' states and districts, confounding the representational and accountable aspects of campaigning. Finally, insofar as the funding for many of these groups comes from a relatively small number of donors, they could have undue influence over the content of the messages and thus, possibly, on the candidates and the election results. Outside money changes the picture considerably, but the consequences thus far are unclear. In only three Senate races in 2012 did candidates benefitting from outside independent spending win; in fact, according to one analysis, "adding outside money to the mix actually lowered a Senate candidate's chances of winning."[83]

7.6 REFORMS

This tangle of election finance laws, practices, and problems screams for reform. What should be done depends on the values to be advanced. Faith in the integrity of campaigns is essential to the legitimacy of the electoral system and to keep people committed to participating. Establishing such integrity calls for eliminating aspects that smack of undue influence and unfairness; for many, it also depends on limiting overall spending. Representation and accountability suffer when voters are deprived of competitive candidates and, perhaps, when their representatives' campaigns are funded by sources outside their constituencies. Senators and representatives should be responsive to their constituents and the national good, but if special interests and wealthy donors influence election results, responsiveness could be muddled. Campaign finance rules affect the effectiveness and efficiency of parties; and if some of the critics are correct, the imperatives of campaign finance interfere with reasoned deliberative decision making in Washington. All these values—deliberative judgment, effectiveness, efficiency, responsiveness, representation, accountability—are affected by the extent to which members of Congress spend too much time raising money. Moreover, these considerations are intertwined; a solution to any one problem is not necessarily compatible with another. Consequences often are unclear.

Too Much Is Too Much: Impose Limits

Spending. Assume that somehow spending should and could be limited. Where should the maximum be set? At the presidential level, there is no obvious number. How much is enough and how much is too much? One hundred million dollars? One billion? Two? The amounts set by FECA have proved far too low, which is why the public financing system collapsed. For congressional elections, setting spending limits at low or even moderate levels constitutes, in effect, an incumbents' protection act. Such seems to be the case in state judicial elections.[84] House challengers need much more than incumbents to make a decent run. What is the magic number? If current practice is any guide—and it is only in general terms that ignore the particularities of each constituency and contest—perhaps $1.5 million is a reasonable ceiling.[85] In the Senate, the number could easily be 10 or 20 times that in a large state; but should that number be determined by state population, by the voting population, or perhaps by the actual number of voters in the last comparable election? Should the limit be affected by the costs of media coverage (think North Dakota versus New Jersey)? To produce a fair race, challengers should spend a good deal more than incumbents. Could—should—such a law ever win passage or pass constitutional muster? Any limit probably would have to be a national limit, applicable everywhere, but election campaigns are not alike everywhere. They differ in costs, competitiveness, and importance at any one time. There might be some negative consequences. If money buys advertising, and if advertising stimulates interest and turnout, then cutting spending will reduce participation. Setting limits is a blunderbuss approach. It also requires a change of heart among Supreme Court justices or a constitutional amendment.

Contributions. The flip side of the coin, limiting contributions to prevent corruption and undue "fat-cat" influence, has survived judicial scrutiny, at least in terms of how much an individual may contribute to a single candidate, party, or PAC. Reformers are scratching their heads trying to counter the *McCutcheon* decision that removed the overall cap on a person's donations. Short of a judicial reversal or a constitutional amendment, one suggestion is to enact legislation forbidding members of Congress from soliciting or encouraging donations over a certain limit, say $50,000 or $100,000. That is unlikely, and if it were to pass, it probably would not work. Taking big donors out of the picture, however it might be done, requires some substitute form of financing. At any rate, wealthy donors have a handy alternative: independent spending.

Focused Contributions

Many pundits, scholars, and former congressmen support confining campaign contributions to members' constituents, thus eliminating out-of-state or out-of-district donations.[86] The notion is attractive because it reinforces the representational linkages between members and their constituents, potentially strengthening accountability and responsiveness, and perhaps even reducing the costs of election campaigns. There are objections. One is the claim—almost certainly to be upheld by the courts—that anyone has the right, under the First Amendment, to support any candidate for public office anywhere. Another goes to the nature of representation, which is both dyadic and collective. Someone may be poorly represented by his own congressman or senator, but his policy preferences can be represented quite well by legislators elsewhere. Should he not be able to support those candidacies? Or take the case of, say, a liberal Democrat who happens to like her Republican senator who is part of a GOP majority in the Senate. Suppose she wants to help the Democrats to take control of the Senate as a way to promote her policy preferences. One option is to vote against her senator to help change the makeup of the Senate; but she likes him. Another option is to support Democratic challengers to Republican senators in other states. Doing so serves the goals of policy representation and responsiveness on a collective, party-based basis. Following the logic of this reform proposal, a citizen also should be barred from assisting in the campaign legwork for any but her own senator or representative. That will hit, among others, college students who vote in their home state but want to work for the election of a candidate in whose district the college lies.

Lobbyists and Contractors

A proposal to constrain undue influence and conflicts of interest comes from Mann and Ornstein: prohibit lobbyists, any holder of a government contract, or any company that receives more than a small amount of subsidy or tax break from making campaign donations to congressional candidates.[87] Aside from First Amendment concerns that render this notion unlikely and maybe impossible, this proposal would decimate campaign chests, forcing a fundamental overhaul in campaign finance. That of course is the purpose. Defining "small subsidy" is tricky at best.

Black Boxes

Two scholars have offered an intriguing reform.[88] Suppose that anyone could contribute, even without limit, to a candidate's campaign but the recipient could not know the donor's identity, thus removing the possibility of influencing the candidate. Contributions would flow into a "secret donation booth" for the candidate's campaign. Surely, one can argue in response, contributors will tell candidates that they contributed, but would their professions of support be credible? Anyone could say, "I supported you with ten thousand dollars," but would the candidate believe it? Donors caught lying lose all credibility and probably access to members of Congress, which should reinforce honesty and credibility. Donors could produce a canceled check or credit card statement to prove their donations, so some lengthy quarantine on release of financial records would have to be put in place; that constitutes an unprecedented government intrusion into the private financial activity of citizens, fouls up disclosure efforts and FEC oversight, and will face tough challenges in court.[89] This system might work for campaign committees, but it does nothing to inhibit independent spending and thus would not affect either the total amount of spending or the potential imbalances among candidates. One wonders what the judiciary might say.

Timing of Fundraising

Because senators and representatives devote so much time and energy to fundraising, one solution might be to constrict the period during which members could solicit or accept funding, not allowing any solicitations or donations until, say, March or April of an election year.[90] That reform would affect only candidates' own campaign funds and any leadership PACs they have established; it would not stop fundraising or spending by independent outside groups. Even if the reform were constitutionally permissible, it could easily be evaded. Members, their campaign directors, and outsiders could collect commitments well ahead of time, against which candidates could spend their own funds or secure loans, with the actual cash flowing in on the appointed day.

Independent Spending

One proposal to control independent spending is to require that independent advertising on behalf of candidates be approved by them and made subject to their veto, just as they must publicly "approve" their own TV and radio ads. The benefits are obvious: candidates could maintain control over and be responsible for their campaign ads. This reform, however, requires that the constitutional equivalence of campaign spending with free speech be overturned, and it does nothing to limit ads taken out by outside groups *against* candidates. Should such a requirement apply to messages dispersed via social media? If it could be done for campaign advertising, might it apply in the commercial realm such that a manufacturer would have the final say over independent endorsements of or advertising for its products?

A popular but radical proposal is simply to reverse the Supreme Court's decisions to reinstate the ban on corporate, union, or other group advertising for or against candidates. The fear after Citizens United was that corporations would drop tens of millions of dollars into a campaign, influencing the result and winning favors from the candidate if she or he wins. Another concern is that foreign influences could creep into elections, depending on control of the stock of corporations. Both fears are real but perhaps overblown. Many corporations and unions in need of congressional support hesitate to support challengers to incumbents whose good will they need. More importantly, corporations that have direct exposure to consumers, such as retail stores, must tread carefully, lest their political activities alienate customers. The Target Corporation in 2010 publicly supported a Minnesota gubernatorial candidate who opposed same-sex marriage; many of its customers rebelled, costing Target their business. Large corporations of this type have not been contributing much, at least not publicly, but they could.

The 501(c)(4) social welfare groups draw the attention of reformers because of their heavy engagement in electioneering. Enforcement has been lax and can be messy, as was shown when, in May 2013, the Cincinnati office of the Internal Revenue Service, whose job is to review the tax exemption applications of such organizations, was accused of unfair scrutiny of and delay in processing the applications of conservative groups. Even-handedness may not even be possible, given the huge workload and need to find shortcuts to determine on which groups to focus, but such discretion is open to abuse. The Obama administration in early 2014 proposed legislation to alter the legal status of 401(c) entities.

Disclosure

Many who have given up on substantive reforms seek to ensure that the public knows who is contributing to candidates and who is spending independently. Currently, the FEC collects and reports on donations above $200 to parties, candidates, PACs, Super PACs, and 527 organizations. A number of bills introduced in Congress aim at extending transparency to all committees and organizations. One such bill passed the House in 2010 but died in the Senate. In July 2012, a filibuster prevented the Senate's taking up another version, New York senator Charles Schumer's DISCLOSE ("Democracy Is Strengthened by Casting Light on Spending in Elections) Act. It would require outside groups to report publicly their top donors, force corporate CEOs to appear in ads funded by their corporate treasuries, and prohibit ads by companies that had received federal funding under the Troubled Assets Relief Program or are more than 20 percent foreign funded. GOP objections focused on singling out corporations while giving unions a pass and on constitutionality. After the *McCutcheon* decision, Senator Angus King (I-ME) and representative Beto O'Rourke (D-TX) introduced the Real Time Transparency Act of 2014, calling for 48-hour reporting to the FEC of contributions, including cumulative gifts of $1,000 in any year from individuals or joint fundraising committees.

Disclosure requires record keeping, reporting, and then FEC analysis and publication; these can be expensive and time-consuming, which only adds to the cost of election. Maybe more worrisome, in addition to invading one's privacy, mandatory disclosure could subject some contributors to forms of punishment or retaliation from bosses or colleagues. Although the Supreme Court has upheld disclosure requirements in election law, it has recognized that disclosure of unpopular activities could be dangerous and thus could be blocked. One case concerned donations to the

National Association for the Advancement of Colored People in the 1950s, then a potentially dangerous activity for southerners.[91] Exemptions from disclosure requirements have also been upheld for members of the Socialist Workers Party and the American Communist Party.[92]

Critics argue that disclosure is unlikely to bring about the anticorruption benefits its proponents seek. All the scandals, corruption, and other nasty effects that have occurred in the past 40 years came during a time of mandatory disclosure of spending and contributions—except for 501(c)(4) groups. Nor is there evidence that transparency has improved public trust in government or reduced the reality or perceptions of corruptive practices. Moreover, unless disclosed data are handled well by the media—and there are doubts about that—there is little likelihood that the average voter will search out the information, let alone be swayed by it. Finally, it is possible, perhaps likely, that disclosure could inhibit contributory participation in elections.[93]

Enforcement

More than a few reformers, understanding that little can be done to change the rules, simply want the existing rules rigorously enforced. The FEC has not functioned as hoped, allowing donors to slip through contribution limits and reporting requirements. Some critics see it as an example of regulatory capture wherein those it is supposed to watch over have become its masters or at least have benefited from the FEC's benevolent protection. Others see the FEC as intrusive and harmful to individuals' rights. Its six members, by law evenly divided between Democrats and Republicans, usually cannot get four votes even to enforce is own rules whenever doing so would more negatively affect one party than the other. According to Public Citizen, blockage by split votes rose from about 1 percent in 2007 to more than 18 percent in 2012.[94] The FEC's weakness and laxity tempt some groups to ignore reporting requirements and others to defy outright its regulations.

In the FEC's defense, enforcement can be difficult. For example, one problem is that 527 and 501(c) groups and Super PACs can pop up, raise and spend money, and disappear long before the FEC staff gets around to studying them. By then the election is over and the organization may have gone out of business, making it difficult to impose fines and impossible to affect its future operations.

In an ideal world, politicians would agree that a strong and neutral election overseer is in everyone's interest; but this is not an ideal world. Given the partisan conflict in Washington and the benefits candidates and groups receive from weak regulations and enforcement, and given fears that the "other" party might be advantaged, there is little pressure to give the FEC real teeth; often it is hard enough to confirm presidential appointments to the FEC. A few critics have suggested outright abolition. An alternate proposal that makes sense but stands little chance of approval is to attack the gridlock by changing the membership of the commission to an odd number, say five or seven members, with all but one divided between the two parties, as now; those commissioners then recommend one or two to the president for his nomination to the Senate. Forcing the Senate to confirm the nominee will require a touch of the magic wand. A second tactic might be legislation requiring the FEC to reissue its rules as a package from time to time, including new rules, and requiring an up or down vote on the package—as is done currently for the closing of military bases. The hope is that such an arrangement will avoid partisan opposition to specific rules. The dangerous default, of course, is that Congress might simply ignore the package, in effect killing the FEC.

Public Funding of Elections

For many reformers, public funding remains the Holy Grail. They note that the Supreme Court probably would not oppose it if its ruling on state-level funding schemes is any indication.[95] *If* the Treasury could be tapped, *if* funding levels approached what candidates themselves raise, and *if* the independent expenditure genie could be put back in the bottle, public funding might work. Direct provision of funds to candidates' campaign committees seems simple and fair, would level the playing field, would constrain the costs of elections, and would avoid the potentially undue influence of donors. The perennial objection to public funding asks why anyone should provide tax money to fund the campaign of those he or she opposes.

Applying public funding to congressional elections leads to nightmarish complexity and cost. Should all districts be treated the same way? Public funding probably will bring out many more candidates, all of whom would, if they were viable and the law were fair, be entitled to some funding. On the House side alone, this means at least 870 candidates every two years at, perhaps, $1.5 million—a total of $1.3 billion. Add in perhaps another 300 or so third-party or independent candidates for another half billion dollars for the general election. Extending public financing to the primaries probably doubles the total. Funding for Senate races adds hundreds of millions. How should primary and third-party candidates be chosen for public funding, and what formula determines how much they will receive? Following the third-party model used for the presidential system, they might have to raise and spend their own money and then be reimbursed.

Most variants of public funding seek to leverage public money to encourage small donations from the public. Providing tax deductions—or, better yet, credits—for small contributions might incentivize more citizens to participate, reconnect them to their representatives, and possibly reduce dependence on wealthy donors and PACs. Deductions were allowed under FECA but were ended by tax reform in 1986. Federal matching funds is another favorite proposal. The "Fair Elections Now Act" introduced in three recent Congresses would match or overmatch contributions of $100, provided that candidates agreeing to this provision could not accept large donations.

Bruce Ackerman, Ian Ayres, and Lawrence Lessig have proposed a different approach calling for government to provide each registered voter with a $50 or $100 voucher—"patriot dollars" or "Grant and Franklin" vouchers—to support his or her favorite candidates or parties. Recipients would forego larger contributions. Ideally this system would empower voters, habituate them to contributing to elections, and render large contributions less important.[96] Leaving aside the issue of where the money is to come from, this system is unlikely to solve most of the problems of campaign finance unless it became the sole source for campaign donations. Although tapping small donors has become an art form, it is not likely to generate enough money to satisfy most candidates; moreover, limiting big contributions hurts challengers more than incumbents.

Any plan to strengthen competition must fund challengers more generously than incumbents. That, of course, violates any equality principle, cries out for a complex formula that weighs incumbent vulnerability, and has run into trouble in the courts.

It defies logic to think that incumbents will ever vote for such legislation. More importantly, no matter how and where lines were drawn, someone in some locality and situation surely would be disadvantaged.

Do These Systems Work?

Public funding, common in other countries, has been tried in 25 American states in several forms. Fourteen states provide funds directly to candidates, subject to overall spending limits and to a limit or ban on private money. Ten states make grants, typically funded by a $5 income tax check-off or add-on, to qualified political parties, usually to fund party conventions—not for spending for or against candidates. In 8 states, the full amount goes to whatever party the taxpayer designates; if none is designated, those funds are evenly split among qualifying parties. Seven states incentivize taxpayers to contribute to candidate campaigns, parties, or even PACs by means of tax deductions or credits of between $25 and $100. In some cases, the condition for tax deductions is that the money goes to candidates who agree to spending limits.[97]

Because these funding systems differ and provide varying levels of funding, because few studies have been able to encompass long periods of public financing, and because elections and campaigns are confounded by other factors such as state term limits, scholars have not been able to provide a definitive assessment of their success. Some studies of Arizona and Maine suggest that public funding attracts more candidates into the primaries, inclines candidates to spend more time interacting with voters, reduces incumbents' advantages, and may enhance competitiveness. Other studies, even of the same states, disagree, noting that incumbents continue to win by large margins and that the numbers of minority and women candidates did not increase dramatically, at least in the early stages of public financing.[98] Full funding of state legislative elections clearly works much better than does partial funding.[99] One recent book looking at multiple states concluded that their finance reforms have neither stopped the growth of campaign spending nor altered citizen attitudes about the political system.[100] Questions about the consequences of public financing in the states are far from settled; and even if they were, there remains a huge difference between state-level election contests and those for seats on Capitol Hill in Washington.

Funding the Parties

Suppose public financing were available not to candidates but instead to the major political parties and at a modest level to minor ones that had demonstrated electoral viability. Alternatively, if public funding is not in the cards, why not at least remove current limits on parties' fundraising and spending? That puts them on a comparable basis with the 527 and 501(c) groups. The parties would behave strategically, thinking in terms of national results and collective representation, investing heavily in close and/or particularly important races, while ignoring safe or hopeless ones. Presumably less money would be wasted, and competitiveness would be enhanced. If combined with curbs on spending by independent groups and maybe even wealthy candidates— both requiring a change of mind by the Supreme Court—making parties the hub of campaign financing could have all sorts of positive consequences, not the least of which might be providing a shield for members of Congress from the pressures exerted by special interest contributions.

For those favoring stronger responsible parties, campaign money is an effective means to that end. Controlling campaign funds might help leaders recruit and promote better candidates and enforce some level of party orthodoxy on them. If party money were the only money, party leaders could prevent wayward or offbeat candidates from competing under the party label. The paradox of campaign finance laws since 1971 is that they have curtailed party funding relative to that of candidates and independent groups. That is not to say that parties have become irrelevant; they continue to raise and spend considerable amounts and play a significant role. However, giving them additional resources to carry out those functions described in chapter 5 advances a number of key values without cost.

End Campaign Finance Restrictions

A radical solution is the simplest: just remove all restrictions on spending and contributions while insisting on absolute and timely disclosure. Doing so would enhance competition by allowing wealthy donors to fund challengers who otherwise might not compete. Allowing unlimited large contributions might reduce pressure on incumbents who should be governing rather than wasting time soliciting small and modest chunks of money.[101] The proposal does not affect independent groups, but the hope is that candidate committees would draw money away from them.

Twenty-five years ago this author and a colleague proposed something of this sort.[102] The suggestion was for *enough* public funding to provide a "grubstake" for general election candidates of the major parties and other candidates whose poll numbers were high or whose parties had proven viability in the last election. Perhaps $400,000 is a reasonable amount to allow a candidate the opportunity to get out his or her message broadly and frequently enough to inform potential supporters and attract their contributions. Except for requiring full and immediate disclosure of all contributions and expenditures over, say, $500, all other restrictions on spending and contributions would be dropped. A somewhat more radical version, as hinted above, is to give this money to the parties rather than the candidates. Funding for this—or any other public grant or tax credit—could come from general revenues. Better yet, why not fund it with a tax imposed on all campaign contributions or independent election spending that exceed $5,000? That either raises a lot of money or discourages hefty spending by individuals and groups. Perhaps a tax on unused money left over in campaign accounts might work as well.[103] Forcing major donors who give to 527 and 501(c) committees to share their wealth with candidates and parties might encourage them to change their focus, thus reducing their influence. One can anticipate legal and constitutional roadblocks to these schemes, but they are worth consideration.

7.7 CONCLUSION AND PROSPECTS

Fixing campaign finance problems could bring about the competition needed to ensure accountability and to enhance representation and responsiveness. Removing some of the fundraising pressure might free up senators and representatives to spend more time on their legislative work, making government more effective. It appears to be a win–win–win proposition.

Every proposal confronts objections and contains hidden consequences for all seven of the values this book espouses. There is no magic bullet. It is as certain as the sun's rising and setting that, whatever the reform, donors will work to find ways around the rules. Fundamental values are in conflict: equality and equity versus freedom and liberty. Protecting donors' privacy is inconsistent with accountability. Reforms are laden with unproven assumptions, such as the notion that money from individuals is more pure than money from PACs, or the notion that small contributions from citizens are healthier for the system than those from rich individuals or groups. In sum, it is hard to identify a satisfactory solution. The toothpaste has escaped the tube, and it is hard to imagine practical reinsertion strategies.

Reforms to constrain spending require a Supreme Court reversal of its decisions equating campaign spending with free speech and giving personal citizenship rights to corporations. Alternatively, a constitutional amendment is needed—an extremely unlikely prospect. In September 2014, the Senate began debate on an amendment to overturn Citizens United and give Congress other powers, but it was blocked as debate began. Assuming that a future Court would change its mind on spending, the ball would be in Congress' court to act, but any action would be perceived as hurting incumbents and their parties. The track record does not breed optimism.

What might trigger reform? Not public opinion. A Pew Research Center poll in 2012 found little public concern on the topic and not much knowledge or awareness.[104] To a question about the "main effect of increased outside spending" on the election, 24 percent reported negative views, 27 percent were neutral, and 49 percent had no opinion.[105]

Results on specific issues are a bit more informative but hardly represent a surging demand for reform. A 2012 CBS–*New York Times* Poll asked, "Which one of the following two positions on campaign financing do you favor more: limiting the amount of money individuals can contribute to political campaigns or allowing individuals to contribute as much money to political campaigns as they'd like?" By a two-to-one ratio, respondents preferred limits. A slightly higher ratio preferred limits on "groups not affiliated with a candidate."[106] In June 2013, Gallup reported that 50 percent of respondents would, if they had a chance, vote for a law that provided full campaign funding by the federal government and banned all private donations. Nearly as many, 44 percent, would vote against such a law. Seventy-nine percent would support a law limiting how much House and Senate candidates could raise and spend; only 19 percent would oppose it.[107]

It has long been believed that only massive scandals or evident corruption could trigger a public reaction that demands reform, such as FECA and Arizona's pathsetting system. BCRA followed a decade of misbehavior. Raymond J. La Raja's historical account of campaign reform challenges this notion. Usually, the goals were less noble: "In summary, campaign finance reform is about gaining partisan electoral advantages. It is most likely to succeed when one party faces heightened uncertainty about gathering sufficient resources to win presidential elections. Trying to alter rules that impact congressional incumbency—which indirectly helps the minority party—is for more difficult and unlikely to happen." He insists that another "condition for successful reform is that it must clearly enhance the influence of an important faction in one party that feels threatened by the status quo." That faction teams up with a faction in the other party fascinated by the progressive "clean government" model.[108] John Samples agrees in starker terms: "those who write campaign finance laws seek primarily to repress and harass those who would challenge their power." Reform movements represent the self-interest of many coupled with good intentions of the few.[109]

Successful campaign finance reforms, like other legislative achievements, emerge from the product of multiple forces whose individual contributions cannot be measured. According to Paul Herrnson, BCRA was enacted because of public pressure, outside interest group mobilization, political scandal, awareness of the growth in soft money spending, the bipartisan efforts led by McCain, Feingold, Shays, and Meehan, and some unorthodox legislative tactics. He concludes that changing the election finance system "requires winning the approval of individuals who have succeeded under the current campaign finance system, who view politics in light of their personal experiences, and who consider themselves experts on campaigns and elections."[110] The key to reform thus lies in the self-interest of members of Congress. Real reform is likely to occur only when the burdens of raising money and the bad consequences of independent spending become too much to bear for the members themselves. The next step is finding common ground—not easy in this day of bitter partisanship. It may be that, given the Supreme Court's rulings and the difficulty in getting Congress to address fundamental reform, trying to regulate campaign contributions and spending is a fool's errand.

QUESTIONS TO CONSIDER

1. Is negative advertising bad?
2. Should debates between candidates be changed? How and why?
3. Is media coverage unfair? How would one study that proposition?
4. Is campaign spending a problem? If so, among the many reform choices, which best meets your criteria for good government?

NOTES

1. Michael M. Franz, Paul B. Freedman, Kenneth M. Goldstein, and Travis N. Ridout, *Campaign Advertising and American Democracy* (Philadelphia: Temple University Press, 2008); Alan S. Gerber, James G. Gimpel, Donald P. Green, and Daron R. Shaw, "How Large and Long-Lasting Are the Persuasive Effects of Televised Campaign Ads? Results from a Randomized Field Experiment," *American Political Science Review* 105 (2011): 135–50.
2. Federal Communications Commissions, "Broadcast Station Totals as of December 31, 2013," https://apps.fcc.gov/edocs_public/attachmatch/DOC-325039A1.pdf..
3. Diana Owen, "The Campaign and the Media," in Janet M. Box-Steffensmeier and Steven E. Schier, eds., *The American Elections of 2012* (New York and London: Routledge, 2013): 21–47; Marjorie Randon Hershey, "The Media: Different Audiences Different Campaigns," in Michael Nelson, ed., *The Elections of 2012* (Los Angeles, London, New Delhi, Singapore, and Washington, D.C.: CQ Press, 2014): 97–118.
4. Eitan D. Hersh and Brian F. Schaffner, "Targeted Campaign Appeals and the Value of Ambiguity," *Journal of Politics* 75 (2013): 520–34.

5. *A Report on the 2008 Presidential Nomination Ads: Ads More Negative Than Previous Years*, http://www.brookings.edu/research/papers/2008/07/0630-campaignads-west/. However, negative *newspaper* ads in the *New York* Times declined from 1996 to 2008. Emmett H. Buell Jr. and Lee Sigelman, *Attack Politics: Negativity in Presidential Campaigns since 1960*, 2nd ed. (Lawrence: University Press of Kansas, 2009).

6. John G. Geer, *In Defense of Negativity: Attack Ads in Presidential Campaigns* (Chicago and London: University of Chicago Press, 2006); Kyle Matters and David P. Redlawsk, *The Positive Case for Negative Campaigning* (Chicago: University of Chicago Press, 2014).

7. John Sides, Keena Lipsitz, and Matthew Grossmann, "Do Voters Perceive Negative Campaigns as Informative Campaigns?," *American Politics Research* 38 (2010): 502–30; Franz, Freedman, Goldstein, and Ridout, *Campaign Advertising*: 134; Keena Lipsitz, *Competitive Elections and the American Voter* (Philadelphia: University of Pennsylvania Press, 2011); Daniel Stevens, "Separate and Unequal Effects: Information, Political Sophistication and Negative Advertising in American Elections," *Political Research Quarterly* 58 (2005): 413–25.

8. Kim L. Fridkin and Patrick J. Kenney, "Variability in Citizens' Reactions to Different Types of Negative Campaigns," *American Journal of Political Science* 55 (2011): 307–25.

9. Deborah Jordan Brooks and Michael Murov, "Assessing Accountability in a Post-Citizens United Era: The Effects of Attack Ad Sponsorship by Unknown Independent Groups," *American Politics Research* 40 (2012): 383–418; Conor M. Dowling and Amber Wichowsky, "Attacks without Consequence? Candidates, Parties, Groups, and the Changing Face of Negative Advertising." *American Journal of Political Science* 59 (2015): 19–36.

10. Richard R. Lau and Gerald M. Pomper, *Negative Campaigning: An Analysis of U.S. Senate Elections* (Lanham, MD: Rowman & Littlefield, 2004); Kim L. Fridkin and Patrick J. Kenney, "The Dimensions of Negative Messages," *American Politics Research* 36 (2008): 694–723; Richard R. Lau, Lee Sigelman, and Ivy Brown Rovner, "The Effects of Negative Political Campaigns: A Meta-Analytic Reassessment," *Journal of Politics* 69 (2007): 1176–1209; Bryce Corrigan and Ted Brader, "Campaign Advertising: Reassessing the Impact of Campaign Ads on Political Behavior," in Stephen K. Medvic, *New Directions in Campaigns and Elections* (New York and London: Routledge, 2011), chap. 5; Daniel Stevens, John Sullivan, Barbara Allen, and Dean Alger, "What's Good for the Goose Is Bad for the Gander: Negative Political Advertising, Partisanship, and Turnout," *Journal of Politics* 70 (2008): 527–41.

11. Kathleen Hall Jamieson and Paul A. Waldman, "Watching the Adwatches," in Larry M. Bartels and Lynn Vavreck, *Campaign Reform: Insights and Evidence* (Ann Arbor: University of Michigan Press, 2000), chap. 4; Kim Fridkin, Patrick J. Kenney, and Amanda Wintersieck, "Liar, Liar, Pants on Fire: How Fact-Checking Influences Citizens' Reactions to Negative Advertising," *Political Communication* 32 (2015): 127–51.

12. L. Sandy Maisel, Darrell West, and Brett Clifton, *Evaluating Campaign Quality: Can the Electoral Process Be Improved?* (New York: Cambridge University Press, 2007).

13. Nelson W. Polsby, Aaron Wildavsky, Steven E. Schier, and David A. Hopkins, *Presidential Elections: Strategies and Structures of American Politics*, 13th ed. (Lanham, MD, Boulder, CO, New York, Toronto, and Plymouth, UK: Rowman & Littlefield, 2012): 184–90; Robert S. Erikson and Christopher Wlezien, *The Timeline of Presidential Elections: How Campaigns Do (and Do Not) Matter* (Chicago and London: University of Chicago Press, 2012), chap. 4.

14. John Sides and Lynn Vavreck, *The Gamble: Choice and Chance in the 2012 Presidential Election* (Princeton, NJ, and Oxford: Princeton University Press, 2013), chap. 6.

15. George Farah, *No Debate: How the Republican and Democratic Parties Secretly Control the Presidential Debates* (New York, London, Toronto, and Melbourne: Seven Stories, 2004).

16. Bush quoted in Newton N. Minow and Craig L. La May, *Inside the Presidential Debates: Their Improbably Past and Promising Future* (Chicago and London: University of Chicago Press, 2008): 67.

17. *Ibid.*, 104–05. William L. Benoit, *Political Election Debates: Informing Voters about Policy and Character* (Blue Ridge Summit, PA: Lexington Books, 2013).

18. Larry M. Bartels, "Campaign Quality: Standards for Evaluation, Benchmarks for Reform," in Bartels and Vavreck, *Campaign Reform*, 1–61; Benoit, *Political Election Debates*, chap. 3.

19. Quoted in Alan Schroeder, *Presidential Debates: Fifty Years of High-Risk TV*, 2nd ed. (New York: Columbia University Press, 2008): 305.

20. L. Sandy Maisel and Mark D. Brewer, *Parties and Elections in America: The Electoral Process* (Lanham, MD, Boulder, CO, New York, Toronto, and Plymouth, UK: Rowman & Littlefield, 2012): 316–22.

21. Owen, "The Campaign and the Media" (2013); Hershey, "The Media: Different Audiences Different Campaigns"; and Hershey, "The Media: Coloring the News," in Michael Nelson, ed., *The Elections of 2008* (Washington, D.C.: CQ Press, 2010): 122–44.

22. Dan Weaver, *The American Journalist of the 21st Century: U.S. News People at the Dawn of a New Millennium* (Mahwah, NJ: Erlbaum, 2007); Dave D'Alessio and Mike Allen, "Media Bias in Presidential Elections: A Meta-Analysis," *Journal of Communication* 50 (2000): 133–56.

23. "The Media: Coloring the News."

24. Natalie J. Stroud, *Niche News: The Politics of News Choice* (New York: Oxford University Press, 2011).

25. Bruce Buchannan, "Campaign Reform: Insights and Evidence," in Bartels and Vavreck, *Campaign Reform*: 217.

26. *It's Even Worse Than It Looks*, 182.

27. Douglas L. Kriner and Andrew Reevers, "The Influence of Federal Spending on Presidential Elections," *American Political Science Review* 106 (2012): 348–66.

28. Gary C. Jacobson, *The Politics of Congressional Elections*, 8th ed. (Boston: Pearson, 2013): 29.

29. Richard F. Fenno Jr., *Home Style: House Members in Their Districts* (Boston: Little, Brown, 1978).

30. David R. Mayhew, *Congress: The Electoral Connection* (New Haven, CT, and London: Yale University Press, 1974).

31. Jacobson, *Politics of Congressional Elections*, chap. 3, and Paul S. Herrnson, *Congressional Elections: Campaigning at Home and in Washington*, 6th ed. (Los Angeles, London, New Delhi, Singapore, and Washington, D.C.: CQ Press, 2012).

32. Bartels et al., *Campaign Reform: Insights and Evidence*: 223–24; Herrnson, *Congressional Elections*: 308–09.

33. David Gura, "So What Can $6 Billion Buy You?," American Public Media Market Place, http://www.marketplace.org/topics/elections/campaign-trail/so-what-can-6-billion-buy-you?/; AnnaMaria Andriotis, "10 Things the Beauty Industry Won't Tell You," http://www.marketwatch.com/story/10-things-the-beauty-industry-wont-tell-you-1303249279432/.

34. Center for Responsive Politics, "Expenditures," http://www.opensecrets.org/pres12/expenditures.php/.

35. Henry A. Kim and Brad L. Leveck, "Money, Reputation, and Incumbency in U.S. House Elections, or Why Marginals Have Become More Expensive," *American Political Science Review* 107 (2013): 492–504.

36. http://www.opensecrets.org/overview/topraces.php?cycle=2012&display=currcands/.

37. http://www.opensecrets.org/overview/topraces.php.

38. Larry Powell and Joe Coweart, *Political Campaign Communication: Inside and Out* (Boston: Allyn & Bacon, 2003): 217; and Melissa M. Smith, "The Future of Campaign Finance Laws," in Melissa M. Smith, Glenda C. Williams, Larry Powell, and Gary A. Copeland, *Campaign Finance Reform: The Political Shell Game* (Lanham, MD, Boulder, CO, New York, Toronto, and Plymouth, UK: Lexington, 2010): 124.

39. http://www.fec.gov/press/bkgnd/cf_summary_info/2010can_fullsum/14sendisb10.pdf/; http://www.opensecrets.org/overview/topself.php

40. *Self-Financed Candidates in Congressional Elections* (Ann Arbor: University of Michigan Press, 2006).

41. Jacobson, *Politics of Congressional Elections*: 89.

42. http://www.opensecrets.org/overview/topself.php.

43. Alexander Fouirnaies and Andrew B. Hall, "The Financial Incumbency Advantage: Causes and Consequences," *Journal of Politics* 76 (2014): 711–24.

44. Federal Election Commission, "Presidential Campaign Disbursements through December 31, 2012," http://www.fec.gov/press/summaries/2012/tables/presidential/Pres2_2012_24m.pdf/.

45. Federal Election Commission, "Presidential Receipts through June 30, 2008," http://www.fec.gov/press/summaries/2008/tables/presidential/Pres1_2008_18m.pdf/.

46. Robert G. Boatright, "Campaign Finance in the 2012 Election," in Box-Steffensmeier and Schier, *American Elections of 2012*: 138.

47. Federal Election Commission: "Presidential Pre-Nomination Campaign Receipts through January 31, 2012," http://www.fec.gov/portal/presidential.shtml/.

48. Mark J. Hetherington and Bruce A. Larson, *Parties, Politics, and Public Policy in America*, 11th ed. (Washington, D.C.: CQ Press, 2010): 122.

49. Gary C. Jacobson and Samuel Kernell, *Strategy and Choice in Congressional Elections* (New Haven, CT: Yale University Press, 1981).

50. Janet Box-Steffensmeier, "A Dynamic Analysis of the Role of War Chests in Campaign Strategy," *American Journal of Political Science* 40 (1996): 352–71; Jay Goodliffe, "War Chests as Precautionary Savings," *Political Behavior* 26 (2004): 289–315.

51. Thomas Strattman, "Money in Politics. A (Partial) Review of the Literature," *Public Choice* 124 (2005): 135–56.

52. Jacobson, *Politics of Congressional Elections*, chaps. 3 and 5; and Paul S. Herrnson, *Congressional Election*, chap. 9.

53. 424 U.S. 1.

54. Federal Election Commission, "Political Action Committee Summary by Type," http://www.fec.gov/disclosure/pacSummary.do/; Center for Responsive Politics, "Business–Labor–Ideology Split in PAC & Individual Donations to Candidates, Parties Super PACs and Outside Spending Groups," http://www.opensecrets.org/overview/blio.php/.

55. https://www.opensecrets.org/pacs/

56. *Colorado Republican Committee v. FEC*, 518 U.S. 604.

57. David Magleby and J. Quin Sonson, eds., *The Last Hurrah? Soft Money and Issue Advocacy in the 2002 Elections* (Washington, D.C.: Brookings, 2004); Magleby, "Campaign Finance: Adapting to a Changing Regulatory Environment," in Medvic, *New Directions*, chap. 2; and Raymond J. La Raja, *Small Change: Money, Political Parties, and Campaign Finance Reform* (Ann Arbor: University of Michigan Press, 2008).

58. Hetherington and Larson, *Parties, Politics, and Public Policy*: 110.

59. Nicholas Confessore, "I.R.S. Ignored Complaints on Political Spending by Big Tax-Exempt Groups," *New York Times*, May 14, 2013: A14.

60. https://www.opensecrets.org/pacs/superpacs.php?cycle=2014.
61. *McConnell v. FEC*, 540 U.S. 93 (2003).
62. 551 U.S. 449 (2007).
63. *Davis v. FEC*, 554 U.S. 12 (2008). In 2011 the Court invalidated an Arizona law that provided additional public funding to candidates if they were competing against candidates who raised their funds privately and were able to attract substantial amounts of money. *Arizona Free Enterprise Club v. Bennett*, 564 U.S. __ (2011).
64. 130 S. Ct 876. In 2012 it reversed a Montana Supreme Court decision allowing restrictions on corporations. *American Tradition Partnership, Inc., FKA, Western Tradition Partnership, Inc., et al. v. Steve Bullock, Attorney General of Montana, et al.*, 565 U.S. ___ (2012).
65. *SpeechNow.org v. Federal Election Commission* 599 F.3d 686 (D.C. Cir. 2010).
66. Marian Currinder, "Campaign Finance: Campaigning in a Post-Citizens United Era," in Nelson, *Elections of 2012*: 121.
67. *Vermont Right to Life Committee, Inc. v. Sorrell*, 12-2904-cv (2d Cir. 2014).
68. http://www.opensecrets.org/pres12/superpacs.php/.
69. http://www.supremecourt.gov/opinions/13pdf/12-536_e1pf.pdf/.
70. http://www.opensecrets.org/pres12/indexp.php/.
71. http://www.opensecrets.org/bigpicture/wherefrom.php?cycle=2010/.
72. http://www.fec.gov/press/bkgnd/cf_summary_info/2010can_fullsum/2allhistory2010 .pdf/
73. Federal Election Commission, "24-Month Financial Activity of House Candidates (January 1, 2011–December 31, 2012), http://www.fec.gov/press/summaries/2012/tables/congressional/ConCand3_2012_24m.pdf/; and "24-Month Financial Activity of Senate Candidates (January 1, 2011—December 31, 2012)," http://www.fec.gov/press/summaries/2012/tables/congressional/ConCand2_2012_24m.pdf/.
74. *Rethinking American Electoral Democracy*, 2nd ed. (New York and London: Routledge, 2011): 178.
75. *Honest Graft: Big Money and the American Political Process*, rev. ed. (Washington, D.C.: Farragut, 1990).
76. Strattman, "Money in Politics," provides a balanced overview of key studies.
77. Melissa Smith, "Future of Campaign Finance": 129.
78. Michael S. Rocca and Stacy B. Gordon, "Earmarks as a Means *and* an End: The Link between Earmarks and Campaign Contributions in the U.S. House of Representatives," *Journal of Politics* 75 (2013): 241–53.
79. Ryan Grim and Sabrina Siddiqui, "Call Time For Congress Shows How Fundraising Dominates Bleak Work Life," *Huffington Post*, January 8, 2013.
80. Quoted in Hetherington and Larson, *Parties, Politics and Public Policy*, 127.
81. Center for Responsive Politics, "Spreading the Wealth," http://www.opensecrets.org/bigpicture/wealth.php?cycle=2012/; "Candidate to Candidate Giving," http://www.opensecrets.org/bigpicture/cand2cand.php?cycle=2012/. See Currinder, *Money in the House: Campaign Funds and Congressional Party Politics* (Boulder, CO: Westview Press, 2009).
82. http://www.opensecrets.org/outsidespending/fes_summ.php?cycle=2012/; http://www.opensecrets.org/outsidespending/fes_summ.php?cycle=2014.
83. Boatright, "Campaign Finance in the 2012 Election": 160; Currinder, "Campaign Finance": 135–40.
84. Chris W. Bonneau and Damon M. Cann, "Campaign Spending, Diminishing Marginal Returns, and Campaign Finance Restrictions in Judicial Elections," *Journal of Politics* 73 (2011): 1267–80.

85. That is roughly twice the amount ($800,000) Jacobson estimates is needed to make a House race competitive as of 2010. *Politics of Congressional Elections*: 54.

86. Mickey Edwards, *The Parties versus the People: How to Turn Republicans and Democrats into Americans* (New Haven, CT, and London: Yale University Press, 2013): 80; David Adamany, "The Unaccountability of Political Money," in John R. Johannes and Margaret Latus Nugent, *Money, Elections, and Democracy: Reforming Congressional Campaign Finance* (Boulder, CO, San Francisco, and London: Westview, 1990): 94.

87. *It's Even Worse Than It Looks*: 160.

88. Bruce Ackerman and Ian Ayres, *Voting with Dollars: A New Paradigm for Campaign Finance* (New Haven, CT: Yale University Press, 2002).

89. Kenneth Mayer, "Answering Ayres," *Regulation* (Winter 2001): 24–29.

90. L. Sandy Maisel, "The Incumbency Advantage," in Johannes and Nugent, *Money, Elections, and Democracy*: 134.

91. *NAACP v. Alabama*, 357 U.S. 449 (1958).

92. *Brown v. Socialist Workers '74 Campaign Committee (Ohio)*, 459 U.S. 87 (1982) and *Federal Election Commission v. Hall-Tyner Election Campaign Committee*, 459 U.S. 1145 (1983).

93. John Samples, *The Fallacy of Campaign Finance Reform* (Chicago and London: University of Chicago Press, 2006): 273–86; Raymond J. La Raja, "Political Participation and Civic Courage: The Negative Effect of Transparency on Making Small Campaign Contributions," Political Behavior 36 (2014): 753–76.

94. http://www.citizen.org/documents/fec-deadlock-statement-and-chart-january-2013.pdf/.

95. *Arizona Free Enterprise Club v Bennett (2011)*.

96. Ackerman and Ayers, *Voting with Dollars*; and Lawrence Lessig, *Republic, Lost: How Money Corrupts Congress—And a Plan to Stop It* (New York: Twelve, 2011).

97. National Conference of State Legislatures "Public Financing of Campaigns: An Overview: Updated January 23, 2013," http://www.ncsl.org/legislatures-elections/elections/public-financing-of-campaigns-overview.aspx/.

98. Michael G. Miller, *Subsidizing Democracy: How Public Funding Changes Elections and How It Can Work in the Future* (Ithaca, NY: Cornell University Press, 2014); Kenneth R. Mayer, Timothy Werner, and Amanda Williams, "Do Public Funding Programs Enhance Electoral Competition?," in Michael P. McDonald and John Sides, eds., *The Marketplace of Democracy: Electoral Competition and American Politics* (Washington, D.C.: Brookings, 2006); Patrick D. Donnay and Graham P. Ramsden, "Public Financing of Legislative Elections: Lessons from Minnesota," *Legislative Studies Quarterly* 20 (1995): 351–62; Patrick Basham and Martin Zelder, "Does Cleanliness Lead to Competitiveness? The Failure of Maine's Experiment," in John Samples, ed., *Welfare for Politicians: Taxpayer Financing of Campaigns* (Washington, D.C.: Cato, 2005); and U.S. General Accounting Office, *Campaign Finance Reform: Early Experiences of Two States That Offer Full Public Funding for Political Candidates,* GAO-03-453, May 2003.

99. Miller, *Subsidizing Democracy*.

100. Shaun Bowler and Todd Donovan, *The Limits of Electoral Reform* (Oxford: Oxford University Press, 2013), chap. 5.

101. Streb, *Rethinking*: 173–78.

102. Johannes and Nugent, "Conclusion: Reforms and Values," in *Money, Elections, and Democracy*, chap. 15.

103. Maisel, "The Incumbency Advantage," *ibid*.

104. Pew Research Center for the People & the Press, "Public Priorities: Deficit Rising, Terrorism Slipping, Tough Stance on Iran Endorsed," http://www.people-press.org/2012/01/23/public-priorities-deficit-rising-terrorism-slipping/.

105. Pew Research Center for the People & the Press, "Little Public Awareness of outside Campaign Spending Boom" (August 2, 2012), http://www.people-press.org/2012/08/02/little-public-awareness-of-outside-campaign-spending-boom/; WP Politics, "Washington Post–ABC News Poll," http://www.washingtonpost.com/wp-srv/politics/polls/postabcpoll_031012.html/.

106. http://www.nytimes.com/interactive/2012/01/19/us/politics/19poll-documents.html?_r=0/.

107. Lydia Saad, "Half in U.S. Support Publicly Financed Federal Campaigns—Vast Majority Supports Limiting Campaign Spending and Contributions," *Gallup Politics* (June 24, 2013), http://www.gallup.com/poll/163208/half-support-publicly-financed-federal-campaigns.aspx?utm_source=alert&utm_medium=email&utm_campaign=syndication&utm_content=morelink&utm_term=All%20Gallup%20Headlines%20-%20Politics]/.

108. La Raja, *Small Change*: 95.

109. Samples, *Fallacy of Campaign Finance Reform*: 288.

110. Herrnson, *Congressional Elections*: 297–98; see Diana Dwyre and Victoria A. Farrar-Myers, *Legislative Labyrinth: Congress and Campaign Finance Reform* (Washington, D.C.: CQ Press, 2001).

CHAPTER 8

How to Think about the
Policy Makers

> The tyranny of the legislature is really the danger most to be
> feared and will continue to be so for many years to come . . . .
> the tyranny of executive power will come in its turn, but at a
> more distant period.
>
> —Thomas Jefferson to James Madison, 1789

The next chapters focus on the policy makers—the Congress, presidency, judiciary, and executive bureaucracy—their interactions, the policy processes, and Madison's warning. The values of concern go to the heart of governance and its limits: effectiveness, efficiency, reasoned deliberative judgment, representation, responsiveness, and accountability. The goal is to understand how reform proposals for one institution affect not only it but also the others, the macro political landscape, and the policy-making processes. Doing so requires a framework and strategy because instituting reforms willy-nilly to fix this or that problem is a recipe for chaos and an invitation to all sorts of unintended consequences.

8.1 A FRAMEWORK FOR ANALYZING REFORMS

There are two fault lines that splinter government and politics today: the enduring institutional rivalry between branches of government and polarized, acrimonious partisanship. The framers clearly were concerned about efforts of presidents and Congress to dominate each other, and many of them dreaded political parties. Thinking of these forces as intersecting and largely interdependent lenses through which reformers view today's problems will clarify the problems and prescribe solutions.

Parties for Good and Bad
Much of the public today believes that Washington substitutes partisanship and electioneering for governing. They want reforms that moderate or circumvent partisanship to restore Congress and the presidency to the way they operated in a pre-party, or at least weak, party environment. Bipartisanship or nonpartisanship, cooperation, and negotiating across party boundaries are the goals. Paradoxically, although favoring bipartisanship, voters think about public policy in a partisan fashion.[1]

There is a radically different vision that perceives partisanship as helping voters sort out who should govern, assists them in holding government accountable, and serves as the primary, perhaps the only, mechanism for surmounting the barriers that the Constitution erected between the houses of Congress and between the Congress and the presidency. Reforms adopting this vision focus on removing or surmounting the structural hurdles that prevent a more responsible partisan approach to governing. Bluntly stated, strong disciplined parties staunchly at odds with each other work wonderfully in a parliamentary form of government, where governing institutions are fused and where one party "wins it all" and earns the right to govern relatively unfettered by the other, whose job it is to criticize, identify alternative policies, and gird for the next election. In the American system of separated institutions that share power, however, those same kinds of parties can backfire and create a stalemate whenever different parties control the institutions. Thus, when thinking about reforms, one can take either of two paths. The first is to reform the institutions to resemble what they were intended to be in the 1780s, which implies weakening the parties and promoting nonpartisan structures and procedures. *The other is to do the exact opposite*: either change fundamentally to a parliamentary system (an unrealistic option) or remodel the institutions so as to make it easy for one party to control all of them. In short, weaken *or* strengthen partisan governance; undermine *or* bolster the parties; render government structures and procedures less *or* more partisan. Reforms that fail to be explicit about their intentions about parties and fail to choose between weak and strong parties are bound to have frustrating consequences. Splitting the difference or tinkering around the edges is likely to make matters worse. This is one case when half a loaf is *not* better than none.

Constitutional Relationships—Pick One

The other lens for evaluating reforms is structural: the constitutional relationships between the institutions of government. There are three logical power relationships: (1) presidential primacy or dominance, (2) congressional primacy or dominance, and (3) presidential–congressional or constitutional balance.[2] These two lenses—parties and institutions—must be brought into focus; one's choice of the options they present affects, indeed must determine, one's views on reforms.

Presidential Primacy. Because a president represents a national constituency whose attention he commands when speaking from the bully pulpit and because of the president's technical and political advantages as head of the federal executive branch, it might be sensible to posit that the presidency should be the dominant partner in policy making. The presidency and executive bureaucracy under such an arrangement should have the primary function of policy initiation and implementation, and the presidential role in pushing legislation through Congress should be exceedingly strong. That leaves to Congress the functions of discussion and public debate, post facto oversight of the executive's actions, representation, and constituency service—not unlike the legislatures in most parliamentary systems. Assuming there will be no constitutional rewriting to give presidents such authority, this form of institutionalized upper hand could come through one of two reformist mechanisms that more or less align with the partisan–nonpartisan choices mentioned above. Either the president might dominate via a strong presidentially led national party that exercised discipline over its congressional members or he might acquire enough small grants of power and advantages to make him the strongest among a collection of players in a pluralist bargaining game on Capitol Hill.

The first means to presidential pre-eminence, a "presidential-responsible party" model (sometimes called the "Jeffersonian" model honoring the president who first used party to lead Congress), resembles a parliamentary fusion-of-powers form of government. As explained in chapter 5, this perspective portrays policy making and democratic politics as a popular choice at election time between two well-organized, disciplined, and ideological political parties, each of which offers a distinct and coherent platform of policies to the voters. At elections, each party's presidential candidate, having a substantial degree of influence over the nomination and campaigns of congressional candidates, leads his party. The winner becomes president and *de facto* leader of Congress. He and his colleagues on the Hill govern until the public chooses the other party in a subsequent election. Government is effective and efficient; policy deliberation is pretty much confined to the president and his advisors, along with other party leaders.

Congress contributes to effectiveness and efficiency by following and endorsing the lead of the president and his advisors. There is no danger of congressional upstaging of or disagreeing with the president, and there is no interference with his execution of the laws. The executive bureaucracy follows the president's lead in all matters; and the judiciary ideally would resonate with the views of the president and his party. Popular representation comes primarily via the deliberations of the party from the grass roots on up to the highest party council that take into account the public's wishes and needs. Because the public knows precisely whom to blame, accountability comes easily: re-elect or dismiss the president's party at the next election.

Concerns that (a) government could become dangerously powerful and intrusive, (b) Congress will become merely a "rubber stamp" for the presidency, (c) the judiciary would lose its independence and authority, and (d) the bureaucracy could become politicized accompany this model, as do fears of losing congressional deliberation and ruining policy responsiveness to members' individual constituencies. The only check on excessive executive power is the ballot box. A miscalculation could be disastrous. The minority party cannot stop the president and his party. The minority has two tasks: criticize the governing coalition and prepare for the next election. Historically, American government on occasion seemed to resemble this model: the first couple of years of the presidency of Woodrow Wilson, Franklin Roosevelt's first term, and Lyndon Johnson's "Great Society" 95th Congress.

Presidential primacy need not require major constitutional changes or establishment of responsible political parties. A combination of specific grants of authority from Congress, unilateral presidential executive actions, and the clever use of existing presidential and party resources would do the trick, albeit probably on a lesser scale. Perhaps congressional deliberation concerning the national good would conclude that presidential leadership and power are essential to governing.

A slightly different perspective—classic pluralism—views Congress and indeed the federal government as the arena in which interest groups and their elected representatives engage in a process of bargaining and accommodation, producing "the public interest" as a byproduct of their self-interest.[3] Politics is neither a clash of two overarching views of the public good as represented in the two parties nor simply a process in which elected representatives exercise wisdom and prudence to accept strong presidential direction. Rather, politics is a battle among self-seeking groups,

CHAPTER 8 • How to Think about the Policy Makers   161

each of which is represented in Congress by members, groups of members, and elements of the political parties. Interests find representation as well in the departments and agencies of the executive branch. Decisions are products of bargaining and horse-trading. One implication, quite contrary to the responsible party model, is that there ought to be multiple political parties, each representing specific interests; at the least, the two parties should be highly decentralized and open to all interests. Party pressures on members of Congress would be nonexistent.

This deliberative and/or interest group approach to presidential dominance is less programmatic and less dangerous than the party model. That first model emphasizes effectiveness and efficiency. This milder version of presidential primacy recognizes the importance of representation, responsiveness, and reasoned judgment in both branches of government, and it counts on the president to use his structural, legal, and political advantages, along with shrewd political skills, to dominate Congress. Accountability comes less from the threat of voters' ousting the governing party than through the close relationships between members of Congress and the citizens and groups supporting them. One might think of this as a "Hamiltonian" version of politics, named after Alexander Hamilton, a strong proponent of vigorous executive leadership in a separation-of-powers system.

Congressional Primacy. Madison recognized that Congress, not the president, must have the final say on policy. Legislatures better represent and are closer to the people because each member has fewer constituents than the president and because members of the House, at least, have shorter terms of office that force them to be more attentive to constituents. Presidents, on the other hand, are the products of essentially national, thus mixed and unclear, majorities. They are, it is argued, in a sense, false representatives, whereas true representation comes from the legislature.

This "Whig" model, as it has been called, refers to the party that rose up to challenge "King" Andrew Jackson, who had transformed the presidency into a powerful office for, and answerable to, the masses. This congressional supremacy model traditionally has enjoyed less support from academics, but it has not been ignored.[4] The country has experienced periods of clear congressional dominance during the two decades before the Civil War, the period immediately thereafter, and the 1920s, to cite three. During the heyday of liberal Democratic ascendance (from Franklin Roosevelt's presidency through that of Lyndon Johnson), frustrated Republicans could not be blamed for salivating over this approach.

Legislative supremacy, like presidential dominance, could be built on the same two frameworks described above for the presidency. One is a congressionally, rather than presidentially, centered party—strong, disciplined, and responsible. The majority party in Congress chooses its leadership and gives it substantial powers like those wielded by House speakers in the late nineteenth century or, some claim, for the past 20 years. Policy decisions are determined by the wishes of a majority of the majority party, as has been the case recently when Democrats and Republicans both followed this "Hastert" rule articulated by former Republican Speaker Dennis Hastert of Illinois. An extreme rendition of this model has presidential candidates being nominated at national conventions dominated by the national congressional party leaderships or by congressional caucuses. Presidents retain some of their powers, but they become junior partners to strong House and Senate leaders—something resembling a parliamentary democracy with the president as the administrator of congressionally determined policy and chief of state for ceremonial functions. Emphasis is on effectiveness, efficiency, and party-based accountability. Representation and responsiveness are more collective than individualized. Under its senatorial power to confirm judges and high-level presidential executive appointments, its authority to reshape the federal judiciary and executive branch structures, and the power of the purse, Congress would enjoy considerable influence over both the judicial branch and the executive bureaucracy.

Those who distrust strong parties but prefer congressional dominance might opt for the alternate scenarios that envision Congress either as a venue for calm and reasoned deliberation by independent statesman-legislators attuned to constituency wishes or as the place for interest group bargaining as described above. In either case, congressional activity is freed from presidential influence because presidential powers would be rescinded or curbed. Multiple representational styles and different majorities in the Senate and House, each with different terms of office and different kinds of constituencies, characterize this model and determine final legislative products.[5] Only then is policy turned over to the executive for implementation, always subject to the supervision and direction of Congress. This version of congressional supremacy probably implies less, rather than more, government; it emphasizes reasoned consideration and caution. The focus is less on effectiveness and efficiency or a simple national party-based electoral accountability than on representation, responsiveness, and local accountability. In the minds of congressionalists, whether Congress follows a highly partisan or bi- or nonpartisan deliberative model, there is no doubt which branch should reign supreme.

Constitutional Balance. A third possible configuration of national power splits the difference between the two other approaches, envisioning power being shared more or less equally by the two branches, each of which in its own way represents the American people. This sometimes is referred to as the Madisonian model, in deference to his writings in the *Federalist*. Policy making in this view results from interactions between autonomous and essentially equal institutions, each structured differently, each with its own powers, and each playing its own role at different stages of the policy process. Although parties may exist and play a key electoral role, their influence in bringing about policy decisions is secondary to and supportive of the *institutional* roles and functions of Congress and the presidency. Congressional committees, for example, deliberate in a bipartisan fashion over the details of laws, relatively free of party pressures. One interpretation sees the president's role as initiating policy proposals based on the president's national and international political focus and his command of the bureaucracy, where executive expertise resides. Congress's task is to apply representational perspectives to the president's proposals, in effect applying a political barometer of popular acceptability to them. The legislature then ratifies, amends, or rejects the initiatives in accord with the public's wishes as filtered by senators and representatives—while serving as a backup policy initiator in case the president falls down on the job.[6] If both institutions are in accord, policies flow in a relatively, but always compromised, effective and efficient manner balancing national and local preferences. If not, it is a sign that one side has come to a reasoned disagreement with the other, that one institution perceives a threat to its independence and authority from the other, or that the constellation of interests that the two institutions represent are in conflict over policy. It is not hard to imagine issues for which a national presidential perspective would clash with the more parochial views of representatives' districts. An accommodation must be forged if there is to be new policy.

Accountability comes through the electoral process, with representatives and senators subjecting their positions and actions to the scrutiny of their individual constituencies. Effectiveness and efficiency probably would not match what one would get from a strong party system, whether led by the president or by Congress. Representation and responsiveness, on the other hand, would be strong, constituency focused, and varied, with presidents, executive agencies, senators, and members of the House representing and responding to their publics in different ways. The result probably would be a more limited set of public policies. Those who fear big government might be more satisfied; those who dread gridlock would be horrified. One potential locus of tension in this model is the executive bureaucracy, as both presidents and legislators struggle to maintain control over and give direction to departments and agencies as they implement legislation. Presidents and legislators often see matters differently. Table 8.1 summarizes the models.

Maintaining the balance, once established, would be tricky, given the institutional and political incentives to expand power and aggrandize status that Madison recognized so well. The task of watching over the rivalry, at least in terms of the formal powers of the two branches, would fall largely on the judiciary, historically the referee between the branches. Additionally, the good sense of the American people, speaking at election time, would be crucial. Unfortunately, neither the courts nor the voters have impeccable records.

Fundamentally, one's evaluation of the performance of government institutions and prescriptions to fix performance flaws depend squarely on one's frame of reference and on the questions one asks. Whether or not reformers are conscious of these three models and their variations, many if not most of their suggestions align with one or another of them, however inadvertently. The danger is trying to remedy the weaknesses of one branch without considering effects elsewhere. Different models, if

Table 8.1 Models of Presidential–Congressional Relations

POTENTIAL SOURCES OF POWER ↓	PREFERRED MODEL OF DISTRIBUTION OF POWER		
	PRESIDENTIAL PRIMACY	CONGRESSIONAL PRIMACY	CONSTITUTIONAL BALANCE
Partisanship	Strong and disciplined parties led by and based in the presidency	Strong and disciplined parties led by and based in the Congress	Weak decentralized parties functioning in bipartisan fashion; relatively minor role in Congress
Incremental advantages and "bargaining chips"	Constitutional and statutory grants of power; inherent and situational advantages of office	Constitutional and statutory grants of power; effective representation of citizens and interests	Constitutional and statutory grants of power; balanced advantages between Congress and the presidency

realized, are bound to promote stronger or more limited government, more or less effective and efficient government, easier or more difficult—and different kinds of—accountability. They locate the locus of reasoned deliberative judgment differently, and they celebrate different forms of responsiveness and representation. The next chapters focus directly on these reforms.

QUESTIONS TO CONSIDER

1. Which of the models above makes the most sense to you? Which branch should have primacy?
2. What is the better approach: the partisan or the bipartisan/nonpartisan model?

NOTES

1. Laurel Harbridge, Neil Malhotra, and Brian F. Harrison, "Public Preferences for Bipartisanship in the Policymaking Process," *Legislative Studies Quarterly* 39 (2014): 327–55.
2. David J. Vogler, *The Politics of Congress* (Boston: Allyn & Bacon, 1983), chap. 1; LeRoy N. Rieselbach, *Congressional Reform: The Changing Modern Congress* (Washington, D.C.: CQ Press, 1994), chap. 2; Roger H. Davidson, David M. Kovenock, and Michael K. O'Leary, *Congress in Crisis: Politics and Congressional Reform* (Belmont, CA: Wadsworth, 1969): 15–36; and John S. Saloma III, *Congress and the New Politics* (Boston: Little, Brown, 1969), chaps. 1–2.
3. David B. Truman, *The Governmental Process*, 2nd ed. (New York: Knopf, 1971); Carol Greenwald, *Group Power* (New York: Praeger, 1977). For a critique, see Theodore J. Lowi, *The End of Liberalism*, 2nd ed. (New York, Norton, 1979).
4. An early volume defending this proposition is Alfred De Grazia, ed., *Congress: The First Branch of Government: 12 Studies of the Organization of Congress* (Garden City, NY: Anchor Books/Doubleday, 1967).
5. Willmoore Kendall, "The Two Majorities," *Midwest Journal of Political Science* 4 (1960): 317–45.
6. Arthur Maass, *Congress and the Common Good* (New York: Basic Books, 1983); John R. Johannes, *Policy Innovation in Congress* (Englewood Cliffs, NJ: General Learning Press, 1972); Johannes, "The President Proposes and Congress Disposes—But Not Always: Legislative Initiative on Capitol Hill," *Review of Politics* 36 (1974): 356–70.

CHAPTER 9

✒

Congress

In republican governments, the legislative authority necessarily
predominates. The remedy for this inconveniency is to divide the
legislature into different branches; and to render them, by different modes of election and different principles of action, as little
connected with each other as the nature of their common functions and their common dependence on the society will admit.

—JAMES MADISON, *The Federalist No. 51*

9.1 WHAT'S WRONG WITH CONGRESS?

Complaining about Washington is an industry unto itself; grousing about Congress is
that industry's Wall Street. Congress's standing in the polls has been running last
among a score or more of public and private institutions, dipping into single digits
and rarely approaching even 20 percent. Is the public correct about congressional
incompetence?

One scholar's "report card" shows that Congress essentially meets 23 of his
37 benchmarks for a sound legislature, leading him to conclude that "it would not be
inaccurate to claim that, in both the absolute and relative senses, it is a pretty good
legislature."[1] The achievements of some Congresses support that evaluation, such as
the 89th of 1965–1966 that produced much of President Johnson's Great Society program or the 111th, in 2009–2010. That Congress passed more than 380 new laws, such
as the Lilly Ledbetter Fair Pay Act, the American Recovery and Reinvestment Act, the
Helping Families Save Their Homes Act, the Credit CARD Act, the Family Smoking
Prevention and Tobacco Control Act, the historic Patient Protection and Affordable
Care Act ("Obamacare"), and the Dodd–Frank Wall Street Reform and Consumer
Protection Act. Then came the 2010 elections that gave Republicans control of the
House, exacerbated the divisions between the House and the Democratic-controlled
Senate, and led to legislative logjams in 2011–2012. That 112th Congress was the least
productive Congress in modern history, enacting only 283 laws, with few major pieces
of legislation. The elections of 2012 settled nothing; Congress passed the fewest bills in
2013 since 1947, brought about a government shutdown, and earned it the *Washington
Times*'s lowest rank ever in its legislative futility index.[2] Nothing changed in 2014 or
the early months of 2015.

Two books by veteran Congress watchers Thomas E. Mann and Norman J. Ornstein
sum up matters: *The Broken Branch: How Congress Is Failing America and How to Get*

It Back on Track, published in 2006, and, six years later, *It's Even Worse Than It Looks: How the American Constitutional System Collided with the New Politics of Extremism.* They highlight policy and operational failures, decrying the partisan warfare they dubbed "tribalism." Congress is neither productive nor a pleasant place to work. As former congressman Mickey Edwards wrote, "True, it's dysfunctional. It's a mess. It's a cafeteria food fight, kindergarten name-calling, a collection of whines, pouts, and threats to pick up one's marbles and go home."[3] Think of almost any negative adjective to describe member conduct or the legislative process, and it has been used to describe Congress.

It is a mistake, however, to view these critiques as unique to today or to place all the blame on party polarization. The problems run deeper. Many of today's criticisms filled the pages of publications 20, 40, 100 years ago. In 1946, two years before President Truman campaigned against a "do-nothing" Congress, a distinguished scholar wrote about *Congress at the Crossroads.*[4] Another in the 1960s titled his book the *Deadlock of Democracy.*[5] Twenty years later a U.S. senator labeled Congress *The Sapless Branch,*[6] while a former member of the lower chamber described a *House out of Order.*[7] Congress was "in crisis," screamed the title of yet another volume, one of whose authors followed up with *Congress against Itself.*[8] One scholar suggested that Congress was so inept that it should "eschew the legislative" role and focus on constituency service.[9] Titles of magazine articles circa 1990 were typical: "Government by the Timid" (*Time*), "Why Congress Doesn't Work (*Reader's Digest*), "House of Ill Repute" (*The New Republic*), and "Nobody Here but Us Chickens" (*Time*). Asked where he got material for jokes, humorist Will Rogers more than 80 years ago reportedly replied that he merely watched Congress in action. The problem seems endemic and almost permanent, not transitory or attributable to today's partisan rancor. Looking for causes, reformers round up the usual suspects: members, structures, procedures, and presidential–congressional relations. If effective, efficient, and deliberative government is missing, and if the public feels unrepresented and unable to hold Congress accountable, just look at these four sets of problems.

9.2 BLAME THE MEMBERS

Polarized Partisanship

The charge is simple: members are self-centered, focused on re-election, and polarized in their behavior; they substitute partisanship, cynicism, and "my way or the highway" philosophies for deliberation and compromise. Winning elections and becoming a majority, which used to be the *means* to governing, has become the *end*, with Capitol Hill activity the means. There once was a distinct campaign and election season that gave way to a governing season; now the two are one. Campaigns and fundraising are incessant, cutting deeply into the time and energy needed for legislating and overseeing the executive bureaucracy. Scoring points against the other party, forcing tough, embarrassing votes on the other side (to be used at campaign time), blocking their initiatives, and doing all of this very visibly so as to appeal to one's base constituents seem to be today's values. Party-line voting, when a majority of one party opposes a majority of the other, has not been so frequent in a hundred years; and on those votes members support their parties roughly 90 percent of the time. There is no

Democrat more conservative than any Republican and no Republican more liberal than any Democrat.[10]

Most observers see this extremism rooted in the ideological division of the American people.[11] Since a primary function of Congress is representation, and if the public is seriously divided on major issues,[12] it is not surprising that divisiveness shows up in Washington. Indeed, *the* fundamental problem may be that Congress cannot legislate precisely because its members represent their own constituents, or at least their base voters, *too well*! Encouraging divisiveness are interest groups that each hold passionate positions on one specific issue. They threaten members by keeping score of their "wrong" votes on that issue and supporting challengers in party primaries—forcing liberals further to their left and conservatives further to the right. Partisan and ideological media remind members that their votes will be put under a microscope. Demographic patterns underpin polarization, especially the conversion of the South from a Democratic bastion before 1970 into a rock-solid Republican stronghold or the reverse shift in the coastal regions and New England. Democrats and liberals dominate cities and inner suburbs, whereas Republicans hold sway in rural and small town areas and outer suburbs. The redrawing of congressional district lines every decade reinforces these demographics. The consequence is that the vast majority of House seats are safe for one party or the other. Once upon a time, the electoral competitiveness in one's district required a careful balancing act within the constituency in addition to weighing constituent interests against those of their parties or the nation. One could beg off of voting with one's party if either conscience or constituency tugged the other way. Now, as constituencies are more homogeneously liberal or conservative, members find themselves in perfect synch with their supporters. Even if they seek wiggle room to oppose the party–constituency–interest group triumvirate, they seldom find it. And when almost all members of a party's caucus or conference are similarly trapped, rancorous partisan behavior rules the day.

Strangers in the Night

Contentiousness and a lack of comity bordering on incivility swamp the Capitol, partly because of the partisanship and partly because members have become strangers.[13] As former Senate majority leader Tom Daschle (D-SD) put it, "Because we can't bond, we can't trust. Because we can't trust, we can't cooperate. Because we can't cooperate, we become dysfunctional."[14] Not that many years ago, members came to Washington with their families, setting up residence in or near the District of Columbia. Members interacted with each other socially, in the gym, at lunch, or at dinner parties. Many spouses knew other spouses, and members' children played with each other. Political differences remained, and battles were hard fought; but relationships were civil. After a hard day, opponents often repaired to a local watering hole for a drink together. Liberals like Senator Ted Kennedy (D-MA) were best friends with hard-core conservatives like Senator Orrin Hatch (R-UT). That pattern has given way to the "commuter congressmen" who rent apartments near the Hill or sleep in their offices. They fly home Thursday nights to be with constituents and return the following Monday evening or Tuesday morning, thus establishing a *de facto* two- or three-day work week. When members are in town, they are torn between their legislative duties and other activities. Fundraisers and receptions take up many evenings.

The consequences are acute: Congress is not in session very much, making it hard to legislate. Committee activities vie with floor votes and other appointments. According to the *New York Times*, the House in 2013 worked less than any nonelection year since 2005, averaging 28 hours per week, with the Senate not far behind.[15] Many of those hours consisted of partisan palaver and disagreeable diatribes. More important, too many members behave as though their colleagues on the other side of the aisle are not temporary opponents but rather enemies to be vanquished.

What? I Did Something Wrong? Congressional Ethics

Reform measures from 1968 through 2007 established and reinforced ethics committees in each chamber, instituted the House Office of Congressional Ethics to police ethical violations, strengthened lobbying disclosure, and banned gifts from lobbyists. Along with partisan-driven emphases on ethics charges, these have reduced much of the questionable behavior that characterized the "good old days." The House Ethics Committee, for example, aided by the Office of Congressional Ethics, took 20 disciplinary actions between 2009 and 2014.[16] In January 2015, the House required its freshman members to undergo the same one hour ethics training previously required of staff. Problems remain, such as the conflict of interest raised by migration of hundreds of former senators and representatives and thousands of staff members to K Street to join law and lobbying firms. Who knows what motivates a member or staffer whose focus is on a subsequent, certainly more lucrative, career downtown? The "Honest Leadership and Open Government Act" requires lawmakers to make timely public disclosures that they are negotiating for such jobs and that there may be conflicts of interests. According to one reporter, "only seven disclosures have been made public in the House since the law was passed in 2007—although more than 200 lawmakers during that time have resigned, were defeated in a primary, or announced their retirement. Only six disclosures have been made public in the Senate, despite 39 lawmakers leaving between 2008 and 2012."[17] In June 2014, Senators Michael Bennet (D-CO) and Jon Tester (D-MT) offered legislation forbidding members of Congress from becoming lobbyists after they retire and require a six-year wait for staff members to do so.

Two other ethically suspect behaviors are ownership of the stock of companies whose fortunes members of Congress can influence and stock trading by members and staffs (and their families) involving "insider" information. Such trading is illegal, but defining it and dealing with it can be messy. So in 2012 Congress passed and the president signed the "Stop Trading on Congressional Knowledge" Act (STOCK), causing some members to sell stocks or move investments into mutual funds to avoid public scrutiny and criticism. In April 2013, Congress repealed portions of the law, weakening disclosure provisions. Congress has not acted on the matter of members' owning securities in companies that may come under their committees' jurisdictions. At least in the 1990s, there was evidence that congressional stock trading yielded above-market results.[18]

A final concern is congressional junketeering. Traveling, sometimes to exotic locations, on congressional business is one thing; accepting travel opportunities from interest groups or using funds from one's own PAC to cover costs for family members is another. Despite disclosure rules and other limits, in 2013 legislators and staffs took more trips of this type than since 2007, when the reforms were enacted.[19] In mid-2014, the House Ethics Committee changed the reporting system to eliminate some of the data previously required to be reported on members' personal disclosure forms, but, faced with severe criticism, rescinded the changes.

9.3 STRUCTURES CAUSE PROBLEMS

The Senate: The Ultimate Gerrymander

Anglers know that lake or stream structure is the secret to finding fish. So too, scholars concerned about representation, effectiveness, accountability, responsiveness, deliberative judgment, and efficiency look to the legislature's structure. The U.S. Senate, in which each state has two seats, presents representational equity problems.[20] One California senator represents about 66 times as many people as does a colleague from Wyoming. Six senators from New York, California, and Texas represent a quarter of the nation's population; so do 62 senators from 31 other states. Senators from 26 states, with about 18 percent of the U.S. population, theoretically can outvote the others who represent 82 percent of the people. Thus the criteria of representation and collective accountability face challenges. In the 2010, 2012, and 2014 elections, for example, 46 Democratic winners received over 40 percent more votes than the 54 Republican winners.

There are other consequences. It is virtually impossible to pass a bill that distributes federal dollars on a formula basis that does not spread the wealth to most or all states, often with perverse inequalities. In 2010, Alaskans benefitted from federal largesse to the tune of $4,680 per capita; Wyoming residents got $4,180, followed by citizens of Delaware ($3,700), New Mexico ($3,310), Vermont ($3,270), and North Dakota ($3,220). At the other end, residents of most of the most populous states received less than $2,000.[21] Small-state senators can focus on fewer issues for their more homogeneous constituencies, whereas senators from large heterogeneous states must attend to just about everything under the sun. Smaller states have been a factory for producing Senate leaders: Democrats Mike Mansfield (Montana), Robert C. Byrd Jr. (West Virginia), George Mitchell (Maine), Thomas Daschle (South Dakota), and Harry Reid (Nevada); and Republicans Howard Baker (Tennessee), Robert Dole (Kansas), Trent Lott (Mississippi), William Frist (Tennessee), and Mitch McConnell (Kentucky). Is there a lesson here?

House Size and Districts

The principle that each House member represents the same number of people falters because of the requirement that a state contain a whole number of congressional districts. Montana and Wyoming each have one U.S. representative despite the roughly 450,000 population difference. In the 1790s, each member represented roughly 34,000 Americans; 50 years later, the average was about 70,000. Today the number exceeds 700,000. For almost a century, the size of the House has remained constant. Interestingly, one of the constitutional amendments Congress considered in 1789 but did not adopt would have provided that the size of the House of Representatives would grow along with the population to ensure that members would remain in close touch with constituents. The size of House districts mark it as an outlier among legislatures in developed democratic countries.

The decennial redrawing of House districts attracts reformers' attention. Redistricting and gerrymandering (rigging boundaries in contortionist fashion to favor particular candidates or parties) are blamed for safe seats, ideological extremism and intransigence, polarization, low voting turnout, poor representation and responsiveness, and just about anything else one can imagine. Undoubtedly redistricting affects these matters, but scholars have demonstrated that the effects are far less important than appear on the surface and are short lived, dissipating after the first couple of elections held under the new boundaries.[22] Moreover, many of the weirdly shaped districts, clearly the product of political decision making, seem almost inevitable because redistricting efforts must accommodate physical barriers such as mountains, comply with mandates of the Voting Rights Act and Supreme Court decisions to protect minorities, and meet state goals such as competitiveness and respect for existing country or city lines.

Redistricting affects the calculations of strategic politicians, triggering large numbers of retirements, summoning into combat good challengers, and leading to large seat swings.[23] It temporarily reduces turnout in newly designed districts; affects people's familiarity with incumbents; and often leads to changes in incumbents' interests and voting behavior.[24]

Crass gerrymandering, on the other hand, influences margins of victory—facing new voters is bound to change patterns of support or opposition—but the effects in the vast majority of cases are not dramatic. Gerrymandering's effect on incumbent re-election is uncertain; one study found that, after controlling for all other relevant factors, redistricting actually leads to fewer re-elections.[25] Redistricting before the 2012 elections mattered in several states, such as Wisconsin and Pennsylvania, where the statewide vote for representatives favored Democrats, but Republicans ended up with a majority of seats. Conversely, in Democratic Illinois, Republicans picked up 45 percent of the vote but only a third of the seats.[26] One tabulation of 2012 results suggests that, overall, districting changed maybe two dozen results that year, with a net gain of one seat for Democrats.[27] Another study simulated redistricting possibilities by running thousands of different districting plans for a number of states. The electoral biases found in the simulations differed little from what the actual districts showed.[28]

Does gerrymandering make some seats safer for one or the other party? Yes— some. In blue states Democratic congressmen may become safer, whereas in red states Republicans benefit. Much depends on the redistricting strategies that vary from partisan gerrymandering that seeks more seats for a given party to bipartisan gerrymandering that protects incumbents of both parties to competitive gerrymandering in pursuit of stiffer competition in as many districts as possible.

Some studies conclude that districts become safer *between* redistricting events than immediately after. Demographic changes and social mobility that concentrate Democrats in "their" districts while dispersing Republicans more broadly to more districts, along with increased and strong voter loyalty to candidates of their parties, are the key.[29] Racial gerrymandering concentrates minority voters in "majority minority" districts, with mixed consequences. Congress holds more black and Hispanic representatives than ever, but the "bleaching" of the surrounding districts (making them more white and Republican) may actually weaken the influence that minority voters could otherwise have if they constituted significant voting blocs in more districts.[30] Redistricting can help one party at one period of time and the other at different times, depending on district partisanship, changing demographics, incumbent–constituency relationships, and better campaigning.[31]

Polarization of the parties may be killing Congress, but the best studies show that one cannot simply blame gerrymandering, although it is not entirely innocent.[32] For example, why is it that polarization has increased at roughly the same rates in both the House and the Senate when Senate "district" (i.e., state) boundaries have not changed? Why is it that, although the number of one-party dominant districts as measured by presidential election results is no different today from averages over the past 60 years, there is so much ideological polarization and rigidity in the House?

9.4 COMMITTEES AND SUBCOMMITTEES BRING COMPLEXITY

A modern legislature without a sophisticated committee system is implausible. Currently there are 21 standing committees in the House, with 98 subcommittees, and 20 in the Senate (73 subcommittees), plus 4 joint committees. Size is an issue: Senate committees average 21 members (of 100), whereas House committees average 39 members but go as high as 60.

Committees and subcommittees present problems because they serve the purposes of three sometimes crosscutting entities: members, the institution, and party.[33] Members use committees to advance their careers by becoming policy experts, by accumulating and exercising power within the House and Senate, and/or by taking good care of their constituents by steering federal funds back home.[34] Committee membership largely determines the types of interest groups that can be tapped for campaign contributions; service on the House Financial Services or Senate Banking panels, for instance, is especially lucrative. Second, committees serve their parent chambers by providing the division of labor, the expertise, and the detailed work needed for policy making and oversight. Third, the majority party relies on committees to produce policies to promote its objectives and thus to retain majority status. These purposes often are incompatible; indeed, it is the conflict among them that leads to many congressional weaknesses and complicates the task of reformers. For example, reform efforts face the tension between (a) the presumably bipartisan or nonpartisan *institutional* goal of expert and negotiated lawmaking that calls for relatively independent, bipartisan, and self-directed committees and (b) the highly *partisan* goal of promoting one party and undermining the other as both jockey for position for the next election.

Getting Appointed Is Important

Committee and subcommittee assignments raise issues, in large measure because some committees are more attractive than others; yet committee size must be limited to be efficient and spread the workload. Sometimes, to deal with multiple claimants for a seat on a given committee, leaders simply add seats to committees, making them unwieldy.

   Processes for assignments vary between the parties and chambers, evolving over the years to give more influence to party leaders. Because members seek committee seats to serve their own interests, committee membership often is biased. Farm-state legislators dominate agriculture committees; urban legislators gravitate to committees handling education, housing, and social welfare; southerners from districts and states with military bases or defense industries have had a penchant for the armed services; and so on. The problem is representational: should committees be stacked with "interested" members to encourage expertise and commitment, or should they more broadly represent the chamber as a whole to incorporate multiple views on any topic? If the former, will parochial interests determine national policy? If the latter, will disinterest on the part of many committee members concentrate policy making in the hands of a few? Scholars cannot agree on whether panels are in fact unrepresentative "preference outliers" or on the consequences if they are.[35]

Workload Matters

Members serve on multiple committees and subcommittees—on average 6 assignments for representatives and 11 for senators—which means that they spread themselves thinly. Thus (1) members choose what they want to devote time and effort to in their committees, meaning that for some issues, few representatives or senators are involved in crafting legislation; and (2) members, especially senators, depend on staffs. Those unelected policy makers have become numerous and hugely influential, providing information to their bosses and doing much of the deal making and some agenda setting as well.

Jurisdiction Problems

Some committees have exceedingly broad jurisdictions, such as Ways and Means or Energy and Commerce in the House; others are narrowly focused, creating an imbalance in workload and power. Jurisdictional lines frequently overlap, leading to incoherence, inefficiency, and rivalries for influence over any given policy. Accountability for policy is often hard to pinpoint. The House has at least 11 committees with jurisdiction over aspects of environmental policy. The National Commission on Terrorist Attacks upon the United States (the "9-11 Commission") found that 14 different House committees shared jurisdiction over antiterrorism efforts. The Environmental Protection Agency and Defense Department, one way or another, each must deal with as many as 90 different panels. In 2009, a bill addressing global climate change was sent to 9 House committees.[36] When seeking to regulate some of the side effects of trading securities derivatives following the financial collapse of 2008, reformers faced a somewhat incongruous problem. The House Financial Services Committee regulated the Securities and Exchange Commission (stocks and bonds), but the Agriculture Committee controlled much of the derivatives trading business by virtue of its jurisdiction over the Commodities Futures Trading Commission (farmers use futures contracts to make their costs and revenues more predictable). Merging the Securities and Exchange Commission and Commodities Futures Trading Commission makes good sense, but neither the Obama administration, Congressman Barney Frank (D-MA), or Senator Chris Dodd (D-CT) dared to force the issue for fear of stoking rivalries between the Agriculture and Financial Services Committees that could undermine what became the Dodd–Frank Law.

Committee jurisdictions do not align neatly with government functions or executive agencies, creating obstacles to effective deliberation and efficiency. A lack of jurisdictional correspondence between ostensibly comparable committees of the two chambers compounds the problem. A House committee, based on its jurisdiction and experience, may shape a bill one way. It then gets worked over by a Senate committee, with a different jurisdictional perspective, that dramatically alters the original, creating difficulties for the measure back in the originating chamber and perhaps dooming it to ultimate failure.[37] Jurisdictional sloppiness can have advantages by subjecting proposals to a multiplicity of perspectives, but it exacts a price. Congress has developed techniques to deal with these problems, such as informal or formal agreements among committee chairs or referral of bills in whole or in part to several committees. These give leaders leverage in pursuit of their policy goals.

Committee chairs and their allies strive mightily to establish, retain, and expand jurisdiction over policy areas.[38] Undertaking investigations, writing bills in certain ways, conducting oversight hearings, or pleading to have bills referred are routine tactics. How much these retard reasoned deliberative judgment and efficiency is unclear but probably nontrivial. When President Bush pushed to create the Department of Homeland Security, pulling pieces from dozens of executive departments and agencies, the effort had its counterpart on the Hill as the newly renamed Homeland Security and Governmental Affairs Committee competed with other panels for authority over that department. On the House side, a temporary committee became a standing committee, but its effort to claim the security turf faced myriad hurdles and created problems for the leadership.[39]

Who Leads?

Committee and subcommittee leadership is crucial. In what is called the "textbook" Congress, before the 1970s reforms, committee seniority dictated chairmanships and ranking minority positions, as it *de facto* does today in the Senate. House leaders, working through their parties' Steering Committees, established firm control over selection of chairs, often ignoring seniority. Republicans, moreover, impose a six-year term limit on committee leaders, ensuring turnover. For naming subcommittee chairs and ranking minority members, the selection systems vary by committee in the Senate. House Democrats on a committee bid for subcommittee memberships and chairmanships in order of seniority, subject to approval by all committee Democrats. Republicans are less democratic; the full committee chair appoints subcommittee chairs, but she or he can be overruled by a majority of fellow partisans. In most cases, the elected party leaders "guide" these processes to ensure that competence, party concerns such as loyalty and fundraising, and leaders' preferences are honored. Special rules ensure leadership control over Appropriations Committee subcommittees and the House Rules Committee.

9.5 THE PARTIES

In the late 1960s and 1970s, a series of reforms broke the power of House committee chairs by giving party caucuses and party leadership additional authority and by instituting a "subcommittee bill of rights" that dispersed committee power to subcommittees. That meant fragmentation and incoherence that eventually provoked an even greater centralization of power in the hands of the leadership, particularly under Republican speaker Newt Gingrich in 1995–1996. He and his successors, enjoying the benefits of the "conditional party government" discussed in chapter 5, conquered the committees and imposed discipline on their parties. Speaker Hastert's practice, readopted by Speaker John Boehner, that no legislation goes to the floor of the House without approval by a majority of the majority party, ensures a highly partisan agenda and all but demolishes hopes for bipartisanship. Leadership's power clashes with the historical quasi-autonomy of committees. Lately the Republican speaker's control has been fiercely tested by House adherents of the Tea Party who are not swayed by traditional perquisites and often split from the leadership. These developments constitute either a blessing or a curse, depending on what one thinks of party control of the legislative process. If a majority of the majority party chooses its party's leaders, if those leaders dominate committees (or bypass them entirely), and if the leaders dictate strategy and process, those who favor a bi- or nonpartisan legislature based on committees' policy expertise have lost the battle for a moderate and compromising, problem-solving Congress. The more centralized the direction and control, the greater the risk of discouraging committee innovation and creativity, not to mention what happens to cooperation across party lines. Conversely, proponents of strong and disciplined parties relish the control of the leadership, wishing only that their party controlled both chambers and the White House as well so that they could govern in a unified fashion, enhancing the effectiveness, efficiency, and collective accountability of Congress.

9.6 PROCEDURES—HOW DOES ANYTHING GET DONE?

Because Congress is a real legislature, as opposed to a rubber-stamp parliament, the way it conducts business is important, complex, and confusing. Procedures affect results, advantage and disadvantage different groups, and foster a bias toward the status quo, almost guaranteeing that policy changes will be incremental and slow rather than massive and rapid.

The House

To be considered on the House floor, almost all bills must have a "rule," a simple resolution drafted by the Rules Committee and passed by the House that sets the terms of debate and the amending process. The rule turns the House into a committee of itself, the Committee of the Whole House on the State of the Union, with a quorum of 100 instead of the normal 218, making it easier to conduct business. Rules can be open (amendments are allowed), closed (no amendments are allowed), or modified open/closed (some amendments are allowed). Many specify which amendments may be offered and the order in which they are considered. The opportunity to offer amendments and have them considered is essential to a collaborative and deliberative process, and thus whoever controls the Rules Committee controls the flow and, in effect, the content of legislation. Until the 1960s, independent Rules chairmen had a throttle-hold on legislation, but that period gave way to today's majority party control of the committee. Party leaders use the Committee to limit or prevent the minority party's ability to amend bills, which triggers anger and retaliation. The battle, often in front of TV cameras—frequently becomes one of positioning for partisan advantage, rather than deliberative discussion and decision making.

Whereas in the past almost all rules were open or at least modified open, in this century three-quarters to four-fifths of all rules are restrictive.[40] Adopting a bipartisan approach to reform requires modifying the Rules Committee's "traffic cop" function and reducing the leaderships' influence and appointment powers. Unless assignments to Rules were to be merely random, however, someone has to appoint its members, and whoever does that will have influence. As always, the question pertains to the model one prefers.

The Senate

In the upper chamber, the majority leader has advantages.[41] Relying on the "right of first recognition" to speak, he controls the pace and scheduling of floor activity, usually needing some cooperation from the minority leader. He often can prevent unwanted amendments, and he has other powers delegated to him by his colleagues, Senate rules, or tradition. Nonetheless, individual senators have considerable autonomous power, using filibusters, holds (whereby one senator can prevent deliberation on a bill until his or her objections have been dealt with), and parliamentary tactics of all sorts to disrupt and obstruct majority strategy. The combination of individual members' prerogatives and party-centered tactics has altered the traditional flow of the legislative process. Genuine policy-based deliberation, at least on the floors of the House and Senate, scarcely exists because debaters do little more than talk past each other in platitudes.[42] Unorthodox lawmaking has replaced textbook lawmaking, with consequences for the deliberative and responsive nature of Congress.[43]

Of all procedures that upset people, the Senate filibuster and its junior cousin, the "hold," are notorious. Critics see filibusters as undemocratic and obstructionist, whereas defenders cite the need to slow down and improve Senate deliberation, the value of protecting the minority, and the protection of small states.[44] They argue that members passionately concerned about an issue should have more say than those with only passive interest. If Congress wants to make fundamental changes that affect the entire nation—civil rights is the classic example—it should pass such laws only with large bipartisan majorities. Originally, senators placed holds on bills or on confirmation votes for presidential appointments because they were not ready to vote. Today, the more common motives are to delay, to hint at a filibuster, to block action, or to gain bargaining leverage—often on unrelated matters.

Filibusters on legislation were relatively rare until the 1970s and were reserved for the most profound of issues. Measuring the number or threat of filibusters by the number of cloture petitions—petitions introduced by 16 members that, if approved by 60 votes, end a filibuster—reveals an interesting history. From 1917 (when Rule 22 instituted the cloture petition) to 1970, there were 58 cloture petitions filed, an average of 2.9 per Congress. From 1971 to 1990, there were 365, an average of 36.5. From 1991 through 2012, the comparable number was 954, or 86.7 per Congress. In 2013–2014 alone, 253 petitions were filed.[45] Filibusters against presidential executive and judicial nominations have skyrocketed. In President Obama's first five years in office, there were more cloture motions on nominations than in all previous years combined since

1968, when the practice began. The threat of filibusters has become so routine that almost all unanimous consent agreements—the Senate's procedural equivalent of a House rule that specifies the duration and nature of the debate and amending process—include a provision that 60 votes are needed to pass a bill or even to proceed to consider it. Even when cloture is invoked, the Senate can be exposed to another 30 hours of debate on the measure; and once the Senate has passed a bill, objectors can filibuster the motion to send it to a conference committee to iron out differences between House and Senate versions.

Honoring a hold is at the discretion of the majority leader, and under recent reforms holds must be made public after three days; but leaders never deny a hold, and the rules on transparency can be evaded if several members team up to put successive holds on the same measure. In the past, filibusters could bring Senate business to a halt; for decades, however, Senate leaders have resorted to a multitrack system in which the Senate simultaneously considers a number of pieces of legislation. If one is subject to a filibuster, it is shoved aside until some compromise is reached, and the Senate proceeds to the other bills.

Majority leaders confront filibusters in other ways. They can divide or combine bills or add controversial bills to "must-pass" legislation. They sometimes can bypass normal procedures, taking bills to conference with the House, where essentially new legislation is written. More dramatically, they can retaliate by cutting off the minority's ability to offer amendments by "filling the amendment tree." Senate rules limit how deep the amending process may go (generally one can amend a bill, amend the amendment, offer a substitute bill, and amend the substitute—no more). Because they control the floor, majority leaders can offer or allow their colleagues to offer all allowable amendments. The minority is shut out. As soon as the leader fills the tree, he files a cloture motion to attack any filibuster that might arise on the amendments. From a leadership perspective, this merely is a way to expedite action and prevent minority obstructionism; from the minority's perspective, this denies their participation in lawmaking and protects majority party members from having to vote on tough issues raised by the minority. This sort of action–reaction–retaliation–reaction cycle is one of the causes of the Senate's current problems.

One other maneuver is common, using the budget process to enact legislation that otherwise would be filibustered. The 1974 Budget and Impoundment Control Act included a provision for reconciling the "official" congressional budget passed early in the year with projected spending requirements of certain existing laws. Reconciliation bills are not subject to filibuster, meaning that a bare majority of senators can pass them. Leaders have found ways to shoehorn all sorts of legislative provisions into reconciliation bills, including, in 2010, key aspects of the Obama health insurance bill that had been negotiated with the House leaders. The "Byrd" rule, named after the late senator Robert Byrd (D-WV), forbids extraneous matters from being included in reconciliation bills, but leaders have found ways around it.

White House and the Capitol: Can They Work Together?

Focusing only on Congress misses much of what affects that body. At the other end of Pennsylvania Avenue resides the president; their interactions and battles explain success and failure in governing. Who initiates policy? Who should have the final say? How can the two branches work together more effectively? Can the institutional and partisan impasse be broken? These questions are grist for chapter 11's mills, but they surely shape congressional activity.

9.7 FIXING THE PROBLEMS: REFORMING CONGRESS

There has been no dearth of reform efforts. From 1961 to 2004, one scholar counted about three dozen proposals covering just about everything.[46] Proposals continue to flow generously. Reforms are tricky because any proposal designed to address one aspect of congressional operations could undermine others. Thinking about reform requires engagement with the perspectives of the last chapter. How can the system best foster the ideal blend of effectiveness, efficiency, accountability, representation, responsiveness, and deliberative decision making? Which branch—presidency, Congress, or both jointly—should dominate policy making? What are the means of so doing—strong parties and partisanship, weak parties and bipartisanship, or non-partisan behavior? What reforms are needed for members, structures, processes, and interbranch relationships to implement these choices? The framework for the analysis is pictured in Table 9.1. The reader's task is to fill the cells with appropriate reforms.

Members of Congress
Reforms to change member behavior cluster into five categories:

- "Throw the bums out" and bring in a "new breed" of congressmen;
- Reduce partisanship and ideological extremism;
- End the perpetual campaigning and fundraising; focus members on policy making, overseeing the executive bureaucracy, and representing and serving constituents;
- Restore decency, civility, and honor; and
- Ensure integrity and high ethical standards.

Turnover. Turnover can be achieved naturally, via election results, or artificially, via term limits. Turnover from elections, resignations, and retirements is significant. From 1992 through 2012, an average of almost 63 House members, about 14.5 percent, left by these means in each election cycle. The Senate averaged almost 11 departures per cycle; one must go back to 1990 to find fewer than 8.[47] When the 114th Congress convened in January 2014, the House had 70 members who were not there 2 years earlier and the Senate 16. The average length of service in the House in the 112th Congress (2011–2013) was just under 10 years, down a bit from the previous seven Congresses; close to half had fewer than 6 years of experience. In the Senate, the average service was 1.9 terms (under 12 years), down from century-long averages. For some critics, these are insufficient. More importantly, those departures have not often changed party control of specific seats and even less often altered the voting patterns of the occupants of those seats. The solution, it is argued, is to limit member's length of service, usually in the form of a 12-year maximum.

Table 9.1 Reforming Congress—An Analytical Perspective

INSTITUTIONAL PRIMACY →	PRESIDENTIAL PRIMACY		CONGRESSIONAL PRIMACY		CONSTITUTIONAL BALANCE	
Control of Congress by → **Source of problem in need of reform ↓**	Presidentially led strong national parties	Bipartisan or nonpartisan majorities	Congressionally led strong national parties	Bipartisan or nonpartisan majorities	Two separate strong parties*	Bipartisan or nonpartisan majorities
Members						
Structures						
Processes						
Interbranch relations						

*Extremely unlikely, probably impossible, scenario: strong national parties focused on presidential elections functioning alongside separate congressionally centered parties focused on congressional elections and internal governance of Congress

Term Limits and Their Effects

Proponents of term limits claim that limits would accomplish the following:

- Limit the power of incumbency, injecting more competition into elections and thus moderating the winners;
- Bring to Washington "fresh faces" and "citizen legislators" with new ideas who are untarnished by political machinations and partisanship;
- Break the bonds between interest groups and members of Congress;
- Reduce the influence of party leaders on members;
- Improve representation;
- Reduce excessive focus on re-election and end perpetual campaigning by fostering a willingness to serve a bit and then depart in favor of another generation of legislators;
- Establish a greater sense of trusteeship with its focus on national problems;
- Change the inefficient operating procedures within the two chambers; and
- End budgetary impasses and deficit spending and put the government's fiscal house in order.

Despite some contradictions, the arguments are seductive. The president and 36 governors are term limited, so what is sauce for the executive goose should be sauce for the legislative gander. Several states sought to impose limits on U.S. senators and representatives, but the Supreme Court deemed such legislation unconstitutional. Term limits have received favorable support from at least 60 percent of the public for decades, rising into the 70 percent range at times.[48] Given voters' propensity to re-elect incumbents, such support seems strangely inconsistent. People think that *other* members of Congress should be booted out, not their own.

The assumptions behind congressional term limits do not lack for challenges. Leaving aside why one would want amateur citizen legislators in the hotbed of Washington politics—imagine a "citizen surgeon" operating on one's spine, a "citizen accountant" doing one's taxes, or a "citizen quarterback" in the Super Bowl—and forgetting for a moment that Congress just might need members with institutional loyalty and memory of how things used to work, it is worth considering who would be the likely replacements for term-limited members. For Senate elections, the most common serious candidate is a veteran of the House of Representatives, a governor, or a senior state legislator. There are exceptions, especially in recent years and especially on the Republican side, but the pattern is clear. The House is somewhat different. In House primaries, relatively or totally inexperienced amateurs outnumber politicians, as seen in the spate of doctors, dentists, and pizza store owners who emerged, sometimes successfully, as candidates in 2010 and 2012.[49] Indeed, the propensity of state legislators to challenge incumbents has diminished over time, as the value of state legislative positions grew more attractive.[50] Nonetheless, it is the experienced politician who most often wins, not the political newbie; and there is little reason to think this pattern will change with term limits. Although a few citizen-legislators succeed, one should anticipate the continued flow of professional politicians to Capitol Hill.

Term limits by definition would increase competition *at the end of incumbents' terms when seats become open.* Open seats always attract strategic politicians who fare much better than amateurs. However, there would be little real competition in the intervening elections. Decisions by professionals to challenge incumbents are taken carefully, and they are reduced in rough proportion to the incumbents' electoral success in the previous election. Perhaps "termed-out" state legislators might be inclined to compete in congressional elections before the federal representative's term ends, but that is uncertain at best. If they did compete, there likely would be a crowding-out effect in which state legislators displace other qualified candidates in congressional races. The net effect on competition probably is a wash.[51] An interesting consequence of term limits likely will be that, at redistricting time, those doing the redistricting will target the districts of termed-out members to further partisan goals. Such seems to be the case in the states.[52]

It is not obvious that intense competition in any given—most likely 12th-year—election automatically will produce a more moderate winner. Since most constituencies are strongly red or blue, competition in the primaries would be intense, emphasizing ideological purity. Thus the candidates in general elections would more likely represent party extremes. As for eagerness to "serve and depart," one must be suspicious. On the one hand, it is not self-evident that a parade of short-term legislators facilitates good government. Legislators in states and localities with term limits are learning that experience and expertise fall victim to turnover.[53] On the other hand, few professionals eagerly leave Washington; if they cannot run for Congress again, they might well choose to follow the well-established pattern of joining lobbying firms or interest groups. Does that enhance their legislative productivity in a positive fashion? Amateurs coming to Washington are not immune to "Potomac fever" either; far from all of them would be eager to leave the Capitol after ingesting the water.

House newcomers may be less aligned with and dependent on interest groups, but it is almost certain that they benefited from interest group money during their campaigns, thus opening or solidifying the channels of communication with the groups. Once in office, they certainly come to rely on interest groups for information and electoral help, as do veterans. As for ushering in reforms of legislative procedures, prospects are unclear. Mavericks such as some Tea Party types come not to legislate but to protest and obstruct; they care little about procedural reform that would increase efficiency. Inexperienced but serious newcomers need time to learn the ropes; if not, their eagerness to change could be destructive as much as constructive. Moreover, while acclimating themselves to Congress, they need guidance from veterans, probably party leaders—precisely those who support traditional procedures.

Will term limits affect how congressmen behave as their terms near their end? No one knows, but an interesting study of members of Congress in their last six months before leaving the House found that lame-duck representatives were four times as likely to miss roll-call votes as they had been before; and centrist members were likely to shift their votes either to the right or to the left. Absent re-election pressure, members can do what they wish. Whether that is good ("statesmen doing the right thing") or bad ("shirking" their representational obligations or currying favor with future employers) is for the reader to decide.[54]

Evidence from the States
One need not rely on speculation to evaluate term limits. Federalism provides state laboratories in which limits have been tested for almost 25 years. Fifteen states have

term limits for their state legislatures; and 6 had them but either repealed them or lost them to state supreme court rulings. The consequences of limits depend on the nature, size, and professionalism (salaries, length of legislative session, size of staff, terms of office, member seniority) of the legislature being studied. Furthermore, findings depend on when the studies were done; impressive early effects often fade as legislative leaders, staffs, lobbyists, and governors adapt. Young renegades become seasoned veterans. Caution is advised: most studies are based on surveys of legislators, which are notoriously slippery. Furthermore, states differ; there is a world of difference between Congress and California's legislature and between New York's and Montana's.

Overall, the experience of the states has *not* supported the hopes of term-limit advocates. There is no persuasive evidence that term limits have improved state governing effectiveness and efficiency, strengthened reasoned deliberation and decision making, or enhanced representation, responsiveness, or accountability.[55] Disaster has not occurred, and some good things have happened, but the case is far from persuasive.

Membership. Turnover has increased, but term limits have not filled legislatures with citizen legislators and have not had a noticeable effect beyond national trends on the racial, gender, or occupational backgrounds of legislators. They have not significantly affected competitiveness (and may have reduced it for most elections); have not noticeably enhanced voter turnout; have not weakened the power of incumbency at election time; and generally have not "turned over" seats from one party to the other. Typically, successful candidates for the state legislature remain the professional politicians. In professionalized legislatures, termed-out legislators, as well as many nearing their limits, tend to run for the other chamber, local or county offices, or statewide positions.

Behavior and Performance. Term limits do seem to affect legislators' behavior, often inclining them toward a trustee model in which they are less concerned with the particularistic policy, pork, and service desires of their districts and more focused on statewide issues and matters they deem important. The correspondence between a state's (not individual constituencies') aggregate policy preferences and legislators' voting records is stronger in term-limited states. How much of that is attributable to legislators' eyeing their next elected state position is unknown but not implausible. On the other hand, there is little evidence that term limits affect the volume of legislative activity, especially bills passed. Legislators remain no less interested in campaigning, getting re-elected, and looking for postlegislative careers.

Institutional Power. Greater turnover means losing experience and expertise, and that can affect respect for legislative procedures and power centers. Party leaders in term-limited legislatures serve for short periods of time. To compensate, some state legislative party leaders have sought to develop a career ladder, grooming the next round of leaders. Effects vary. Where leadership powers were substantial, term limits seem to have weakened them; where leadership powers were weak, there has not been much change or there has been a strengthening. Depending on the state particulars, term-limited members believe either that they don't need leadership help or that leaders cannot deliver what they need (because the leaders themselves are limited); or, recognizing their inexperience, they are more inclined to take guidance from the elected leadership.

The loss of committee veterans undermines the power and institutional memory of legislative committees. Term limit–induced turnover undercuts legislative professionalism and the benefits it brings, including comity and civility. If legislators are less expert and less specialized, the power and influence of legislative staffs should gain, at least in those legislatures like Congress, where staffs are strong and large. Evidence is mixed. Much depends on the state, with staffs becoming busier but sometimes less competent when member turnover induces greater staff turnover. Overall, most studies conclude, staffs have grown in importance.

External Forces. The influence of lobbyists seems to have grown, although not everywhere. Lobbyists report having to work harder and longer as dependence on them for information has increased. More certain is the effect of limits on legislative–executive relations. Term-limited legislatures play a lesser role in crafting state budgets than do others. They experience fewer gubernatorial vetoes, perhaps because governors get their way on legislation or have crafted their proposals to account for legislative preferences. Term-limited legislatures seem less inclined to oversee the bureaucracy and to press career civil servants who know that, long after the legislators are gone, they will still be in their offices. The result is a subtle shift of power toward the executive.

Policy Consequences. A couple dozen studies find no hard evidence that policy making has changed because of term limits, although it does appear that it may have become less predictable and perhaps a bit sloppier in some term-limited states. The influx of new legislators seems to bring efforts at innovative legislation, but their inexperience and lack of know-how doom their efforts. Despite fears that term limits would lead to members' pursuing short-run solutions and quick fixes or to a focus on "big splash" items, it does not appear to have happened. On the other hand, there is some evidence that newcomers under term limits introduce and spend time promoting legislation that repeats previously considered and rejected measures. Term-limited states fare relatively less well fiscally than others, spending more, having lower budget balances, and suffering lower bond ratings. Again, however, these findings do not apply everywhere, may be spurious, may be a function of methodology, and thus have been disputed.[56]

Despite the public's favorable view of term limits, term-limited state legislatures receive no more favorable public approval than those that are not. Voter turnout has been unaffected, but in some states campaign spending has risen. Speculatively, assuming that Democrats are more inclined to build political and legislative careers than are Republicans, by diminishing the traditional legislative career path, term limits might favor the party (usually Republicans) that is less oriented toward careerism in legislatures. Whether this would apply to Congress is unlikely, given its higher prestige.

To conclude, term limits on balance appear to have weakened legislatures, probably more so in the lower chambers than in the upper ones. The effects depend on a host of factors, especially the stringency of the term limits (length of allowed service, eligibility to seek a seat later on in the same chamber or in the other one) and the level of the legislature's professionalization before limits were enacted. The lessons for reformers of Congress are not absolutely clear, but in general they suggest that term limits would not solve that body's ills, would not make for much if any improvement, and could well inflict damage, rendering it weaker relative to the presidency and executive branch and quite possibly more dependent on staffs and interest groups. There is little to worry about, however, because the likelihood of imposing term limits on Congress is slim to nonexistent. A constitutional amendment, or a reversal of the 1995 *U.S. Term Limits v. Thornton* Supreme Court case, would be required, and neither is in the offing.

Member Behavior

Little can be done to change human nature, but reforms might give sociability a boost. One proposal is to construct or purchase several apartment buildings for members to rent at reasonable, probably subsidized, rates, thus encouraging them to move their families to the Capitol without such negative financial consequences. How this would play with taxpayers is predictable, but a concentrated effort at persuasion and strong bipartisan backing might make it possible. A common proposal is to change the work schedule in both chambers. The Senate in the 1980s planned to try a three-week-on and one-week-off schedule, but members clung to their Tuesday-to-Thursday schedule. In 2007 Democrats proclaimed a five-day work week that met some success but faded away; and in 2011 the House Republican leadership announced a two-week-on one-week-off schedule that came under fire from Democrats because it put the House schedule out of synch with the Senate's and led to low productivity.[57] Back home, members meet constituents, raise campaign money, and engage in media and public relations events.

Schedule changes might incline members to bring their families to Washington, perhaps inducing a degree of comity and civility to help grease the legislative wheels. A schedule change might help solve the workload problem that today crams a lot of activity into those few days each week and results in long sessions, long and complex omnibus bills, poorly attended floor proceedings and debates, and the devastating year-end crush. Aligning House and Senate schedules would be beneficial as well. Short of increasing time on the job, the only other way to address the problem of institutional overload is to restrict the numbers of bills that may be introduced, as several state legislatures have done, or put limits on the number of measures reported out of committee. One can predict many "exceptions" to such rules.

Most members resent having to spend so much time hustling campaign dollars. The reforms in chapter 7 address this problem, but there is little chance of enactment. Extending House terms to four years might reduce some of the money-raising pressure, giving representatives a bit more time to focus on their duties. A bigger problem is ideological extremism, which on an individual basis is hardly subject to controls. Structuring elections in a fashion to reduce partisanship—using the top-two runoff system, for example—might make a difference, but experience in California and Washington is insufficient to make that claim.

The bottom line is that changing member behavior is probably impossible to do legislatively or constitutionally. Nor is public pressure likely to make a difference. The public perceives widespread corruption and weak ethics among senators and representatives, but people tend to love their own members.[58] The consequences of any reform designed to alter behavior are likely to be many and unforeseen. What is called for is a greater sense of personal responsibility, decency, accommodation, and courage. In today's ideological and polarized political world, where members represent their constituents all too well and face incredible scheduling pressures, that may be too much to ask.

Get Your Tools and Fix the Structures!

Add Senate Seats. Short of abolishing the Senate or stripping it of meaningful powers, one reform has drawn attention: enlarge the Senate by giving bigger states more seats. At the constitutional convention, Charles Pinckney proposed a sliding scale that would do just that. Small states, naturally, resisted. More recently, Larry J. Sabato proposed giving the 10 largest states two additional senators and the next 15 one each, bringing the number of senators to 135.[59] Not only would this improve the Senate's representational character and prevent senators representing a small portion of the citizenry from being able to block those representing the vast majority, but also it would help distribute the workload. With members having fewer committee and sub-committee responsibilities, they would have more opportunities to learn the details of legislation and to engage more carefully in overseeing the executive branch. Adding to the number of senators might improve responsiveness to constituents and counter the tendency of senators to see and listen to only some of the subconstituencies back home.[60] In addition, Sabato would give former presidents and vice presidents seats as "national senators" who could bring different perspectives and experience to bear. Alternatively, national senators might be elected on a national at-large ballot. The model for this is the mixed representational system found in many cities wherein some city council members are elected from and oriented toward their districts (think states), whereas others are elected at large to focus on broader citywide (national) matters and interests.

The scheme intrigues but raises problems. Adding one or two senators would not yield truly fair representation—California and Wyoming would still differ—although it would improve matters. Second, the plan conflicts with the federal rationale for state equality. How important that is depends on one's view of federalism. Third, a larger Senate does nothing to reclaim the already lost tradition of reasoned floor debate and deliberation, to enhance comity and civility, or to reduce or better manage partisan squabbles. With more members, the Senate might come to resemble the House, with its strident partisanship and dependence on centralized leadership. What happens when the population of one of the larger states is surpassed by that of an-other; must it give up one of its senators? Fourth, more senators means more campaign spending, with all that entails.

An alternative is weighted voting—giving each senator a number of votes proportional to his or her state's population. That would promote "majority rule" and might reduce the inefficient state-by-state distribution of federal spending. A radical proposal is to change the very principle of representation. Instead of representing the populations of the states, suppose the Senate's constituencies were reconstituted as a single multimember nationwide district, with 33 or 34 members elected every two years, either using a proportional representation party list system or allowing voting for individual candidates. Revisiting chapter 4 might be worthwhile to think about the consequences. For example, with a high minimum threshold for victory, the dominance of the two major parties would continue; lowering it might elect an occasional third-party senator. For any of these proposals, a constitutional amendment would be required; but that is essentially impossible because the Constitution guarantees each state two senators and forbids amendments that would deprive any state of equal suffrage in the Senate without its consent. An amendment changing that provision would have to be passed by three-quarters of the states, including those whose relative influence in the Senate would be diminished. There is one intriguing argument on this score. Only 13 states constituted the original union; all others were creatures of the federal government and arguably do not have quite the same claims to sovereignty—or, some argue, even to equal representation in the Senate.[61]

Enlarge the House. There are at least six arguments for enlarging the House of Representatives. If, as Kristina C. Miler has shown, members perceive and are attentive to only about a third of their constituencies,[62] reducing the size of districts by increasing their number makes it easier for legislators to engage more constituents. That improves representation, policy and service responsiveness, and dyadic accountability. Perhaps public approval of Congress might improve.

Second, with more seats, any given state's districts come closer to matching the average size of districts in other states. Third, more seats probably mean that minority groups will have a greater say in the election of some members and be able to send more of their own to Washington. Fourth, adding seats means fairer representation (and maybe more federal money) for larger states. Fifth, the added numbers ease some of the representational crudeness of the Electoral College that gives smaller states greater influence than their populations warrant. Finally, adding members implies a workload reduction for each, allowing more time to read, think, attend committee meetings, deliberate, debate, and interact with colleagues—or, alas, to spend more time on fundraising and media appearances. How many seats would be appropriate? Brian Frederick, for one, thinks that 675 representatives would be about right, following the "cube root law" that sets the size of the average constituency as the cube root of the general population—which seems to be the international standard for lower chambers of legislatures.[63]

Arguments abound in opposition.[64] Modern transportation and communication, for example, already handle the problems of connecting people to their representatives. Additional seats will constrain members' ability to speak on the floor. Coalition building, already difficult across the party divide and across the multiplicity of constituency interests coast to coast, probably will be more difficult. The tasks of leadership become more complicated. Getting to know and understand one's fellow legislators already is impossible; adding hundreds more makes it harder. Committees, often too large for efficient participation, will have to grow in size or number, undermining deliberative efficiency and leading to pressures to create more subcommittees to give each member a chance to play some important role. With smaller, probably more homogeneous constituencies—almost certainly more purely liberal or conservative—partisanship, ideological rigidity, and narrowness of focus likely will increase, detracting from effectiveness and deliberative judgment.

Finally, additional members mean additional costs. Based on current expenditures for running the House, every additional seat will cost about $3 million.[65] For 675 members, the added operating costs approach three-quarters of a billion dollars. Moreover, the House chamber must be expanded; additional office buildings must be constructed; and committee rooms require remodeling. More members undoubtedly will fuel the lobbying industry, and the "care and feeding" of members of Congress by executive agencies will require more employees and expenditures.

Few members of Congress have thought the matter important; one can count on a single hand the number who have cosponsored a bill as mild as mandating a study of the size of the House.[66] The public does not seem overly enamored of the idea of expansion either.[67] In sum, the proposal to grow the House pits the values of better representation, local accountability, and responsiveness against those of effectiveness, efficiency, and deliberative judgment. Whether it strengthens or weakens Congress relative to the presidency is an open question. One might think of the opposite approach, a *reduction* in the size of the House. Increasing the size and therefore heterogeneity of constituencies could enrich electoral competition and force members to balance a greater variety of constituent views and interests—more like the Senate. Moderation might ensue. As each member becomes more important, constituents' attention to them might become more acute.

House Districts and Gerrymandering

Who Should Draw the Maps? There must be a better way to skin the redistricting cat, a thesis that raises two questions: who should do the redistricting and what should be their objectives? Most reformers advocate removing the drawing of constituency lines from the hands of politicians. Some think that civil servants should do the job, as in Britain. Others argue for judges to do it, as they often do when legislatures and governors cannot agree or when a redistricting plan is judged to discriminate against minorities. Some advocate for a neutral computer algorithm to solve the problems. Still others think that having at-large elections, or having just a handful of multimember districts in large states, would eliminate the problems. Probably the most popular solution is to establish independent, non-, or bipartisan bodies for the task.

Computer algorithms depend on assumptions, and they can be manipulated to achieve whatever goals their designers wish. Garbage in, garbage out. Letting judges do the job injects the judiciary into politics even more than it already is; and why assume that judges are nonpolitical? In many states they are elected, often after tendentious partisan contests; those who are appointed are chosen by political governors and confirmed by political legislators.

Letting civil servants do the job assumes that they have no partisan interests or that they could set such inclinations aside. In Iowa, the officially nonpartisan Legislative Service Agency (the legislature's bill-drafting service) draws the maps, which the legislature votes up or down, with no amendments. If after three tries the legislature has not agreed, the Iowa Supreme Court undertakes the job—which it has not had to do since the system was adopted. Civil servants, like politicians, must follow guidelines set down by law as to what are the priorities to be sought.

Forty-two states rely on the legislative process to draw the lines, putting the careers of U.S. representatives at the mercy of state legislators and governors. Some rely on special commissions to advise the legislature or to undertake the redistricting task. Five states employ backup commissions in case the normal process fails. In six states—Alaska, Arizona, California, Idaho, Montana, and Washington—the commissions are independent. All sorts of restrictions and rules dictate how the commissions work, and no two states do it exactly the same way.[68] Commissioners usually are appointed by combinations of legislative leaders, governors, Supreme Court justices, and others. Even nonpartisan commissions, however, are subject to political considerations. Most states specify a balance of Democrats and Republicans plus a tie breaker. The questions then become who gets that job and who selects the tiebreaker? Randomly selecting a citizen does not guarantee nonpartisanship. In New Jersey, the chief justice of the supreme court selects the "odd" commissioner, but judges cannot always be counted on to be impartial. Asking the appointed Democrats and Republicans to pick a neutral tie breaker has worked, but it could easily lead to deadlock. In Arizona, the Commission on Appellate Court Appointees creates a pool of 25 nominees, 10 from each of the two largest parties and 5 others. The top 4 party leaders of the legislature choose 1 commissioner each, and these appoint a fifth from the pool to serve as chair. That person, however, may not be a member of any party already represented on the commission. If the 4 deadlock, the Appellate Commission appoints the chair. Hawaii has a similar plan. In late 2014, the Arizona legislature sued to invalidate the commission approach on the grounds that the initiative that created it deprived the legislature of its constitutional authority; the Supreme Court will rule on it in 2015. California in 2008 adopted an even more interesting twist that was put into play after the 2010 census: a 14-member commission that must include 5 Democrats, 5 Republicans, and 4 members from neither party. A state government auditor selects 60 "qualified" registered voters from an applicant pool from which legislative leaders may strike names. The auditor then picks 8 commission members by lot, and those commissioners pick 6 additional members. Final approval of any districting map requires votes from 3 Democratic commissioners, 3 Republican commissioners, and 3 of the others.

Do commissions produce better results? Scholars have gone fishing in this pond and have caught a promising, if mixed, bag. One study, for example, shows that the use of commissions correlates with lower levels of partisanship in the voting behavior of representatives from commission-designed districts.[69] Another finds that commission-drawn plans survive judicial scrutiny better than legislatively built ones.[70] A third concludes that commission-drawn districts increased the likelihood that incumbents faced opposition, often by strong challengers. Electoral margins did not drop, however, and there was no increase in incumbent defeats.[71] These findings could be attributable to the particular states and years under study; and of course correlation does not equate with causality. Across the board, commission-drawn districts do not seem to be much more competitive than others; incumbents are not more likely to lose in this type of district than in others.[72] The new California system created a dozen open seat districts for the 2012 elections; put a third of the state's U.S. representatives into districts represented by other incumbents, forcing incumbents to compete against each other; changed the constituency makeup, sometimes radically, in many districts; and apparently caused some representatives to drop out of the races. Competition overall increased, which in turn seems to have led to higher spending than would otherwise be predicted.[73]

There are no guarantees about any particular results. A perfectly balanced commission is as likely to protect both parties' incumbents as to draw districts that would be highly competitive. In sum, the jury is still out. Meanwhile, some scholars maintain that it is preferable to put the responsibility squarely in the hands of elected officials, state legislators, who can be removed by the voters if they do a poor job of redistricting.[74] That is a nice idea, but how many voters will reward or punish an incumbent for her vote several years ago on such an obscure matter?

What Goals Should Be Emphasized? The goals to be pursued in redistricting are clear. Districts should: (1) be equal in population, (2) be compact and contiguous, (3) not harm racial minorities and not waste their votes by spreading them thinly across several districts, and/or should provide districts in which they can elect their own representatives, and (4) respect existing political boundaries and preserve communities of interest.[75] Some states (5) seek to maximize competition. District designers often seek (6) to protect incumbents, or at least keep them in districts in which they reside, and (7) to maximize one or the other party's number of seats in a state. These objectives are not compatible. One must prioritize, and that is where things become interesting. Keeping communities of interest together usually conflicts with the goal of competition. To ensure sound prospects of electing a black or Hispanic candidate or to give incumbents the best shot at re-election, districts must concentrate their supporters, which implies boundaries that violate the compactness requirement and "loading up" other districts with the other parties' supporters. To foster competition in strongly Democratic urban or strongly Republican rural areas, district lines may have to stretch a long distance and cut across several city or county boundaries. So much for compactness or protecting communities of interest. Some criteria may not make sense. If the purpose of the exercise relates to *elections*, should not districts be composed of equal numbers of eligible or actual *voters* rather than equal numbers of *people*?

The ostensible purpose of creating as many competitive districts as possible is that such districts lead to better representation, responsiveness, accountability, and the election of moderates.[76] Several decades of political science research have tested that assumption, yielding rather ambiguous results. Recently, Thomas L. Brunell mounted a frontal challenge on both empirical and normative grounds.[77] He argues that the country needs more, not fewer, safe one-party districts. Homogeneous districts make for greater voter satisfaction because, since people like winning, there will be more people who supported the "winner" in any given district. Approval of one's member, and maybe of Congress, will be higher. Fewer votes get wasted because huge majorities will support their favorite candidate. The few who voted for the losing candidate would be better off in a neighboring district that elects the candidate of the party they prefer. For example, if the partisan proportions in a pair of 600,000 constituent districts were 80–20 Democratic and 80–20 Republican, 240,000 voters are disappointed; if the ratios are more competitive, say 55–45 in each, 540,000 lose and go unrepresented. Nonmajoritarian outcomes will be less likely because, in diverse and closely divided districts, independent or third-party candidates now deny the winners a majority. General elections should cost less, reducing the pressures for constant fundraising. Furthermore, at least conceivably, members who know they are safe might be freer to vote as trustees, on behalf of national priorities, than hew to the narrower wishes of thin majorities of their constituents. Finally, with fewer competitive districts, the swing ratio declines, leading to greater stability—small swings in voting behavior will less likely tip control of the House to the other party. Imagine a state roughly evenly divided between Democrats and Republicans that has five congressional districts. Creating two safe districts for each party means that one of the parties is sure to win 40 per of the seats—not radically different from its 50 percent share of voters. If all five districts are made competitive, four or all five could easily tip to one party in any election by narrow margins in each district, leaving the losing party with zero or perhaps 20 percent of the seats—far from its 50 percent share of voters. Which is the more representative system?

Some skepticism is in order. Safe districts are not immune from competition; the difference is that it usually occurs in the *primaries* and is intense because the winner is guaranteed victory in November. Depending on who votes, the primaries could produce extremist candidates, just as is the case in districts that are competitive overall. Turnout, notoriously low in primaries, would rise, as would spending. And if electoral safety is assured, what forces will keep representatives attentive to their constituents?

What information should mapmakers have when designing districts? Today's technology provides political and demographic data previously unavailable, thus making the task of gerrymandering much easier. What if those drawing district lines were denied political information, as in Iowa, for example, where the legislative staff that prepares the maps is not allowed to consider where incumbents live or how given neighborhoods voted in past elections? Under such a veil of ignorance, district designers might produce more diverse and competitive districts. Where partisans are concentrated, the mandates of "compact and contiguous" probably make for safe districts. Not knowing voting or demographic patterns, on the other hand, could make it difficult to follow the mandates of the Voting Rights Act and Justice Department rulings that call for taking care of minority groups. In the end, as is true for almost all reforms, there is no magic bullet that avoids negative consequences.

Prospects for Reform. There has been a slight trend in the direction of the nonpartisan commission-type system, supported by pressure from various "good government" groups. The most important cases of successful reform were the result of statewide initiatives and referendums, often triggered by egregious districting decisions; but more than half of the states do not allow that approach. It is possible that Congress might act under the authority of the Voting Rights Act or in response to a judicial order to push states to adopt independent commissions.[78] More likely, argues Heather K. Gerken, is an approach that takes advantage of politicians' self-interest and fear of embarrassment or lawsuits.[79] Citizens and organized groups should take advantage of software programs and census data to generate districting maps that lawmakers or the courts could adopt. She points to an Ohio redistricting contest that enticed residents to come up with alternative maps, producing sensible alternatives. Public opinion pressure might follow. She also advocates establishing model districting commissions that, with public fanfare and media attention, operate parallel to official state redistricting efforts, focusing a spotlight on the process, generating alternatives, and providing bases for lawsuits against official mapping plans—a prospect few governors and state legislators relish. Some foundations have picked up this idea, funding such experiments. But again, it is the assumptions and goals that go into a redistricting effort that determine the final effects. If reformers' goals are simplistic, and if their assumptions are wrong, so will be the consequences.

Repairing the Structure: The Committee System

Members and Chairs. At the heart of the reform agenda is a simple question: should each chamber of Congress function on a centralized and highly partisan basis or on a decentralized non- or bipartisan pattern? For those seeking the former, power must flow to the elected party leaders, and party leaders must be able to control and direct committee operations and floor procedure. They must control appointment of committee and subcommittee members. Oversized party ratios on committees favoring the majority party are in order, rather than making sure that committee membership reflects the party ratios in the parent chamber. That implies loading up committees in highly unrepresentative ways, subordinating members' goals to those of the parties, rewarding or punishing members by assignments, and controlling committees' agendas. Whatever the formal mechanisms for making assignments and picking chairs, in the end party leaders make the call. Under such a model, committee and subcommittee staffs will be party based, with majority and minority staffs serving their respective members.

For those preferring the opposite model, decentralizing power to committees and operating them on a bipartisan fashion is crucial. Former congressman Mickey Edwards wants nonpartisan and random committee selection to make all committees representative of their parent chambers. Perhaps committee membership should be subject to term limits to ensure turnover—although that can weaken institutional memory and member expertise. He suggests that each committee have a majority chair and a minority vice chair, the latter of whom could bring bills forward for committee consideration and could call his or her own witnesses at hearings. Chairs should be chosen democratically by supermajorities of their committees (or maybe the full chamber) to ensure bipartisan support and operations.[80] They should be term limited, as is now Republican practice. All staffs are to be nonpartisan, chosen on the basis of professional qualifications, and they serve members of both parties. Party leaders once again must defer to committees and their chairs for legislative initiative and for facilitating the legislative process across party lines.

The nature of subcommittees becomes relevant. The argument for greater independence for subcommittees is built on a need for expertise and specialization, norms that once characterized the House and, to a degree, the Senate. However, subcommittees are small and less representative; and the number of active participants in subcommittee activity generally is small. Broader, larger, and more representative committees counter subcommittee narrowness and bring numerous perspectives to bear. Committee chairs have a stake in making sure that whatever comes out of their committees can pass on the floor, and thus they have a strong incentive to produce high-quality legislation that, ideally, has support from members of both parties. That, of course, means that party leaders may not get from the committees what they want.

Jurisdictional Reforms. To promote effectiveness and efficiency in the bipartisan model, it makes sense to balance committee workload and authority, rationalize jurisdictional overlap, and reduce turf battles. Under a partisan approach, doing so is not as important; sometimes leaders like to have differences among committees to give them flexibility in their efforts to drive partisan legislative agendas—not to mention using assignments to reward loyal members and punish wayward ones. House leaders sometimes overcome committee squabbles by writing and promoting their own legislation, either before or after committees have acted.

The creation of more joint committees may offer possibilities. Currently there are four (Library, Printing, Taxation, and Economic), only one of which actually holds hearings and issues reports (the Joint Economic Committee). In the past, members sometimes have proposed such panels to deal with new matters that did not fit the jurisdictions of standing committees. The last successful example of a joint committee was the Joint Committee on Atomic Energy after World War II. Advocates of the partisan model of Congress probably find joint committees problematical because, if not tightly controlled—House and Senate leaders would have to agree—such units could develop considerable clout and autonomy. Those interested in nonpartisanship or bipartisanship might welcome such committees as a solution to jurisdictional squabbling, to facilitate policy making when each party controls one chamber, and/or as a way of creating a counterforce to party leaders. Arguably, joint committees can offer greater efficiency in terms of time, staff resources, and coordination; and their mixed membership might enhance their deliberative capabilities. Interestingly, few reformers even consider this option; and even fewer senators and representatives push it.

Reform of the leadership depends on the preferred model. The roles of the speaker constitute an inherent conflict. On the one hand, he or she is supposed to be the presiding officer and symbol of the chamber, ensuring fairness, dignity, and efficiency. On the other hand, the speaker is the elected leader of his or her party. Mickey Edwards wants the speaker to be nominated by a bipartisan group, with 60 or more percent of the votes of all the chamber's members required for election.[81] Indeed, he proposes to remodel the House chamber so that Republicans and Democrats no longer are separated by an aisle. He advocates having only one lectern in the House to be shared by both parties, rather than one on each party's side of the chamber, and eliminating separate cloakrooms to force members to mingle across party divisions while waiting to proceed to the floor. A series of bipartisan retreats and social events, he thinks, will encourage members to see each other as people, not "wearers of the letter D or R."

New Congressional Procedures
In the Senate. Filibuster reform for years stood atop most reform agendas but failed because few senators wanted to eliminate the right of "extended debate." Even members of the majority party appreciate the fact that someday they will be in the minority and may want to filibuster. Several reform proposals have attracted attention. One is to constrain filibusters or lengthy holds by exempting certain kinds of legislation from the threat. Finding objective criteria to define such measures, however, is tricky. Perhaps some dollar amount, number of people affected, or a bill's relevance to fundamental rights is the answer. Another proposal is to allow only one filibuster per bill, ending the current situation that allows filibusters on the motion to proceed, on amendments, on the bill itself, and on a motion to go to conference with the House.

Under current procedures, filibusterers need only announce their intention to filibuster or object to a unanimous consent request for consideration of a bill and, presto, they've won the day, as the majority leader moves on to another subject. If they actually engage in a traditional talkathon, it is up to the leader to have 50 members ready to respond to a quorum call because the filibusters would love nothing more than to have to recess the Senate for lack of a quorum. They then can go home, enjoy a nice dinner and sleep, and then return the next day refreshed and ready to continue talking. Thus the suggestion: change Rule 22 to allow three-fifths of senators *present and voting*, rather than the currently required 60 senators, to invoke cloture on legislation and allow cloture petitions to be brought up on the floor at any time, with a short lay-over (two or three hours), rather than the current two days. The burden then shifts and forces filibusterers to hold the floor out of fear of a sudden 60 percent cloture motion—even if it were only 60 percent of 50 members—and talk until they give up out of sheer exhaustion. A related idea is to require 41 affirmative votes to maintain a filibuster in the face of a challenge by, say, one-fifth of the members present. Holding "real" filibusters at the end of a session still will kill legislation because, given congres-sional calendars, so much of what is important gets settled in the last few weeks. On top of that, dyed-in-the-wool filibusterers won't give up. Indeed, their behavior might look like heroism to their constituents and Washington allies.[82]

Reformers such as former Senator Tom Harkin (D-IA) urge the establishment of a sliding scale of votes needed to invoke cloture. Sixty votes would be required to impose cloture at first; then the number of votes needed drops to 57 for a few days, then to 55, 53, and eventually only to 51. The rationale addresses one of the supposed purposes of the filibuster, namely, to ensure adequate debate while driving the Senate to a final vote. The reform is not without flaws.[83] For example, the time required to ratchet down to 51 votes for constructive debate could be put to better uses, and for those concerned with protecting minority rights, the proposal is anathema.

Presidential appointments now are protected from filibusters. Employing a tactic known as the "nuclear option," the then Senate majority leader Harry Reid (D-NV) changed the rules in November 2013. On a nomination for an appeals court seat, Reid raised a point of order to assert that only a majority is needed to confirm appointees other than Supreme Court justices. The presiding officer at the time, Vermont senator Patrick Leahy, ruled against Reid, who appealed the ruling. Requiring only a majority of senators, the appeal succeeded, 52–48, effectively ending the 60-vote cloture precedent. In the end, absent further invocation of the "nuclear option" to end or limit filibusters on normal legislative matters—which has been threatened—changing Senate Rule 22 prob-ably is impossible, since it requires a two-thirds vote of senators present and voting.

As discussed above, one cause of, or response to, obstructionism is the majority leader's practice of preventing the minority party from offering amendments. Limit-ing the majority leader's ability to fill the amendment tree would be in order, as would guaranteeing by rule that a certain number of amendments may be offered by the minority if supported by, perhaps, five senators for each. Holds on legislation can be constrained by forcing senators who want to delay legislation to object publicly to unanimous consent agreements or to engineer a cloture-proof coalition to block a bill's consideration. At the very least, any trace of anonymity could be ended. Curtail-ing the practice of holds requires courage on the part of majority leaders, and it might even cost them their jobs.

House Procedures. Unlike the Senate, where the minority or even an individual can engage in obstructionist tactics, in the House the danger is just the opposite: ma-jorities can run roughshod over minorities. Advocates of strong party government do not object, but many others do, and they propose remedies to prevent the Rules Committee from manufacturing closed rules to frustrate the minority's efforts to amend legislation.[84] For example, requiring a supermajority, say 60 percent, to adopt any restrictive special rule governing legislation might incline the Rules Committee to allow amendments. Some have suggested that Rules Committee membership be divided equally between the parties, thus preventing unfair decisions. Perhaps a permanent rule change allowing consideration in the Committee of the Whole of any germane amendment that had a minimum number of co-sponsors—perhaps 50 or 100—could work. Another idea is to guarantee the minority party the ability to offer at least one or two first-order amendments to any pending bill. All these would open up the process without gravely injuring majority party control. Majority party skeptics retort that the minority will simply use amending opportunities to force majority party members to cast embarrassing votes. Currently, the minority uses the "motion to recommit" a bill that has just passed the House back to committee with instructions to amend it—the last and often only chance minorities have to change a bill before final passage—for that purpose. To which one might respond: so what? Are not members supposed to stand up for what they believe in and vote accordingly? Certainly existing rules mandating that bills and committee reports on them be available three days before floor consideration should be rigorously enforced; waivers issued by the Rules Committee should be allowed only for genuine emergencies.

One reform popular with outside observers, but not many members, is to institute formal debates in the House and Senate. "Oxford-style" debates pit small groups of members against each other, debating broad issues and approaches to major public policy problems. "Lincoln–Douglas" debates between the majority and minority leaders, but confined to major issues of principle, are an intriguing idea. Perhaps at the beginning of each Congress, and monthly thereafter, such debates could take place, with prime-time television coverage. For these and other debates, a fact-checking outside source should serve as referee to ensure that neither side could make up its own facts or make unrealistic claims. The point of these proposals is to inject genuine deliberation and reasoned debate into the process.

One Last Idea. Larry Sabato and others have raised questions about "the unthinkable"—an accident or a massive terrorist attack that incapacitates most members of Congress and leaves the country without a functioning government.[85] The Constitution provides for presidential succession and for gubernatorial appointments to fill Senate vacancies, but the only comparable provision for the House is the reference to special elections. Even if some representatives survive such a catastrophe, how could the House function with a handful of members? Could the House and Senate carry out their roles in choosing a new president or replenishing the vacant line of succession? The country lacks any provision for handling temporary but serious and widespread incapacitation of the membership of the House. Answers to these questions are not easy, but they deserve reformers' thought.

9.8 ARE REFORMS POSSIBLE?

The story of reform efforts has been well told, as individuals, parties, groups, and special committees and commissions on the Hill—not to mention hundreds of outsiders—sought to clear up jurisdictions, modernize structures, streamline procedures, enhance accountability, and improve fairness and efficiency.[86] There have been significant successes, such as the 1946 Legislative Reorganization Act, the House committee and subcommittee reforms of the early 1970s, the 1974 Budget and Impoundment Control Act and a series of successor efforts to control budgets, an overhaul of Senate committees in 1977, and the reforms of committees and subcommittees in 1995. Have reforms balanced the contrary dictates of effectiveness, efficiency, representation, responsiveness, accountability, and reasoned deliberation to improve Congress? Most experts agree that reforms have achieved some—but far from all—of their objectives, often at the margins and usually only temporarily.[87] However, they have carried all sorts of unintended consequences, contributing to the demise of the traditional textbook legislative process and ushering in Sinclair's "Unorthodox Lawmaking" as a standard feature of Washington politics.

The sunshine revolution of the 1970s—open committee meetings, recorded floor votes, electronic voting, televised proceedings—sought transparency and accountability. In addition to subjecting members and committees to the close scrutiny of the media and lobbyists, the reforms turned Congress into a well-publicized and media-conscious forum for partisan struggles, one-upmanship, pandering, grandstanding, and "gotcha" politics. Moreover, there is little evidence that the reform actually stimulated citizen attentiveness to Congress; if anything, the greater transparency helped turn off Americans and turn their suspicions about Congress into utter disdain. Reforms tend to create situations that themselves deteriorate, leading to reforms of the reforms in a continuing cycle; some, such as Senator Reid's attack on the filibuster for presidential nominations, trigger reactions. Republicans retaliated with all sorts of delaying and obstructionist tactics. One danger is that modest reforms negate possibilities for fundamental change. Tensions between centralization and decentralization of authority in the committee system, and more broadly between party leadership and committee autonomy, offer another example. It is hard to argue that the current situation is somehow a salubrious culmination of reform efforts.

What will cause serious reforms? Lawrence Evans points to four sources that have driven, and might again drive, such efforts: (1) public opinion, especially in the context of a scandal; (2) interest group pressure, probably from "public interest" groups; (3) partisan imperatives that help parties achieve electoral and policy goals; and (4) the personal interests and power goals of members of the Senate and House. The reality is that the public has no measurable interest in broad-based congressional reform; and when there is interest, it tends to focus on "sexy" topics like campaign funding and gerrymandering. Imagine what is needed to fire up a crowd of Americans about changing committee jurisdictions or adding seats to the House! Interest groups typically are narrowly focused on discrete outcomes; they might be interested in some minor jurisdictional or procedural matters, but except for a few public interest organizations, one is likely to get a long yawn when trying to drum up support from groups. Evans finds that the "recent history of congressional reform indicates that the collective interests of the legislative branch usually play second fiddle to more parochial goals, that is, to partisanship or the narrow interests of particular members and constituencies."[88] Committee jurisdictional reform, for example, asks too many legislators to give up the personal power structures on which they have built careers and influence. E. Scott Adler, indeed, claims that members' electoral interests trump all other considerations to prevent jurisdictional reform.[89]

Parties use reforms to advance their agendas; committee leaders and other members support or resist them according to how the reforms affect their powers and ambitions. A good example of resistance of this sort is the 1974 Budget Act whose purpose was to give Congress equal footing with the president in determining budget priorities and making taxing and spending decisions. Rather than change jurisdictions or perhaps combine the appropriations committees with the taxing committees (Ways and Means in the House and Finance in the Senate), the only way reformers could make progress was to affirm those committees and add a new layer of budget committees on top—hardly a step in the direction of efficiency. One veteran student of Congress concluded that "the prospect of large-scale jurisdictional reform in the House is virtually nil, because, as we have seen, it would disrupt too many members' reelection and power interests."[90] Perhaps most sadly, according to Paul J. Quirk and Sarah A. Binder, "neither the House nor the Senate seems capable of debating institutional reforms in an open and deliberative manner. . . . Congress does not change often for the sake of any broad conception of performance. Most change is driven by partisan or group goals, and only rarely do the needs of Congress as an institution come to the fore in episodes of reform."[91] As Stephen E. Frantzich and Claude Berube argue, reforms confront the magnitude problem: comprehensive reforms contain too many costs for too many people; reforms that are small contain too few benefits.[92] In short, barring disaster or superscandal, or unless one party controls both houses by an overwhelming majority, there is little prospect for serious institutional reform. Even under such circumstances, members would need to choose between much more party control and much less, as pointed out earlier. Such choices are exceedingly hard to make.

There remain, however, several strategies worth considering. One is to use the "commission" approach used for military base closings. A bipartisan commission recommends closings, and its recommendations must be accepted or rejected as a whole; there can be no modifications pushed by individual senators or representatives. Congress tried this approach to solve the budget crises following the financial crash of 2008. It created the Bowles–Simpson Commission, a bipartisan group whose task was to devise a definitive long-term budget solution. If a supermajority of commissioners were to endorse its report, the plan would go to the House and Senate floors for an up or down vote. Although a majority of the commission supported the Commission's recommendation, not enough did so to move the measure to a congressional vote. The same idea might be applied to the reforms alluded to above. It would not be hard to put together a commission of current and especially former senators and representatives of both parties, scholars, and others to review congressional performance and propose a package of reforms to be accepted on an all-or-nothing basis, accompanied by considerable public relations fanfare. Their first task would be make the tough choices described in this chapter and outlined in Table 9.1; if they could not, no genuine reform could result. Making those choices is unlikely.

Second, sometimes when faced with an impasse, Congress devises a "doomsday" bomb of sorts to force itself into action. The budget deal of 2011, for example, established a committee to come up with a solution to several crosscutting problems. If that committee could not do so, the federal budget would be cut across the board in what is known as "sequestration." The expectation was that Republicans would not want that to happen because defense spending would be cut and Democrats would fear it because of the cuts in domestic programs. The bomb did go off. Members of both parties complained bitterly and sought to win exemptions from the cuts, but the sequestration prevailed and had the effect of reducing the deficit. The same approach, perhaps combined with the reform commission, might work for reforming Congress if an appropriate "bomb" could be manufactured. One difficulty is that for any given reform, one party or the other, one committee or another, or one group of members or another might prefer the effects of the explosion to the proposed reforms. With-holding salaries, forcing people off desirable committees, sharp reductions in office budgets, and similar punitive devices could be concocted as the price for failure to support reforms.

A third approach is less dramatic but might be more effective. Precisely because reforms face resistance from current members, committees, and parties, it would make sense that any reform effort include a provision that the reform would not go into effect for a period of time—say five or six years—to exempt current members and current operations from its effects. Obviously this means delaying "good" reforms, but it might mean that reforms stand a chance of being adopted.

Fourth, consideration should be given to sunset provisions for structural and procedural arrangements. What if all committee jurisdictions expire every 10 years? The temptation probably would be simply to re-enact them, but at least the opportun-ity would be there to reconsider, reflect, and reform—especially if renewal depended on passing a commission recommendation described above. What if the biennial ap-proval of House rules had to be approved by two-thirds of the members instead of a simple majority? The need for positive action opens the door for change.

Finally, as Eric M. Patashnik has written with respect to policy reforms, often side payments are required to entice a senator or representative to support general-interest reforms that might have particularistic costs to him or her.[93] To the extent that passing reforms requires "greasing the wheels," there must be an ample supply of benefits to members—tons of pork dumped on their constituencies, policies adjusted to favor the members, and so on. That is the definition of inefficiency, but it might do the trick. Nor is there be any guarantee against slippage back into old patterns of be-havior, along with reforms of the reforms to restore elements of the *status quo ante*. Most changes in Congress come not as deliberate theory-based calculations but rather as reactive adaptations to new issues that arise, new players, and new partisan align-ments. In the end, it will require an unusual alignment of the stars, as well as of mem-bers, committees, parties, and interest groups, to bring about needed institutional change. Most importantly, successful comprehensive reform requires a master plan, a theory, to guide it and to ensure that all the pieces cohere into a rational whole. The reader can judge which of the models described earlier best provides that master plan. Until then, the ball is in the court of the members themselves to rise above parochial and self-interested concerns and focus on what would enhance institutional effective-ness, efficiency, and deliberative judgment.

QUESTIONS TO CONSIDER

1. How was redistricting done after the 2010 census in your state? Was it fair? What were the goals of those doing the redistricting, and what were the consequences?
2. What is the best way to redistrict? Who should do it, and what values and criteria should drive the effort?

3. Should the sizes of the House and Senate be increased?
4. If you could enact three reforms dealing with Congress, which would they be—and why?

NOTES

1. Andrew J. Taylor, *Congress: A Performance Appraisal* (Boulder, CO: Westview Press, 2013): 2–13, 189. See John R. Hibbing and Elizabeth Theiss-Morse, *Congress as Public Enemy: Public Attitudes toward American Political Institutions* (New York: Cambridge University Press, 1995).
2. Stephen Dinan, "Capitol Hill Least Productive Congress Ever: 112th Fought 'about Everything,'" *Washington Times*, January 9, 2013, http://www.washingtontimes.com/news/2013/jan/9/capitol-hill-least-productive-congress-ever-112th-/print/; U.S. Congress, *Congressional Record*, http://www.gpo.gov/fdsys/pkg/CREC-2013-03-13/pdf/CREC-2013-03-13-pt1-PgD196.pdf/.
3. Mickey Edwards, *The Parties versus the People: How to Turn Republicans and Democrats into Americans* (New Haven, CT, and London: Yale University Press, 2013): 171.
4. George Galloway, *Congress at the Crossroads* (New York: Crowell, 1946).
5. James McGregor Burns, *Deadlock of Democracy* (Englewood Cliffs, NJ: Prentice Hall, 1963).
6. Joseph S. Clark, *Congress: The Sapless Branch* (New York: Harper & Row, 1964).
7. Richard Bolling, *House out of Order* (New York: Dutton, 1965).
8. Roger H. Davidson, David Kovenock, and Michael O'Leary, *Congress in Crisis: Politics and Congressional Reform* (Belmont, CA: Wadsworth, 1966); Davidson and Walter J. Oleszek, *Congress against Itself* (Bloomington and London: Indiana University Press, 1977).
9. Samuel P. Huntington, "Congressional Responses to the Twentieth Century," in David B. Truman, ed., *The Congress and America's Future*, 2nd ed. (Englewood Cliffs, NJ: Prentice Hall, 1973): 38.
10. Roger H. Davidson, Walter J. Oleszek, and Frances E. Lee, *Congress and Its Members*, 13th ed. (Los Angeles, London, New Delhi, Singapore, and Washington, D.C.: CQ Press, 2012): 264–65, 270; C. Lawrence Evans, "Parties and Leaders: Polarization and Power in the U.S. House and Senate," in Jamie L. Carson, ed., *New Directions in Congressional Politics* (New York and London: Routledge, 2012), chap. 4.
11. Keith T. Poole and Howard Rosenthal, "The Polarization of American Politics," *Journal of Politics* 46 (1984): 1061–79; Jon R. Bond and Richard Fleisher, eds., *Polarized Politics: Congress and the President in a Partisan Era* (Washington, D.C.: CQ Press, 2000); Jeffrey M. Stonecash, Mark D. Brewer, and Mark D. Mariani, *Diverging Parties; Social Change, Realignment, and Party Polarization* (Boulder, CO: Westview Press, 2003); Sean M. Theriault, *Party Polarization in Congress* (Cambridge: Cambridge University Press, 2008).
12. Alan I. Abramowitz and Kyle L. Saunders, "Is Polarization a Myth?," *Journal of Politics* 70 (2008): 542–55; and Abramowitz, *The Polarized Public? Why American Government Is So Dysfunctional* (Boston: Pearson, 2013). For an opposing view, see Morris P. Fiorina, with Samuel J. Abrams and Jeremy C. Pope, *Culture War? The Myth of a Polarized America*, 2nd ed. (New York: Pearson/Longman, 1996).
13. Eric M. Uslaner, *The Decline of Comity in Congress* (Ann Arbor: University of Michigan Press, 1996).
14. Quoted in Walter J. Oleszek, *Congressional Procedures and the Policy Process*, 9th ed. (Los Angeles, London, New Delhi, Singapore, and Washington, D.C.: CQ Press, 2014): 435.
15. Jeremy W. Peters, "Senate Prepares to Wrap Up Sluggish 2013," *New York Times*, December 15, 2013.

16. Public Citizen, "The Case for Independent Ethics Agencies: The Office of Congressional Ethics Six Years Later, and a History of Failed Senate Accountability," October 2014, http://www.citizen.org/documents/OCE_Briefer.pdf/.

17. Billy House, "How Lawmakers Skirt the Law to Keep Their Next Jobs Secret," *National Journal*, January 21 2014, http://www.nationaljournal.com/daily/how-lawmakers-skirt-the-law-to-keep-their-next-jobs-secret-20140121/.

18. Alan J. Ziobrowski, Ping Chen, James W. Boyd, and Brigitte J. Ziobrowski, "Abnormal Returns for the Common Stock Investments of the U.S. Senate," *Journal of Financial and Quantitative Analysis* 39 (2004): 661–76.

19. Katie Barrows, "Caught Our Eye," *LegiStorm*, February 3, 2014, http://www.legistorm.com/pro_news/view/id/740.html/.

20. Sanford Levinson, *Our Undemocratic Constitution: Where the Constitution Goes Wrong (And How We the People Can Correct It)* (New York: Oxford University Press, 2006), chap. 2.

21. Adam Liptak, "Small States Find outside Clout Growing in Senate," *New York Times*, March 11, 2013: A1.

22. Chad Murphy and Antoine Yoshinaka, "Are Mapmakers Able to Target and Protect Congressional Incumbents? The Institutional Dynamics of Electoral Competition," *American Politics Research* 37 (2009): 955–82.

23. Marc J. Hetherington, Bruce Larson, and Suzanne Globetti, "The Redistricting Cycle and Strategic Candidate Decisions in U.S. House Races," *Journal of Politics* 65 (2003): 1221–34.

24. Danny Hayes and Seth C. McKee, "The Participatory Effects of Redistricting," *American Journal of Political Science* 35 (2009): 1006–23; M. V. Hood III and Seth C. McKee, "Stranger Danger: Redistricting, Incumbent Recognition, and Vote Choice," *Social Science Quarterly* 91 (2010): 344–58; Matthew Hayes, Matthew V. Hibbing, and Tracey Sulkin, "Redistricting, Responsiveness, and Issue Attention," *Legislative Studies Quarterly* 35 (2010): 91–115; Michael H. Crespin, "Serving Two Masters: Redistricting and Voting in the U.S. House of Representatives," *Political Research Quarterly* 63 (2010): 850–59.

25. John N. Friedman and Richard T. Holden, "The Rising Incumbent Reelection Rate: What's Gerrymandering Got to Do With It?," *Journal of Politics* 71 (2009): 593–611.

26. Griff Palmer and Michael Cooper, "How Maps Helped Party Keep Edge in the House," *New York Times*, December 15, 2012: A10.

27. William J. Miller, "Why Redistricting Matters," in Miller and Jeremy D. Walling, eds., *The Political Battle over Congressional Redistricting* (Lanham, MD, Boulder, CO, New York, Toronto, and Plymouth, UK: Lexington Books, 2012), chap. 20.

28. Jowei Chen and Jonathan Rodden, "Unintentional Gerrymandering: Political Geography and Electoral Bias in Legislatures," *Quarterly Journal of Political Science* 8 (2013): 239–69.

29. Alan I. Abramowitz, Brad Alexander, and Matthew Gunning, "Incumbency, Redistricting, and Decline of Competition in U.S. House Elections," *Journal of Politics* 68 (2006): 75–99; Andrew Gelman and Gary King, "A Unified Method of Evaluating Electoral Systems and Redistricting Plans," *American Journal of Political Science* 38 (1994): 514–54.

30. Charles Cameron, David Epstein, and Sharyn O'Halloran, "Do Majority–Minority Districts Maximize Substantive Black Representation in Congress?," *American Political Science Review* 90 (1996): 794–812.

31. Scott W. Desposato and John R. Petrocik, "The Variable Incumbency Advantage: New Voters, Redistricting, and the Personal Vote," *American Journal of Political Science* 47

(2003): 18–32; Richard Born, "Partisan Intentions and Election Day Realities in the Congressional Redistricting Process," *American Political Science Review* 79 (1985): 305–19.

32. Nolan McCarty, Keith T. Poole, and Howard Rosenthal, "Does Gerrymandering Cause Polarization?," *American Journal of Political Science* 53 (2009): 666–80; Jamie L. Carson Michael H. Crespin, Charles J. Finocchiaro, and David W. Rohde, "Redistricting and Party Polarization in the U.S. House of Representatives," *American Politics Research* 35 (2007): 878–904; Abramowitz, Alexander, and Gunning, "Incumbency, Redistricting, and the Decline of Competition"; Buchler, "Resolved, the Redistricting Process Should be Bipartisan," in Richard J. Ellis and Michael Nelson, eds., *Debating Reform: Conflicting Perspectives on How to Fix the American Political System*, 2nd ed. (Washington, D.C.: CQ Press, 2011): 216–27.

33. Gary Cox and Mathew McCubbins, *Legislative Leviathan*, 2nd ed. (New York: Cambridge University Press, 2007); Keith Krehbiel, *Information and Legislative Organization* (Ann Arbor: University of Michigan Press, 1991); Forrest Maltzman, *Competing Principals: Committees, Parties and the Organization of Congress* (Ann Arbor: University of Michigan Press, 1997).

34. Richard F. Fenno Jr., *Congressmen in Committees* (Boston: Little, Brown, 1973).

35. Thomas Gilligan and Keith Krehbiel, "Organization of Informative Committees by a Rational Legislature," *American Journal of Political Science* 34 (1990): 531–64; Timothy J. Groseclose, "Testing Hypothesis of Committee Composition," *Journal of Politics* 6 (1994): 440–58; Richard L. Hall, "Participation and Purpose in Committee Decision Making," *American Political Science Review* 81 (1987):105–28; and John Londregan and James M. Snyder Jr., "Comparing Committee and Floor Preferences," *Legislative Studies Quarterly* 19 (1994): 233–66.

36. Oleszek, *Congressional Procedures*, 19.

37. Roger Larocca, "Committee Parallelism and Bicameral Agenda Coordination," *American Politics Research* 38 (2010): 3–32.

38. David C. King, *Turf Wars: How Congressional Committees Claim Jurisdiction* (Chicago: University of Chicago Press, 1997).

39. Davidson, Oleszek, Lee, and Schickler, *Congress and Its Members*: 198.

40. *Ibid.*, 221.

41. Chris Den Hartog and Nathan W. Monroe, *Agenda Setting in the U.S. Senate: Costly Consideration and Majority Party Advantage* (New York: Cambridge University Press, 2011).

42. Gary Mucciaroni and Paul J. Quirk, *Deliberative Choices: Debating Public Policy in Congress* (Chicago: University of Chicago Press, 2006): 187–89; Andrew J. Taylor, *The Floor in Congressional Life* (Ann Arbor: University of Michigan Press, 2012): 133–42.

43. Barbara Sinclair, *Unorthodox Lawmaking: New Legislative Processes in the U.S. Congress*, 4th ed. (Los Angeles, London, New Delhi, Singapore, and Washington, D.C.: CQ Press, 2012).

44. Thomas E. Mann and Norman J. Ornstein, *It's Even Worse Than It Looks: How the American Constitutional System Collided with the New Politics of Extremism* (New York: Basic Books, 2012): 84–91; Mann and Ornstein, *The Broken Branch: How Congress Is Failing America and How to Get It Back on Track* (Oxford and New York: Oxford University Press, 2006), *passim*; Lauren C. Bell, *Filibustering in the U.S. Senate* (Amherst, NY: Cambria, 2011); Sarah A. Binder, *Politics or Principle? Filibustering in the United States Senate* (Washington, D.C.: Brookings, 1997); Richard A. Arenberg and Robert B. Dove, *Defending the Filibuster: The Soul of the Senate* (Bloomington and Indianapolis: Indiana University Press, 2012).

45. U.S. Senate, http://www.senate.gov/pagelayout/reference/cloture_motions/clotureCounts.htm.

46. Lawrence Evans, "Politics of Congressional Reform," in Paul J. Quirk and Sarah A. Binder, eds., *The Legislative Branch* (Oxford and New York: Oxford University Press, 2005), chap. 17.

47. Norman J. Ornstein, Thomas E. Mann, Michael J. Malbin, and Andrew Rugg, *Vital Statistics on Congress*, http://www.brookings.edu/research/reports/2013/07/vital-statistics-congress-mann-ornstein/, tables 2.7 and 2.8.

48. Lydia Saad, "Americans Call for Term Limits, End to Electoral College: Virtually No Partisan Disagreement on These Long-Discussed Constitutional Reforms," *Gallup Politics* (January 18, 2013).

49. Gary C. Jacobson, *The Politics of Congressional Elections*, 8th ed. (Boston: Pearson, 2013), chaps. 3 and 6; Paul S. Herrnson, *Congressional Elections: Campaigning at Home and in Washington*, 6th ed. (Los Angeles, London, New Delhi, Singapore, and Washington, D.C.: CQ Press, 2012), chaps. 2, 3, and 9.

50. Cherie Maestas and Melissa Stewart, "Recruitment and Candidacy: Ambition, Strategy, and the Choice to Run for Congress," in Carson, *New Directions in Congressional Politics*, chap. 2.

51. Nathaniel Birkhead, Gabriel Uriarte, and William Bianco, "The Impact of State Legislative Term Limits on the Competitiveness of Congressional Elections," *American Politics Research* 38 (2010): 842–61.

52. Brian F. Schaffner, Michael W. Wagner, and Jonathan Winburn, "Incumbents Out, Party In? Term Limits and Partisan Redistricting in State Legislatures, *State Politics & Policy Quarterly* 4 (2004): 396–41.

53. David W. Chen and Michael Barbaro, "Across Country, New Challenges for Term Limits," *New York Times*, September 10, 2008: A1.

54. Lawrence S. Rothenberg and Mitchell S. Sanders, "Severing the Electoral Connection: Shirking in the Contemporary Congress," *American Journal of Political Science* 44 (2000): 316–25.

55. The following represent the author's conclusions from the vast literature on term limits, including Trick Farmer, John David Rausch Jr., and John C. Green, *The Test of Time: Coping with Legislative Term Limits* (Lanham, MD, Boulder, CO, New York, and Oxford: Lexington Books, 2003); Thad Kousser, *Term Limits and the Dismantling of State Legislative Professionalism* (Cambridge, UK: Cambridge University Press, 2005); Stanley M. Caress and Todd T. Kunioka, *Term Limits and Their Consequences: The Aftermath of Legislative Reform* (Albany: SUNY Press, 2012); Matthew C. Moen, Kenneth T. Palmer, and Richard J. Powell, *Changing Members: The Maine Legislature in the Era of Term Limits* (Lanham, MD, Boulder, CO, New York, Toronto, and Oxford: Lexington Books, 2005); Karl T. Kurtz, Bruce Cain, and Richard G. Niemi, *Institutional Change in American Politics: The Case of Term Limits* (Ann Arbor: University of Michigan Press, 2007); Marjorie Sarbaugh-Thompson, Lyke Thompson, Charles D. Elder, John Strate, and Richard C. Elling, *The Political and Institutional Effects of Term Limits* (New York: Palgrave–Macmillan, 2004); John M. Carey, Richard G. Niemi, and Lynda W. Powell, *Term Limits in the State Legislatures* (Ann Arbor: University of Michigan Press 2000); Kathryn A. DePalo, *The Failure of Term Limits in Florida* (Gainesville, FL: University Press of Florida, 2015); Carey, Niemi, Powell, and Gary F. Moncrief, "The Effects of Term Limits on State Legislatures: A New Survey of the 50 States," *Legislative Studies Quarterly* 31 (February 2006): 105–34; Jeffrey R. Lax and Justin H. Phillips, "The Democratic

Deficit in the States," *American Journal of Political Science* 56 (January 2012): 148–66; Gerald C. Wright, "Do Term Limits Affect Legislative Roll Call Voting? Representation, Polarization, and Participation," *State Politics & Policy Quarterly* 7 (2007): 256–80; Susan M. Miller, Jill Nicholson-Crotty, and Sean Nicholson-Crotty, "Reexamining the Institutional Effects of Term Limits in U.S. State Legislatures," *Legislative Studies Quarterly* 36 (2011): 71–97; Katerina L. Robinson, "Shifting Power in Sacramento: The Effects of Term Limits on Legislative Staff," *The California Journal of Politics and Policy* 3 (2011); Travis J. Baker and David M. Hedge, "Term Limits and Legislative–Executive Conflict in the American States," *Legislative Studies Quarterly* 38 (2013): 237–58; Marjorie Sarbaugh-Thompson, John Strate, Kelly Leroux, Richard Elling, Lyke Thompson, and Charles D. Elder, "Legislators and Administrators: Complex Relationships Complicated by Term Limits," *Legislative Studies Quarterly* 35 (2010) 57–89; H. Abbie Erler, "Legislative Term Limits and State Spending," *Public Choice* 133 (2007): 479–94; Daniel C. Lewis, "Legislative Term Limits and Fiscal Policy Performance," *Legislative Studies Quarterly* 37 (2012): 305–28; Jeff Cummins, "The Effects of Legislative Term Limits on State Fiscal Conditions," *American Politics Research* 41 (2013): 417–42; Lilliard E. Richardson Jr., David M. Konisky, and Jeffrey Milyo, "Public Approval of U.S. State Legislatures," *Legislative Studies Quarterly* 37 (2012): 99–116; Andrew B. Hall, "Partisan Effects of Legislative Term Limits," *Legislative Studies Quarterly* 39 (2014): 407–29.

56. Luke Keele, Neil Malhora, and Colin H. McCubbins, "Do Term Limits Restrain State Fiscal Policy? Approaches for Causal Inference in Assessing the Effects of Legislative Institutions," *Legislative Studies Quarterly* 38 (2013): 291–326.

57. Oleszek, *Congressional Procedures*: 149, 240.

58. Rarely since 1976 has even a quarter of the public viewed congressional ethics and honesty as highly important. Frank Newport, "Congress Retains Low Honesty Rating," *Gallup Politics* (December 3, 2012).

59. Larry J. Sabato, *A More Perfect Constitution: 23 Proposals to Revitalize Our Constitution and Make America a Fairer Country* (New York: Walker & Company, 2007), chap. 2.

60. Wendy J. Schiller, *Partners and Rivals: Representation in U.S. Senate Delegations* (Princeton, NJ: Princeton University Press, 2000).

61. See the debate between Bruce I. Oppenheimer and John J. Pitney Jr., "Resolved, the Senate Should Represent People, Not States," in Ellis and Nelson, *Debating Reform*, chap. 13.

62. *Constituency Representation in Congress: The View from Capitol Hill* (Cambridge, UK: Cambridge University Press, 2010).

63. Brian Frederick, *Congressional Representation & Constituents: The Case for Increasing the U.S. House of Representatives* (New York and London: Routledge: 2010). See also Jeffrey W. Ladewig and Mathew P. Jasinski, "On the Causes and Consequences of and Remedies for Interstate Malapportionment of the U.S. House of Representatives," *Perspectives on Politics* 6 (2008): 89–107.

64. See the debate pitting Frederick against C. Lawrence Evans and Nicholas J. Bell, "Resolved, the Size of the House of Representatives Should Be Increased to 675 Seats," in Ellis and Nelson, eds., *Debating Reform*, chap. 9.

65. Ida A. Brudnick, "Legislative Branch: FY2013 Appropriations," Congressional Research Service, May 2, 2013: 26, http://www.fas.org/sgp/crs/misc/R42500.pdf/; Ornstein, Mann, Malbin, and Rugg, *Vital Statistics*, table 5-10.

66. Miler, *Constituency Representation*: 157.

67. Frederick, *Congressional Representation*, chap. 6.

68. National Conference of State Legislatures, "Redistricting Commissions: Legislative Plans," http://www.ncsl.org/legislatures-elections/redist/2009-redistricting-commissions-table.aspx/; Miller and Walling, *The Political Battle over Congressional Redistricting*.

69. David G. Oedel, Allen K. Lynch, Sean E. Mullholland, and Neil T. Edwards, "Does the Introduction of Independent Redistricting Reduce Congressional Partisanship?," *Villanova Law Review* 54 (2009): 57–59.

70. Jeffrey C. Kubin, "The Case for Redistricting Commissions," *Texas Law Review* 75 (1996): 837–72.

71. James B Cottrill, "The Effects of Non-Legislative Approaches to Redistricting on Competition in Congressional Elections," *Polity* 44 (2012): 32–50.

72. Abramowitz, Alexander, and Gunning, "Incumbency, Redistricting, and Decline of Competition."

73. Eric McGhee, "California's New Electoral Reforms: The Fall Election," *Public Policy Institute of California*, November 2012, http://www.ppic.org/main/publication_show.asp?i=1039/.

74. Thomas L. Brunell, *Redistricting and Representation: Why Competitive Elections Are Bad for America* (New York and London: Routledge, 2008): 116.

75. See Charles S. Bullock III, *Redistricting: The Most Political Activity in America* (London, Boulder, CO, New York, Toronto, and Plymouth, UK: Rowman & Littlefield, 2010), chap. 3.

76. John D. Griffin, "Electoral Competition and Democratic Responsiveness: A Defense of the Marginality Hypothesis," *Journal of Politics* 68 (2006): 911–21. He shows that competitiveness across districts correlates positively with congruence between district ideology and members' ideology. He also finds that within districts, as districts become more competitive over time, congruence between district ideology and member ideology increases, especially for junior members and more moderate members.

77. Brunell, *Redistricting and Representation*; Brunell and Justin Buchler, "Ideological Representation and Competitive Congressional Elections," *Electoral Studies* 28 (2009): 448–57.

78. Ryan P. Bates, "Congressional Authority to Require State Adoption of Independent Redistricting Commissions," *Duke Law Journal* 55 (2005): 333–71.

79. "Getting from Here to There in Redistricting Reform," *Duke Journal of Constitutional Law and Public Policy* 5 (2010): 1–15.

80. Edwards, *The Parties versus the People*.

81. *Ibid.*, 101–04.

82. Steven S. Smith, *The Senate Syndrome: The Evolution of Procedural Warfare in the Modern U.S. Senate* (Norman: University of Oklahoma Press, 2014).

83. Arenberg and Robert B. Dove, *Defending the Filibuster*: 75–76.

84. Reforms discussed below are summarized in Taylor, *The Floor in Congressional Life*: 181–200.

85. *More Perfect Constitution*: 69–75.

86. Christopher J. Deering and Steven S. Smith, *Committees in Congress*, 3rd ed. (Washington, D.C.: CQ Press, 1997); James A. Thurber and Roger H. Davidson, eds., *Remaking Congress: Change and Stability in the 1990s* (Washington, D.C.: Congressional Quarterly, 1995); Julian E. Zelizer, *On Capitol Hill: The Struggle to Reform Congress and Its Consequences, 1948–2000* (New York: Cambridge University Press, 2004); Nelson W. Polsby, *How Congress Evolves: Social Bases of Institutional Change* (Oxford and New York: Oxford University Press 2004); Davidson and. Oleszek, *Congress against Itself*; Roger H. Davidson, ed., *The Postreform Congress* (New York: St. Martin's Press, 1992); C. Lawrence Evans and Walter J. Oleszek, *Congress under Fire: Reform Politics and the Republican Majority*

(Boston and New York: Houghton Mifflin, 1997); Leroy N. Rieselbach, Congressional Reform (Washington, D.C.: CQ Press, 1986); Rieselbach, *Congressional Reform in the Seventies* (Morristown, NJ: General Learning Press, 1977); Rieselbach, *Congressional Reform: The Changing Modern Congress* (Washington, D.C.: CQ Press, 1994); Burton D. Sheppard, *Rethinking Congressional Reform* (Cambridge, MA: Schenkman Books, 1985); Evans, "Politics of Congressional Reform," chap. 17, and David W. Rohde, "Committees and Policy Formulation," in Quirk and Binder, *Legislative Branch*, chap. 7.

87. E. Scott Adler and John D. Wilkerson, "Intended Consequences: Jurisdictional Reform and Issue Control in the U.S. House of Representatives," *Legislative Studies Quarterly* 33 (2008): 85–112; E. Scott Adler, *Why Congressional Reforms Fail: Reelection and the House Committee System* (Chicago: University of Chicago Press, 2002).

88. Evans, "Politics of Congressional Reform": 516.

89. *Why Congressional Reforms Fail.*

90. Rohde, "Committees and Policy Formulation": 220.

91. "Congress and American Democracy: Assessing Institutional Performance," in Quirk and Binder, *The Legislative Branch*: 543–45.

92. *Congress: Games and Strategies*, 4th ed. (Lanham, MD, Boulder, CO, New York, Toronto, and Plymouth, UK: Rowman & Littlefield, 2012): 350.

93. *Reforms at Risk: What Happens after Major Policy Changes Are Enacted* (Princeton, NJ, and Oxford: Princeton University Press 2008): 171; Diana Evans, *Greasing the Wheels: Using Pork Barrel Projects to Build Majority Coalitions in Congress* (New York: Cambridge University Press, 2004).

CHAPTER 10

↝

The Presidency

Energy in the Executive is a leading character in the definition of
good government.

—ALEXANDER HAMILTON, *The Federalist No. 70*

Americans have a love–hate relationship with their presidents. When times are good, people credit their chief executives; when times are bad, blame falls on the White House, perhaps because citizens suffer from the illusion that presidents "run the country."[1] The presidency is much less in the sights of reformers than Congress, but reform proposals typically show up in times of trouble. Is the 2000 Florida presidential election a fiasco? End the Electoral College! Has Franklin Roosevelt won four straight elections? Limit presidential terms. Did President Nixon misuse his spending authority and continue an unpopular war? Enact a budget act and the War Powers Act. Are presidential staff members engaged in illegal support of military groups in Central America? Put restraints on them. Is the presidency becoming imperial? Check it. Is it imperiled? Strengthen it. Although scholars, pundits, politicians, and everyday Americans vacillate between wanting a stronger and a weaker president, everyone has a stake in making this institution effective, efficient, accountable, and responsive and in making sure that the occupant of that office has every opportunity and incentive to make sound and reasoned decisions.

10.1 THE MATTER OF POWER

At the heart of the issue is a debate between those who see the presidency as excessively strong and dangerous and those who counter that in fact it lacks adequate authority. The former group argues that presidents have too much power—some expressly granted by the Constitution, some delegated to him by laws enacted by Congress, and some claimed to inhere in the office by virtue of Article II's "executive power," "take care," and "commander-in-chief" clauses. These claims culminate in a theory of the "unitary executive" under which presidents hold plenary authority over the executive branch and thus over the implementation of legislation and regulatory matters, regardless of congressional intent. So, for instance, presidents, who since the early 1970s are legally prohibited from impounding (not spending) funds that Congress has appropriated for various purposes, now issue "signing statements," in which they state that sections of the legislation they are signing into law violate their constitutional authority. Their use goes back as far as President Monroe, but it became common under President Reagan, who issued 276 statements, a quarter of which were made when the president thought his constitutional powers to direct the executive branch were being infringed.[2] President George W. Bush issued 161 such statements, typically citing constitutional issues. President Obama campaigned against them, but he quickly adopted their use once in office—nearly 30 by the end of 2014. Involved in many signing statements are directives to executive agencies to delay the implementation of laws or not to enforce them at all. Obama, for example, instructed the Justice Department not to defend the Defense of Marriage Act in court and not to enforce sections of the Controlled Substance Act when a number of states decided to allow the growth and distribution of marijuana for medicinal and private recreational use. In signing a bill requiring prior notification to Congress of any release of prisoners from the Guantanamo Bay detention center for accused terrorists, Obama said he disagreed with the law because it constrained his ability to negotiate. In May 2014, he agreed to trade five prisoners held in Guantanamo for one American soldier held by the Taliban without informing Congress.

Signing statements are contentious. Critics in Congress see them as a threat to the rule of law—precisely what the president is sworn to enforce—through which Congress gives policy direction to executive agencies. Presidents Bush and Obama insisted that they could countermand such provisions. Defenders point to the need for presidents to be able to supervise and direct the executive branch in administrative matters. Although Congress responds with increased oversight of presidential actions,[3] the only certain checks on presidents—impeachment and conviction by Congress, a denial of funding for government programs, or Supreme Court decisions forbidding presidential action—are extremely unlikely. Presumably, a constitutional amendment could stop them, but that is not going to happen. The result is that this presidential behavior now is a *de facto* "reform" constituting a new type of veto that strengthens the president's hand.

Moreover, presidents regularly evade congressional wishes legally (by transferring funds from one account to another, for example) or illegally (as happened when the staffs of presidents Reagan and Nixon stashed away piles of money for banned projects). In a crisis, or if the other branches resist, presidents in effect can emulate President Andrew Jackson's challenge to the judiciary: "John Marshall has made his decision, now let him enforce it." According to critics, these claims of authority become doubly dangerous when presidents become isolated and fail to engage members of Congress on a regular and equal basis, as is called for by the constitutional balance model described in chapter 8.[4]

Others, however, argue that these critics have it all backward. In fact, they claim, the president is in peril of losing, or at least not being able effectively to use, his authority. Presidential powers are unduly constrained by the courts, statutes, the *de facto* independence of the executive branch's bureaucracy, and the American free enterprise system that puts direction of the economy beyond his control although the public holds him accountable for it. These commentators find that the presidency lacks the ability to command effectively; he cannot push his legislative agenda through Congress; he has lost control of the budget; and he cannot get the bureaucracy to administer as he wishes.

10.2 ACCOUNTABILITY: HIRING
AND FIRING PRESIDENTS

Everyone wants the president to be accountable. That raises questions of presidential elections and length of service. First, however, there is one precondition reform worth thinking about: eligibility. Why must a president be a natural-born American citizen, as required by the Constitution? It makes as much sense to require that he or she had run a business or served in the military. The issue arose when there was talk about possible candidacies of former California governor Arnold Schwarzenegger and Michigan governor Jennifer Granholm, neither of whom was born in the United States, and it exploded when critics questioned the birthplace of President Barack Obama. A constitutional amendment would be required, and it is hard to imagine that it would generate a lot of opposition; but there has been little pressure for one.

10.3 THE ELECTORAL COLLEGE

Problems and Criticisms

"Electoral College, Electoral College, that's all I hear," the man shouted; "why don't you pick on some others for once—Boston, Haverford, Amherst, or Oberlin?" The writings "picking on" the Electoral College have devoured far too many trees, but the debate rages on, fueled by close elections or snafus such as the one in Florida in 2000. The rules of the game are well known. Voters in each state cast their presidential votes for one or another slate of electors, most of whom are party loyalists unknown to the voters but who are pledged to cast their votes for the presidential candidate who collects the most popular votes in that state. After the November election, electors meet in their state capitals to cast their votes, separately, for president and vice president. Votes are counted on January 6 before a joint session of Congress. A majority (270) of electoral votes is necessary to win; if no one gets a majority, the House of Representatives decides, with each state's delegation getting one vote. The arguments for and against this system are familiar.[5]

1. It is undemocratic, unrepresentative, and unfair—a system devised to keep the election out of the hands of citizens. In the late eighteenth century, communication and travel were difficult and slow. Most voters could not know the candidates; election had to be by some other group of informed citizens. Today, knowing just about everything about the candidates is easy. The framers knew that states *as states* had to be involved if there was hope of ratifying the Constitution, and so each state got two electors to reflect its two senators, thus reaffirming the values of federalism and protecting the smaller states. At the same time, the rest of the electors are distributed on the basis of population as measured by the numbers of its representatives. The District of Columbia gained its three electors by the Twenty-Third Amendment. This argument about federalism impresses neither those who believe federalism itself is no longer important nor those who insist on strict "one person, one vote" voter equality. Small states are amply protected in the Senate.

That the states all have votes supposedly forces presidential candidates to seek broad geographical support and to preach the same message everywhere, rather than play to regional idiosyncrasies. Supporters of the College point out that the largest states are the most heterogeneous, with the greatest mixture of ethnic groups; that gives minorities added Electoral College importance to offset their lower turnouts. The problem with this argument is that a good number of large and medium-size states—California, New York, Texas, New Jersey, Illinois, Massachusetts—are usually locked up by one or the other party. So candidates skip them and go after the battleground states whose voters are evenly divided and whose electoral votes will determine the outcome. According to George Edwards's count, presidential and vice presidential candidates in 2008 made no campaign appearances in 26 states, up from 20 in 2004.[6] He also questions the concept of "small-state interest" because most small states have little in common (Rhode Island and Wyoming, Vermont and North Dakota, Delaware and Idaho) and because presidential candidates seldom campaign on issues particularly salient to small-state voters. Moreover, first-term presidents allocate their travel to states much the same way as do candidates, favoring competitive states and skipping over the small ones.[7]

2. A related argument concerns voting fraud. Allegations of fraud in several states would trigger recounts and other delays, but they would affect the election of a president only if the votes from those states were needed to determine the victor. That would be relatively rare. The converse argument is that precisely because relatively few popular votes in a very competitive state can determine all of that state's electoral votes, denying a candidate the 270 votes or pushing an opponent barely over that total, there is a positive incentive toward cheating. Much of the flap over requiring photo ID cards to vote focuses on this issue, with Democrats complaining that Republicans are trying to suppress voter turnout among likely Democratic voters. Interestingly, some of the states trying to impose ID regulations are safely in the GOP camp.

3. Although electors chosen by state legislatures were expected to be well-informed citizens who understood both state and national issues and who could deliberate carefully and wisely, today they are robots who follow the wishes of a plurality of the voters in their states. In fact, they have done so almost from the get-go. In about half the states they are bound by law to support the popular vote winner, but constitutionally they are independent, which leads to the possibility that one or more electors would opt not to vote according to the results of state balloting. In a close race, one or more of these unfaithful electors could deny victory to a candidate who won "fair and square." Indeed, there have been some 156 women and men who technically have not voted or voted the "wrong way," but almost half of them had no choice because the candidates to whom they were pledged died. Since 1900, there have been 10 such faithless electors, the last in 2004. The good news is that it has never mattered, and it would only do so in the closest of elections.

4. The unit or winner-take-all rule that casts all of a state's electoral votes for the popular vote plurality winner is claimed to be unfair, to distort election results, to discourage turnout, and, because the electoral vote margin exaggerates the popular vote differences, to convince winners that they have more of a "mandate" than the popular vote warrants. Size of state matters in terms of a citizen's voting power—the probability that one person can affect the selection of a president—and big states have a huge advantage.[8] A 1-vote margin in California determines 55 electoral votes; carrying the 13 smallest states by 100 percent of the popular vote in each commands 44.

This means that strategic candidates focus on big payoff "swing" states that are not fore-gone conclusions, such as Pennsylvania, Wisconsin, Florida, Ohio, Virginia, Colorado, and North Carolina. Currently, only Maine and Nebraska abjure the unit rule, allo-cating the 2 electoral votes that represent the two senators to the statewide victor and 1 electoral vote to winners in each of the House districts. The unit rule may have pernicious effects on electoral turnout. If a state clearly is going to go "red" or "blue" in the presidential race, the incentive to trudge to the polls diminishes; and that could affect results in congressional and state office races. Perhaps worst of all, the unit rule is perverse in that the total number of electoral votes a state has depends on popula-tion, not voters, including those people who would prefer to vote for candidate X. If candidate Y wins the popular vote, in effect the electoral weight accounted for by X's supporters goes to Y!

   5. The Electoral College regularly produces presidents who fail to attract the sup-port of a majority of voters. Minority presidents are common, having occurred 18 times in close elections, including presidents Lincoln, Woodrow Wilson (twice), Truman, Kennedy, Nixon (1968), George W. Bush, and Bill Clinton (twice). The culprit is a third-party candidate. Defenders of the system retort that the Electoral College makes certain what voters might not: make a majority decision, often by decisive margins.

   6. According to some commentators, the contingency plan for when no candi-date wins a majority of electoral votes is flawed. When that happens, the House of Representatives chooses from among the top three popular vote getters. The catch is that the House delegations could favor the candidate who came in second or third in the popular vote, as in 1824, when a good dose of wheeling and dealing robbed Andrew Jackson, who finished first among four candidates, of the presidency. There also is the real possibility of a 25–25 deadlock (the District of Columbia has no voting representation in the House), an invitation to all sorts of bargaining scenarios. Voting by states rather than by individual choice challenges the value of fair representation as well. According to one calculation, the Electoral College came close to electoral count deadlocks that would have triggered a House election in 1836, 1856, 1860, 1948, 1960, 1968, and 1976.[9] The Senate selects the vice president from the top two finishers. Cynics' political mouths water at the prospect of the House choosing a president of one party and the Senate picking a vice president of the other!

   7. Worst of all, according to most commentators, is that a winner of the popular balloting can lose the electoral vote. In 1876, Samuel J. Tilden won the popular vote plurality and apparently the requisite numbers of electoral votes. Amid all sorts of Reconstruction Era shenanigans in the South, there was a dispute over which 20 elec-tors from Florida, Louisiana, Oregon, and South Carolina were duly chosen. After Congress failed to decide, it set up a special commission, evenly divided between Democrats and Republicans, with one Supreme Court Justice as tiebreaker. That Jus-tice, Joseph Bradley, was a Republican, and—surprise!—the Commission accepted the Republican electors, giving the presidency to Rutherford B. Hayes, who had re-ceived about a quarter of a million fewer popular votes than Tilden. Twelve years later Grover Cleveland edged out Benjamin Harrison in the popular vote, 48.6 to 47.8 per-cent, but he lost the Electoral College by 65 votes. In 2000 Al Gore beat George W. Bush in popular votes, 48.4 to 47.9 percent, but because of the contested result in Florida requiring a Supreme Court decision to settle, Bush won. There have been a

number of close calls. In 1948 a swing of about 30,000 votes in several states would have elected Governor Dewey instead of Harry Truman; in 1960 a switch of under 12,000 votes in five states would have given Nixon the presidency, and slightly different results in Missouri and Illinois would have tossed the race into the House. A swing of about 54,000 votes in three states would have created the winner–loser problem in 1968; and in 1976, 11,117 votes in Ohio and under 7,500 in Hawaii would have elected Ford despite a convincing popular victory for Carter. Some skeptics claim that when elections are that close, they are in effect tied because of the imprecision in counting ballots; and thus appropriate tie-breaking methods should be used rather than trying to recount the votes. Some historians claim that more than a few of the founding fathers believed that almost all elections would end up in the House and that the electoral vote was a sort of primary election to eliminate lesser candidates.

8. The Electoral College plays strange games with third parties. The winner-take-all rule makes it all but impossible for a third-party candidate to compete successfully on the national level. Few people want to "waste" their votes supporting a candidate who will not win the most votes in their state. Defenders of the College tout its role in preserving the two parties. Skeptics scoff, arguing that it takes a lot more than abolishing the Electoral College to change the fundamental nature of the party system. Strangely, the College can give a third-party candidate power to frustrate majorities. His or her very presence can deny another candidate an electoral majority and swing the election the wrong way. In the 2000 Florida case, for instance, Ralph Nader picked up more than 97,000 votes. Almost all experts believe that a strong majority of Nader supporters there would have voted for Al Gore had Nader not been on the ballot, giving Gore enough votes to edge out Bush. Moreover, by winning just one or two states in a close race, such a candidate could deny the major candidates a majority of electoral votes and force the election into the House, where the states that supported the third-party candidate could cut some pretty interesting deals.

9. Finally, the American people, by margins of two or three to one, or more, consistently want to replace it.

For opponents of the Electoral College, the conclusion is apparent: change the system to address these problems or, better still, trash the system altogether. Defenders say that the system almost always works and that most proposed cures would be worse than the disease. They point out, for example, that electoral votes are tabulated easily and quickly, regardless of the closeness of the popular vote, almost always leading to a decisive victory that other systems could not produce as easily. Sometimes having an imperfect system that makes decisions is better than a perfect one that is subject to delays and imprecision—especially in a time of heightened and bitter polarization nationally. What are the reform alternatives?

Reforming the College—Proposals

1. *Eliminate the electors.* Since the electors follow the wishes of their states' voters, why not just get rid of them and eliminate the possibility of renegade electors who could create havoc in close elections? Doing so saves a few dollars as well. Reformers are reluctant, fearing that doing so reduces the pressure for fundamental change.

2. Keep the Electoral College but *allocate votes by congressional districts* as do Maine and Nebraska. This plan preserves the federalist dimension while enhancing representation, bringing electoral and popular votes into closer correspondence. It would incentivize candidates to contest more states, or areas of states, than they now do. That of course involves time and money. Recently a number of state Republican parties have promoted this reform, especially in those states that President Obama narrowly won in 2008 and 2012, such as Colorado, Wisconsin, and Pennsylvania. Critics demur, noting that this scheme would not accurately represent the public's voting preferences. Distortion remains because of the difference in the sizes of House districts across the states and because of the constant two electors accorded each state regardless of its population. It is not at all clear that candidates would contest many more states and districts because relatively few—certainly under 100—congressional districts are competitive. Rational candidates skip the safe ones to focus intensely on those "swing" districts. Strange things could happen. Nationally, one could win 270 districts, and thus electoral votes, by the slimmest of margins and get creamed in the others—yet still be elected with many fewer popular votes than another candidate. The congressional district plan inserts a Republican bias into the Electoral College because, owing to the concentration of Democratic voters in a limited number of House districts and the dispersion of Republican voters across more districts, there are notably more Republican-leaning districts than there are districts leaning Democratic, although there may be more potential Democratic votes in total. This plan might inject new considerations into redistricting strategies every 10 years. Several scholars have retroactively compared the district plan to the existing unit rule system in the elections since 1960—assuming, of course, that the changed method of counting would not have affected people's votes or campaign strategy.[10] In all but 1960, the same winners would have emerged, although with smaller margins than actually occurred. In 1960, Nixon would have become president. The same is true in 2012; Mitt Romney won more districts than did President Obama. Assuming that third-party candidates with concentrated regional appeal would emerge, it is quite possible that they could win enough districts to deny the major candidates a majority of electoral votes, throwing the election into the House.

3. A similar proposal is *to allocate electoral votes on a proportional basis* within the states, ideally using fractions of a vote to guarantee accurate correspondence to the popular vote. (Although assigning electoral votes in a fashion other than the unit rule is a state prerogative, splitting them into fractions would require a constitutional amendment.) If electoral votes were not split, rounding fractions up or down to a whole number, this plan would have the same strange results as the district plan. Indeed, following this formula would have forced the elections of 2000, 1996, 1992, and 1968 into the House. In other years it would have significantly reduced the electoral margins enjoyed by the winner. In 1880 and 1896 it could have led to runner-up presidents. Candidates might give scant attention to small, generally safe, states because it would take a substantial popular vote shift to swing one of the states' three or four electoral votes; instead they would go hunting in big competitive states—where relatively small changes in popular votes could translate into two or three more electoral votes. They might also focus on states that already are leaning in their direction, hoping to increase the margins enough to land an extra electoral vote or two. Clearly, strategies would change.

A proportional plan encourages third-, fourth-, and more party candidates to enter the race. Picking up 5 percent of the vote in a large state could mean a couple of electoral votes. The preventative usually is said to be the requirement of a minimum percentage of votes to qualify for any electoral votes—something like what the Europeans do in their multimember parliamentary districts. Trying to set that cutoff would instigate a battle royal between third parties and the two major ones. Last, imagine the nightmare of counting, owing to the fact that to calculate an accurate percentage of the popular vote, states would need *precise* counts not only of how many votes a candidate won but also of how many valid votes were cast overall for all candidates. In close contests, a fraction of a percent can swing an electoral vote; across several states, that might determine the result. Recounts and the inevitable lawsuits take time, money, and energy.

4. The most popular reform is *simple direct national election* in which every vote counts equally. The advantages are many. People would easily understand the process and results, which is not always the case now. There would be no more runner-up presidents: the winner wins, period. All votes would count equally, encouraging turnout. Fraud would be less likely if only because it would be hard to cheat enough to make much of a difference. Candidates would have to campaign everywhere to secure every possible vote, putting considerable pressure on them and costing them and their supporters a lot more money than they now spend.

Defenders of the Electoral College find two flaws with direct popular election. First is the possibility that several minor parties will collect enough votes to deny a majority of popular votes to any candidate—increasingly likely when the two major parties are pretty much equal in strength across the nation and when all sorts of special interests can form political parties to appeal to small but intensely motivated constituencies. Elections require a contingency system: election by Congress, a runoff between the top two candidates, or some other mechanism. Runoffs are costly and impose a burden on citizens who had already voted twice that year (primaries and general election), probably leading to lower turnout and thus a blow to representation and accountability. The alternatives to a runoff are a plurality vote system with a minimum vote requirement for victory, perhaps 40 percent, or an instant runoff balloting system, as described in chapter 4.

A second concern occurs in the event of a close election. Under the Electoral College system, a close national popular vote may be inconsequential if enough states with enough electoral votes clearly swing for one or the other candidate. At the worst, as in 2000, one must recount disputed ballots in only one or two states whose electoral votes can decide the election. With a national popular election, a close result—say a difference of a half percent—could lead to a call for recounts. The problem is that every single ballot throughout the country, as well as absentee and provisional ballots, would have to be recounted and checked for validity—difficult in the day of electronic voting machines with no paper backup. That could take weeks or months, running up against, or scooting past, the day set for inauguration, implying that the speaker of the House would serve as acting president.

5. Creative theorists have come up with *all sorts of other plans*. One is the National Bonus Plan, awarding 102 electoral votes (2 each for the states and District of

Columbia) to whichever candidate wins a plurality of popular votes nationwide. That presumably eliminates the possibility of a runner-up president. Like any popular vote scheme, it raises the problems of a recount in a close election. Based on a proposal of the Center for Voting and Democracy, a number of states have agreed to a compact that assigns all their electoral votes to the winner of the national popular vote, regardless of how the vote in these states turns out. The catch, however, is that they will not cast their votes that way until enough states sign up to guarantee the plan's success. That has not occurred. As of late 2014, 11 states with 165 electoral votes—61 percent of the 270 needed—have passed the legislation, as have 32 legislative chambers in 22 states and D.C.[11] The plan accomplishes the goals of direct election without having to amend the constitution. Larry J. Sabato's proposal described in the last chapter to enlarge the Senate, as well as proposals to enlarge the House, would have the effect of bringing the electoral vote closer to the popular vote.[12] Alternatively, he proposes simply adding to the number of electors by giving a state one more elector for each percentage point of the national population over 2 percent that a state has. Doing so would add about 75 electors.

There is no guarantee that any one of these reforms can achieve its objectives. The reason is that changing the rules could change the list of candidates, the behavior of the parties, campaign strategies, and/or the way voters think and cast their votes; it could also affect how the media covers the races. One consequence of reform is unknown consequences.[13]

Prospects for Reform

Hurdles and challenges accompany all reform proposals, the biggest of which is that many of the proposals require a constitutional amendment, which 13 states can block. Ten amendments that bear directly or indirectly on the election of presidents have been adopted: only one, the Twelfth Amendment, made serious changes in the Electoral College. That is not for want of proposals; there have been more than 700. Reforms depending on coordinated action by a large number of states may raise issues about the interstate compact clause of the Constitution that requires congressional approval.[14] There also are technical problems with some of the plans that require an accurate count of the national popular vote. Currently there is no one official tabulation, and the Florida experience of 2000 is a reminder that counting votes is imprecise and messy. Although Congress came close to sending an amendment to abolish the Electoral College to the states in 1969–1970 in response to the close 1968 election and despite the 2000 fiasco in Florida, nothing has happened. It probably will take another case that egregiously violates the plurality principle to trigger action. Such events have been rare, but the current polarized political landscape might give rise to more. At the same time, contemporary politics might make opponents that much more dogmatic about resisting change.

10.4 THE TWO-TERM LIMIT

Why Two?

Presidential terms have implications for governmental effectiveness and accountability, and they affect the balance of power between the White House and Congress.

The Twenty-Second Amendment, passed in response to Franklin Roosevelt's four elections as president, limited a president to two terms plus a fraction of an unfinished term of his predecessor. The notion that presidents should not overstay their visit remains popular, but it does raise questions. Is a president in his or her final term liberated to "do what is right" rather than what is needed for re-election? Might it make the chief executive unnecessarily reckless as he tries to build a legacy? Or will it constrain him to a hapless and frustrated lame-duck status whereby members of Congress and the executive bureaucracy merely need to wait him out before continuing with their own priorities? The historical record suggests that the correct answers are yes, yes, and yes; one can find examples of them all. What is known is that presidential approval ratings almost always drop in their second terms; and it is generally agreed that second termers occasionally suffer from a touch of hubris. Many have misinterpreted their "mandates" and have overreached, leading to a tendency to substitute executive orders for painful and often unsuccessful legislative negotiating. Other characteristics include burnout and exhaustion, loss of creativity, massive departures of "first-string" cabinet officials and key staff, difficulties in appointing top-notch replacements, scandals such as President Reagan's secret funding of rebels in Nicaragua or President Clinton's sexual escapades, in-fighting within his party as people jockey for position for the next election, an increased focus on foreign problems, and the almost inevitable midterm loss of congressional seats.[15]

Presidential success with Congress tends to decline, and the media turn their attention away from governance and toward the next election. Administrative performance flounders—witness President Bush's experience with Hurricane Katrina and the Iraq–Afghanistan war and the rollout and implementation of President Obama's Affordable Care Act. How much of that is the result of presidential inattention or exhaustion cannot be determined, but it does raise interesting questions.

Reforms

Although the two-term limit has many defenders, others think it needs to be changed or eliminated because in a democratic republic the voters should determine who governs and for how long.[16] After all, the founders considered and then rejected a term limit. Moreover, there is little evidence that capping a president's tenure prevents misbehavior. Some of the worst examples of the "imperial" presidency occurred after the Twenty-Second Amendment was in effect. One camp advocates repealing the amendment to allow presidents to seek a third term, although most probably would not do so. Opponents argue that eight years is enough; indeed, it may be too much for that high-pressure job. They contend, moreover, that rotation is healthy to prevent stagnation. If presidents suffer in their second terms, they speculate, matters would be even worse in a third term.

Another camp advocates a single six-year term on the grounds that four years is insufficient to make major policy changes—the first year is taken up by filling administration posts and getting a handle on the job, and the third and fourth years focus on re-election—but eight years is too long if an ineffective president is re-elected. A single fixed term won support from scholars and presidents such as Johnson, Nixon, and Carter. A constitutional amendment to make the change has been introduced more than 150 times.[17] The arguments are that a single term would accomplish the following:

1. Reduce the level and importance of politics, removing concerns about re-election;
2. Allow more time for policy planning, enactment, and implementation;
3. Free presidents from special interests, giving them more freedom; and
4. Limit the intense pressure and exhaustion that come with eight years in the office.

Opponents defend the importance of re-election as a means to enforce caution and accountability. Worse, if a president is inept, the country is stuck with him for two more years than would otherwise be the case; if he is successful and popular, the country is denied his leadership. Nor is it clear that presidents should be immune to the pressures and vicissitudes of interest groups and congressional action. In short, argue Thomas Cronin and Michael Genovese, the single six-year term "represents the last gasp of those who cling to the hope that we can separate national leadership from the crucible of politics."[18] Part of the debate over a single term concerns whether it would make the president a lame duck the minute he takes office. One test of that hypothesis is to observe how presidents in their second four-year term have functioned; and on that matter, the record is ambiguous. Presidents have not abandoned their partisanship to become statesmen above the partisan fray, if the records of Nixon, Truman, Reagan, Clinton, George W. Bush, and Barack Obama are any indication. Even presidents with one six-year term have responsibilities to their parties' next nominees and to their congressional and gubernatorial candidates. Whether a single six-year term can be compared to a second four-year term, however, is debatable.

Professor Sabato suggests a six-year term with the option of a two-year extension, determined by a national "confirmation" election.[19] The idea is to give presidents enough time to accomplish their major goals without having to face a challenger while also giving him the option to bid for extra time by means of a plebiscite wherein the president's record, not his ability to compete with an opponent, is the sole issue for voters to decide. He claims that this would also free up a president from the threat of a renomination challenge, allowing the president to govern from the center of his party rather than having to cater to its extreme wings. The problem with this scheme is that six years for a bad president are six bad years for the nation; and if there are 6 or 8 good years, why not more? Furthermore, the scheme requires a constitutional amendment specifying when and how the added two years would be decided.

Closely related to terms is the matter of when a newly elected president takes office.[20] Currently there is about a 10-week interregnum period between election and inauguration, starkly different from the British system in which the new prime minister takes office immediately after the election. The inauguration on January 20 gives presidents time to think, to assemble at least the core of his administrative and advising team (it may take a year or more to complete the task), and to figure out how to turn campaign promises into policies and budgets. At the same time, important and dangerous events can occur during transition; planning must go on; international meetings may be held; and a host of decisions must be made. Famed presidential scholar and advisor Richard E. Neustadt referred to these as the "hazards of transition."[21]

People and governments during that time may fairly ask, who really is in charge and can make decisions? The proposed reform is to move inauguration up considerably; but doing so requires moving up the timing of the count of electoral ballots from January 6, which in turn means moving up the casting of electoral votes in the state capitals—both of which could cause havoc if the November popular election did not result in a clear winner.

10.5 EFFECTIVENESS IN GOVERNING THE EXECUTIVE BRANCH

The Problem: Can a President Govern?

A president is the chief executive officer of the government—an entity of about 2.75 million civilian and 1.4 million military employees spread across 15 departments, 70 independent agencies and government corporations, 68 boards, commissions, and committees, and 4 quasi-official offices and agencies. Departments and most of the agencies, like the Central Intelligence Agency, National Aeronautics and Space Agency, Small Business Administration, and Central Intelligence Agency, are totally subject to presidential direction. Others, such as the Securities and Exchange Commission, the Consumer Financial Protection Bureau, the Federal Communications Commission, and the Commodity Futures Trading Commission, have quasi-legislative rule-making, administrative, and adjudicatory powers. Agencies of this type enjoy considerable, and sometimes absolute, independence from the White House and exercise their powers in ways that do not necessarily accord with presidential wishes. How does the chief executive control and direct these entities, especially when each of them tends to see matters from its own perspective? Where is the accountability to the public?

Complicating matters are three conditions. First, departments and agencies are established by, function under laws written by, and are funded by the Congress and its committees and subcommittees. Those units have vested interests in protecting and/or directing "their" agencies, not infrequently counter to presidential wishes. They sometimes prefer to embed new programs in independent regulatory agencies so keep them as far from presidential control as possible.[22] Second, the various social and economic interest groups that agencies and departments deal with have strong incentives to protect them and keep them "loyal" and responsive to the groups' interests, regardless of presidential wishes. Groups that find themselves in mutually beneficial relations with government agencies will support laws, court rulings, and governmental procedures that help the agencies retain power and operating autonomy.

The third challenge to presidential leadership is the tension between the "presidential government" (the president, his staff, and top-level administrators whom he appoints) and the "permanent government" (the department and agency employees who carry out the day-to-day work of the government). Whether hired through the traditional Office of Personnel Management merit procedures or employed directly by agencies for their particular skills and expertise, the bureaucrats and professionals who administer public policy have their own understanding of what should or should not be done to implement and improve laws and regulations. Their policy preferences frequently differ from those of the presidential-appointed political executives to whom they report. Most of them are more loyal to the departments and agencies in which they work than to the president and his appointed executives. Moreover, civil servants are hard to remove from office; hence the term "permanent government." Presidents usually want to change things, advancing or retarding government programs and spending, based on ideological or political imperatives; the permanent government, on the other hand, often has a stake in preserving the status quo and thus resists change.

Because a majority of bureaucrats are Democrats or Independents leaning in a Democratic direction, there are tendencies, varying by agency and administration, to support more liberal policies than Republican presidents want and to support the status quo against retrenchment. Presidents Nixon, Reagan, and George W. Bush, especially, felt frustrated by the permanent government and tried to "conquer" or at least counter the federal establishment. Thus are raised a full stable of issues and problems including the power to hire, fire, and organize the executive branch; coordination and leadership; authority; and secrecy—all involving questions of effectiveness, efficiency, and reasoned judgment.[23]

The size of executive agencies, the nature of their responsibilities, and the characteristics of the workforce create difficulties. They put great pressure on the political executives in the second and third tiers of administration who walk a fine line between loyalties up to their bosses (the president and his agency heads) and loyalties down the chain of command to the bureaucrats on whom they must depend. Complicating the matter is the short time most political appointees are in office—about two years. A perennial danger is that these appointees, even including the heads of agencies and secretaries of departments, "go native" to adopt the agency's or department's perspectives rather than those of the White House. Faced with these difficulties, presidents may become frustrated and lash out or at least try to circumvent normal executive agency procedures. That can lead to dangerous actions, often violating standards of good administration and sometimes skirting the edges of legality or even going beyond.

The drivers of reforms for these problems are twofold. On the one hand are *administrative* values concerning the operational effectiveness and efficiency of executive branch units. Adherence to these values can have the effect of strengthening departments and agencies but weakening presidential control. On the other hand are *political and policy* values that strengthen the presidency but diminish the authority and independence of department and agency heads and perhaps undermine bureaucratic effectiveness, efficiency, and responsiveness to their clients and the public. Choosing between these goals depends on how one prioritizes the seven criteria discussed in chapter 1. The two cannot coexist in any measure of completeness. Chapter 11 will address some of the purely administrative issues; here the focus is on presidential matters.

Solutions: A Collective Presidency and Vice Presidency?

Some scholars have thought that the United States needs a collective presidency—two or three co-presidents, perhaps one for domestic policy, one for foreign and national security policy, and one for economic policy. A recent book proposes a dual, bipartisan presidency. One goal is to enhance reasoned deliberative judgment, effectiveness, and safety; the co-presidents would have a major incentive to come to agreement across party lines to "do the right thing."[24] Another objective is to dampen down the "swollen head effect" that seems to infect even the most humble politicians once they become head of government and chief of state. The scheme has problems, even in an ideal world. How do two presidents from different parties avoid deadlock? Who makes the final decisions when they disagree? For a tripartite presidency, who makes the final decision when domestic, economic, and foreign policy spheres overlap? How would the two or three co-presidents be elected—as a team or separately? How does the public hold the presidency accountable?

A half century ago, there were some proposals for a multiple vice presidency, roughly along the lines of the multiple presidency, with each of three vice presidents overseeing one policy area: national security, economic policy, and domestic policy. These vice presidents would be the president's chief advisers and go-to administrators, taking many burdens off the president's shoulders and perhaps displacing some of the powerful but unelected White House staffs. Problems abound. What happens when the vice presidents disagree, forcing the president to choose? Precisely how much authority would the vice presidents have—unless it were significant, the scheme makes no sense—and would cabinet members and other officials go behind their backs to seek direct access to the boss? What happens if a vice president disagrees with the president's policy? Which one succeeds to the presidency if the office becomes vacant?

A more popular reform at one time was to abolish the office entirely. For many years vice presidents had but three jobs: to attend funerals for heads of state around the world, to preside over the Senate (which is seldom done and strains the notion of separation of powers), and to wait until something terrible happened to the president. Occasionally a vice president did damage to the president, as was the case when Nixon's vice president Spiro Agnew resigned in disgrace, or to presidential candidates, when their vice presidential candidates seemed to lack sufficient *gravitas*. Such was the case of Dan Quayle, George H. W. Bush's vice president, and Sarah Palin, Senator John McCain's running mate. Both became the butt of countless jokes.

In rebuttal are arguments that strong vice presidents in fact serve the nation well, taking some of the burdens off the chief executive, giving him independent advice, and just "being there" when the country needs to know that there is a clear successor. The vice president's role has changed greatly, as vice presidents Rockefeller, Mondale, Gore, Cheney, and Biden assumed tasks of coordinating one or more areas of policy, traveling for the president, negotiating with House and Senate leaders, playing a heavy political role in promoting the administration, and raising campaign money. Nonetheless, it remains true that vice presidents are at the mercy of presidents as to how, when, and where their talents might be used.

One perennial complaint is that the selection of vice presidential running mates leaves too much discretion to presidential candidates, who may be motivated by political ticket balancing rather than by considerations of good government; and it denies voters a separate say on who will be a heartbeat away from the Oval Office. Suggested reforms focus on letting the party convention or some other party group select the party's vice presidential candidate and on forcing presidential candidates to pick running mates months before the election, during the primary season, to give voters a clearer picture. As Cronin and Genovese put it, "Even the most casual of political science students can discern most of the trade-offs and the deficiencies" in these suggestions."[25]

Solutions: Appoint and Infiltrate

To combine the values of presidential leadership and accountability with overall governmental effectiveness, efficiency, and responsiveness, students of the presidency sought ways to establish a stronger connection between the president and federal agencies. The most obvious means for so doing seems to be presidential appointments. Gary Rose and others, for example, favor re-establishing patronage—a modern version of the old spoils system—to let presidents appoint at least 100,000 administrators across the government.[26] This would allow his loyalists to penetrate and infiltrate the bureaucracy, giving it a presidential direction and overcoming internal resistance. In addition to questions of practicality—precisely how presidents would make the appointments and how long it would take—there are potentially serious consequences. Such a tactic likely would demoralize and undermine the civil service, leading to bureaucratic resistance; and it would be easy to see how presidents might make purely political appointments to offices requiring neutrality and expertise. Still, presidents do need to have their people in key administrative positions if they are to govern effectively and faithfully for the voters who supported them.

Presidents currently appoint about 3,000 executive branch officials. In addition to about 1200 heads of departments and agencies and their top-level administrative teams, who must be confirmed by the Senate, presidents appoint "Schedule C" employees who are exempt from the civil service hiring processes and serve in a variety of policy-related and politically sensitive capacities, often as middle managers and functional specialists. A president's top-level administrators also control the roughly 7,900 members of the Senior Executive Service. These are mostly careerists who, in return for higher pay and status, serve wherever the political executives need them to take on important program and policy responsibilities. They are expected to render loyalty to their political superiors.[27]

The Challenges. When President Kennedy came to office in 1960, he had 286 positions to fill in the highest ranks of secretary, deputy secretary, undersecretary, assistant secretary, and agency administrator. President Clinton had 914. Of course, presidents don't personally make all these choices, let alone the Schedule C appointments; they have the Presidential Personnel Office in the Executive Office of the President (EOP) as well as advisors of all sorts to help. A major problem is that it takes presidents a long time to select and clear these nominees. A year into the Obama administration, the president had submitted to the Senate only three-quarters of his 422 top positions, roughly the same proportion as his two predecessors.[28]

Appointing the presidential government is challenging for at least two reasons. The first is the restricted availability of good people who are willing to undergo the rigors of the appointment and confirmation process. A high-level appointee will make less money and work longer hours than she did in the private sector; will fill out pages and pages of documents and statements; is sure to be scrutinized without mercy by the press; will be investigated by the Federal Bureau of Investigation and the Internal Revenue Service; and must undergo dozens of interviews. She surely can expect to be pounded by senators of the other party during confirmation hearings. The ordeal reduces the number of talented and willing people who might be appointed.[29] Matters are worse in a president's second term, after a president has made an army of enemies and the likelihood of great accomplishments is limited.

The second hurdle is the confirmation process. Presidents formally submit tens of thousands of nominations annually, mostly for military promotions and minor positions; and virtually all of these receive Senate confirmation. Only about 400 to 500 are for important administrative posts; and for some of these, at least, presidents are under pressure from members of Congress to appoint specific people—perhaps former members or former staff persons, prominent home-state politicians or executives, and so on. The prenomination give-and-take between White House and key members of the Senate, especially, is a long-standing practice and often determines presidential options.[30]

Depending on which party controls the Senate, nominations may face opposition, long delays, or a refusal even to vote on the nominee. Holds and filibusters have become common. Under President Obama, Republican senators filibustered a record number of executive branch nominations, but that problem may now be solved via the "nuclear option" described in the last chapter. During the first year of President George H. W. Bush's administration, it took the Senate an average of 51 days to confirm presidential nominees; under Obama, it was 61 days. Obama managed to fill only 64 percent of the total in his first year versus 86 percent for Reagan, 80 percent for George H. W. Bush, 70 percent for Clinton, and 74 percent for George W. Bush. For all presidential executive branch nominations from Clinton's second term to Obama, the average time between nomination and confirmation was 3.7 months. Failure-to-confirm rates, which ran about 5 percent from the 1960s through the early 1990s, jumped to the 15 percent range thereafter.[31] The Senate rarely votes to reject a nominee—the last such vote was in 1989 when senators rejected their former colleague John Tower of Texas to be the secretary of defense—but occasionally it either does not act or returns the nomination to the president. Sometimes presidents give up, withdraw their nominations, and make different ones. Ideological differences as well as ethical questions are the major reasons for blockage and delay.

To get around the roadblocks, presidents resort to other tactics. One is to take advantage of the Senate's recess between sessions, or during sessions when the Senate is not in operation, to appoint someone who may serve until the end of that session of Congress. Since 1981, presidents made more than 650 recess appointments.[32] Senate leaders countered this tactic by running one session (2012) right up to the beginning of the next Congress, in January 2013, thus eliminating the intersession "recess" altogether. Obama ignored it and made four recess appointments, setting off a storm of protests and legal challenges. The president then renominated the four whom the Senate subsequently approved. Senators tend to view recess appointments as a violation of their advice and consent powers and as presidential chicanery. One set of recess appointments to the National Labor Relations Board, made during a 3-day hiatus between pro-forma Senate sessions, turned into a Supreme Court case in 2014.[33] In that case the Court ruled unanimously but in a limited fashion, allowing recess appointments when Congress recessed for 10 or more days.

Presidents also get around Senate foot dragging by appointing officials on a temporary "acting" basis, but only for a limited time, usually 210 days. A third tactic—used to ensure coordination of executive departments, agencies, bureaus, and offices dealing with a common problem, to get around confirmation delays that leave key positions empty, and to maintain White House control over policies—is to designate someone *outside* of the normal chain of command to take charge. Frequently they are dubbed "czars" for a policy area, and their range of activity might be as broad as energy policy or as narrow as facilitating the payments from British Petroleum to victims of the offshore oil spill. A good definition is "an executive branch official who is not confirmed by the Senate and is exercising final decision-making authority that often entails controlling budgetary programs, administering/coordinating a policy area, or otherwise promulgating rules, regulations, and orders that bind either government officials and/or the private sector."[34] These czars have been cabinet-level secretaries, lower-level department executives, agency heads, or special appointees within an agency. More often in recent years they have been someone in or hired into the White House staff, and so they do not require Senate confirmation. President Obama has been the most aggressive in the use of czars, appointing 50 or more of them, thereby touching off a strong reaction in the Senate. Senators have four complaints:

- Presidents have neither constitutional nor general legislative authority to create offices and empower officials.
- They do not have blanket power to appoint officials who exercise executive authority without the Senate's advice and consent.
- Authority to make executive decisions results only from law, not presidential directives.
- Czars and their decisions are not subject to congressional oversight.

Congress cannot compel them to testify under oath at hearings; when they do show up before a congressional committee, it is not uncommon for them to refuse to answer questions on the claim of "executive privilege"—the long-established doctrine that purely internal advisory or policy discussions with the president are shielded from congressional access and scrutiny. Imposing a czar atop one or more executive departments has other consequences. Because they have no official authority over budgets or personnel, these officials must rely on lower-level executives to carry out their wishes; that does not always work as well as hoped. Furthermore, when a czar is put in charge of departments and agencies that do have their own secretaries or administrators, a measure of demoralization sets in, given the access the czar has to the president—which department and agency heads may not have.

Reforming the Process. Fixing the appointment and confirmation process is serious business if the president is to be chief executive in fact and is to be able to do what he promised as a candidate. Two studies for the Brookings Institution in 2001 and 2010 made a number of sensible reform proposals, some of which could be done by executive order and some of which require legislation.[35]

For example,

1. Simplify the forms used to gather information on appointees and the use of the same forms by the White House and the Senate.
2. Reduce the number of positions subject to required Federal Bureau of Investigation full-field investigations.
3. Modify codes of ethics imposed on political appointees.
4. Raise salaries for top-level administrators.
5. Institute a Senate rule requiring a confirmation vote on presidential nominees within 45 days of the nomination and placing a limit thereafter on Senate

holds. (A gentleman's agreement between majority and minority leaders would also do the trick, but it could easily be broken.)

6. Allow a joint majority of each party of a Senate committee dealing with a nomination to report it for floor consideration without hearings.

7. Cut by one-third the number of layers of political appointees within an executive department or agency, and limit Senate confirmation to positions at or above the assistant secretary level in departments and the top three levels in independent agencies.

8. Restore presidential executive reorganization authority (discussed below).

The 112th Congress took some steps on these recommendations, reducing by 163 the number of executive positions for which confirmation is required.[36]

One unsuccessful congressional attack on the czars was an effort to prevent funding their salaries. After a failed 2009 attempt, in April 2011, Congress included in a short-term funding measure a provision eliminating money for several czar positions that happened to be vacant at the time; in signing the bill President Obama indicated he would ignore the ban, arguing that it conflicted with his executive authority of supervise the executive branch. In short, the use of czars "transform[s] a system of government based on accountability to one in which most power rests unchecked in the executive branch."[37] The only solution left for Congress is to legislate that all officials, czars or anyone else, exercising significant executive authority must be confirmed. Such a measure would surely be vetoed.

Solutions: Reorganize

More coherent and functional organizational structures might improve government performance and presidential control. Presidents no longer have the authority they once had to reorganize, consolidate, or eliminate units of the federal executive branch, a congressional grant of power that expired in the 1980s. The obvious reform is to reinstate that authority. Before the Supreme Court ruled it out,[38] Congress used a "legislative veto" to let presidents structure the executive branch while maintaining ultimate control. It worked like this: Congress would grant a president or an executive agency authority to do something—reorganize governmental units, build dams on a river, spend money on a project whose particulars were not at the time clear—and watch what was happening. If the executive decision struck legislators as wrong, they would pass a resolution of disapproval, ending the matter. Sometimes that was a concurrent resolution (passed identically by both House and Senate) and sometimes it was a simple one-chamber resolution. In reality, it often became a single committee decision, undermining the principle that vetoing an executive action should be a collective decision of Congress. The legislative veto combines congressional setting of broad goals, presidential and executive discretion and action, and ultimate congressional say-so. Between 1932 and 1983, Congress approved 125 resolutions overturning presidential, departmental, or agency actions, of which 24 were related to reorganizations. The veto could be the solution to presidential organizational decisions as well as a host of executive branch actions, but the Court declared it an unconstitutional violation of the separation of powers and the "presentation clause" of the Constitution. One should note that, although formally banned, it survives in many other informal ways with respect to executive agency actions, retaining for Congress some measure of control.

Solutions: Bypass the Executive Agencies

The Predicament. In an era of more limited government, presidents could rely on cabinet members to lead and control their departments and to give the presidents the best possible advice. For reasons explained above, that strategy no longer suffices. Because they cannot rely on the advice they get from the heads of agencies and departments and because these executives do not always meet presidential performance or loyalty expectations, presidents over the years moved to develop their own experts. The evolution began when Franklin Roosevelt built a small personal staff in the White House. Later, based on recommendations from the Brownlow Commission, Congress in 1939 established the EOP, an institution intended to be a neutral and efficient organization to help presidents coordinate and oversee the growing federal establishment. In its early years, it had a modest list of functions and contained only several units, such as the Bureau of the Budget and the White House Office (staff), but the EOP evolved, taking on more functions and powers. Beginning with Richard Nixon in about 1970, presidents shifted its focus from coordination and management to political control and direction. Today the EOP consists of 11 units, including the powerful Office of Management and Budget, the White House Office, the National Security Staff, the Council of Economic Advisers, and the Office of the Vice President. EOP units come and go, sometimes out of necessity (a new issue cannot be handled by the departments and agencies) and sometimes to demonstrate presidential concern and commitment to a new problem such as drugs or poverty.

The White House Office has morphed from a small and loyal group of generalist and anonymous presidential assistants into a complex organization of specialists that now contains several councils, policy and support staffs of all sorts, legal offices, and so on.[39] The staff's job, and that of the EOP, evolved from ensuring that presidents get the *best advice from the executive departments* and agencies to providing *advice independent of those units.* The two functions—coordinating and managing the flow of advice, and giving advice, are inherently in conflict. As John Hart described it, the work of today's EOP "necessarily overlaps, second-guesses, and often conflicts with the work done in the departments and agencies," leading to an adversarial relationship between the executive branch and the White House. One consequence is that the president becomes removed from the operations of government and those who run it, and he depends more and more on, first, a limited number of cabinet officers (State, Defense, Justice, and Treasury) and, second, his White House staff.[40] Thus arises the dangers of "palace guard government," wherein the president is surrounded by loyalists who filter information he needs, protecting him from what they see as biased information and pressure from government offices (including his own cabinet officers), and who serve as veritable courtiers and "yes men" who squabble among themselves for the president's attention.[41] Isolation, recklessness, and groupthink may result, along with turf warfare within the staff, mixed messages, and mistrust between and within the presidential and bureaucratic establishments.[42]

Reforms. One reform seeks to downsize the EOP and White House staff, cutting back on their roles as policy advisors and advocates while emphasizing their original functions of coordination, oversight of budgets, management of the advice-giving processes, and assistance to presidents in their everyday tasks. This move would reduce their power, diminish the tension between the White House and the rest of the executive branch, and end the isolation of presidents. At the same time, the functions of policy planning, policy implementation, and advising presidents could return to the heads of the executive departments and agencies, where they once resided.

Coordination, however, is needed more than ever. Some observers suggest that it can be supplied by consolidating departments and agencies into a limited number of cabinet-level departments, as President Nixon once proposed in his plan to create a smaller number of "superdepartments." These behemoths would be tasked with long-term planning as well as short-term implementation and coordination. The alleged advantages are several. First, there would be less duplication and overlap in the executive branch, advancing the goals of efficiency. Second, the superdepartment heads would be much stronger and more important, allowing them to exert influence on the president and perhaps prevent him from making big mistakes. Third, this reform could lighten the burdens on presidents and streamline the White House staff, allowing them to focus on truly important issues.

The downsides to these ideas are obvious. Consolidating executive units simply makes for much larger and unwieldy departments, stretching the scope and range of command while making the jobs of departmental leadership all that more difficult. Can one superdepartment secretary actually run such a large entity? More powerful departments pose a threat to presidential authority and control, especially when their proposals find support on Capitol Hill. Moreover, consolidation might depress, rather than enhance, the objective of gaining multiple perspectives on problems, especially if those "supersecretaries" prove to be skillful at dominating their rivals and subordinates. Environmental protection, for example, looks different when viewed from the vantage points and responsibilities of the many departments and agencies; under one supersized unit, would those differing views get to a president's desk?

To foster multiple perspectives while retaining centralized control, presidents have established cross-functional advisory and coordinating councils such as the National Security Council, Domestic Policy Council, and National Economic Council. These are composed of the heads of relevant departments and their top deputies to ensure breadth and multiple perspectives, but they are staffed by members of the White House Office to give presidents control over their agendas and deliberations. These structures can be useful, but one of their primary effects is to strengthen the hand of those White House staffers assigned to orchestrate and support the councils.

Those who worry about excessively powerful White House staffs suggest that the top dozen or so presidential aides should be subject to Senate confirmation. The goals are to enable senators to bring pressure on them and to cut them down to size, ensuring that that they might be a bit less ambitious and haughty. Those who relish greater congressional authority and fear presidential primacy presumably support this idea; those who see the need for strong and independent presidential staffs shudder in horror. The proposal raises separation-of-powers questions. Others have suggested that to broaden the vision of participants, key staff members of the White House, EOP, and departments and agencies be interchanged for periods of time, hopefully moderating the antagonism between the EOP and the executive branch agencies. This proposal would have utility for the civil servants in the EOP and agencies, but presidential appointees in EOP and White House staff members seldom are in office long enough to warrant spending months on these exchange programs.

The dangers of isolation and groupthink are serious, but no obvious remedy exists. Ideally, the president's inner circle of trusted White House staffers should include a devil's advocate or, to use biblical terms, a "prophet," whose job is to challenge emerging consensus decisions and to remind the president of human fallibility. Holding up a policy mirror to the president and his advisors might invite a second or third look at what seem to be obvious decisions. The weakness in this notion is obvious: how can Congress or anyone force a president to listen to his devil's advocate?

The two-term limit and need for reelection present another problem: presidents must focus on short-term matters. There is no institutional locus for long-term planning or integration of domestic, international, and economic policies as are found in energy, trade, or environmental issues. A number of scholars and veteran government hands have proposed a planning unit within the EOP, composed primarily of neutral, relatively nonpolitical types—perhaps including the elite of the civil service—to handle this task. The idea confronts one stark reality: policy planning groups, such as in the State Department, have not had great success. Their plans frequently repose on dusty shelves, are dismissed as "unreal," or are buried amid the blizzard of crises and emergencies that swamp the parent department or agency. Presidents and their staffs, focused on immediate issues, seldom take seriously planning that is divorced from decision making, budgets, and implementation.

Presidential Authority and Practices

Unlike Congress, which is composed of 535 members, the president is a unitary actor sitting atop his White House structure, which sits atop the executive bureaucracy. Constitutionally, he possesses "executive power" and thus can issue orders, directives, proclamations, and memoranda to administrative officials. These constitute one form of executive direct action enabling presidents to institute or change management practices, give direction to departments and agencies, and mandate or forbid specific actions.[43] Not all are successful, as departments and agencies sometimes fail to carry out the orders.[44] Many of these orders have a legislative flavor and are used to undertake action in the absence of specific legislative authority or to preempt or maneuver around congressional wishes.[45] Examples are legion: Washington's proclamation of Neutrality in 1793; Truman's 1948 order to integrate the armed forces; Eisenhower's order sending federal troops to Little Rock, Arkansas, to enforce the Supreme Court's decision against racial segregation; Nixon's 1969 order establishing racial hiring quotas on federal projects; Clinton's "don't ask, don't tell" policy for homosexuals in the military; Reagan's order giving the Office of Management and Budget the authority to review all federal regulations using cost–benefit analysis; and a long list of presidential national security directives. President Obama, frustrated by congressional inaction on a series issues, announced under his "We Can't Wait" policy that if Congress didn't agree to his priority policies in, for example, environmental protection, gun violence, energy, and education, he would do all he could on his own, via executive orders. He did so repeatedly on these and other matters such as immigration policy and government subsidies for health insurance for members of Congress. Several times he changed provisions of the Affordable Care Act. His supporters pointed out that his use of executive orders is comparable to that of presidents Ford and George H. W. Bush; his critics argue that he has used them on more substantive matters in defiance of congressional authority. In 2014, a case challenging his use of executive authority on greenhouse gas emissions made its way to the Supreme Court.

Some of the most controversial exercises of presidential direct action have occurred since 9/11. Presidents Bush and Obama, claiming constitutional or inherent presidential authority to do whatever they judged best to protect the American people, issued commands concerning antiterrorism tactics. These included setting up the detention center for "enemy combatants" in Guantanamo Bay, Cuba; prosecuting both public and covert wars in Iraq, Afghanistan, and Pakistan; interpreting the laws on torture; instituting warrantless wire taps and other forms of electronic surveillance; mandating National Security Agency record keeping of Internet and telephone records; and stretching the authority granted by Congress in the PATRIOT and Foreign Intelligence Surveillance Acts. Presidents point to their executive authority, to their position as commander in chief, and to their oath of office: "I do solemnly swear that I will faithfully execute the Office of President of the United States, and will to the best of my ability, preserve, protect, and defend the Constitution of the United States." The assumption is that the "office" constitutes something close to a blank check in times of crises and emergencies. This is the theory of the unitary executive mentioned at the outset of this chapter. Based on the oath and the "take care" clause, the theory asserts that the president is quite literally *the* responsible chief officer of all things in the executive sphere, and therefore he on his own can determine what is and is not constitutionally permitted and thus what should or should not be done, regardless of congressional instructions to administrators. President George W. Bush reigns as champion claimant of unitary executive authority, having invoked the notion scores of times, forcing executive agencies into compliance, ignoring congressional wishes and directives, and at times simply ignoring provisions of the law. His effort to centralize and control regulatory policies is perhaps the best example outside of the national security sphere.[46]

Many constitutional scholars, lawyers, and civil libertarians judge these unilateral claims of and use of executive powers to be of dubious legality. Sanford Levinson, for example, asked whether his readers would support a change in the oath to read "best of my ability, *do whatever I believe necessary to defend the interests* of the United States."[47] Not surprisingly, members of Congress object as well, occasionally referring to "monarchical powers." However, short of a constitutional amendment (virtually impossible), clear and forceful legislation (subject to presidential vetoes), a denial of funding (rarely done because of the ancillary damage it causes and because Congress seems incapable of passing normal appropriations bills), or severe brow beatings of department or agency heads at hearings (which have little effect), there is little Congress can do. Frustration and rage follow, frequently leading to the default congressional response: obstructionism and resistance on other policies and appointments. Worse, in 2014, amid talk of impeachment, House Republicans commenced a lawsuit against President Obama.

Lame-duck presidents in their last weeks in office, especially when a president of the other party has been elected, have issued and authorized agency heads to issue "midnight" orders or regulatory rules that proved highly controversial. Outgoing presidents are not above trying to bind the incoming administration or forcing it to take unpopular actions, should it choose to cancel those orders. Although most such rules are merely the culmination of years-long efforts, some clearly are issued to lock in a policy that had faced heavy resistance. Making matters worse, some are promulgated without following normal procedures required under the federal Administrative Procedures Act that requires notices of rule making and opportunities for public comment, among other provisions. Such actions do not sit well on Capitol Hill, spurring some reform proposals forbidding outgoing administrations from issuing any rules or regulations during their last three or four months in office. Recently the Administrative Conference of the United States made a series of recommendations to curb this behavior. The key proposals were that such rules should be issued only after consultation with an incoming administration, should include explanations of the timing of their issuance, should not take effect until 90 days after the new administration has taken office, and should not pertain to internal governmental operations and structures. It also suggested that Congress authorize agencies to delay the implementation of such rules for 60 days without having to issue any formal reasons.[48]

Prospects for Reform

For all reform proposals, the issues are simple yet contentious. Should the government's chief executive officer be able to choose the people on whom he must rely to carry out the pledges he made at election time? Should he be able to organize the executive branch structures as he sees fit to carry out his policies? Should he be able to issue executive orders that involve policies and actions of the government without clear legislative permission? Should he be able to act in a unilateral fashion, at least in emergencies? Similarly, should Congress maintain at least some real control over executives and the bureaucracy to ensure that it is operating effectively, efficiently, and honestly, implementing policies in accord with congressional intent? One's answers depend on one's location on the continuum between presidential and congressional supremacy and on one's reading of constitutional grants of power.

There are three hurdles en route to reform. The first, as Matthew J. Dickinson put it, is that "the significance of an administrative reform is inversely proportional to the likelihood of its implementation."[49] Given the limited opportunities they have for achieving anything significant, and in the face of inevitable crises and emergencies, presidents focus on creating new policies and changing the direction of government, not on altering structures, procedures, and institutions. They especially avoid institutional reform, however sensible it might be, if reforms undermine the very staffs that presidents rely on and if doing so will eat up a lot of time, energy, and political capital. Presidents could make some major changes by executive order, but they rarely have the time or inclination; moreover, they can be mistrustful of reformers, suspecting that lurking beneath the most innocent-looking and efficiency-seeking reforms are political and policy agendas. Plus, presidents tend to like the authority that has become centralized in the White House and the EOP. Why would they decentralize power just because academic or management experts think it wise? Why would they abandon the powers they think they need to deal with terrorism, national and international catastrophes, important policy issues, and other emergencies? Why would they concede to Congress the ability to further frustrate their goals? If anything, their natural inclination would be to reform by expanding, not limiting, their authority.

The second hurdle is that each department and agency serves a key representational and responsiveness function. Think about farmers and the agribusiness, veterans, labor unions, the education establishment, Wall Street and businesses, environmentalists, western ranchers, cities and urban dwellers, scientists, and so on. Each interest has its own department or agency. Almost all government units deal with and in a sense represent constituencies that rely on the department or agency for help and support and in turn provide political support for it. Each such interest comes complete with its own formal organization, lobbyists, and even private foundations. They will resist as best they can any alteration in what often is a cozy relationship. This cuts both ways; interests will support or oppose presidential and congressional control of executive departments and agencies depending on how it affects them. Convenience and opportunism, not constitutional theory or legal realities, are paramount. Yet without support from these interests, reformers have little chance of success.

Third, significant reform ultimately depends on Congress. Chairs and members of its committees and subcommittees relish the legislative and oversight authority they enjoy over departments and agencies. They are little more likely to support executive branch changes that jeopardize that authority than they are to surrender their own jurisdictions within the House and Senate—certainly not when the organized interests and government agencies object. That, in part, is why at times Congress strongly supports the independence of certain agencies against presidential control efforts; conversely, at other times congressional committees seek to rein in agencies that pursue policies that run afoul of their preferences. To be sure, Congress has at times acted to reorganize the executive and even the EOP, but usually that comes as a follow-up to some crisis, scandal, or major snafu. The creation of the Department of Homeland Security is the best recent example. It is noteworthy that Congress has not reinstated the reorganizational authority that presidents had prior to President Reagan. Nor are most members of Congress eager to take actions that might enhance any presidential powers, especially those that smack of presidential unilateralism. The president or perhaps the judiciary will try to block any restrictive moves they take. Reforms, therefore, are likely to come in bits and pieces, reacting in an ad hoc fashion to particular events or uses of executive power. The prospects for any wholesale changes are slim.

QUESTIONS TO CONSIDER

1. Is the presidency imperial or imperiled? On what basis can one decide?
2. Should the Constitution be changed to allow non–native born Americans to be president?
3. What is the best way to reform the presidential election system—and why?
4. Should the president be given a freer hand in appointing high-level executives and in reorganizing the executive branch? Are congressional controls too limiting or too weak?
5. Is the presidential staff system dangerous? What are alternative models?

NOTES

1. Hugh Heclo and Lester M. Salamon, eds., *The Illusion of Presidential Government* (Boulder, CO: Westview, 1981).
2. T. J. Halstead, "Presidential Signing Statements: Constitutional and Institutional Implications," Congressional Research Service report RL33667, April 13, 2007, cited in

228 THINKING ABOUT POLITICAL REFORM

Roger H. Davidson, Walter J. Oleszek, Frances E. Lee, and Eric Schickler, *Congress and Its Members*, 14th ed. (Los Angeles, London, New Delhi, Singapore, and Washington, D.C.: CQ Press, 2012): 296.

3. Scott H. Ainsworth, Brian M. Harward, and Kenneth W. Moffett, "Congressional Response to Presidential Signing Statements," *American Politics Research* 40 (2012): 1067–91.

4. Arthur M. Schlesinger Jr., *The Imperial Presidency* (New York: Popular Library, 1974); Charles M. Hardin, *Presidential Power and Accountability* (Chicago: University of Chicago Press, 1974); and Theodore J. Lowi, *The Personal Presidency: Power Invested, Promise Unfulfilled* (Ithaca, NY: Cornell University Press, 1985).

5. Judith A. Best et al., *The Choice of the People? Debating the Electoral College* (Lanham, MD: Rowman & Littlefield, 1996); Gary Bugh, ed., *Electoral College Reform: Challenges and Possibilities* (Farnham, UK, and Burlington, VT: Ashgate, 2010); Tara Ross, *Enlightened Democracy: The Case for the Electoral College* (Dallas: Colonial Press, 2004); George C. Edwards III, *Why the Electoral College Is Bad for America*, 2nd ed. (New Haven, CT, and London: Yale University Press, 2011); Nelson W. Polsby, Aaron Wildavsky, Steven E. Schier, and David A. Hopkins, *Presidential Elections: Strategies and Structures of American Politics*, 13th ed. (Lanham, MD, Boulder, CO, New York, Toronto, and Plymouth, UK: Rowman & Littlefield, 2012), chap. 6.

6. Edwards, *Why the Electoral College Is Bad*, chap. 1.

7. Brenden J. Doherty, "Electoral College Incentives and Presidential Actions: A Case for Reform?," In Bugh, *Electoral College Reform*, chap. 11.

8. Lawrence D. Longley and James D. Dana Jr., "The Biases of the Electoral College in the 1990s," *Polity* 25 (1992): 123–45.

9. Edwards, *Why the Electoral College Is Bad*, chap. 4.

10. Polsby, Wildavsky, Schier, and, Hopkins, *Presidential Elections*: 236.

11. http://www.fairvote.org/national-popular-vote/.

12. Larry J. Sabato, *A More Perfect Constitution: 23 Proposals to Revitalize Our Constitution and Make America a Fairer Country* (New York: Walker & Company, 2007): 148–51.

13. Darshan J. Goux and David A. Hopkins, "The Empirical Implications of Electoral College Reform," *American Politics Research* 36 (2008): 857–79; Andrew Gelman, Jonathan N. Katz, and Gary King, "Empirically Evaluating the Electoral College," in Ann N. Crigler, Marion R. Just, and Edward J. McCaffery, *Rethinking the Vote: The Politics and Prospects of American Election Reform* (New York and London: Oxford University Press, 2004): 75–88.

14. Robert W. Bennett, *Taming the Electoral College* (Stanford, CA: Stanford University Press, 2006).

15. Michael B. Grossman, Martha Joynt Kumar, and Francis E. Rourke, "Second-Term Presidencies: The Aging of Administrations," in Michael Nelson, ed., *The Presidency and the Political System*, 6th ed. (Washington, D.C.: CQ Press, 2000), chap. 8; John C. Fortier and Norman J. Ornstein, eds., *Second Term Blues: How George W. Bush Has Governed* (Washington, D.C.: American Enterprise Institute and Brookings Institution, 2007).

16. David Karol and Thomas E. Cronin, "Resolved, the Twenty-Second Amendment Should Be Repealed," in Richard J. Ellis and Michael Nelson, eds., *Debating the Presidency: Conflicting Perspectives on the American Executive*, 2nd ed. (Washington, D.C.: CQ Press, 2010), chap. 4.

17. For much of the following, see Thomas E. Cronin and Michael A. Genovese, *The Paradoxes of the American Presidency*, 2nd ed. (New York and Oxford: Oxford University Press, 2004): 329–32.

18. *Ibid.*: 332.

19. Sabato, *More Perfect Constitution*: 87–93.
20. Sanford Levinson, *Our Undemocratic Constitution: Where the Constitution Goes Wrong (And How We the People Can Correct It)* (Oxford and New York: Oxford University Press, 2006): 98–101.
21. *Presidential Power and the Modern Presidents: The Politics of Leadership from Roosevelt to Reagan* (New York: Free Press, 1990), chap. 11.
22. David E. Lewis, "Policy Durability and Agency Design," in Jeffery A. Jenkins and Eric M. Patashnik, *Living Legislation: Durability, Change, and the Politics of American Lawmaking* (Chicago and London: University of Chicago Press, 2012), chap. 9.
23. Joel D. Aberbach, "The Executive Branch in Red and Blue," in *The Annenberg Democracy Project, A Republic Divided* (Oxford and New York: Oxford University Press, 2006), chap. 6; Joshua D. Clinton, Anthony Bertelli, Christian R. Grose, David E. Lewis, and David C. Nixon, "Separated Powers in the United States: The Ideology of Agencies, Presidents, and Congress," *American Journal of Political Science* 56 (2012): 341–54.
24. David Orentlicher, *Two Presidents Are Better Than One: The Case for a Bipartisan Executive Branch* (New York and London: New York University Press, 2013).
25. *Paradoxes*: 314.
26. Gary L. Rose, *The American Presidency under Siege* (Albany: State University of New York Press, 1997); Robert Maranto, "Thinking the Unthinkable in Public Administration: A Case for Spoils in the Federal Bureaucracy," *Administration & Society* 29 (1998): 623–42.
27. David E. Lewis, *The Politics of Presidential Appointments: Political Control and Bureaucratic Performance* (Princeton, NJ, and Oxford: Princeton University Press, 2008), esp. chap. 2.
28. William A. Galston and E. J. Dionne Jr., "A Half-Empty Government Can't Govern: Why Everyone Wants to Fix the Appointments Process, Why It Never Happens, and How We Can Get It Done," *Governance Studies at Brookings*, December 2010: 9.
29. Nancy Kassebaum Baker and Franklin Raines," Uncle Sam Wants Few Good Appointees," *Los Angeles Times*, April 5, 2001: A17. See their *To Form a Government: A Bipartisan Plan to Improve the Presidential Appointments Process* (Washington, D.C.: Brookings, 2001).
30. Mitchell A. Sollenberger, *The President Shall Nominate: How Congress Trumps Executive Power* (Lawrence: University of Kansas Press, 2008).
31. Galston and Dionne, "Half Empty"; Jon R. Bond and Kevin B. Smith, *Analyzing American Democracy: Politics and Political Science* (New York and London: Routledge, 2013): 500.
32. Davidson, Oleszek, Lee, and Schickler, *Congress and Its Members*: 315.
33. *National Labor Relations Board v. Noel Canning*.
34. Mitchel A. Sollenberger and Mark J. Rozell, *The President's Czars: Undermining Congress and the Constitution* (Lawrence: University of Kansas Press, 2011): 7. Much of the following relies on this book.
35. Kassebaum and Raines, *To Form a Government*; Galston and Dionne, "Half-Empty Government."
36. P.L. 112–166, the *Presidential Appointment Efficiency and Streamlining Act of 2011*.
37. Sollenberger and. Rozell, *The President's Czars*: 167.
38. *Immigration and Naturalization Service v. Chadha*, 462 U.S. 919 (1983).
39. See http://www.whitehouse.gov/.
40. John Hart, *The Presidential Branch: From Washington to Clinton*, 2nd. ed. (Chatham, NJ: Chatham House, 1995): 50.
41. Dan Rather and Paul Gates, *The Palace Guard* (New York: Harper & Row, 1974); George E. Reedy, *The Twilight of the Presidency: From Johnson to Reagan* (New York: New American Library, 1987).

42. Irving L. Janis, *Victims of Groupthink: A Psychological Study of Foreign Policy Decisions and Fiascoes* (Oxford: Houghton Mifflin, 1972).

43. Phillip J. Cooper, *By Order of the President: The Use & Abuse of Executive Direct Action* (Lawrence: University of Kansas Press, 2002). Graham G. Dodds, *Take Up Your Pen: Unilateral Presidential Directives in American Politics* (Philadelphia: University of Pennsylvania Press, 2013). The next paragraphs borrow from these sources.

44. Joshua B. Kennedy, ""Do This! Do That!' and Nothing Will Happen": Executive Orders and Bureaucratic Responsiveness," *American Politics Research* 43 (2015): 59–82.

45. Michelle Beico and Brandon Rottinghaus, "In Lieu of Legislation: Executive Unilateral Preemption or Support during the Legislative Process," *Political Research Quarterly* 67 (2014): 413–25.

46. Christopher S. Kelley, "Rethinking Presidential Power—The Unitary Executive and the George W. Bush Presidency," paper prepared for the 63rd Annual Meeting of the Midwest Political Science Association, April 7–10, 2005, Chicago, IL; Kelley, ed., *Executing the Constitution: Putting the President Back into the Constitution* (Albany: State University of New York Press, 2005).

47. *Our Undemocratic Constitution*: 109.

48. "Administrative Conference Recommendation 2012–2: Midnight Rules," http://www.acus.gov/sites/default/files/Final-Recommendation-2012-2-Midnight-Rules.pdf/.

49. "The Executive Office of the President: The Paradox of Politicization," in Joel D. Aberbach and Mark A. Peterson, eds., *The Executive Branch* (Oxford and New York: Oxford University Press, 2005), chap. 5: 164.

CHAPTER 11

⤳

President, Congress, and the Policy Process

The defect must be supplied, by so contriving the interior structure of the government as that its several constituent parts may, by their mutual relations, be the means of keeping each other in their proper places . . . ; each department should have a will of its own. . . . Ambition must be made to counteract ambition. The interest of the man must be connected with the constitutional rights of the place.

—JAMES MADISON, *The Federalist No. 51*

Presidential–congressional relations determine public policy. This chapter focuses on three specific arenas in which those relations are tested and frequently found wanting: legislating, budgeting, and national security policy. All raise questions about the effectiveness, efficiency, rational deliberative judgment, and accountability of each branch and of their joint policy-making processes.

11.1 PROBLEMS OF SHARED POLICY MAKING CALL FOR REFORMS

Whether policy initiatives come from presidents or members of Congress, lawmaking requires cooperation. Policy flows most easily when the same party controls the House, Senate, and White House; when not, and especially when poisonous partisanship and ideological polarization characterize their relationships, troubles arise, leading to delay, gridlock, and a good dose of nastiness. What is to be done? Answers depend on which of the three modes of interbranch relations—presidential primacy, congressional dominance, or constitutional balance—and which model of political parties one prefers.

Neutral Reforms, More or Less

Citing a "constitutional dilemma" of "failed government" exhibited in the inability of the branches to cooperate, James L. Sundquist several decades ago offered a range of considerations that still today can guide the way to greater cooperation.[1] He wanted to arrange the structures, process, and powers of the House, Senate, and presidency to facilitate effective, efficient, and rationally deliberative legislating in a fashion that makes holding government accountable as easy as possible. His preferred reform was to institute party government, or at least come as close as possible, by arranging the odds to maximize chances that the same party controls all three branches. Not surprisingly, this notion finds little favor with the public; an April 2014 Gallup poll found that only 32 percent of the public favored unified government compared with 36 percent who thought it better to have different parties control different branches of government. Almost one-quarter said it makes no difference.[2]

The deck can be stacked toward more unified government. One way is to increase House terms to four years and Senate terms to eight (half elected every four years) and hold congressional elections at the same time as presidential elections. This reform eliminates midterm elections, avoiding the predictable loss of seats by the president's party. All policy makers and their challengers would face the electorate at the same time, giving voters the chance to pronounce their judgment on the *collective* governance provided over the past four years by the "in" party while giving the "out" party the opportunity to offer an alternative vision. A side benefit would be to improve the lives of representatives, who have the shortest terms of office of any major democratic nation, by reducing some of the pressures of ongoing campaigning and fundraising.

Sundquist suggested that candidates run as a team on a common set of policy positions. Doing so assumes that all candidates of a party share common views or at least that they refrain from overtly disagreeing with the party's platform. For congressional candidates, that could deprive them of the strategy of running for Congress by running against Congress and against Washington. It might facilitate the political education of the voters and perhaps stimulate turnout, with everyone focusing on the same important issues. Debates between the parties' candidates would be substantive and coherent. Combined with sufficient internal party discipline and cohesion to prevent candidates from abandoning their party's platform if doing so could enhance their prospects at the next election, these proposals would bring the U.S. system to resemble the parliamentary model under presidential strong-party leadership. Greater cooperation, effectiveness, and easier accountability follow.

The problems with this scheme are several. Eight years is a long term for senators, and half of them would always be running with, and half separate from, their parties' presidential candidates. That makes for two "classes," one tied to presidential and party plans and one relatively free from them. What if the voters confounded the plan by splitting their tickets and installed for four years—not two as currently happens—one party in the House and another in the Senate and/or presidency? Such results could double the duration of today's gridlock and obstructionism. The good news for those who like this idea is that ticket splitting has declined from its 1972 high to the levels of the late 1950s and early 1960s. Nonetheless, in a close election year, even a miniscule amount of ticket splitting could throw the institutional arrangements awry. To counter that possibility, ballots could be standardized to make it easy to cast a straight party vote. Alas, some states, as a way to counter straight ticket voting, have done just the opposite. Research shows that ballot forms matter, at least at the margins.

Another negative concerns the possibility of a unified government that can do "bad" things for four rather than two years. The framers deliberately picked two-year terms to give voters a finer degree of control over government and to provide the possibility of mid-presidential term corrections if public policy veers off course. Would longer terms insulate legislators from their constituents, giving them a dangerous sense of freedom to vote against their party or the folks back home? Could this just be another way to subordinate congressmen to stronger presidents? Since presidential candidates draw the most news coverage and voter attentiveness, the power question depends in part on who determines the platform and, especially, who nominates the candidates. If nominations are conducted as at present, a party's slate could lack cohesiveness, with the likelihood that a number of the representatives and senators would jump ship on some issues.

Other versions of this plan feature three- and six-year terms. Depending on particulars, these would: (a) add a year to House terms, cut one from presidential terms, and keep the Senate as is; (b) add one year for the House and two for the president, while keeping the Senate at six; or (c) change both House and Senate terms to three while giving the president a six-year term. Whereas presidents and members of the House appreciate longer terms, senators do not want theirs halved. Reducing a presidential term by a year probably would be a negative.

To achieve its goals, this reform must make it impossible, or at least difficult, for third-party candidates or independents to win seats. The reason is that, in an election resulting in narrow margins in the House and Senate or no majority party in either, third-party or independent senators or representatives could hold bargaining power far exceeding what their numbers warrant. That means that voters could not have much confidence in the promises of the parties because the final legislative products would owe much to those third-party or independent legislators. Party-based effectiveness thus falters, and accountability blurs. Sundquist offered another possibility: hold the congressional elections separately, a couple weeks after the presidential election, so that in selecting senators and representatives voters know which party owns the White House for the next four years and could vote accordingly. If current experience holds, this scheme could fail miserably. Typically, many of the voters who show up at the polls primarily because of the presidential election do not reappear two years later, and the "normal" balance of the parties returns. If that occurred under this scheme, the result could be exactly the opposite of what is intended, and presidents might well face a Congress of the other party.

Give the Presidency the Upper Hand in Policy Making

For those who prefer that the president have a stronger position in the lawmaking process, reform proposals abound. One set assumes strong and responsible parties controlled by the presidential candidates. Conceivably, presidents might wield a veto over the nominations of their parties' House and Senate candidates; or at least, if campaign contributions could be legislated to flow through the parties led by presidential candidates, they could control congressional campaign war chests. Presidents might be given some control, perhaps a veto, over the congressional committee assignment process. These are radical ideas that only avid presidentialists could support. One less dramatic proposal is to empower the president to present Congress with a finite number of legislative proposals on which Congress must act, voting them up or down, within a defined time frame, maybe three months. This fast-track, take-it-or-leave-it approach parallels proposals requiring Senate confirmation votes on presidential appointments to executive positions. Ceding the initiative to the White House puts

Congress in a defensive and reactive position. The complexities are apparent. When if at all may Congress amend a presidential proposal? What happens if the House or Senate takes no action? Surely no one would suggest that the proposal should become law. One imagines a president using one of his "must act" cards to try to force consideration of a substitute for a bill he does not want that is about to be reported to the floor from a committee.

Another Sundquist idea is to award a victorious president a number of "bonus" seats in Congress—enough to guarantee him a reasonable majority in each chamber. Perhaps these could be former presidents, vice presidents, governors, senators, and representatives—to bring into office seasoned politicians who have no election concerns. Questions abound. Exactly how many should there be, how are they selected, by whom, and from what areas of the nation? Might their status paradoxically render them independent of party leaders and presidential directives? Thinking through the possibilities makes for a dizzying brain game. Someone has to prepare a master list from which enough names are picked to meet the quota needed for a given year. Someone has to rank order the names on the list. What happens to those selected if they are not needed after the next election—do they automatically remain in the legislature or at least on the list? Possibilities are endless, but the addition of extra legislators committed to support a president would surely give him the upper hand on Capitol Hill.

Proponents of a stronger presidency argue for an item veto to allow presidents to negate parts of any piece of legislation (discussed below). Forty-four governors have some variant of that power. An item veto on one bill could be used as a bargaining tool to influence congressional action on another, dramatically altering the balance of power between the branches. To be sure, Congress can override a veto, but that task is daunting. As of February 2015, only 110 of 1,498 regular (i.e., not "pocket" end of congressional session) presidential vetoes have been overridden; since 1977, it is 16 of 131.[3] A de facto item veto has emerged through presidential "signing statements" described in the last chapter.

No, Give Congress a Stronger Hand

Veto Politics. Suppose the reformer's goal is to give Congress the upper hand over the presidency and executive branch or at least to bring the two branches into balance. One reform to accomplish this is to change the number of votes needed to override a veto, reducing it from two-thirds to three-fifths. Not only might that lead to more overrides (but probably not *all that many* more), but also it would change the bargaining game considerably, reducing the credibility of a veto threat—which probably is more important than an actual veto. Vetoes themselves often are not final because vetoed bills frequently are amended and sent back for presidential approval.

Legislative Veto. A second reform is formally to resurrect the constitutionally banned legislative veto, described in the last chapter. A mild form of this tool is the "waiting period" version that states that once the executive has decided how to implement a congressional mandate, action must wait to give Congress time to decide to initiate legislation to stop it. Such legislation, naturally, is subject to presidential veto. One consequence would be to stall what might otherwise be urgent executive actions, but that could be countered by limiting the waiting period. Congress, it should be noted, has continued to insert legislative vetoes of all sorts into hundreds of laws, and presidents continue to ignore them or, frequently, comply with them informally. Indeed, the informal practice of an executive agency's "coming into agreement" with a committee remains a way to ensure compliance with congressional wishes.

Debate. Some scholars and a few members of Congress have suggested that the United States institute a version of the British "Question Hour," a weekly or biweekly exchange during which the prime minister faces questions from members of the House of Commons. This reform requires the president, with department and agency heads, to appear before one or both chambers. The ostensible goals are to force presidents and administrators to think deeply about their policies and to educate the public. Frequently these British episodes deteriorate into circuslike exchanges that give the prime minister a chance to devise clever and witty retorts to dismiss criticisms and counter political point making. As always, there is the issue of which questions may be put to the executive, by whom, and how they are to be worded. Presidents hold press conferences and easily deflect reporters' queries, but that should be harder to do when facing chairs of powerful committees and party leaders in a televised forum. Still, the challenge would be to compel the respondents to provide straightforward answers.

Oversight. A fourth set of policy-related reforms focuses on the rivalry for control over the implementation of laws by the executive branch. The president is the chief executive officer, but Congress is a board of directors that wants to ensure compliance with its laws. Congress does not lack oversight tools. Senate confirmation proceedings extract commitments from presidential nominees for executive offices. Congressional committees annually hold hundreds of hearings and conduct investigations of all sorts, using them and reports on proposed legislation to issue reams of instructions. Congress requires thousands of reports from executive agencies; it has access to the work of inspectors general in executive units and the investigative staffs of the Government Accountability Office; and staffs maintain regular interaction with executive offices. Most important is the power of the purse. Annual spending bills to pay for government operations afford the appropriations committees enormous influence over bureaucratic behavior. Amid conflicting pressures from constituents who want less government in theory but more in practice, from interest groups of all sorts pushing this way and that, and from an inquisitive and demanding media, senators and representatives have the incentive and potential to steer executive actions, press for compliance with legislative directives, and promote efficiency. How well do they do their jobs?

Most observers agree that the oversight record is inconsistent and in need of improvement. Sometimes Congress is aggressive—when scandals or executive maladministration are obvious; when "hot" new issues arise; when the media are on the hunt; when committees and subcommittees see opportunities to expand their jurisdictions; when committee staffs are entrepreneurial; and especially when different parties control the presidency and Congress.[4] A few committees systematically conduct hearings to watch over agencies under their jurisdiction and push them in the "right" direction, but they are a distinct minority.[5] Moreover, the focus often is less on policy evaluation and effectiveness than on program administration, inefficiencies, mistakes, opportunities to embarrass the president, budget cutting, and either attacking or protecting favored agencies, bureaus, and even individuals. The task frustrates many members. Said one, "You feel sometimes as though you are trying to wrestle an octopus. No sooner do you get a hammerlock on one of his tentacles than the other seven are strangling you." According to another, "To do it right, you have to hear an endless stream of witnesses, review numerous records, and at the end of it you may find an agency was doing everything right. It is much more fun to create a new program."[6]

The amount, intensity, and quality of oversight are functions of (a) the extent of policy differences between Congress and the president and executive agencies and (b) the costs to the members in terms of time and energy for what, if done systematically, often is tedious and unglamorous.[7] Executive cooperation varies; some agencies, especially in the national security area, hesitate to share information or documents, using high-level secrecy classifications or simply stonewalling to duck issues. The ace in the hole for presidents and top administrative officials is executive privilege, a doctrine that pits the political version of an unstoppable force against an immovable object. Presidents from Washington's time claimed the right to unfettered executive discussions protected from the prying eyes of Congress, lest external pressures and the fear of being "found out" deter open and honest dialogue among presidential advisors. Nonetheless, Congress must have information to carry out its constitutional duties. Congress acknowledges executive privilege, but when it becomes excessive, seems to be abused, is used to cover up mistakes, or interferes with congressional investigations, legislators grow furious and retaliate. They can make a public spectacle of presidential or executives' refusal to cooperate; issue subpoenas or contempt of Congress citations; legislate in a punitive fashion; or refuse to confirm presidential nominees or ratify treaties. In theory, Congress can cut off funding for presidential or departmental programs, but that is dangerous and self-defeating. Congress has supported and initiated lawsuits, the most famous of which was *U.S. v. Nixon*,[8] in which the Supreme Court affirmed the existence of executive privilege but made it clear that privilege has little standing when criminal activity is involved. The judiciary maintains its right to inspect even the most sensitive documents *in camera* to determine the validity of presidential claims and to separate truly confidential documents from others. The result, as in the Nixon Watergate tapes case, can be to compel the president to give Congress what it wants. Otherwise, for the most part, the courts have trod this ground carefully. The historical record and the advice of many constitutional lawyers are simply to let the separation-of-powers system resolve these disputes on a case-by-case basis; let the forces of constitutional checks and balances play out.[9]

To solve the congressional time pressure problem, several reforms discussed in earlier chapters are available, especially extending the Washington work week to five full days. Perhaps increasing the numbers of senators and representatives to provide more overseers would foster better oversight, as might bolstering committee staffs; but enlarging staffs can bring its own problems when ambitious staff members become excessively entrepreneurial in digging up new projects and generating additional work. Structurally, there are options. Both Senate and House have committees responsible for oversight, and 9 House and 4 Senate committees have subcommittees dedicated to that purpose. However, too many chefs in the kitchen—too many subcommittees claiming oversight authority over a given agency or bureau (with some attacking and some defending the unit)—make it hard to cook up effective oversight, inadvertently strengthening presidential rather than congressional control.[10] Reformers might consider whether centralized oversight committees in each house or oversight subcommittees in each legislative committee better facilitate effective oversight; currently, it seems that each has advantages in particular situations. In recent years, the House Oversight Committee has been active, but whether the goal is to ensure proper administration and improve executive performance or to highlight differences between the parties and harass the executive is not a bad question to ask.

Reorganization of the committee system to clarify jurisdictions could improve oversight. A radical but intriguing suggestion is to take advantage of the natural antipathy between the parties by putting oversight under the control of the "out" party— Democrats when the GOP holds the White House and Republicans if there is a Democratic president—regardless of which party has a majority in the House and Senate. That could lead to more than a little political harassment and grandstanding. Making sure that senior members serve on oversight committees and subcommittees might ameliorate the danger, unless those members had become too cozy over the years with the administrators they are supposed to watch over. Imposing sunset provisions on laws to force executive agencies periodically to demonstrate their effectiveness and to prove administrative efficiency gives Congress the opportunity to evaluate the policies and programs; but too many such provisions could overwhelm all participants. For all these remedies, care must be taken not to invite micromanagement of agency actions or to inject legislators' personal preferences into administrative functions; these can threaten effective, efficient, and reasoned decision making and enforcement.

Each of these reforms faces an uphill climb. Given the crush of multiple priorities, improving oversight is not a topic dear to most members, and voters are unlikely to apply pressure. Reform involves stepping on the toes of members and committees, as well as tangling with executive agencies. Most reforms other than reconstitutionalizing the legislative veto can be done legislatively or by internal mechanisms.

Can't They Work Together?

If one hesitates to advantage either the presidency or Congress but seeks cooperation and balance, some options may be available. One, suggested a century ago by President Taft, is to link the two branches by amending the Constitution to allow members of Congress to serve in high-level executive ranks, perhaps even as cabinet secretaries or agency heads. Former Wisconsin Democratic congressman Henry Reuss, an inveterate institutional reformer, in 1979 proposed that 50 legislators should take such positions. Congress could specify which offices were eligible; the president then submits a list of 50 nominees; and Congress accepts or rejects the list en bloc.[11] The scheme faces challenges. The House and Senate might not agree on the offices involved or on accepting the president's nominees. It is easy to imagine eager-beaver representatives and even senators vying for inclusion on the list, using their and their friends' votes on presidential initiatives to pressure the chief executive. It would be easy to block his list or force him to amend it, perhaps to include some of the other party's members if it were in the majority, raising the possibility that his political opponents would serve in his administration. Presidential selection of committees and subcommittee chairs for this honor could undermine congressional oversight of executive agencies or at least create a conflict of interest. If presidents picked other members, would their newly enhanced stature threaten the chairs of some of the committees and subcommittees on which they sit? Regardless of who is chosen, could these "legislative executives" handle the workload?

The reverse has also been proposed: allow heads of executive agencies, or their top deputies, to serve in Congress as nonvoting members. Their presence could bring expertise and facilitate deliberations in committees or even on the floor. A cynic might remark that, given the concentration of power in the White House, it should be White House staff, not line administrators, who should become faux legislators. The Question Hour idea, above, is related: heads of executive agencies and departments would appear before the House and Senate to engage with the legislators. As far back as the 1860s, Congress debated legislation requiring cabinet members to appear on the Hill when legislation affecting their departments is being considered. Beyond the problems of time management, it should be clear that this and the previous proposals constitute good examples of how a practice—elected members of the House of Commons serving as Government ministers—that fits the parliamentary system does not translate to a separation-of-powers system. History shows that if the parties in Congress and the president want to cooperate, they do not need artificial mechanisms to do so; if they choose not to cooperate, it is unlikely that any reforms like these would help.

11.2 IMPROVING FISCAL POLICY AND THE BUDGET PROCESS

Problems and Failures

What a record! An $18 trillion federal debt, combined with multiples of that in potential unfunded future liabilities. Inability to pass all 12 appropriations bills by the first day of the new fiscal year to fund government operations—only twice in more than 40 years and not since 1995! And when, as in fall 2013, everyone expects Congress at least to pass a continuing resolution to allow government to spend at the previous year's rates until appropriations bills are passed, a two-week shutdown of government! Pitched battles regularly occur over raising the debt ceiling to let the government borrow to pay its obligations, even as legislators fear cutting spending on popular programs. The machinations of 2011 and 2012 are illustrative. Facing the need to raise the debt limit, President Obama and House speaker John Boehner negotiated feverishly into July. Obama and Democrats resisted big cuts and demanded increased tax revenues; Boehner, under pressure from his right wing, insisted on slashing spending. Neither could accept the other's terms, so they devised a patchwork that included short-term increases in the debt ceiling and some budget cuts; and they agreed to establish a "supercommittee" to work out a more definitive solution. If the committee could not agree or if Congress failed to enact its recommendations, there would be across-the-board spending cuts in defense to inflict pain on Republicans and in domestic programs to make Democrats suffer. This "doomsday" plan was going to force both sides to compromise. Alas, the committee members could not agree; and the cuts—"sequestration" in Washington argot—automatically went into effect, establishing a new, lower spending base that would affect subsequent budget deliberations. A late 2013 budget deal pulled back slightly on the sequestration, but the impact remains.

Things were not ever thus. There were five surplus years between 1947 and 1957. As recently as fiscal year 2001 the government ran a surplus. There was a time, now probably past the memories of most observers, when Congress enacted most appropriations bills on time. What went wrong, and how can it be fixed?[12]

Spending. Traditionally, Congress establishes new programs by enacting authorization legislation written by its committees, often based on presidential proposals. Authorizations usually set a maximum on expenditures, and then the House and Senate appropriations committees in a dozen separate bills determine precisely how much money may be spent in a given year. The executive branch then writes the checks. Appropriations bills are supposed to deal only with "how much" money is to be available, not with policy matters; but by including negative limitations ("none of the funds herein may be used for . . .") and sometimes specific substantive provisions, appropriators can make policy. Conversely, authorizing committees can create programs that carry mandatory, often open-ended, funding provisions that escape appropriators' controls, such as the big-three entitlement programs: Social Security, Medicare, and Medicaid. These and others like the Highway Trust Fund operate outside of normal congressional processes. Hence their designation as "uncontrollable," meaning that their funds are raised and spent automatically and cannot be touched without changing the underlying laws that created the programs. Some programs borrow money, whereas others enter into contracts that must be honored. In addition, interest on government borrowing, costing more than $220 billion annually, must be paid to holders of Treasury bonds. Together, mandatory spending programs constitute more than three-fifths of federal expenditures, and few politicians want to touch them for fear of electoral retribution. The rest of the government's spending is discretionary, but most covers defense spending, salaries, or transfers to state and local governments.

Revenue. About 85 percent of revenue comes from income taxes and payroll taxes (Social Security, Medicare). Revenue would be a trillion dollars greater, enough to produce budget surpluses, were it not for tax expenditures—"loopholes" such as tax deductions, different tax rates for different types of income, credits, and exemptions in the tax code to encourage citizens to pursue particular governmental (and private) goals. These provisions at times cause two persons with identical incomes to pay vastly different amounts of tax. Credits for such things as mortgage interest, child care, environmentally friendly home improvements, and employers' cost of providing health insurance are almost impossible to kill because beneficiaries, and the legislators they elect, fight like mad to preserve them. The Senate Finance Committee and the House Ways and Means Committees have primary responsibility over taxes, but other committees get their fingers into the pie from time to time.

The Budget. Until the late 1960s, revenue and tax policy processes, although essentially uncoordinated, were orderly. Most changes came at the margins, and deficits were manageable. Much of the success reflected the actions of the senators and especially representatives sitting on taxing and spending committees. In the House, appropriators tended to be senior fiscal conservatives who functioned in a largely nonpartisan fashion. Roughly the same was true for Ways and Means members who controlled the tax code. On the executive side, the 1921 Budget and Accounting Act gave presidents control of spending requests from the various departments. It set up the Bureau of the

Budget in the Treasury Department, an office subsequently transferred into the Executive Office of the President in 1938 and renamed during the Nixon administration, with some new authorities and duties, as the Office of Management and Budget (OMB).

The process went like this. Usually in February, the president, relying on the OMB, sent a proposed budget to Congress, estimating revenues and expenditures. Periodically, he would propose legislation having fiscal implications. The budget process pits executive agencies against the budget examiners in the OMB who, theoretically, are solely concerned with dollars and cents, leaving policy issues to White House interactions with department and agency heads. In fact, policy preferences and questions about program efficacy slip into OMB analyses, complicating presidential decisions. Congressional committees considered the legislative proposals, whereas the House Appropriations Committee focused on spending, finally reporting 13 (now 12) appropriations bills to the floor. The House Committee tended to cut the president's spending requests, but the executive agency and presidential appeals to the Senate's appropriators restored some of the House cuts.[13]

Because of deficits caused by the explosion of new programs in the 1960s, because President Nixon was more active than his predecessors in impounding (withholding) funds Congress had appropriated, and because of partisan divisions between the branches, Congress by the early 1970s had had enough. The result was a momentous reform: the 1974 Budget and Impoundment Control Act, designed to block presidential impoundments (at which it has succeeded) and to create a *congressional* budget. After receiving the presidential budget, the House and Senate, relying on their newly created Budget Committees and the nonpartisan but influential Congressional Budget Office (CBO), and employing a set of procedural rules to facilitate action, was to enact a concurrent House–Senate resolution establishing a budget. This allowed legislators a macro view of revenues and expenditures, on which basis they were to set spending, revenue, and deficit (or surplus) targets. The budget bill allocated sums to 20 functional categories, such as defense, energy, and transportation, and to each committee handling matters affecting the budget. In spring, the appropriations and tax committees would do their work, guided by the budget resolution. Ideally, in mid-September Congress would adopt a second, binding resolution adjusting the overall targets and requiring committees to report legislation to bring their previous actions in line with the final budget resolution. Those bills would be rolled into an annual omnibus reconciliation bill to be considered under expedited rules in both chambers.

The reform faced challenges, such as its complexity and timeline; and the budget resolutions expressed wishful thinking more than realism. As representative David Obey (D-WI) said in 1985, "the only kind of budget resolution that can pass today is one that lies."[14] In 1980, Congress moved the reconciliation process from September to May to avoid having to cut back funding promises made earlier. Despite rules to the contrary, substantive policy amendments slipped into reconciliation legislation. Members carved out all sorts of exemptions and employed "emergency" supplemental appropriations to violate the budget resolution's targets. Deficits rose steadily, so Congress in 1985 again pulled out its reform pen, passing the Balanced Budget and Emergency Deficit Control Act ("Gramm–Rudman–Hollings I," or GRH-I, named after its sponsors). GRH-I set tougher deadlines and mandated that if actual spending and taxing did not come close to the budget resolution's targets, mandatory and

painful sequestration would follow. Most of the budget—debt interest and entitlement programs—was exempted from the sequestration, which was supposed to be
handled by the General Accounting Office; but the Supreme Court ruled that sequestration was an executive function, not one to be handled by a congressional agency,
the Government Accountability Office. So Congress turned sequestration over to the
OMB by passing the 1987 Balanced Budget and Emergency Deficit Control Reaffir-
mation act (GRH-II), which set more realistic targets. They didn't work either because
deficits and congressional credibility marched in opposite directions. Congress went
back to the drawing board to produce the 1990 Omnibus Budget Reconciliation Act
and the Budget Enforcement Act. These promised deficit reduction via a multiyear
plan, modified the deficit targets of GRH, and instituted a "pay-as-you-go" (PAYGO)
system requiring that any spending increases or tax reductions be offset by tax hikes or
entitlement program cuts. Sequestration for budget violations continued, but within
specific spending categories (defense, international, and nondefense programs). Rules
changes made it easier to challenge spending that broke the rules. Here, at least, was
discipline! Although President Clinton and Republicans waged budgetary and political wars that included a government shutdown in 1995–1996, the new budgetary
rules, some 1997 legislation limiting spending, and an incredibly strong economy that
boosted tax revenue led to surpluses for fiscal years 2000 and 2001.

Substantial tax cuts, antiterrorist programs after 9/11, the Iraq war, and the ex-
piration of the PAYGO requirements set spending soaring, and the Great Recession
following the financial collapse in 2008 slashed tax revenues, leading once again to
skyrocketing deficits. When they captured the House in the 2010 elections, Republicans pushed through a rule forcing offsetting reductions if spending for entitlement
programs were increased. Tax cuts, however, were exempted; so any reduction in revenue did not have to be offset, putting more upward pressure on deficits. Then followed the debt ceiling and supercommittee saga related above.

Implications. The saga of failed reforms amounts to a congressional confession
that willpower is lacking; spending is pleasure, whereas taxing is pain. The reforms
failed to achieve their fiscal goals, but they have altered power relationships. Congress's efforts to force itself to be responsible have failed for several reasons: (1) ideological differences over fiscal policy; (2) split party control of House, Senate, and
White House; and (3) sharp internal divisions among House Republicans. Creating
the Budget Committees inserted another layer into the process, causing delays and
inviting turf and policy battles. The timetable probably was unrealistic, as was the assumption that a budget resolution in, say, June of one year can accurately predict
revenue and spending 4 to 16 months into the future. The traditional role of the appropriations committees as guardians of the Treasury gave way to a spending ethos,
and party leaders, by appointing members to the Budget Committees, have established more party control over what was a more independent and decentralized process, inevitably ratcheting up partisan and ideological warfare. Deadlines are not
met—Congress failed entirely to enact a budget for fiscal years 2003, 2011, 2012, and
2013—and enforcement of budgetary decisions is lax. A recent example occurred in
August 2013, when both the House and the Senate were unable to pass housing and
transportation spending bills that hewed to the limits set in their budget resolutions;
members wanted more spending. Said Stan Collender, a former Budget Committee

staffer, "You've got a situation where it's not so much that the process is broken, it's that no one wants to implement it because it forces them to do things that they wouldn't otherwise want to do. . . . So, rather than do any of those things, there's much less penalty for just not complying with the process."[15]

The glass is not entirely empty, however. Presidential impoundment excesses have ended; Washington focuses on budget issues in a way never before seen; and the 1990 Omnibus Budget Reconciliation Act and Budget Enforcement Act, along with the 1997 Balanced Budget Act, did bring budget successes under President Clinton. Recently, discretionary spending growth has been minimal, thanks largely to the 2012 sequestration. Deficits, although high, are declining. Thanks in part to the CBO, Congress holds a somewhat stronger budget posture *vis à vis* the president than was the case previously. The CBO functions as a budget scorekeeper, and members turn to it for estimates of the budgetary implications of legislation. Its "word" becomes gospel in the budget wars. Despite these successes, the congressional budget "fix" has not worked. Are there reforms that might?

Reforms

Balanced Budget Amendment. The hope of conservatives is a constitutional amendment mandating a balanced budget every year or, in other versions, over several years. The goal is to force more analytical and deliberative judgments on specific spending and taxing items. Opponents fear rigidity; unless there were loopholes to deal with emergencies, the amendment could lead to fiscal disaster. They argue, further, that clever politicians will always find ways around budgetary strictures, such as pushing expenditures into a subsequent fiscal year to avoid a current deficit.

As always, details reveal the devil. There must be room for emergency spending, subject to some supermajority vote in Congress and presidential acquiescence. Drafting language defining "emergency" and deciding how to handle inflation is tricky. Trustworthy estimates of spending and revenue are essential; whose estimates, the OMB's or the CBO's, are to be used? Do they include costs of proposed legislation or only "baseline" numbers linked to current programs? What happens when deficits differ from estimates because of a late drop in revenue caused by a weakened economy? Representative Justin Amish (R-MI) proposed a stark solution: look backward rather than forward, setting a given year's total spending at a level no higher than the average of the total nonborrowed revenues in the prior three years. Federal spending would drop significantly; any surplus thus generated would be applied to retiring some of the nation's debt. One could modify this proposal to allow for modest growth.

Who enforces a balanced budget? Would the courts be dragged in somehow? Who could bring a lawsuit against a president or Congress for busting the budget? In an economic or national security crisis, what happens if the required supermajority cannot be marshaled? The leverage available to senators and representatives whose votes were absolutely needed would be mind-boggling.

Multiyear Budgeting. The idea of a biennial budget has been kicking around for decades. In March 2013, the Senate passed a nonbinding amendment to its fiscal year 2014 budget resolution calling for a two-year cycle to give Congress time to conduct due diligence on fiscal issues. Overall budget strategy and enacting substantive legislation would occupy the first year, followed in the next by appropriations and reconciliation. In addition to fostering more reasoned and deliberative decisions, this could enhance congressional oversight.

The negatives are substantial. Although biennial budgets might work for long-term capital projects and military procurement, and perhaps some programs where spending is determined by predictable demographic trends, it is incapable of addressing shorter-term issues, such as abrupt changes in the economy's performance, inflation, foreign policy developments, or domestic catastrophes. If forecasting the economy for next year is difficult, projecting it out another year is bound to be futile. If it worked, however, biennial budgeting could give a slight breather to budgeters and appropriators on the Hill and might help a bit in facilitating long-term thinking.[16] The downsides, however, would seem greater than possible advantages.

Alternate Frameworks. Currently the government budgets on a cash accounting basis. Revenues and expenditures are counted when they actually occur, tempting legislators to enact policies whose costs do not appear for some time after the benefits, and electoral rewards, are enjoyed. In accrual accounting, on the other hand, costs are recognized when commitments occur, giving a better picture of economic and budgetary consequences. The CBO "scores" the future costs of new laws, but its assumptions must accord with the letter of existing law, although changes are certain to alter revenue or spending. Some have proposed "generational" accounting to make explicit the cost burdens of today's programs on the future generations that have to pay the bills. For programs like Social Security and Medicare, it is argued, the results will induce caution in expanding them. The catch, obviously, is the ability to predict the future.

Beginning in the 1960s, a pie-in-the-sky movement proposed that, every year or two, budgets for a given program should be recalculated from scratch. This was a zero-based budget wherein every program and item must be justified annually. It quickly became apparent that this is impossible. The idea vanished.

Another reform idea is to segregate trust funds, including the big entitlements that run independent of the taxing and spending process, from the rest of the budget and to divide the remainder among capital projects and operations. For years the Social Security Trust Fund has generated large surpluses that, when offset against operating and capital deficits, made annual deficits look smaller, confusing the debate in Washington and misleading voters. Those funds were moved "on budget" in the 1960s partly to offset spending for the Vietnam War and partly to provide a more accurate picture of the government's impact on the economy. Both forms of the budget could be available, improving transparency. Traditionally, borrowing has been justified to invest in infrastructure, such as highways, bridges, and education; but experts discourage it for current consumption and normal government operations that current tax revenues should pay for. They argue that if people want government benefits, they should pay for them, not pass the costs on to their grandchildren. Differentiating capital and operational costs can improve the quality of the debate, perhaps yield wiser judgments, focus attention, and thus serve the goal of accountability. There is at least one glitch. Are programs like education or medical care an investment in human capital, or are they merely ongoing government operations? Legislators eager to enact their favorite programs would find ways to classify them as capital investments, with an eye to borrowing to fund them.

Budget Enforcement. The PAYGO provisions of the 1990 Budget Enforcement Act did not end deficits but did slow their growth. The recent "CUTGO" version (extra spending must be financed by cutting other programs) exempted tax cuts. Resurrecting the original version across the board could restrain spending, but whether Washington would agree to do so is far from clear. A related proposal is to convert the annual congressional budget resolution from a concurrent to a joint resolution, giving it the force of law and, reformers hope, compelling compliance from the appropriations committees. Involving the president might be messy. First, he might have to disavow the budget that he provides in February. Second, it would lead to his direct involvement in congressional budgeting, causing delays and exaggerating existing political fighting. His veto power would be a game changer. Again, recent congressional willingness to ignore the legal requirement to enact a budget—the Senate has passed only five budget resolutions since 2002, and in 2013 there was no effort to merge the House and Senate versions—does not augur well for such a plan.

Tax Expenditures. A number of reformers suggest that the focus shift from government spending to the trillion dollars' worth of taxes that are not collected. They insist that if politicians want to achieve certain goals, they should enact appropriations and write the checks up front, transparently. This reform will be hard to achieve. Beyond figuring out which tax deductions and credits should be eliminated—all have passionate defenders in the executive branch, on Capitol Hill, in the offices of K Street lobbyists, and throughout the entire country—there are reasonable objections. Philosophically the claim is that taxpayers' money is theirs, not the government's, so let them keep it if that advances a governmental goal. Doing so also might be more efficient because there is no transaction cost—no need to create new executive units to administer the programs or to collect and disburse the money. The only cost is a miniscule one for the Internal Revenue Service as it processes tax returns. The negative consequence of tax expenditures is that they make it hard to have a rigorous and rational discussion of the purposes of the programs funded this way. One might, for example, want to discuss the wisdom of encouraging home ownership or of the best way to provide health insurance. Such a discussion would occur if the government were writing subsidy checks for these purposes; but when they are funded by not collecting taxes, that conversation becomes unlikely.

Item Veto. As mentioned above, presidents have lusted after the item veto to kill spending they dislike and to attack pork barrel spending that provides funds for, among others, a railroad museum in Pennsylvania, a Teapot Museum in North Carolina, and an indoor rain forest in Iowa. When Republicans captured control of Congress in the 1994 elections, they enacted a version of the item veto. Under their law, after signing an appropriations bill, the president had five days to transmit a message listing items he wanted rescinded. These cuts would take effect automatically unless Congress passed a "disapproval bill," which the president could veto, but with the possibility of an override. The law also allowed the president to veto tax breaks that affected 100 or fewer taxpayers or 10 businesses, and he could "cancel" any new provision that would expand entitlement benefits. President Clinton in 1997 used the power on 82 provisions worth about $870 million; Congress blocked his efforts to rescind another $1.1 billion and to cancel a handful of tax breaks. Several members of Congress sued, but the Supreme Court chose not to rule on the matter because the legislators lacked standing to sue—none of them suffered a personal, concrete injury. Eventually a hospital and some Idaho potato farmers who had lost money when their tax breaks were ended sued and won. The Supreme Court ruled that presidents have no constitutional authority for this form of veto; bills must be vetoed in their entirety.[17] Subsequently, President Obama in 2010 proposed a new version of rescission authority, but it failed of enactment. More recently, the House in early 2013 passed a bipartisan bill providing for such authority over the objections of leaders of the Appropriations Committee. Under its provisions, a president would have 10 days after an appropriations bill became law to submit to Congress a list of items for which appropriations had been made; if brought to the floor, these cuts would face an up or down vote in each house. The bill died in the Senate, where leaders and the Appropriations Committee members objected.

Arguments to amend the Constitution to include the item veto are straightforward.[18] First, it has worked, both for the United States in 1997 and in the states. It can and does save some money and induce budget discipline. Second, although the framers intended presidents to approve or veto whole bills, the nature of appropriating has changed dramatically over the years. No longer does Congress pass a dozen discrete measures; more often, because Congress fails to act by the start of a new fiscal year, they roll appropriations bills into omnibus measures, and then they infuse the bills (or accompanying reports) with all sorts of special interest provisions, pork barrel spending, and other riders to mandate or forbid spending. Third, the item veto might cause presidents to rely less on constitutionally dubious signing statements when they want to hold back on spending. It would also focus accountability for spending, whereas now presidents can throw up their hands and blame Congress for bridges that go nowhere. Vetoing an entire bill to get at several particular items is like using a cannon to kill a mosquito.

The negatives are equally powerful. The Constitution is clear; and omnibus appropriations bills long preceded the item veto movement. Nor is the item veto a solution for deficits; the amounts involved constitute not even a rounding error in federal spending. Besides, it could apply only to discretionary spending, not mandatory programs where the big bucks reside. If presidents wish to cut spending, they are free to propose and press for cuts in subsequent years. Would presidents really veto popular tax credits or deductions? Opponents value the congressional power of the purse, claiming that senators and representatives are at least as likely as, perhaps more likely than, presidential advisors to know what spending needs to occur. Furthermore, not only members of Congress want to include "special projects" in appropriations bills; there are plenty such items that were promoted by presidents. Giving the president the item veto inhibits the logrolling and "greasing of the legislative wheels" that often help forge majorities in the House and Senate.[19] It might also induce legislators to "pad" appropriations bills with extra spending measures for unneeded but popular programs, letting the president take the heat for cutting them. The strongest argument is that the item veto could dramatically shift the balance of power. Presidents could threaten to cut favorite programs of legislators to win their approval of his priorities, further enhancing what many see as an excessively powerful executive. If a president truly has strong objections to spending, he ought to have the courage of his convictions and veto the whole bill, if only to send a message.

An item veto's impact depends on its precise nature—whether presidents could veto titles, sections, paragraphs, words, whole numbers, digits, or even punctuation marks. In Wisconsin, the late governor Pat Lucey was a master at striking out words and numbers to reshape laws, sometimes drastically, even to reverse a provision's meaning. A lot also depends on congressional authority to override. To balance the item veto, a constitutional amendment changing the override provision from two-thirds to three-fifths might make sense. Unless the constitutional language defining the veto is crystal clear, however, serious litigation is sure to follow.

Reinstatement of Traditional Budget Norms. The biggest barriers to better budgeting are the political pressures to spend more without raising taxes and the partisan disagreement that shapes everything on Capitol Hill. With only two-fifths of the budget subject to annual adjustments, most of which is for defense and government salaries, the battles over the remainder are bound to be intense. Before the 1974 Budget Act, discipline came from the tension between the president and the congressional guardians of the Treasury and within Congress from the tussles between House and Senate appropriators. Pervading it all was a belief that a balanced budget was desirable, if not attainable. Regular legislative order, placing responsibility on committees and their chairs, controlled the processes. All that is now gone. Absent such norms, all the mechanical and legal gimmicks in the world are unlikely to control deficit spending. The good news, if that it is, is that the battles between Tea Party Republicans and Democrats, and the sequestration, have imposed some semblance of fiscal discipline.

11.3 REFORMING NATIONAL SECURITY POLICY MAKING

Perhaps no tension between the branches is more important than the struggle over direction and control of foreign and national security policy and, in particular, the use of military force. Ask almost any pundit, journalist, or scholar about the role and power of Congress in these areas, and the odds are she will answer with something like, "Congress tinkers at the margins of foreign policy, usually pandering to domestic political needs; on the big, tough issues, it defers to the president, abdicating its authority." Such a response contains a good element of truth, but it also misleads.

Constitutionally, a president is situated to dominate. He is the official voice of the country, commander in chief of the military, and chief executive. These constitute the claim to policy leadership and to almost blanket power to use the military when presidents judge it to be in the interests of national security or to implement treaty obligations. Congress is not powerless, however. It possesses constitutional authority to tax and spend for the "common defense," to regulate commerce with foreign nations, to raise and support armies, to provide and maintain a navy, to make rules for the army and navy, to utilize state militias to repel invasions and provide for their arming and discipline, and to make all laws "necessary and proper" for the foregoing. Only Congress can declare war—the framers originally said "make war" but switched in recognition of emergencies. That opening has been large enough to drive a tank through. Indeed, presidents have committed U.S. forces hundreds of times. Wars and other hostilities, however, are only part of what constitutes U.S. foreign and defense policy.

Crises and War—Who's in Charge and Who Should Be?

National security policy can be thought of in four sometimes overlapping and imprecise categories: (1) crises, (2) the use of force, (3) strategic policy (what should be done?), and, for want of a better word, (4) structural policy (how should it be done?). Presidents dominate crises because they hold the constitutional and institutional advantages, because decisions must be made quickly, because secrecy is paramount, and because Congress is not equipped for such action. Defining "crises," naturally, pits White House lawyers against those on Capitol Hill. The president and a small circle of advisors make crisis decisions. These usually are rooted in an existing foreign policy consensus or ideology, and they turn on immediate information. Congress seldom plays a significant role. Political challenges come later, when presidential decisions turn out poorly or when casualties mount and popular opinion turns. The only reform that makes sense in crisis situations is a mandatory consultative arrangement involving congressional leaders (see below). No commander in chief would agree to be bound by such an arrangement, although presidents do occasionally choose to engage congressional leaders if only to protect themselves against subsequent criticism.

Crises frequently involve the use of force. The framers wanted Congress to control that decision, at least with respect to the initiation of conventional wars. Although Congress declared war only five times, it frequently provided legislative authorization to presidents to engage in military action, as was the case in Vietnam, Iraq (twice), and Afghanistan. At other times, presidents relied on a claim of inherent authority or on international treaty obligations. Few would object to clearly defensive military action, but what constitutes "defensive" in the post–Cold War era makes for acrimonious debate. Once forces are committed, presidents dominate the action. It is exceedingly hard for senators and representatives to change presidential deployment decisions or military strategies and tactics. It borders on a cardinal sin to deny American forces engaged in harm's way what the military brass says is needed. It can happen, however; Congress eventually cut off funding for the Vietnam conflict and ended other ventures.

Following two decades of what some term "consent without advice"—congressional deference to the White House—and in reaction to Vietnam, Congress in 1973 passed the War Powers Resolution (WPR) "to insure that the collective judgment of both the Congress and the president will apply to the introduction of United Sates armed forces into hostilities, or into situations where imminent involvement in hostilities is clearly indicated by the circumstances." The law specifies the following:

1. Presidents may use military force after a declaration of war, after statutory authorization, or in a national emergency "created by attack upon the United States, its territories or possessions, or its armed forces."
2. Before introducing the military into hostilities, presidents are to consult in "every possible instance" with Congress, and they are to continue consultation thereafter.
3. Presidents are to report to Congress within 48 hours, and periodically thereafter, after introducing forces into hostilities or into the territory, airspace, or waters of another country. The report is to include (a) the circumstances necessitating the action, (b) the constitutional and legislative authority

under which it took place, and (c) the estimated scope and duration of the involvement.

4. Absent congressional authorization, presidents must terminate the use of forces after 60 days, with a 30-day grace period, unless doing so is impossible.
5. Within those 60 days, Congress by concurrent resolution may end the use of force. (This provision was wiped out when the Supreme Court voided the legislative veto.)

Presidents resist, arguing that the law unconstitutionally infringes on their powers.[20] To date there has been no definitive court test, and it is unlikely that the judiciary will wade into the morass. Since 1974, there have been scores of troop or air power commitments, some of which were to protect the lives of Americans or foreign nationals, whereas others were aimed at terrorist or genocidal activities. Examples include the invasion of Grenada (1983); naval activity in the Persian Gulf (1987); deployment of troops to Panama (1989), Somalia (1992–1995) and Haiti (1993–1994); use of troops and airpower in Bosnia and Kosovo (1995–1999); wars in Iraq and Afghanistan following 9/11; application of airpower over Libya in 2011; the killing of Osama Bin Laden in Pakistan in 2011; targeted killings of terrorists; and President Obama's decision to bomb Islamic radicals and reinsert military advisors into Iraq in mid-2014. Some (Iraq, Afghanistan) were authorized by Congress in advance; most were not. Still others were deemed to be continuations of previous authorizations. In early 2015, President Obama asked for congressional authority to use ground troops in the fight against the Islamic State in Syria and Iraq, even while insisting that previous congressional authorizations have granted him authority to act.

Interestingly, presidents occasionally consulted with congressional leaders, and they often complied with the *post facto* reporting requirements even while denying that they had to. Usually the presidents report to Congress "consistent with" or "taking note of"—but not "in pursuance of"—the law's provisions. One count in 2010 put the number of reports at more than 130; it also found 18 cases of nonreporting.[21] Critics note that full reporting may reveal to an enemy all sorts of useful information. At times, such as Carter's and Reagan's sending of military advisers to El Salvador, George H. W. Bush's use of troops in Panama, Obama's use of airpower in Libya in 2011, or Reagan's use of the navy in the Persian Gulf and troops in Lebanon in 1982, presidents deny that their actions constitute introducing forces into "hostilities." Advance consultation has occurred, but often it consists of a briefing a few hours before presidents act.

The terms and extent of the law are anything but clear, and some implications raise eyebrows. There is no definition of "hostilities" or of their "imminence." The law exempts deployments relating solely to training and the use of the navy to protect convoys; but if such forces are attacked, it would seem to allow actions in their defense. Clever presidents can manipulate such forces to entice attacks, as the origins of the Mexican War attest. There is ambiguity about rescue operations inside another country, as occurred in President Ford's efforts in Vietnam and Carter's in Iran. Would attacks by Somali pirates on American private shipping allow presidential action without authorization? Perhaps of greatest concern today: may presidents pre-emptively attack terrorists on another country's soil on the assumption that they are planning to attack the United States or its foreign installations or are recruiting others to do so?

The WPR provisions on consultation are vague: who decides what "every possible instance" means, and who decides which members of Congress must be consulted? Some presidents, such as Obama before going after Osama Bin Laden, consulted with a dozen or more members of Congress; others have consulted with a small handful or none at all. How much information must he give them? Depending on circumstances, the 60/90-day limit may be much too long to prevent serious complications or much too short to allow the military to accomplish its goals. Interestingly, the limit starts with the presidential report; but if presidents fail to report, how does one count to 60? President Reagan pulled troops out of Grenada on the 59th day, following House and Senate passage of resolutions stating that the War Powers Resolution applied to that situation; but he did not acknowledge the Act's applicability.

Strategic and Structural Policies

Strategic policies—defining the national interest, deciding what the nation should do about alliances, trade, aid, arms control—and structural or support matters such as weapons systems, military construction and bases, specific trade and tariff issues, spending, embassy security, intelligence operations, transport, and certain internal military rules—are driven by executive leadership. At the same time, congressional involvement is common and influential; frequently it is determinative.[22] Congressional action is necessary to ratify treaties, to appropriate funds, and to authorize trade and tariff actions; these call for interbranch cooperation. Following World War II, especially under President Eisenhower, "politics stopped at the water's edge," and Congress tended to support the president more in foreign and defense policy than in domestic policy.[23] Since the mid-1970s, Congress has been more assertive, and often more partisan, typically amending authorizing or appropriations bills to block or limit presidential actions. Congress restricted U.S. operations in Angola; forbade U.S. businesses from complying with an Arab boycott of Israel, limited or cut off aid to countries supporting terrorism or violating human rights, imposed an embargo on arms to Greece and Turkey after their 1976 war, prohibited support for groups seeking to overthrow the government in Nicaragua, capped certain missile tests, restricted arms sales, and imposed economic sanctions on Iran. Normally Congress provides presidents escape routes via waivers of statutory restrictions "for national security reasons." Domestic considerations and the demands of groups such as farm or labor organizations, ethnic groups concerned about their relatives abroad, and businesses are what often drive congressional action. A prime example is weapons acquisitions. Building a new warplane or directing elements of its construction (the V-22 Osprey and the F-22 and F-35 fighters come to mind) involves subcontractors and jobs in scores of congressional districts across the country, leading to pressures to produce more planes than the air force or navy might want. Congress even mandated that U.S. military bases abroad burn American coal.

Congress can and does initiate policies, such as human rights bills and economic sanctions exceeding those presidents want. Congress regularly pressures presidents and executive officials via laws, hearings, reporting requirements, investigations, language in reports that accompany legislation, speeches, and media appearances. Annual authorizations for Defense and State Department spending provide handy opportunities. In 1993–1994, legislators prodded President Clinton to press the United Nations for an end to an arms embargo on Bosnia. Recently, legislators pushed for retaliation against China for manipulating the value of its currency and Russia for its adventures in Ukraine. Committees investigate executive actions in the security realm. The deaths of a U.S. ambassador and several staff at the U.S. embassy in Benghazi, Libya, in 2012 triggered a lengthy series of hearings; President Obama's swap of Guantanamo prisoners for an American soldier held by the Taliban in 2014 led to hearings and threats of impeachment for failure to consult with Congress, as required by law. Presidential actions in Iraq, Afghanistan, and Africa have been fodder for committees since 9/11. Presidents know what Congress can do and must factor such actions into their calculations.

Treaties require Senate approval, but in addition to ratification (about 70 percent of the time), the Senate can reject (rare), delay (for decades), amend (rare), add reservations that alter U.S. obligations, and tack on "understandings" to treaties. The House gets into the act to fund treaties and to provide implementing legislation. Presidents frequently get around treaty roadblocks using executive agreements, but even these agreements often need some form of congressional follow-up action. Senators and representatives participate in diplomacy when they confirm ambassadors, conduct trips and investigations, and sometimes attempt direct personal negotiations with foreign officials or seek to block presidential actions. In an unprecedented move that could undermine the president's negotiation position, 47 Republican senators in March 2015 sent a letter to Iranian leaders reminding them that any agreement Iran would work out with President Obama on Iran's nuclear weapons capability could be reversed by subsequent presidents or by Congress.

Oversight of the executive in these areas often resembles oversight in domestic affairs: episodic, reactive, and often driven by partisan motivations. The dangers of micromanagement attributable to domestic pressures are real. In 1978, for instance, Congress enacted a law to purchase copper for the U.S. stockpile to firm up prices to help the American copper companies. To find the money to do so, the law required the sale of tin, which infuriated the Bolivian government, a prime supplier of that metal. More than one admiral or general has thrown up his hands in exasperation at what they consider congressional meddling in details of policy and in operations.

What Can Be Done to Balance the Scales?

Foreign and defense policy is complicated, delicate, and dangerous, which is why Congress often defers to the White House—as well as why on occasion Congress gets its back up and plunges in. President Clinton's withdrawal of forces from Somalia in 1994, to cite one case, was facilitated if not forced by congressional actions.[24] When Congress criticizes presidential strategies and tactics, as the Iraq War demonstrates, it affects public opinion. Critics who opt for the congressional primacy model prefer that Congress assume a greater and more responsible role.

A Fourth Branch. A radical proposal whose provenance dates to the "celebrated Montesquieu" (an eighteenth-century French political philosopher of whom some of the framers were fond) is a constitutional amendment to establish a fourth branch of government to embody the "fœderative" (war and peace) power. As suggested by one authority, the Constitution can be amended to create a Council on War and Peace, composed of 50 experienced national security hands chosen by the state legislatures, who—based solely on *publicly available* evidence—make decisions on war and treaties. The Council takes from the presidency the ability to engage military forces and relieves Congress of the burdens of treaty ratification and oversight of the presidency.[25] Presidents could veto acts of the Council, and Congress always controls the purse strings. To enforce its decisions, the Council could petition for impeachment proceedings or take a president to court. Setting aside the practical impossibility of enacting such an amendment, one must wonder about the councilors' ability to withstand pressures from Congress and the White House. A disagreement among them could constitute a constitutional crisis. What if, the Council having declared war, Congress refuses to fund it or the president refuses to prosecute it? Conversely, what if the Council yells "stop" to a presidential military venture. Who would win? Nonetheless, the principle behind this idea is simple: the decision to commit forces ought to be either shared or undertaken only after broad-based deliberation.

Fix the War Powers Resolution. A second reform seeks to give teeth to the War Powers Resolution. In 2008 a commission chaired by former secretaries of state James Baker and Warren Christopher proposed a "War Powers Consultation Act" to clean up the ambiguous terms of "hostilities" and "imminent involvement in hostilities" by referring to "significant armed conflict." They also sought to strengthen the consultation provisions, an idea advocated with regularity but without results. Congress needs to add to the law language to deal with terrorism and the pursuit of terrorists located in neutral or allied countries, such as Pakistan. The only "hostilities" in some such cases could be those initiated by U.S. drones.

The late senator Robert Byrd (D-WV), one of the staunchest defenders of senatorial prerogatives, proposed the establishment of a special or joint committee, a veritable war council, composed of 18 congressional party and committee leaders. He wanted to require presidents to consult with that group before dispatching any military force, an effort to broaden the network of advisers. Some have suggested that this body be empowered to initiate or stop military ventures, but that would go too far. The point was and is to clarify whom a president must consult.

When the Supreme Court ruled that the legislative veto was unconstitutional, it shot an arrow through the heart of the WPR, taking away from Congress its ability to stop presidential activism abroad. Of course, Congress probably could pass legislation stopping a war, but the president would veto it. Then Congress by two-thirds vote could override the veto. In effect, notes Louis Fisher, one-third of the members of either chamber could continue presidential action against majority congressional opposition.[26] Under the WPR, congressional inaction forces a withdrawal of troops after 60 (90) days, but the question is how to ensure presidential compliance. Passing a concurrent resolution to do so, although not binding, might create pressure to end hostilities. In the end, enforcement of the War Powers Resolution runs up against constitutional challenges and presidential determination. The courts will not entertain suits to compel presidential compliance, and unless Congress is willing to take drastic action, not much can be expected.

Other Possibilities. Defenders of presidential power might advance a third remedy: get Congress out of the business of war and perhaps of national security altogether, giving the president virtually plenary power to determine what is and is not in the country's vital interests, including initiating hostilities. Proponents of congressional dominance or of constitutional balance would have none of this. Congress needs additional muscle, they insist. Perhaps the two-thirds requirement to ratify treaties is too steep a hurdle in today's divided capital. Involving the House directly in treaty approval has been suggested as well, with treaties requiring three-fifths support in both chambers. Explicit congressional approval of executive agreements involving military commitments or promises of financial aid would bolster Congress's role.

The only real powers Congress has are statutory prohibitions and controlling the funding for presidential ventures. Although it is politically impossible to cut off funding that affects the safety of the troops in action, Congress could punish presidents in other ways. In the past Congress legislated to stop funding of presidential actions in Central America. Theoretically, Congress could legislate, probably over a presidential veto, to institute an automatic cut in White House, Defense, and State Department civilian staffs and budgets any time that both chambers determine that presidents failed to comply with the WPR or reached an executive agreement without congressional approval or adequate consultation. That would at least force additional calculations onto presidential plates.

One final proposal is to create in each House a committee on national security policy, combining the defense and foreign affairs, and maybe intelligence, units. The advantage would be to establish powerful panels that would attract the best and brightest members, create the possibility of integrated and coordinated security policies, and establish a genuine congressional counter to the White House and executive. A joint House–Senate security committee would be too big, but suggestions to create three joint committees (foreign affairs, defense, and intelligence) have found support. Attracting dedicated and talented lawmakers to the task is important. Once the Senate Foreign Relations Committee, and to a lesser extent the House Foreign Affairs Committee, were considered choice assignments. Those days are gone. Armed Services Committees, on the other hand, still attract senior members who remain on them for many years, developing expertise and familiarity with military matters and Pentagon officials.

In the end, the only real solutions are to energize senators and representatives, stimulate their interest, and stiffen the congressional backbone. In today's highly partisan era, most serious efforts to check presidents, alter foreign policy, and oversee Pentagon activities come from efforts of the "out" party. Partisan motives, indeed, may be the only way to enhance congressional powers, but that too often means shifting the focus from well-reasoned deliberative, effective, and efficient *national* security policy making to tactics designed to embarrass the president to score political points. It is probably true, as James M. Lindsay said of foreign policy, that congressional assertiveness, obstructionism, or abandonment rests on the breakdown of what once was a security consensus about threats facing the country.[27] The threats may remain, but they are different; and the approaches to counter them are less than clear. All have domestic and political consequences.

11.4 SOLVING GOVERNMENTAL DEADLOCK

"The United States," wrote James L. Sundquist in 1992," is in bondage to the calendar."[28] He was referring to the four-year presidential term and to the lack of a means between elections to remove a president short of impeachment and conviction for "treason, bribery, or other high crimes and misdemeanors." Incompetence, moral turpitude, maladministration, gross exceeding of legal authority, poor leadership, and total loss of popular support do not qualify as reasons to kick out a president. Nor is there a way to break paralyzing partisan deadlock. In a parliamentary system, a majority party can replace its leader or force new elections altogether. The prime minister's self-defense is to beat the legislature to the punch, dissolving it and calling for new elections on his terms. The mutual threat serves the interests of caution. Sundquist and Sanford Levinson, along with other scholars and not a few senators and representatives over the years, suggested the need for something analogous to the parliamentary vote of "no confidence" that topples a government. The Twenty-Fifth Amendment takes care of physical or mental incapacities, and the impeachment process handles crooks and traitors; but there is no way to get rid of presidents who simply are bad at their job or seriously offend the nation's conscience. Remedies aplenty have been proposed. The simplest is adding "maladministration" to the impeachment clause of the Constitution, leaving to the House of Representatives the tasks of defining and proving the charge. Whether such a change would have been enough to convict presidents Nixon for Watergate and its coverup or Clinton for his sexual improprieties and lies is not clear. Impeachment for incompetence could become a partisan weapon; but the requirement of a two-thirds vote by the Senate protects against abuse. Moreover, the very existence of this new impeachment rationale might induce presidents to be more careful and more respectful of Congress.

The alternative reform to deal with irreparable gridlock—and maladministration as well—is the establishment of a constitutional vote of "no confidence and removal" by, probably, an absolute two-thirds of both houses of Congress, followed either by the vice president's becoming president or by a special election to fill the office of the presidency. Indeed, Representative Reuss introduced such a bill in 1974 in reaction to Watergate. The two-thirds number is needed both to counter a presidential veto, which surely would come if removal were possible, and to constitute a barrier against partisan hijinks. The time it takes to raise a charge, hold a debate, and act could stretch out, undermining presidential authority and running a major risk during any crisis occurring during that time.

The idea is attractive, but its appeal rises and falls with presidential behavior. As soon as a crisis passes, such as President Nixon's resignation, the enthusiasm subsides as Washington moves on to the routines of governing. Opting for a special election to pick a new president is the most democratic choice, but it is fraught with problems. Unlike the minority party in a parliamentary system that has its own "shadow" cabinet and is ready to assume power at the drop of a hat, choosing and installing a new president is not instantaneous. Does the incoming president merely fill out the outgoing chief executive's term, or does a new four-year term start anew shortly (how shortly?) after the election? What does that do to the case for simultaneous congressional and presidential terms as a means to facilitate cooperation? How often could Congress invoke no confidence?

The succession question also is complex. If the vice president becomes president under the Twenty-Fifth Amendment, the problem is solved—unless he had been complicit in the presidential behavior that led to the removal. If the vice president does not assume the presidency, must he leave his position on the removal of his boss or selection of a new president? If he stays as vice president, what if the new president is of the other party? Could the removed president become a candidate for the presidency at a later date?

If a president were removed, should there also be elections for the House and Senate as a means of inducing careful consideration of what Congress is about to do and to give the new chief executive a shot at having a Congress of his own party—which presumably is the solution to the deadlock that started the problem? If so, what does that do to the standard two- and six-year terms that run from January to January? Do members elected after such an event merely fill out unexpired terms, or does the dissolution of government reset the clock to the standard two–four–six-year term sequence? Do the terms run from the date of the new election, or should they be altered to commence on January, as now is the case? Timing of the next regular elections is an issue. How are candidates to be nominated, and how are their campaigns going to raise money quickly? Could they and their parties handle a short (six- to eight-week) campaign period? There surely would not be time for the normal primary process, unless it would be permissible to go months without a new president. The mind boggles.

A slightly different version of these ideas is to adopt Sabato's "confirmation election" described in chapter 10. A president losing a vote of no confidence must face the electorate for an up or down vote. The recall election similar to that available in a third of the states is another option. Upon a two-thirds vote of both houses, the president must run alone in defense of his record or against a candidate chosen by the other party. How that candidate is chosen constitutes a problem, as does the timing. Probably the simplest of all possibilities is to institute a vote of no confidence by two-thirds of each chamber, without removal, letting the moral and political onus of such a rebuke rest on the president's shoulders and perhaps leading to resignation or to altered behavior. Note that surviving a no-confidence vote of any kind might have consequences opposite of those intended. It could embolden a president, leading him to be even less mindful of congressional authority and thus moving into a graver stage of gridlock. A no-confidence vote without removal would become a tempting partisan tactic in a divided government situation, and it could have governance repercussions. As Cronin and Genovese point out, the overhanging threat of such a vote could also render a president too timid, afraid of undertaking needed bold leadership that might offend legislators.[29]

The flip side of the deadlock-breaking coin is equally intriguing. Why not let a president, frustrated by obstructionism in Congress, dissolve Congress and call for new elections, as prime ministers do in parliamentary systems? To prevent misuse of such power, one of two conditions should be attached. One is that dissolving Congress also means resignation for the president. Second, as Sundquist suggested, such a presidential move should require the support of a majority of either the House or the Senate. He offered one other possibility to break gridlock: taking the tough issue or issues to the country in a national referendum. As shown in chapter 4, that is not as easy as it might seem.

In the end, fixing breakdowns between the president and Congress defies mechanical or legal solutions. Which values one puts first will shape one's views, as will one's preference for presidential or congressional primacy and the means (strong or weak parties) to it. The sophisticated reformer must think through these issues, making sure that patching one crack does not widen another.

QUESTIONS TO CONSIDER

1. Would you support a change in presidential and congressional terms? Why, and with what consequences?
2. Should the president be empowered to present a limited number of bills to Congress that must be acted on within a limited time frame?
3. Do you think a version of the parliamentary "Question Hour" would work in the U.S. system?
4. How can Congress improve its oversight of executive activity?
5. What would be the best way to establish firm control over budgetary deficits?
6. Does the president have too much power over war-making? If so, what would be the best means for Congress to reassert itself?
7. Would some form of "vote of no confidence" yield more benefit than harm? How can gridlock be overcome?

EXERCISE

Consider Table 9.1. Fill in the cells three ways: (1) with reforms that would achieve each of the three models (presidential primacy, congressional primacy, or constitutional balance); (2) with the reforms best suited for the model you prefer; and (3) with reforms you think stand a chance of being enacted. Then compare your choices to those of your colleagues; why are there differences?

NOTES

1. *Constitutional Reform and Effective Government*, rev. ed. (Washington, D.C.: Brookings, 1992).
2. Jeffrey M. Jones, "Most U.S. Voters OK with Split-Party Control of Congress; Just As Many Favor Divided Control as One-Party Control," *Gallup Politics* (May 22, 2014), http://www.gallup.com/poll/170261/voters-split-party-control-congress.aspx/.
3. U.S. Senate, "Statistics and Lists," http://www.senate.gov/reference/Legislation/Vetoes/vetoCounts.htm/.
4. Joel D. Aberbach, *Keeping a Watchful Eye: The Politics of Congressional Oversight* (Washington, D.C.: Brookings, 1990); Mathew D. McCubbins and Thomas Schwartz, "Congressional Oversight Overlooked: Police Patrols versus Fire Alarms," *American Journal of Political Science* 28 (1984): 165–79; David Parker and Matthew Dull, "Divided We Quarrel: The Politics of Congressional Investigations, 1947–2004," *Legislative Studies Quarterly* 34 (2009): 319–45; Douglas Kriner and Liam Schwartz, "Divided Government and Congressional Investigations," *Legislative Studies Quarterly* 33 (2008): 295–321.
5. Steven J. Balla and Christopher J. Deering, "Police Patrols and Fire Alarms: An Empirical Examination of the Legislative Preference for Oversight," *Congress & the Presidency* 40 (2013): 27–40.
6. Quoted in Walter J. Oleszek, *Congressional Procedures and the Policy Process*, 9th ed. (Los Angeles, London, New Delhi, Singapore, and Washington, D.C.: CQ Press, 2014): 412–13.
7. Robert J. McGrath, "Congressional Oversight Hearings and Policy Control," *Legislative Studies Quarterly* 38 (2013): 349–76.
8. 418 U.S. 683 (1974).

9. Mark J. Rozell, *Executive Privilege: Presidential Power, Secrecy, and Accountability*, 3rd ed. (Lawrence: University of Kansas Press, 2010).

10. Joshua D. Clinton, David E. Lewis, and Jennifer L. Selin, "Influencing the Bureaucracy: The Irony of Congressional Oversight," *American Journal of Political Science* 58 (2014): 387–401.

11. James L. Sundquist, *Constitutional Reform and Effective Government*, rev. ed. (Washington, D.C.: Brookings, 1992): 234–45.

12. James A. Thurber, "The Dynamics and Dysfunction of the Congressional Budget Process: From Inception to Deadlock," in Lawrence C. Dodd and Bruce I. Oppenheimer, eds., *Congress Reconsidered*, 10th ed. (Los Angeles, London, New Delhi, Singapore, and Washington, D.C.: CQ Press, 2013), chap. 13; and Eric Patashnik, "Budgets and Fiscal Policy," in Paul J. Quirk and Sarah A. Binder, *The Legislative Branch* (Oxford and New York: Oxford University Press, 2005), chap. 13.

13. Richard F. Fenno Jr., *The Power of the Purse: Appropriations Politics in Congress* (Boston and Toronto: Little, Brown, 1966); John F. Manley, *The Politics of Finance: The House Committee on Ways and Means* (Boston: Little, Brown, 1970); Allen Schick, *Congress and Money* (Washington, D.C.: Urban Institute Press, 1990).

14. Quoted in Davidson et al., *Congress and Its Members*: 323.

15. Quoted by Paul M. Krawzak, "Don't Blame the Budget Process; It's Politics," *CQ Weekly*, April 8, 2013: 624–27.

16. Aaron Wildavsky, *The New Politics of the Budgetary Process*, 2nd ed. (New York: Harper-Collins, 1992): 433–35.

17. *Clinton v. City of New York*, 524 U.S. 417 (1998).

18. See the debate between Michael Nelson and Robert J. Spitzer, "Resolved, the President Should be Granted a Line-Item Veto," in Richard J. Ellis and Michael Nelson, eds., *Debating Reform: Conflicting Perspectives on How to Fix the American Political System*, 2nd ed. (Los Angeles, London, New Delhi, Singapore, and Washington, D.C.: CQ Press, 2014), chap. 16.

19. Diana Evans, *Greasing the Wheels: Using Pork Barrel Projects to Build Majority Coalitions in Congress* (Cambridge, UK: Cambridge University Press, 2004).

20. Louis Fisher, *Presidential War Power*, 3rd ed. (Lawrence: University of Kansas Press, 2013).

21. Richard F. Grimmett, "The War Powers Resolution: After Thirty-Six Years," Congressional Research Service, April 22, 2010.

22. David P. Auerswald and Colton C. Campbell, *Congress and the Politics of National Security* (Cambridge, UK: Cambridge University Press, 2012).

23. Aaron Wildavsky, "The Two Presidencies" in Wildavsky, ed., *Perspectives on the Presidency* (Boston: Little, Brown, 1975), chap. 19.

24. Douglas L. Kriner, *After the Rubicon: Congress, Presidents, and the Politics of Waging War* (Chicago and London: University of Chicago Press, 2010).

25. Brien Hallett, *Declaring War: Congress, the President, and What the Constitution Does Not Say* (Cambridge, UK, and New York: Cambridge University Press, 2012).

26. Fisher, *Presidential War Power*: 300–02.

27. "The Senate and Foreign Policy," in Burdett A. Loomis, ed., *The U.S. Senate: From Deliberation to Dysfunction* (Los Angeles, London, New Delhi, Singapore, and Washington, D.C.: CQ Press, 2012), chap. 11.

28. *Constitutional Reform*: 199.

29. Thomas E. Cronin and Michael A. Genovese, *The Paradoxes of the American Presidency*, 2nd ed. (New York and Oxford: Oxford University Press, 2004): 334–36.

CHAPTER 12

Unelected Policy Makers

The judiciary . . . will always be the least dangerous to the political rights of the Constitution; . . . [it] has no influence over either the sword or the purse . . . has neither force nor will, but merely judgment.

—ALEXANDER HAMILTON, *The Federalist No. 78*

The true test of a good government is its aptitude and tendency to produce a good administration.

—ALEXANDER HAMILTON, *The Federalist No. 68*

Although the public's attention focuses on the White House and Capitol Hill, the policy-making picture must include the judiciary and the executive bureaucracy. The judiciary's role is important for several reasons. One is the litigiousness of American society—"if you look at me cross-eyed, I'll sue you"—and the propensity of those who lose in the legislative or regulatory arenas to take their cases to the courts. A second reason is the judicial role in protecting American justice and fairness. Courts can advance or retard political participation (who gets to vote?), representation (can congressional district lines be gerrymandered?), and responsiveness (do unlimited campaign contributions shift legislators' attention toward big donors?). The judiciary's ability to void executive agency rulings can wreak havoc with governmental effectiveness and efficiency. Last, the Supreme Court often referees battles between the federal and state governments, between states, and between the president and Congress, tipping the balance of power this way and that. The power and behavior of the judiciary, together with its freedom from normal political accountability, are enough to keep serious citizens awake all night worrying.

The executive bureaucracy "runs" the government and probably has a more direct bearing on people's lives than anyone else in government as it writes rules and regulations to implement the laws, enforces those regulations, prosecutes violators, and administers the day-to-day operations of government. The bureaucracy constitutes the "support staff" to carry out the wishes of the president and Congress. That, however, presents a problem: whose instructions should it follow? Government's effectiveness and efficiency depend on a functioning bureaucracy that is responsive to people's needs, but where is the accountability to the public?

12.1 THE JUDICIARY: PROTECTOR OF OR THREAT TO AMERICAN DEMOCRACY?

Although *Federalist No. 78* assured its readers that the judiciary "is beyond comparison the weakest of the three departments of power," that proposition is open to challenge; and to the extent that the judiciary in fact is powerful, questions arise concerning the men and women who hold judicial positions and concerning the issue of accountability. The focus here is limited to five matters that, in varying degrees, affect governmental as well as judicial effectiveness, efficiency, deliberative judgment, representation, responsiveness, and accountability:

1. Judicial review, the power to declare laws and presidential actions unconstitutional;
2. The size and composition of the Supreme Court;
3. The terms and tenure of its members;
4. The appointment and confirmation processes; and
5. Workload issues.

Judicial Review: What Power!

The Problem: The federal judiciary's power of judicial review is virtually unique among the world's judicial systems. Although most Americans accept the judiciary's authority to void state laws, libertarians and conservatives have rediscovered the Tenth Amendment that reserves unallocated powers to the states as a tool to resist Washington. Upsetting to many, federal courts have voided state laws and constitutional amendments enacted via initiatives and referendums, a blow delivered directly at the voters.[1] Giving nightmares to some critics is the ability of five unelected Supreme Court justices with lifetime tenure to overturn the collective judgment of 535 elected senators and representatives and to stop a president dead in his tracks. Everyone knows the story of the *Marbury v. Madison* case in which Chief Justice John Marshall more or less invented judicial review, an authority that does not appear in the Constitution. Alexander Hamilton in *Federalist No. 78* posited the need for such judicial supremacy, but his view was not universally accepted. Regardless, Marshall staked his claim, and it has survived and thrived. By the end of the 2010–2011 term, the Supreme Court had struck down 166 federal and 1,307 state and local statutes completely or in part.[2] Appellate and district courts have not shied away from declaring laws unconstitutional either, thereby making or unmaking policy; and only a fraction of their decisions receive Supreme Court review. Judicial activism on states' gay marriage bans is but one recent example. When an appeals court rules, its decision affects only the courts within its regional jurisdiction (circuit), potentially leading to inconsistent constitutional understandings from one circuit to another if the courts disagree. When that happens, as in the case of the Patient Protection and Affordable Care Act (Obamacare), the Supreme Court almost always takes the case on appeal.

How can unelected, unaccountable, and unrepresentative men and women in black robes overrule the democratic lawmaking process? Are they that wise? Americans place more confidence in the Supreme Court than in Congress and the presidency, although the poll numbers are not overwhelming; even if they were, confidence hardly justifies the power of judicial review—unless one wishes to argue that democracy requires an undemocratic entity, some "Platonic Guardians," to make it work.[3] The discretion to select which cases to deal with and the divisions between liberals and conservatives create doubts as to whether the justices are simply playing legislative politics in disguise. The occasional basing of enduring *constitutional* determinations on the foundation of sociological, medical, economic, or psychological studies—which if subsequently proved wrong or inapplicable would seem to destroy the rationale used by the Court—exacerbates the problem. Overturning its precedents (about 2 percent of cases) further shakes confidence. It is not as though all nine justices agree, either, on *how* they should exercise the power of judicial review or make any decision. Some base their decisions on what they take to be the original intent of those who wrote the Constitution and the laws; others focus on the words and their context; a few view the Constitution and laws in terms of "evolving standards of democracy" or underlying democratic the "purposes" of the Constitution; and still others simply appear to be pragmatic and thus often inconsistent in their opinions. A constitutional crisis this may not be, but in the minds of some, it comes close, especially for those who see the Court's rulings as out-and-out policy making or constitutional revisionism in service of some ideological stance or personal policy preferences.

There are, of course, some checks and balances. Federal and state lower courts and executive agencies must enforce Supreme Court decisions, and the historical record suggests that cooperation is not always forthcoming. Congress on multiple occasions passed laws to overturn or modify Court decisions, but the Court can nullify them if appropriate cases reach its docket. Congress can add to or subtract from the number of justices on the Court; nine is not sacrosanct. It can restrict the Supreme Court's appellate jurisdiction; and it can create, abolish, expand, or modify appellate and district courts. On a couple of occasions, constitutional amendments, such as the Eleventh, Fourteenth, Sixteenth, and Twenty-sixth, have discarded judicial rulings. Presidents have resisted. Still, the general respect these institutions render to the Court bolsters its autonomy and authority.

Reforms. In addition to personnel issues discussed below, there are at least four possibilities to limit judicial review. One is a constitutional amendment requiring a two-thirds majority of Supreme Court justices to overturn *on constitutional grounds* a federal law or presidential–executive action. Having to build a six-vote majority in most instances will require the justices to reach agreement across liberal–conservative lines. That should build a firmer foundation for the decision, make for a stronger precedent, perhaps remove some of the suspicion that Court rulings are merely political decisions, and strengthen confidence in and support for the rulings. These, in turn, create pressures on lower courts for more faithful adherence to the Court's decisions and on executive agencies and states for more rigorous enforcement; the criterion of effectiveness would be served. The downside is the possibility for delay, indecision, or watered-down rulings; but if the Court's word is to be taken as final, not for a short time but for decades at least, the risks might be well worth it.

A second possibility is to allow Congress to override a Supreme Court decision that voids a federal statute or executive action by a two-thirds vote of each chamber, just as it can override presidential vetoes. Such an amendment would return to the democratic body the ultimate power over law and policy while preserving the judiciary's role and authority. Either the two-thirds Court majority or this override system should reduce pressures for retaliatory congressional lawmaking and executive resistance, which in turn just might give a boost to the Court's trustworthiness in the eyes of the citizenry.

The third approach is to check judicial review by threatening judicial careers. If Supreme Court and appellate court judges were limited in the length of their terms and depended on reconfirmation to remain on the Court, they might be more cautious in the use of their power. The downside, of course, is that failure to reconfirm does not reverse the decision that led to it; the justice is out of a job, but the decision, precedent, and consequences remain. Worse, a system like this might unduly influence justices' judgments, injecting political considerations into constitutional rulings.

The most fundamental reform is a straightforward constitutional prohibition of judicial review. The advantages are clear.[4] No longer could Congress and the president pass the constitutional buck to the judiciary. *They* become responsible for understanding and interpreting constitutional provisions; and their deliberations on such questions are open to the populace—the accountability principle at work. The Constitution presumably would be interpreted in a fashion more responsive to present-day understandings and concerns. The downside of these arguments is easy to see. What restraints are there on Congress? Could emotions of the moment, triggered by some catastrophe, lead legislators to trample on constitutional rights and liberties? Can elected politicians be trusted to inject constitutional thinking into political debates? Indeed, *should* the Constitution be interpreted in light of current social mores and economic thinking? Isn't it supposed to be a permanent set of ground rules for government, an anchor of sorts, a framework for how government is operated, a bastion of basic human rights? It is true that countries lacking written constitutions and judicial review, such as Great Britain, have managed to protect individual liberties; but there are plenty of counterexamples where legislatures or executives determine fundamental rights, leading to unhappy results. The debate over judicial review comes down to a trade-off between limits, safety, and perhaps reasoned deliberative judgment, on the one hand, and representativeness, responsiveness, and accountability on the other.

To the extent that the citizenry should see and understand the Supreme Court, a frequently debated issue is whether its proceedings should be televised, as is done in Canada. Doing so could educate the public, and it might encourage justices to be more precise in questioning the lawyers appearing before them. Such were the arguments of Elena Kagan and Sonia Sotomayor during their confirmation hearings. Conversely, the great fear is that it will turn Court arguments into an entertainment event, tempting justices to "perform" for the camera. Strikingly, Justices Kagan and Sotomayor *now oppose* television in the Court.[5] Perhaps a compromise could be to televise the justices only when they read their opinions from the bench, since these tend to occur only in the most important cases.

Size and Balance: Too Small for the Job?
The Problem. Perhaps the current number of nine Supreme Court justices is insufficient for appropriate representation, efficiency, and the deliberative process, especially given the historical presence on the Court of white males from Ivy League

law schools. The weaknesses of nine lies in (a) the lack of broader representation of women, minorities, and maybe graduates of less prestigious but still high-quality law schools; (b) the power given to five members—some appointed decades ago—in what often is a narrowly and contentiously divided Court; and (c) workload pressures.

Reform. Larry J. Sabato has argued for expanding the size of the Supreme Court to 12 members to help with workload and to enhance diversity and representation.[6] He goes further to suggest that that number be locked in via constitutional amendment to prevent congressional tampering with the Court's size. Sabato prefers an even number to prevent one justice from becoming the powerful "swing" vote and to reduce the Court's propensity to become a "superlegislature." In this way, tie votes merely reaffirm the appellate or state supreme courts' rulings, in his view putting the responsibility where it often belongs. The objection is that the nation needs definitive decisions on so many legal and constitutional matters. When tie votes affirm differing appellate rulings, the results can be contradictory decisions in different circuits, leading to even more law suits in which the litigants hope for the authoritative Supreme Court ruling. Nor is it clear why 12 is particularly good; would not 10 or 14 or 20 be just as valid? An odd number is standard judicial practice; why not 13?

Terms and Tenure: "I Could Serve Forever"

A Problem? Most federal judges hold their jobs "during good behavior." (Judges serving in certain specialty federal courts that derive their authority from legislation instead of the Constitution have limited terms.) It is rare for justices and judges to remain in office until death; only 1 of the last 18 Supreme Court justices left that way. Others retired, albeit at an average age of 75—a figure that would be higher but for several "early" retirements for reasons having nothing to do with old age or illness. From 1911 to 1940, 19 justices served on the Court for an average of 16 years each. From 1941 to 1970, 17 justices averaged 12.2 years. From 1971 to 2005, 12 justices served, averaging 26.1 years.[7] Setting aside comment on what constitutes the good behavior required to remain on the bench, understanding that when the Constitution was written people didn't live as long as they now do, and recalling that no other democratic country and only New Hampshire and Rhode Island in this country provide lifetime appointments, it is not unreasonable to question the long terms of Supreme Court justices and many lower court judges. One problem is that life tenure pushes the power of the judiciary beyond what the framers imagined. Second is the danger that long-serving justices at some point no longer can do the job; effectiveness, efficiency, and perhaps the quality of deliberative judgment suffer. More than one justice has nodded off during Court sessions; and age often brings illness. Chief Justice William Rehnquist missed dozens of oral arguments and meetings in the year leading up to his death from cancer in 2005. Justice William O. Douglas suffered such fatigue and mental lapses in his last year that his colleagues sometimes had to wake him for votes and supposedly hatched a plan to deal with the questionable validity of some of his decisions. Moreover, infirmity inclines justices to rely more and more on their clerks. Another view is that justices in their 70s and 80s are likely to be out of touch with contemporary issues, technology, and thinking, with the accompanying dangers of foisting obsolete views on the public and frustrating responsiveness to current needs. Issues that were prominent when justices and judges first took their offices, and those that constituted the judges' formative adult experiences, have come and gone or at least have been subjected to different understandings that, 20 or more years later, challenger earlier verities.

Justices decide when to retire, often a highly politicized decision. Liberal justices and judges prefer to wait until a Democrat is in the White House; conservatives await a Republican. Both sides are concerned about the ideological status quo on the Court, fearing to give the "other side" an additional seat. Waiting for a president of one's own party entices justices to linger beyond the time their mental capacity and energy warrant. Strategic and delayed retirement gives substantial and enduring influence to presidents who are lucky enough to appoint multiple justices and judges.

Reforms. Two solutions are commonly suggested. The first is to limit the terms of justices and judges. One can pick any number. Sabato, for example, advocates 15 years and would allow a 5-year extension for district and appellate courts—deemed less important in the big picture of judicial matters—subject to Senate approval.[8] Some writers favor 18 for the Supreme Court because it is easily divisible by the number of justices, nine, and makes transition predictable. Forty-seven states limit judicial terms to under 14 years, as do many other countries, so there is ample precedent. Terms could be even shorter, with justices and judges coming up for reconfirmation after, say, 7 or 10 years, but such short terms would produce incessant battles in the Senate and could harm the judiciary's ability to function smoothly over time. One approach is a series of successive fixed terms, each followed by a senatorial confirmation vote. The first term should be long enough to provide the independence and stability the judiciary (especially Supreme Court) needs, perhaps 12 to 15 years. A second term would be shorter, say 8 to 10, followed by a final 5-year term. This combination makes possible continuity with the constraints and checks that confirmation provides.

There is a possibility, however slight, that fixed terms will reduce some of the partisanship and filibustering that impede judicial appointments. Knowing that at worst a "bad" judge or justice will not be on the bench forever might reduce the incentive to block his or her appointment—especially if there were to be a second confirmation after a number of years. This arrangement opens the way for a "deal" in which the parties might agree to alternate confirmation decisions over some period of time; but that would be tricky and require an immense degree of trust. On the other hand, limits could engender more, not less, strategizing by presidents, senators, and interest groups about appointments. Election campaigns might well include a greater focus on, and fights over, judicial appointments than at present. Justices appointed at a young age and scheduled to leave the court in their 50s would be looking for their next opportunities.

The other reform is to institute a mandatory Supreme Court retirement age, probably 70, as in most other democratic nations and 20 states, or maybe 72 or 75 as in other states. This reform will generate turnover, arguably bringing in new energy and ideas and avoiding senility problems. Depending on when justices or judges are appointed, several could hit retirement age in a given year, and then none might do so for many years. Some presidents would appoint several justices and others none. Other effects are less clear.

The same arguments apply to district and appellate court judges. Moreover, for them especially, there has been concern that misbehavior, not to mention incompetence, is too hard to punish. Involuntary removal is rare: only 15 judges in history have been impeached and only 8 were convicted. Judges can be reprimanded, censured, and denied case assignments, but they cannot be removed short of successful impeachment proceedings. Term or age limits solve that problem; broadening the impeachment criteria may be ideal. One successful state-level practice is to allow justices and judges to retire at full pay when the total of their ages and years on the bench reaches 80. Congress also allows judges to continue in "senior status," giving them pay and perquisites but lower caseloads. Its effectiveness is hard to demonstrate, although more judges and justices retire rather than die in office than was the case before the law took effect. An additional financial incentive, perhaps a retirement bonus coupled with a sliding salary scale that declines after the first year of retirement eligibility, may be one way to encourage retirement at a reasonable age. The rebuttal to all these notions is the fact that many judges and justices have served with distinction well into their 80s.

Appointments: "Make Me a Judge"

Problems. Presidential nominations of judges below the Supreme Court are shaped by the practice of senatorial courtesy that gives senators of the president's party much of the initiative for and always a veto on appointments of district court judges from their home states. Partisanship dominates, with nearly 90 percent of district court appointees since 1981 sharing the president's party affiliation. A concern for ethnic and gender diversity has become more important. At the appellate court level, the president, advised by the Justice Department and political advisors, makes the call, but always in consultation with the senators from the states in the appellate court region. Because circuits cross state lines and involve senators of both parties, the politics becomes complex. Still, as true for district judges, shared partisanship with the president accounted for slightly more than 90 percent of appellate appointees between 1981 and 2011; appointment of white males, once standard practice (92 percent under Reagan and two-thirds under George H. W. Bush), dropped to 49 percent under President Clinton and 27 percent under Obama. Except for a few district court situations, all nominees for both sets of courts received the American Bar Association ratings of "exceptionally well qualified," "well qualified," or "qualified," although that designation guarantees neither talent nor judicial wisdom.[9] For the past three or four decades, blatant ideological considerations have become important.

The politics is intense at the Supreme Court level, with presidents almost always—90 percent over history—appointing justices of their own parties. Competence, credentials, and judicial experience are essential; but ideological compatibility—flavored with a good dose of ethnic, gender, and in the past religious and geographical representativeness—trumps all other considerations. Only the certainty of a confirmation battle might incline presidents to temper their ideological preferences just a bit.

Senators of the president's party are eager to confirm his nominees; those from the opposing party resist. Nearly one-fifth of all Supreme Court nominations failed to be confirmed, with the bulk of them occurring in the nineteenth century. After about a 70-year hiatus, the pattern of contentiousness, resistance, obstruction, and denial of confirmations flared up in the 1960s, when civil liberties and civil rights issues moved to the top of the Court's agenda and presidents abandoned any pretenses that they were interested in anything other than ideological compatibility. The liberal swing of the post–World War II Court persuaded Republicans that changes were needed, either in appointing conservatives when Republicans held the White House or in blocking liberal appointments made by Democratic presidents. Democrats are equally hesitant to confirm Republican nominees. The issue is not qualifications; it is political ideology.

The average length of the Senate confirmation process for all three levels of judicial appointments has risen dramatically, often denying the courts their full complement of judges.[10] Under Presidents Johnson, Nixon, Ford, Carter, and Reagan, the average appellate and Supreme Court appointment required no more than 3 months for confirmation; that rose to nearly 5 under President George H. W. Bush and during President Clinton's first term. In Clinton's second term and President George W. Bush's first, an average of 10 months went by before confirmation. That number subsequently dropped, but only to about 6.5 months in Obama's first two years—with a Democratic Senate. Out-and-out confirmation failure rates are up as well. From the time of President Lyndon Johnson to President Reagan, failure rates were about 7 percent for Appellate and Supreme Court nominations; that almost tripled from Reagan's presidency to Clinton's first term. After that it leaped to more than 40 percent.[11] The cause is the fear of tipping the partisan and ideological status quo in these courts one way or another.

The District of Columbia Circuit, whose confirmation rate was below 40 percent between 1991 and 2010, is the prime example. It is especially important, since it handles most federal government appeals and is a prime recruitment source for Supreme Court nominees. Recently, there has been a five-to-five balance, and neither party is willing to confirm a nominee proposed by the other's president. Moreover, because its workload is relatively low, there are proposals to reduce its size to eight, with the continued prospect of tie votes in key cases.

Failure to confirm occasionally includes outright rejection by the Senate, the most famous example of which was Robert Bork's nomination to the Supreme Court in 1987. The Judiciary Committee sometimes chooses not to report a nomination to the floor; and presidents withdraw nominees whose chances of approval prove to be slim. Failure of a home-state senator to return a "blue slip" (a form the Judiciary Committee uses to secure approval of the relevant senators) kills a nomination.[12] Simple inaction or stalling, via a hold or a filibuster until permanent Senate adjournment, has become the most common way of killing a nomination. These tactics led Senate Democratic leaders to invoke the "nuclear option" described in chapter 9 to push through confirmations of district and appellate court judges on a simple majority vote. Supreme Court nominations still can suffer a filibuster.

The consequences of failing to fill vacancies and of delaying confirmations are clear. One study of the 1971–2002 period found that the "greater the vacancy problem on a court of appeals, the longer it takes for the court to dispose of the cases on its docket and the larger the caseload for each judge is."[13] Although the temporary assignment of senior district court judges to appeals courts helps, the workload problem is real.

Attacks during confirmation proceedings on a nominee's character, ideology, and past experience—tactics designed to make political points rather than to examine a nominee's qualifications[14]—can do all sorts of harm, not the least of which is the disincentives they create for future nominees. Some studies show that when judges are pilloried for their previous rulings and pictured as unduly political, their stature drops in the eye of the public. Perhaps worse, such behavior challenges the judiciary's impartiality and leads to the conclusion that it merely functions as a third house of the legislature. No one knows precisely how this behavior affected decisions rendered by federal judges, but it is not implausible that there are ramifications for the act of judging.[15] Last, the wrangling over judicial nominations does nothing positive for the Senate's image or for the relationships among its already fragmented membership. Something, critics claim, needs to be done.

One Fix: Let a Commission Nominate. The selection of federal judges could be done differently. American states use a variety of approaches, ranging from appointments by the legislature to elections to gubernatorial appointments. Most states mix and match, employing one form for the local courts and another for higher courts. The modal pattern for the highest courts resembles the "Missouri Plan" in which the initial appointment is made by a governor from a list of candidates recommended by a commission. The commission's composition varies by state, as do requirements for legislative approval. These justices typically face either a retention election or a reconfirmation by the state's upper legislative chamber.[16]

Reliance on bipartisan or nonpartisan commissions of experts to recommend candidates—or in the extreme even to make appointments—seeks to ensure that professional competence characterizes the judiciary. Commissions have been tried for some federal district court nominations and seem to have had positive benefit, with confirmation rates for judicial candidates nominated by commissions enjoying a confirmation rate 12 percentage points higher than those nominated by governors.[17] Commissions are no panacea, however. They are essentially lawyer driven and thus somewhat inbred. When chosen by state legislative leaders, partisan considerations immediately leap to the forefront. Extending the commission model to appellate courts whose jurisdictions extend across state lines is more complex. Doing it for Supreme Court justices has been proposed by a good number of commentators, but the politics of forming a commission is delicate and surely creates more opportunities for partisan wrangling. Because there probably is no such thing as a truly bipartisan or nonpartisan commission, the primary advantage is that a commission's list of candidates at least has the *appearance* of impartiality and neutrality.

Another Fix: Let's Elect Them. Honoring the values of accountability and participation, almost half the states elect their highest court justices, and somewhat fewer states elect appellate court judges. Election of district court judges is common. Nonpartisan judicial elections are more typical than partisan ones. Although ostensibly democratic, reasonably popular among the public, and perhaps likely to induce sentiment for greater responsiveness to the voters, judicial elections and re-elections are fraught with problems.[18] Citizen knowledge of judicial candidates' qualifications is minimal, leading to potentially irresponsible voting. The public has a hard time distinguishing between the *legality and constitutionality* of matters on which judges rule, on the one hand, and the *substantive merits* of such issues, on the other. Yet that distinction is what separates judicial decisions from legislative decisions. Moreover, when the elections are nonpartisan, voters lack the cue they rely on most, party labels—precisely the cue that is least appropriate when electing "nonpolitical" judges. Millions of dollars must be raised and campaigns organized. The latter takes time and invites the same problems that plague legislative elections; the former opens the judiciary to complaints about excessive spending, potential corruption, and special interest influence. Judges, once on the bench, may have to rule on cases involving their campaign contributors. Elected judges, especially if seeking re-election, find themselves in compromising situations on a regular basis. The strongest yet somewhat cynical argument for electing justices or judges is that their jobs of neutral adjudication have morphed into *de facto* policy making done in the guise of constitutional and statutory interpretation; to that extent, the democratic mandate for direct accountability points to elections.

Anything Better? Other nations select judges differently. Would-be judges in France, for example, orient their education and legal experience toward attaining judgeships and must pass examinations to secure their positions. In the United States many judicial ambitions form later in life, with many shaped by purely political motives. Several other ideas are intriguing, if probably impractical. One is to allow the sitting appellate court judges in a given circuit to nominate judges for the appellate bench. Who would better know and be able to evaluate the qualifications of potential candidates—all of whom presumably are district judges whose cases had been reviewed at the appellate level? Perhaps nominations could be facilitated by consulting candidates' fellow judges of the circuit's district courts. Gerry Spence has suggested random selection of lower-level judges from a list assembled by each district's lawyers who have been involved in trials in that district and thus had experienced the judges' performance on the bench.[19] Judicial, as opposed to executive or legislative appointment, of certain judges and magistrates has ample precedent in the states and around the world.[20] The danger is the creation of an inbred judiciary, a concern to be weighed against the political intrigue and battles that characterize current appointments.

Supreme Court appointments vary as well. The president of France, the president of the National Assembly, and the Senate president each choose three members of the French Constitutional Council, their Supreme Court. The Germans do something similar. Applying that model to the United States would prove interesting, to say the least. Who does the appointing? Would the majority leaders in the House and Senate each appoint two justices and perhaps the minority leaders one each? Would that reduce or exacerbate the wrangling that affects Court appointments? Would all nine appointments occur simultaneously (assuming fixed and limited terms), and if not, how would they be staggered? Once again, what works in one political system does not easily translate to another.

Fixing the Confirmation Process. Regardless of nomination procedures, the senatorial confirmation process remains a huge concern. Several reforms receive support. The first is to make sure that the Senate Judiciary Committee cannot bottle up presidential nominations and deny the full Senate the opportunity to express its judgment—a common occurrence when different parties control the Senate and presidency. Preventing such behavior could be achieved by (a) putting a time limit, perhaps 90 days, on the Committee's work; (b) requiring it to report *all* nominations to the floor, even with negative recommendations; or (c) making it easy for a sizeable minority of senators to discharge the Committee and bring nominations to the floor after an appropriate period of Committee evaluation. As always, these suggestions face pushback. Given that the Committee has other tasks and that some nominations require more study than others, setting an arbitrary standard timeline undermines the close scrutiny and judgment needed. Limiting the Judiciary Committee's discretion strengthens the hands of presidents, and it certainly violates the traditional authority of committees.

Creating a "fast-track" process to combat the possibilities of filibusters or holds for Supreme Court nominations is a second approach. The case for facilitating Senate action on justices and judges is not as strong as it is for executive appointments, but it cannot be dismissed. Critics have long cried for an "up or down" vote—no more filibusters—after the Senate Judiciary Committee has reported a nomination to the floor; that now becomes the norm for district and appellate court judges. If the old system were reinstated, allowing filibusters on all judicial nominations, a proposal by Binder and Maltzman might work. First, create a bipartisan screening commission that makes recommendations to the president; he can choose from that list or bypass it to pick someone else. If he chooses from the list, that candidate receives fast-track consideration in the Senate; otherwise not. They also suggest packaging a series of judicial nominations, presumably to include both liberal and conservative appointees, as a way to entice prompt Senate action.[21] The first proposal could induce presidents to pick less controversial nominees from the commission's list of, presumably, compromise candidates. One can imagine all sorts of gamesmanship in putting together a "package" of appointments, leading to a slate of "B"-team judges when the courts need the first stringers. The politics would be dicey. Extending the new confirmation rule (51 votes rather than 60 to break a filibuster) to Supreme Court nominations after a decent interval might be beneficial—but surely would draw fierce resistance from the party not controlling the White House.

Last, some critics, frustrated by Senate behavior, have proposed a constitutional amendment taking the confirmation function out of the hands of senators and giving it to a bipartisan judicial council or commission. How such a council or commission would be constituted is the question. Would it merely transfer the political battles to that institution, with no guarantee of any less partisanship? A few other observers suggest that the Senate's confirmation function be shared with the House, led perhaps by a special joint committee on judicial nominations. The likely result would be even more partisan warfare and longer delays.

In the end, the preferred method of nominating, appointing, and confirming judges boils down to which values one considers most important and which level of the federal judiciary one is concerned with. Understanding that there is no way on earth to ensure an independent, nonpartisan, nonideological, and highly talented judiciary or to build a flawless judicial appointment process, the choices are limited. Citizens and members of Congress, at least in theory, want judges to be impartial and independent; they also want some accountability and responsiveness, hoping that justices and judges will rule in a fashion that supports policies, rights, and liberties they value. These two goals simply are incompatible. Nor is there much evidence that any one system of appointments is superior to the others; all have consequences. In the end, picking judges is a political process.

Workloads: Too Much to Handle?

Problems. By themselves, but especially in light of vacancies on the bench, heavy workloads threaten the efficient and careful administration of justice. Although the numbers fluctuate, having risen for 25 years but tailed off in the last 10, the data are informative. In U.S. district courts, for the 12 months up to March 31, 2014, a total of 363,820 civil and 66,193 criminal suits were commenced, whereas bankruptcy courts saw 1,038,280 new cases. Federal appellate courts took on 55,623 new cases, settling 56,354.[22] A good portion of the pressure on appeals courts comes from executive or independent agency administrative law judges who deal with issues arising from the actions of their agencies. The more those executive units do, the more legal disputes there are to be settled; and the more cases those judges have, the more that are appealed. Unlike these courts, the Supreme Court has total discretion over its workload, picking for full consideration and argument about 90 of the 8,000 petitions it receives annually. The vast majority simply are rejected; several dozen are handled with summary decisions.

Reforms. Assuming that caseloads constitute a problem, several solutions are available. The first is to raise the bar for entry by increasing the cost of filing lawsuits in district courts and/or by imposing user fees. Initial costs now are $200 to $300. The basic charge for an appeal is $450, with other fees attached.[23] These modest fees neither cover costs nor discourage suits, thus shifting the cost of civil litigation from the plaintiffs and defendants to the taxpayer. They also encourage people who lose in the political arena to take their cases into the judicial arena, inviting policy making by judges. From a purely economic perspective, it seems sensible to raise those fees substantially and impose user charges to cover the costs for this service. The objection is that access to the courts and the judicial process is not a service but a right; and raising the fees places unfair burdens on litigants, especially the poor. Fees for indigents can be waived, of course, and it should be recalled that there is no *constitutional right* to litigate most controversies. In civil cases where good sums of money are involved, charging court costs as a fixed proportion of the amounts sought by the plaintiffs might make sense and, if the rates were high enough, doing so might discourage many questionable filings. On the other hand, it could incline plaintiffs to take their courses out of federal courts and push them to state courts.

A second approach is fee shifting: making the losers pay all or most court costs incurred by both parties, as is done just about everywhere else in the world except the United States and Japan. Common sense suggests that it should discourage frivolous and "iffy" lawsuits that take up a lot of time, but Judge Richard Posner counters that this would not necessarily reduce litigation and actually could increase it, possibly putting more pressure on the appeals courts.[24]

Third, "alternative dispute resolution" (ADR), encouraging or requiring settlement of civil disputes outside the judicial system, has evolved as a *de facto* substitute for civil litigation. Along with legal experts and some attorneys, courts often favor this approach, hiring specialized settlement mediators for the job. One question is whether it is appropriate for judges to push this solution; settlement, after all, can look like a denial of someone's "day in court." Arbitration and mediation *outside* the judicial system has spawned a small industry, exemplified by the American Arbitration Association and the Judicial Arbitration and Mediation Services. Contracts, brokerage or credit card agreements, and the fine-print "conditions of sale" imposed by merchants increasingly require binding arbitration or mediation as an alternative to the judicial process. The more of this that occurs, the lower should be the caseloads in the courts, but the jury is still out, especially on mandatory ADR. According to one authority, "There is substantial evidence that mediation and other ADR approaches can result in enhanced satisfaction, reduced dispute resolution costs, shorter disposition times, improved compliance with a settlement, and other benefits in some contexts." He goes on to point out, however, that all is not perfect. Binding arbitration has become "judicialized"—overly formal and almost courtroom-like in many cases—leading to calls for improved judicial oversight, regulation, and court cases, which contradict the original purposes of arbitration.[25] The strongest objection comes from trial lawyers and advocates for consumers and "the little guys" who more often than not are disadvantaged *vis à vis* corporate entities by such agreements.

A fourth workload reform is to improve the court system itself. Recruiting more clerks and more judges, as well as speeding their appointment and confirmation, will reduce the burden on individual judges and allow for more thorough and less pressured adjudicatory activity, but doing so is expensive.[26] As the dockets of district court judges clogged, Congress added judges—a mixed blessing because their efforts inevitably add to the workload of the appellate courts. The logical solution is to divide the latter, adding one or more new circuits. This seemingly technical solution runs into political problems, however, as the senators from the states in the old circuits hesitate to give up their influence over the appointment of the circuit's appellate and district judges. Senators may also fear the consequences, in terms of excessively liberal or conservative rulings, from the new appellate courts.[27] A related reform was the creation of specialized courts like the existing Tax Court, Court of Federal Claims, Court of Appeals for Veterans Claims, the Court of International Trade, and the military court system. One could imagine others dealing with federal land issues, certain kinds of discrimination cases, specialized criminal matters, labor problems, and the like. The advantage of these courts is expertise and focus; the disadvantage is excessive narrowness of perspective, leading to tension between the specialized trial courts and the generalist appeals courts. Some years ago, a proposal was floated to create a "superappellate" court to deal with the cases involving statutory matters that the Supreme Court now handles on appeal from the appellate courts. This new court would provide expertise and free up the Supreme Court to focus on constitutional questions.

Improving management is a favorite reform topic, but doing so requires both clear goals (efficiency, effectiveness, more careful deliberation, fairness, responsiveness defined as equitable access and legal representation) and appropriate measures of performance.

Such measures might include the number of cases handled, types of decisions rendered, numbers of undecided cases, time it takes to handle a case, frequency of being overturned, percentage of cases settled outside of court, and cost per case. One can think of other goals and measurements, but many are contradictory or inconsistent with key values. Maximizing both efficiency and access, for example, cannot be done. Assuming proper identification of objectives and measures, how are they to be imposed and implemented without realistic sanctions on underperforming judges

Table 12.1 Summary of Judicial Reforms

ISSUE	PROBLEM/ CRITERIA	PROPOSED REFORM	CONSEQUENCES
Judicial review	Accountability of judicial power	Super Court majority to overturn laws on constitutional grounds	Firmer foundation for decisions; moderation of ideological divisions
		Congressional two-thirds veto of Court overturns federal law	Democratic control and judicial responsiveness
		Controls on justices' careers; limited terms	Enhanced responsiveness; risk of politicized judiciary; removing judges doesn't change decisions
		Abolish judicial review	Enhanced democracy; greater responsibility for Congress and president; risk of violations of constitutionally protected rights
Supreme Court size, composition	Efficiency and representation	Increase size of Supreme Court	Better representation; possibly better deliberative judgment and effectiveness; danger of gridlock if number if justices is even; more confirmation battles
Terms and tenure of judges	Effectiveness, efficiency, responsiveness, deliberative judgment	Term limits or age-determined mandatory retirement	Predictable turnover; more democratic responsiveness; enhanced ideological and partisan battles; difficulty deciding on ideal length of term; danger of losing good judges; uncertain political consequences
Appointment and confirmation process	Effectiveness, efficiency, responsiveness, ideological representation, politicization	Nomination by bipartisan Commission	Possibly better judges; possibly less politicization if successful; difficulties of choosing the commissioners
		Election of judges	Politicization; campaign finance; conflicts of interest; danger of ill-informed voters
		Appointment by peers or joint appointment by president, Senate, House	Inbred judiciary; difficulty of agreeing on appointees if branches of government are divided
		Fast-track confirmation	Risk of poor evaluation; political gamesmanship
Workload	Efficiency; effectiveness	Raise cost of entry	Lower caseloads; potential denial of right to trial
		Fee shifting	Discourages lawsuits; uncertain consequences
		Alternate dispute resolution	Lower caseloads; can favor business over consumers
		Better management; more courts	Faster adjudication; increase in appeals; cost

who serve for life? Shame may be the only remedy, and that opens a Pandora's box. Table 12.1 summarizes the major problems and reforms.

12.2 THE EXECUTIVE BUREAUCRACY

Everyone seems to complain about bureaucracy and bureaucrats, and reform proposals abound to cover personal management, budgeting, structural reorganization, contracting, compensation, leadership, and dozens of other topics. Chapters 10 and 11 covered a few of them; the focus here is more general.

Politics, Red Tape, and All That Stuff

Long before he became president, Woodrow Wilson the political scientist argued that politics and administration must be separated. Politics decides what should be done, he said; administrators, hired solely for their talents, carry out the laws and should do it neutrally, dispassionately, and scientifically.[28] Since then, that view has suffered empirically, if not normatively. Decisions made in carrying out the law often make policy. Bureau chiefs and office administrators, although members of the Civil Service, find themselves under pressure from the White House and political executives, from Congress and its members, from interest groups, and from the media and public. Inevitably, they must practice the political arts if they are to do their jobs. No reforms can change that. There remain, nonetheless, complaints that citizens lodge against the civil servants in the executive agencies whom they encounter or merely read about. These include waste, red tape, lack of courteous treatment, delays, inability to get unambiguous answers to questions, being shuffled from one office to another, outsourcing, inefficient management and spending, lack of creativity and discretion, interagency (and sometimes intraagency) battles over jurisdiction, budgets, and authority—the list goes on and on.

Scholars, members of Congress, and presidential appointees are frustrated by bureaucratic behavior. Paul Light, a leading student of the federal service, produced his own list of bureaucratic problems: (1) assigned duties that exceed available resources; (2) a chain of command that blurs and frustrates accountability; (3) leadership by political executives who must undergo unreasonable scrutiny, whose appointments take forever to confirm, and who then stay in office for short periods of time; (4) a workforce insufficiently devoted to helping people and making a difference; and (5) a system that is "battered by one administrative reform after another, all in search of higher performance, but few sharing the same direction."[29] He points to the "thickening" of the federal service in breadth and depth, featuring more layers of leaders and more leaders per layer. As of 2003 there were no fewer than 64 distinct and lofty titles for supervisors such as "assistant principal deputy assistant secretary." Half of the departments used at least 21 of them. Although the number of federal employees has not grown much at all, the number of senior executives has, from 451 in 1960 to 2,592 in 2004.[30] The hierarchy grows tall and wide, often substituting oversight and supervision for implementation and administration, management for productivity. Contrast this with the norm in the private sector that aims at no more than six layers between the top and bottom of units or divisions of a company.

The late James Q. Wilson, one of the most astute observers of bureaucracy, cut to the heart of the bureaucracy problems: *conflicting goals*. He pointed to issues of: (1) accountability or control, getting the bureaucracy to serve the public goals established by elected officials (while presumably following "scientific" modes of management); (2) equity, or treating like cases alike; (3) efficiency; (4) responsiveness, especially to unusual cases that don't fit the normal categories of rules; and (5) fiscal integrity, the proper spending of funds.[31] To these one might add the pressures of representativeness—each agency and department has its own clientele (farmers, veterans, Wall Street, labor unions, etc.)—and the need for reasoned and deliberative judgment. At any given time, these goals conflict, inevitably undermining strategies and behaviors designed to produce better performance. Indeed, better behavior in one area, efficiency or equity or accountability to political superiors, for example, may frustrate or even negate others such as responsiveness to those being served and faithfulness to the law's demands. For many scholars, as for Americans generally, the case against the bureaucracy boils down to the simple plea: Why can't government bureaucracy operate like a business? Why can't it be fixed?

Lots of Laws, but Do They Fix the Problems?

There has been no end of reforms, reform plans, reform commissions, hearings, studies, and legislative enactments, amounting to what Light called "tides of reform," to address these concerns. He notes that these tides—177 laws enacted between 1945 and 2002—pursued four contradictory impulses:

- Scientific management that trusts the federal service and opts for centralized administration;
- Liberation management that trusts the service but prefers decentralization;
- War on waste that does not trust the federal service but likes centralization; and
- "Watchful eye" accountability that neither trusts the federal bureaucracy nor likes centralized management.[32]

During the Clinton administration, Vice President Al Gore led an effort, the National Performance Review, to "reinvent government." At the same time, in 1993, Congress passed the Government Performance and Results Act, which required all federal agencies to develop strategic plans, annual performance plans, and performance reports. Under President George W. Bush, the OMB established the Program Assessment Rating Tool, aimed at better integration of budgets and performance assessment. In 2010, Congress amended the Government Performance and Results Act to get congressional input on strategic plans and to encourage the OMB to deal with crosscutting issues. Collectively, these alphabet-soup efforts sought to institute scientific management, fight waste, improve personnel systems, induce transparency and better oversight, encourage a more entrepreneurial attitude, and empower employees to get results.[33] Many of them have succeeded; federal bureaucracies probably function better today than ever. Personnel and payroll systems are more flexible, at least in some agencies; procurement procedures are improved; there is more emphasis on performance and workforce planning; and managers have greater discretion to achieve their goals.[34] The record, however, remains mixed. For example, Light's 2001 survey found that fully half of all federal employee respondents claimed that the reform efforts made their jobs more difficult; on the other hand, 60 percent of senior executives said that reforms had improved their efforts. Inconsistent evaluations of reform reflect the priorities of different participants: presidents and the OMB, congressional committees, and the department and agency executives themselves.[35] So, why can't government operate like a business?

The answer, that it simply cannot, comes from Professor Wilson. Government bureaucracies and private bureaucracies have things in common, but government bureaucracies: (a) cannot retain and distribute to workers the profits they generate, (b) cannot allocate resources as their leaders might wish, and (c) serve goals not of their own choosing. Worse, those programmatic goals, set by Congress, often are vague because legislators, seeking compromise, cannot agree on specifics. Even when objectives are clear, their achievement is not accurately measurable—unlike the profits a corporation produces. What, for example, is the best way to measure the performance of the Veterans' Hospitals that were much in the news in May 2014, because of horrendous backlogs, or the effectiveness of the Agriculture Department's efforts to support family farms while optimizing farm output? Simply put, the federal government does not invest enough effort or money into specifying performance measures or assessing them; no wonder so many programs fail to demonstrate successful results.[36] Existing goals entice government workers to favor equity over efficiency and to follow prescribed procedures over ad hoc solutions to new problems. Department secretaries and agency heads are not as free as their private-sector peers to hire more employees to complete a job or to pay higher salaries to reward behavior.[37] Purely administrative operating goals are not always agreed on. Does an agency seek primarily to respond to and satisfy its clients and customers? Who, exactly, are they? Are they the same as the citizens and taxpayers to whom departments and agencies owe loyalty, frugality, and effective and efficient administration? Is its goal to spend less or to ensure high employee morale? In the end, can government be more businesslike in the absence of competitors?

Is Reform Possible?

Professor Light has made several important suggestions.[38] First, there is need to clarify federal government goals, prioritize them, and eliminate marginally important programs and activities. When government has too many goals and activities, it cannot possibly hope for effectiveness or efficiency. Nor can it afford the financial and administrative costs, and that means spreading dollars and executive talent too thinly, inevitably undermining key programs. But is there any likelihood that elected officials will chop out any programs their constituents like? Short of program reduction, there are other possibilities, most with mixed consequences. New approaches to budgeting, as mentioned in chapter 11, are one example.

Contracting and Outsourcing. Greater outsourcing and privatizing of government functions is a constant recommendation on the grounds that the private sector can function more efficiently and more effectively than government. By one count, as of 2005, there were 7.6 million nongovernment employees working on government contracts, with another 2.9 million doing work under federal grants.[39] Contracting out government duties can works well in areas where private-sector businesses do what sectors of government do and where there is marketplace competition and thus greater efficiency. Contracting and outsourcing, however, carry drawbacks. Account-ability is one. Agencies must expend considerable effort to work out the numbers that go into contracts with private providers. Then they must direct, monitor, and control contractors who often are not subject to the same requirements in ethics, job security, personnel, or salaries under which government agencies work. Look at the war in Iraq; by all accounts, billions of dollars were wasted, lost, misplaced, or at least mis-used by private contractors working for the State and Defense Departments and the Central Intelligence Agency. Moreover, to the extent that projects are outsourced, agency officials are unlikely to know and retain as much information about them—a loss of institutional knowledge and memory that could come back to bite adminis-trators when things go wrong. Occasionally, contracting with the private sector brings disaster. An example is the case of Edward Snowden, the employee of a consulting firm given access to National Security Agency computers and secrets who took what he knew to the media, leading to massive embarrassment for the government (not to mention endangering intelligence-gathering operations).

Peter Schuck offers a sensible reform: require by law that executive agencies, before beginning to implement a law, undertake a study to see whether the service to be provided can be done more effectively and efficiently by the private sector, and then publish the findings before proceeding. If program goals are explicit, if rigorous cost–benefit analysis is applied, and if the Governmental Accountability Office validates the studies, better results should emerge.[40]

Reorganizing. Reorganization and consolidation of government agencies, along with reducing the overlap and fragmentation of, and rivalries among, agencies and programs are favorite reforms. Does good government require 100 programs dealing with surface transportation, 82 to monitor teacher quality, 80 for economic develop-ment, and 47 for job training? Why are 20 offices or programs devoted to homeless-ness, and 17 different grant programs available for disaster preparedness? Why do multiple regulators oversee the banking industry? Fifteen agencies or offices handle food safety, and 5 work to ensure the federal government uses less gasoline.[41] Why, as President Obama mentioned in a State of the Union message, is the Interior De-partment in charge of salmon while they swim in fresh water and the Commerce Department when they are in saltwater? Presumably, inspectors in the Food and Drug Administration or even the Department of Agriculture might take over once they are smoked or canned—after state fish and wildlife departments have checked the licenses of the fishermen who caught them. What is the unit of analysis: the fish, the water, the fisherman, or the nature of the commerce? Why do three agencies—the Department of Agriculture, the Food and Drug Administration, and the National Oceanic and Atmospheric Administration in the Commerce Department—inspect catfish?[42] Two answers are that each program presumably has a specialized focus and that Congress placed it in its particular departmental or agency to placate specific committees, subcommittees, or individual members. Such factors do not affect private businesses.

Another answer is that the tasks of creating and abolishing departments and agencies, or of reshuffling offices and bureaus within agencies, invite lengthy political fights that are not worth the political capital that presidents and congressional leaders must expend to accomplish the reorganization. Still, structural changes do occur;

some 22 agencies saw themselves or parts of their organizations transferred to the Department of Homeland Security, which in turned spawned new personnel and management systems. Structural reform is driven by multiple goals, some of which are incompatible with each other. In addition to the usual reasons of effectiveness and efficiency, reorganizations are proposed to respond to a public demand for change or action on a burning issue; to represent better the concerns of certain interests or groups; to symbolize concerns of a president when he really doesn't want to take concrete policy action; or to enhance the influence of certain congressional committees.

Put Someone in Charge. Bureaucracies develop their own modes of operation, their own goals and objectives, and their own traditions and values. Bureaucrats' civil service status, their expertise, and their linkages to interest groups, the media, and the public provide independence and power; and those raise concerns of control and direction. To whom is the bureaucracy accountable? Who judges its success and failures, its responsiveness and effectiveness? Presidents, certainly, would like greater control, perhaps best done by means of many more presidential appointments, as discussed in chapter 10. Restoring and invigorating the "M" in the OMB would be one step; strengthening the Government Accountability Office would be another. Placing the vice president in charge of that effort might make sense. Filling all 73 Inspector General positions (whose task it is to ferret out inefficiencies, conflicts of interest, criminal behavior, ethics violations, poor management, and so on within agencies) with hard-charging experienced people and bolstering their authority cannot but help. Naturally, not all agency heads and employees will welcome or cooperate with them. From the congressional perspective, the call is for better—more effective and more regular—oversight. Paul Light suggested the establishment of a joint Committee on Federal Management, largely as a holding tank for staff experts who could assist the House and Senate oversight committees and subcommittees.[43] Obviously these two "solutions"—stronger OMB control and enhanced congressional oversight—are not entirely compatible and invite more presidential–congressional squabbling. Which branch should reign supreme over policy implementation and bureaucratic operations? Nor, arguably, is there compatibility in the goals of Vice President Gore's National Performance Review that sought a bureaucracy that "works better and costs less."

Personnel Management. To address the growth in levels and titles of administrators, Light urged a thinning of government, reducing by half the number of managers and supervisors while cutting the layers and titles. A perennial problem that leads to contradictory reform movements is the centralization–decentralization issue. Should there be, as was the case not all that long ago, a single federal government personnel system, with essentially the same ranks, work rules, and salary schedules in all departments? That allows easy transferability of workers and consistency in personnel practices; it can make presidential control easier, and it could be a means to efficiencies of scale. Or should there be more decentralization of personnel policies and structures to allow managers the ability to utilize their workers in the best fashion *for their agencies and departments* and allow more experimentation with private-sector management techniques, such as enhanced pay-for-performance systems that reward productivity and innovation rather than longevity? Government workers' unions have tended to resist efforts to empower management and impose private sector–like

reforms; presidents and the OMB worry about loss of control caused by decentralization; and Congress is reticent to strengthen agency managers in the face of union
objections and presidential claims of authority.[44] The judiciary gets into the act when
union contracts and statutory management provisions are in dispute, as, for instance,
when the courts voided President Bush's efforts to impose new management systems
on the Departments of Defense and Homeland Security.

As described in previous chapters, the appointment and confirmation processes
for high-ranking political appointees must be improved and made easier if the government is to attract and retain top-notch administrative leaders. At lower ranks,
there is a need for vigor and high performance in the civil service, including easier
and faster hiring and promotion processes and, probably, an "up or out" system. Government cannot afford to retain marginally competent or incompetent workers. Last,
there is need to incentivize young, talented, and well-motivated Americans to seek
jobs in government.

Conclusion. Highlighting the numerous efforts to fix the bureaucracy problem,
Professor Light pleaded for a moratorium on reform efforts, followed by a more careful congressional process for considering reforms. He urged that reforms should
(a) measure and constrain the expansion of the "true" size of the federal government
(including contract employees, grantees, and so on), (b) cull as many of these as possible, bringing the work back inside the civil service, and (c) strengthen oversight
of all federal "employees," inside and outside the government. To this list one might
add three others. First, there should be a greater use of experimental trials of newly
enacted programs before launching wholesale into their implementation. Second, it
would pay to enhance returns on taxpayer investment, such as hiring more Internal
Revenue Service workers to bring in unpaid taxes. Third, Congress and the president
must inject into the system a willingness to cut losses quickly when a new program is
failing or running over budget.[45] For certain, reformers must guard against trying to
apply a "one size fits all" rule to federal agencies.

The record of bureaucratic reforms is one best characterized as incremental change
on an agency-by-agency basis, often spurred by specific events, crises, scandals, or
institutional breakdowns. Reform defies what Professor Wilson called "Big Answers"
to "Big Questions." There are no easy ways to "curb rampant bureaucracy" or "unleash
the creative talents of our dedicated public servants." Government entities cannot
function as do private business bureaucracies. Even the most innocent reforms proposed by presidents are viewed suspiciously by the other party and by legislators and
outsiders. Public management is "a world of settled institutions designed to allow
imperfect people to use flawed procedures to cope with insoluble problems." Bureaucracy is a system "laden with rules" for efficient operation, fairness, and so on, but
also a system that makes citizen and group access very easy.[46] Is that the best to be
hoped for?

QUESTIONS TO CONSIDER

1. Is the power of judicial review something to fret about? If so, what should be done?
2. Are term limits on judges and justices needed? What would be the consequences?

3. Should the appointment system for judges be changed? Should lower-level federal judges be elected?
4. What is the trade-off between making access to the courts more difficult (to control workloads and enhance more careful decision making) and the need to make access to the courts available in the pursuit of justice?
5. Why is improving the executive branch's effectiveness and efficiency so hard?

NOTES

1. Kenneth P. Miller, *Direct Democracy and the Courts* (Cambridge, UK, and New York: Cambridge University Press, 2009).
2. Lawrence Baum, *The Supreme Court*, 11th ed. (Los Angeles, London, New Delhi, Singapore, and Washington, D.C.: CQ Press, 2013): 163.
3. Mark A. Graber, "From Republic to Democracy: The Judiciary and the Political Process," in Kermit L. Hall and Kevin T. McGuire, eds., *The Judicial Branch* (Oxford and New York: Oxford University Press, 2005), chap. 15.
4. Neil B. Cohen, "'What If There Were No Judicial Review?," in Herbert M. Levine *et al.*, *What If the American Political System Were Different?* (Armonk, NY, and London: Sharpe, 1992), chap. 6.
5. Adam Liptak, "Bucking a Trend, Supreme Justices Reject Video Coverage," *New York Times*, February 19, 2013: A15.
6. *A More Perfect Constitution: 23 Proposals to Revitalize Our Constitution and Make America a Fairer Country* (New York: Walker & Company, 2007): 117–18.
7. Sanford Levinson, *Our Undemocratic Constitution: Where the Constitution Goes Wrong (and How We the People Can Correct It)* (Oxford and New York: Oxford University Press, 2006): 127–28.
8. *A More Perfect Constitution*: 112–13.
9. Robert A. Carp, Ronald Stidham, and Kenneth L. Manning, *Judicial Process in America*, 9th ed. (Los Angeles, London, New Delhi, Singapore, and Washington, D.C.: CQ Press, 2014): 119–20.
10. Barry J. McMillion, "Length of Time from Nomination to Confirmation for 'Uncontroversial' U.S. Circuit and District Court Nominees: Detailed Analysis," Congressional Research Service, September 18, 2012.
11. Jon R. Bond and Kevin B. Smith, *Analyzing American Democracy: Politics and Political Science* (New York and London: Routledge, 2013): 595–97.
12. Jon R. Bond, Richard Fleisher, and Glen S. Krutz, "Malign Neglect: Evidence That Delay Has Become the Primary Method of Defeating Presidential Appointments," *Congress and the Presidency* 36 (2009): 26–243.
13. Sarah A. Binder and Forrest Maltzman, *Advice & Dissent: The Struggle to Shape the Federal Judiciary* (Washington, D.C.: Brookings, 2009): 133. What follows is from chapter 6.
14. Logan Dancey, Kjersten R. Nelson, and Eve M. Ringsmuth "Individual Scrutiny or Politics as Usual? Senatorial Assessment of U.S. District Court Nominees," *American Politics Research* 42 (2014): 784–814.
15. Binder and Maltzman, "Advice and Consent: The Politics of Confirming Federal Judges," in Lawrence C. Dodd and Bruce I. Oppenheimer, eds., *Congress Reconsidered*, 10th ed. (Los Angeles, London, New Delhi, Singapore, and Washington, D.C.: CQ Press, 2013), chap. 11.

16. Marvin Comisky and Philip X. Patterson, with the assistance of William E. Taylor III, *The Judiciary—Selection, Compensation, Ethics, and Discipline* (New York, Westport, CT, and London: Quorum Books, 1987), chap. 2. For state judicial appointments, see American Judicature Society, "Methods of Judicial Selection," http://www.judicialselection.us/judicial_selection/methods/selection_of_judges.cfm?state=/.

17. Binder and Maltzman, *Advice and Dissent*: 150.

18. For this and what follows, see Matthew J. Streb, *Rethinking American Electoral Democracy*, 2d ed. (New York and London: Routledge, 2011), chap. 3; Chris W. Bonneau and Melinda Gann Hall, *In Defense of Judicial Elections* (New York and London: Routledge, 2009); and James L. Gibson, *Electing Judges: The Surprising Effects of Campaigning on Judicial Legitimacy* (Chicago: University of Chicago Press, 2012).

19. *With Justice for None* (New York: Penguin Books, 1984).

20. Comisky and Patterson, *The Judiciary*, chap. 2.

21. Binder and Maltzman, "Advice and Consent": 153–55.

22. U.S. Courts, http://www.uscourts.gov/Statistics/FederalJudicialCaseloadStatistics.aspx/.

23. http://www.uscourts.gov/FormsAndFees/Fees/DistrictCourtMiscellaneousFee-Schedule.aspx/; http://www.uscourts.gov/FormsAndFees/Fees/CourtOfAppealsMiscellaneousFeeSchedule.aspx/.

24. Richard A. Posner, *The Federal Courts: Challenge and Reform* (Cambridge, UK, and London: Harvard University Press, 1996), chap. 7.

25. Thomas J. Stipanowich, "ADR and the 'Vanishing Trial': The Growth and Impact of 'Alternative Dispute Resolution,'" *Journal of Empirical Legal Studies* 1, no. 3 (2004): 843–912; "Arbitration: The New Litigation," *University of Illinois Law Review* 1 (2010): 1–60.

26. Russell Wheeler, "Toward a More Perfect Union: A Progressive Blueprint for the Second Term," *American Constitution Society for Law and Policy*, January 2013, http://www.acslaw.org/sites/default/files/Wheeler_-_Filling_Judicial_Vacancies.pdf/.

27. Lawrence Baum, "The Future of the Judicial Branch: Courts and Democracy in the Twenty-First Century," in Kermit L. Hall and Kevin T. McGuire, eds., *The Judicial Branch* (Oxford and New York: Oxford University Press, 2005), chap. 19.

28. "The Study of Administration," *Political Science Quarterly* 2 (1887): 197–222.

29. Paul C. Light, *A Government Ill Executed: The Decline of the Federal Service and How to Reverse It* (Cambridge, MA, and London: Harvard University Press, 2008): 2–3.

30. *Ibid.*: 66.

31. "The Bureaucracy Problem," *The Public Interest* 6 (1967): 3–10; Joel D. Aberbach and Bert A. Rockman, *In the Web of Politics: Three Decades of the U.S. Federal Executive* (Washington, D.C.: Brookings, 2000).

32. Light, *Government Ill Executed*: 166.

33. *The Tides of Reform: Making Government Work, 1945–1995* (New Haven, CT, and London: Yale University Press, 1997).

34. Patricia W. Ingraham, "The Federal Public Service: The People and the Challenge," in Joel D. Aberbach and Mark A. Peterson, *The Executive Branch* (Oxford and New York: Oxford University Press, 2005), chap. 9; Donald F. Kettl, "Reforming the Executive Branch of the U.S. Government," *ibid.*, chap. 11; and Donald F. Kettl and John J. DiIulio Jr., *Inside the Reinvention Machine: Appraising Governmental Reform* (Washington, D.C.: Brookings, 1995).

35. Beryl A. Radin, *Federal Management Reform in a World of Contradictions* (Washington, D.C.: Georgetown University Press, 2012).

36. Peter H. Schuck, *Why Government Fails So Often—And How It Can Do Better* (Princeton, NJ, and Oxford: Princeton University Press, 2014).
37. James Q. Wilson, *Bureaucracy: What Government Agencies Do and Why They Do It* (New York: Basic Books, 1989), chap. 7.
38. Light, *Government Ill Executed.*
39. Light, *Government Ill Executed*, 202. See his *The True Size of Government* (Washington, D.C.: Brookings, 1999).
40. Schuck, *Why Government Fails*, 388–93.
41. "2013 Annual Report: Actions Needed to Reduce Fragmentation, Overlap, and Duplication and Achieve Other Financial Benefits," GAO-13-279SP, April 9, 2013; Ed O'Keefe, "Government Overlap Costs Taxpayers Billions, GAO Reports," *Washington Post*, March 1, 2011, http://voices.washingtonpost.com/federal-eye/2011/03/government_overlap_costs_taxpa.html/; and O'Keefe, "GAO: Overlapping Government Programs Cost Billions," *Washington Post*, February 28, 2012, http://www.washingtonpost.com/blogs/federal-eye/post/gao-overlapping-government-programs-cost-billions/2012/02/27/gIQAnSPdeR_blog.html/.
42. Ron Nixon, "Number of Catfish Inspectors Drives a Debate on Spending," *New York Times*, July 27, 2013: A9.
43. Light, *Tides*, chap. 6.
44. Radin, *Federal Management Reform*, chap. 5.
45. Light, "The Sequester Is an Overhaul Opportunity," *Wall Street Journal*, March 21, 2013: A15; see also Schuck, *Why Government Fails.*
46. Wilson, *Bureaucracy*: 357–77.

CHAPTER 13

Conclusion—Thinking about Reform

> Happy will it be if our choice should be directed by a judicious
> estimate of our true interests, unperplexed and unbiased by
> considerations not connected with the public good.
>
> —ALEXANDER HAMILTON, *The Federalist No. 1*

The reform agenda is overwhelming. From radical constitutional change to tweaking congressional or party rules, and whether dealing with citizens and elections or political institutions, the previous chapters offered a long list of problems and proposed solutions. All are proposed with an eye to bringing about government that is more effective, efficient, accountable, representative, responsive, and participatory—and one in which policies derive from reflective, deliberative, and reasoned judgments of policy makers. As pointed out in chapter 1, these values or criteria are not always mutually enforcing; indeed, by pursuing some of them aggressively, others will suffer. There are trade-offs to be made, and the results depend entirely on one's priorities among the seven values. This chapter's focus is twofold: to reflect on the meaning and consequences of reform efforts and to think about reform strategies and prospects.

13.1 THE LESSONS OF REFORM: WHAT IS INVOLVED?

"Reform" is a loaded word; what some see as progressive reform others view as an assault on traditional values and processes or an invitation to future troubles. Making voting easier seems like a great idea, but it raises concerns about fraud and people's confidence in elections. The notion of facilitating the policy-making process in Washington is not always greeted by applause, let alone fanfare; some appreciate gridlock.[1] What can be said about reforms?

First, probably the most important lesson is that *any reform is a gamble*; no one knows how it will play out. The history of reform produced a mixed record. Some reform efforts have succeeded, and dramatically so, but usually the degree of success is modest; reforms typically make improvements at the margins. For example, the efforts to restructure the committee system in the House of Representatives in the 1970s brought about some operational and jurisdictional efficiencies, but not many.[2] The multiple efforts to make voting easier barely moved the turnout needle; and when they did, sometimes the needle returned or moved in the wrong direction. Legislative efforts to control campaign finance improved disclosure, but they failed to achieve their objectives of controlling spending or making elections more competitive. Simply put, one cannot predict success, and that can hold back cautious politicians who, if they are going to gamble their political capital, will do so on substantive policy matters, not structural or procedural reforms.

Second, it is highly *likely that reforms will disappoint* because expectations are often unrealistic and because reforms seldom deal with the underlying and fundamental causes of problems.[3] Reformers frequently exaggerate the problems they want to fix and fail to look for root causes. Too often, reform efforts assume that changing laws, rules, or practices will alter underlying motivations and interests, thus securing behavioral changes. The reality is that politicians and average citizens have their own interests that ignore, or sometimes conflict with, reformist impulses. Institutional reforms do not necessarily solve election problems. Efforts to change electoral processes, early voting, for example, aimed at generating higher turnouts, assume that people are attuned to and care about politics. Many do, of course, but they are already going to vote. The challenge is to motivate the others, and that is more a cultural and socialization issue than a structural or procedural one. Even if that happened, is there any assurance that the result of higher turnout would be more reflective and responsible voting? Or take reforms of the bureaucracy. According to Paul C. Light, "Reforms fail for many reasons, not the least of which is the burnout that comes from the constant push for reform itself."[4] The problem is that many bureaucratic reforms are politically motivated, seeking goals (cut spending, for example) that don't make it easier for bureaucrats to do their jobs. Reform efforts distract employees, chew up resources, and often undermine each other (to fight waste you need more oversight, which in turns diminishes bureaucratic innovation and entrepreneurial management). Too many reforms come too quickly, frustrating the learning that should occur from previous reformist mistakes. More generally, most reforms are driven by short-term reactions to "bad" political events—campaign finance efforts driven by the Watergate fallout in the early 1970s—or by the interests of specific groups. They raise hopes that are often bound to be dashed.

Third, reformers may *take aim at what they think is the cause of a problem when, in fact, it might not be*. For example, it has been well documented that multimember proportional election schemes are associated with higher voting turnout, a greater sense of political efficacy, and stronger attachments to political parties. What is at dispute is whether that correlation is causal. It might be that these effects are the result of political culture and patterns of democratic development rather than structural causes; moving American electoral districts in the direction of multimember proportional representation might not make a difference at all. Studies have shown that when states adopt direct democracy reforms, participation rates sometimes climb; but is the increase permanent, and does it come because of the reform, or are both the reform and the higher participation results of changes in a state's underlying culture or temporary forces?[5]

Fourth, *reform efforts aimed at one problem often become entangled with other goals*, as reformers seek to piggyback their concerns onto a popular reform proposal. The history of the Help America Vote Act shows how this happens. If there is only one train pulling out of the station heading in the right direction, one is tempted to add additional cars to get a different set of passengers to their destinations that lie somewhere along the tracks. That is politics at work. Simple efforts to improve the voting processes ended up including others, including some that almost look like efforts to discourage turnout.[6]

Fifth, *almost all reforms produce winners and losers*; few, if any, "pure" reforms benefit everyone and redistribute power equitably. One party gains advantages over another, at least in certain regions; the presidency picks up new bargaining chips to use to influence Congress; Congress obtains an operating edge over the executive; the federal government gains power over the states; and so on. Politicians abhor uncertainty, and they relish losing power and influence even less. Is there any wonder why they are cautious about reform—or use reforms to secure partisan or personal advantage? Is it any wonder that only two constitutional amendments affected constitutional structure, the Seventeenth (election of senators) and the Twenty-Second (presidential term limits)?

Sixth, *all reforms come with unintended consequences*. Progressive and populist reforms hurt voting turnout; campaign finance reforms facilitated the creation of PACs, super PACs, and 501(c) groups. New voting machines sometimes made a mess of counting and recounting, and some made election errors easier. The McGovern–Fraser presidential nomination reformers after 1968 did not intend that there be so many primaries or so long and so expensive a process. Reforms to one political institution, the Senate, for example, are bound to affect others, such as the House or the presidency. Changing the Electoral College or switching to multimember districts would affect political parties and the redistricting process. Adding more district courts and judges would impact the appellate courts. One cause of negative unintended consequences might be that reform efforts mistargeted the problem or were too timid, allowing reactions to negate or weaken the intended effects. As LeRoy Reiselbach said about congressional reform,

> The important lesson is that reforms designed to promote one value may have costs in terms of another. Reform evolves incrementally in response to political pressures and reformers' pragmatic motives. Piecemeal changes adopted over a number of years without benefit of a master plan do not always mesh well with another. The record of reform is a record of anticipated and unanticipated results. Desirable outcomes may give way to detrimental ones as political circumstances evolve.[7]

There may be no better way to describe this problem than the title of one book: "That's Not What We Meant to Do."[8]

Seventh, *most reforms are costly*. Think of increasing the size of Congress, modernizing the voting system with better machines, improving election administration at the polls, or issuing photo identification cards. When the Presidential Commission on Election Administration in 2013 took testimony, the most common complaint of election administrators concerned a lack of resources. They described themselves as the least powerful lobby at the state legislature and often the last constituency to receive scarce funds at the local level. The flip side of cost is that reforms aimed at saving money—usually those aimed at making the federal bureaucracy more efficient—seldom produce savings. Nor, probably, should that be a preeminent goal.

The bottom line is that reformers should be cautious, avoid pushing for reforms too quickly, and think more deeply about fundamental issues. The process of improving political institutions and processes needs a theoretical basis to give guidance. Reformers need, first, to prioritize the seven criteria discussed throughout. Is good policy most important? If so, one must look to reforms that promote effectiveness, deliberative and reasoned judgment, and efficiency. Is one concerned about a government that is too powerful? If so, one would seek limits to safeguard rights; and in a democracy, that means a focus on making accountability easy and rigorous. Is the concern about the citizenry? Representation, responsiveness, and participation would then be most important. Worrying about and trying to fix issues of presidential vetoes, the Electoral College, campaign spending, or photo IDs may mislead. These often are symptoms, not causes, of what reformers really should be concerned about; and they are all connected.

Reformers next must define goals and evaluate means, weighing possible benefits against almost certain negative consequences. Especially when prescribing changes in the national political institutions, one should proceed in terms of the models outlined in chapter 8. Which branch, Congress or the presidency, does one want to be primary; or should there be genuine constitutional balance? What would the judiciary's role be in any of the presidential–congressional models? Should the institutions rely on strong parties to function, or should bipartisanship or nonpartisanship be the objective? What sort of a party system is desired to organize politics: two parties or multiple parties? Disciplined, responsible, and centralized parties or weak and decentralized ones? The message here is simple: *one must choose among these options before thinking about specific reforms.*

If strong parties are the chosen means to empowering either Congress or the presidency, one has no logical choice but to opt for a good measure of centralized control. That means handing over the candidate selection and campaign financing processes to party leaders, whether they be located in the White House, Congress, or an independent party leadership. If one disdains strong parties and prefers little party influence, changes must be made in how congressional leaders are chosen, how committee assignments are made, how presidential candidates are nominated, how primary elections are run, how judges and justices are appointed, and so on—all in ways to moderate or weaken party influence. Processes must be rigged to encourage compromise across ideological lines, with some real threat imposed for failure. *No meaningful institutional reform can occur unless there is a clear choice of institutional and partisan models.* For example, a belief that the only way to maximize the value of effectiveness is to ensure presidential dominance over Congress must be accompanied by a significant shift of governmental and political powers to the White House. The president, as leader of his party or as "manipulator in chief," must in some real measure control the fate of legislators. If one prefers congressional primacy, the implications are clear: the president's political life and authority must depend on senators and representatives, or at least on their leaders. And so on. When it comes to fundamental reform, it is likely that half a loaf is worse than no bread at all; compromises on the principles and objectives that guide reforms and half-baked reforms almost certainly will end up with disappointment and undesirable consequences. Filling in the cells of Tables 8.1 and 9.1 would serve reformers' purposes quite well.

13.2 IS REFORM POSSIBLE?

Building Barriers

Reforming government and politics to bring about desirable ends is not impossible, but it is difficult. There are several hurdles, the first of which may be the reformers themselves. Beware of the motives of insiders! Incumbent legislators and executives have many goals, some policy related, some personal and ambition related, some partisan related, and some related to "good government." Reformist impulses usually are trumped by the self-interest motives, and those are almost always short term in scope. When it comes to election-related reforms, incumbents' incentives and disincentives are strategic, often anticipating social or demographic changes that affect their or their parties' electoral prospects. Their motives seldom coincide with those of academics, policy advocates, or the general citizenry.[9] Representatives and senators dread the prospects of losing power, weakening their committee jurisdictions, jeopardizing safe seats, losing their roles in selection of judges, and, in the Senate, foregoing the ability to bollix up floor action. All government programs and procedures have supporters who will retaliate against legislators who vote to reform the programs in a fashion that disadvantages or harms the supporters' interests. If a representative supports 10 such reforms, each of which is strongly opposed by 2 percent of her potential voting support, she will be dead at election time. Fear, especially fear of the unknown, is a mighty force. If presidential authority is at stake, legislators of the president's party often see themselves as his field lieutenants, rather than responsible members of an independent branch of government that has its own job to do.[10] This self-perception is fine if and only if a presidential dominance and strong party model is desired. Presidents themselves might see value in a wide range of reforms, but they have little time, energy, or political capital to devote to such causes.

Second, reforms face institutional and procedural challenges. Winning a majority vote in the House and the 60 votes currently needed in the Senate to get major legislation passed, securing the support of the president, and passing muster with the Supreme Court make prospects for legislative changes unlikely, whether the changes bear on electoral laws or internal congressional systems. Passing a constitutional amendment is almost impossible. Administrative implementation is fraught with potential problems, inefficiencies, and sometimes corruption. Federalism represents a major hurdle to many reforms dealing with elections and administration. Even when political party leaders want to change the candidate selection processes (primaries and caucuses, duration of the nominating season, and so on), they need state legislative cooperation. Policies that make sense nationally sometimes hurt state interests; more often, they don't make it to the action agenda in state capitals. Changes in process and structure must be implemented and enforced. Threatening not to seat delegates from states that violate national party rules on front-loading and scheduling of presidential primaries may be a good solution, but it must be carried out ruthlessly. The problem is that the sanction can end up doing harm to the party and its candidates. Enacting reforms that are fundamental, as opposed to tinkering at the margins, faces heavy odds. *The more thorough the reform, the greater will be the resistance.*

Third, as pointed out above, reforms can run into financial issues. Many of them cost a lot of money, or at least enough to force legislators to think about priorities; and reforms fall low on the priority list. A fourth problem is governmental and public apathy. Not many Americans care about the cloture rule, committee structure, judicial workloads, or closed primary elections. Despite the frequency of elections, problems of election administration become headline news only for a week or two after elections—and then only every other or every fourth year. The urgency of fixing election problems fades, as substantive policy matters take over the media's and the government's attention. In the midst of intense competition for budget dollars, election officials have a hard time advocating for more voting machines.

Overcoming Barriers: What Will It Take to Reform?

Pressure. Reforms require an impetus to get onto the legislative agenda and, especially, emerge successfully and intact. Pressure sometimes comes from an infuriated citizenry or at least well-organized and highly motivated elements of it. Americans demanded election changes at the end of the nineteenth century, and most supported alterations in the presidential nominating system after the 1968 fiasco. It is, however, almost inconceivable that without strong leadership the public could push through enactment of a comprehensive and well-designed reform agenda. Today there are numerous organizations and interest groups dedicated to the cause of better, more responsive, less corrupt, and more effective and efficient government. Of course, not all agree on what those objectives require; few, if any, seem to begin with a sophisticated theory of reform politics. Most see an outrageous practice or some sort of governmental collapse and rush in with solutions. Yet without a theory of reform, without choosing among the policy-making institutions, and without considering the mechanisms of government action (especially party politics), those reforms can backfire.

Politicians. Despite their hesitancy to make changes, and despite the self-interest that often drives their concerns, some incumbent legislators and executives are serious about improving government. They tend to be few in number and not always in the key positions to push their proposals. Successful basic reform requires a good handful of entrepreneurial, motivated, thoughtful, skillful, and well-positioned policy makers who, somehow, can think seriously and conceptually about the big picture (the seven criteria, the issue of institutional primacy, and the role and power of parties), translate that into proposals, and then persuade a critical mass of their colleagues of the need for change. Chances of that happening are essentially nil.

Crisis. James Sundquist years ago opined that, in the end, the only way to get what he defined as "real" reform—a means to break governmental deadlock—was to experience a constitutional crisis and near governmental collapse.[11] That may bring about reform, but what would emerge would be an *ad hoc*, and perhaps rash, response—not a comprehensive solution extending past the current crisis that is based on a theory of government and politics. The reason is that once a crisis is resolved, the impetus for reform passes. Memories are short, and other matters press in on the policy agenda. Adrian Vermeule has described the problem well with respect to the judiciary, using Franklin Roosevelt's court-packing plan as a case study; but his insights go much further. Vermeule points to the "self-negating tendency" of reforms, explaining that conditions that produce a need for reform will also tend to produce a policy, structure, or rules change that reduces the threat and "buys off" the demand for deeper and broader reform. He concludes that exogenous (external) shocks may be necessary, but they are not at all sufficient for reform. Efforts to undertake major changes inevitably run up against accusations that they are *ex parte*, serving someone's or some group's interests, rather than being solutions to underlying problems.[12] Thus, when a crisis sparks demand for reform, the temptation is to apply a band-aid rather than enter the operating room for surgery.

Strategies and Approaches

Some of the reforms described in the previous chapters can be instituted by merely changing party or congressional rules or by imposing administrative regulations on departments and agencies, although doing so is much more difficult than prescribing it. For the bigger items requiring legislative or even constitutional action, there are some possible avenues to pursue in Congress.

Omnibus Solutions. For all the reasons mentioned above, single specific reforms usually raise suspicions and lead to resistance. Some just are not important enough to move party leaders, senators, or presidents; others scare the daylights out of officials. Opposition coalitions are easy to build if the reforms "hurt." Perhaps the only way to surmount this problem is to package a number of reform proposals into an omnibus rule or bill that gives everyone some of what he or she wants. Such a measure would have to be approved as a whole or not at all—no amendments. For example, presidents like an item veto, but most members of Congress disagree. Congress, for its part, could do well if the legislative veto were reinstated to give it more control over executive actions. These could be linked. Or perhaps legislation requiring photo identification to prevent fraudulent voting could be combined with expensive programs of massive outreach and voter education and mobilization. In short, develop an offer that no one can refuse or, at least, that imposes roughly equal pain on all sides in return for equal benefits.

A Reform Commission. There may be a way to get such omnibus solutions. It depends on the willingness of Congress, the president, the judiciary, party leaders, and other affected interests to acknowledge that the only path to serious reform is to admit that they cannot and will not do it themselves and to impose upon themselves some form of mechanism resembling a doomsday machine. Because members of Congress have other fish to fry, and because they are wary of losing power, few of them are likely to be the instigators of reform. Nor are Supreme Court justices, presidents, department and agency heads, or leaders of the national political parties often eager to work hard for major reform. Neither, for the most part, are outside citizens' groups, at least not for reforms that go beyond their particular interests. No one in Washington, Sundquist points out, is "in charge" of government effectiveness and efficiency; no one is paid to worry about representation, responsiveness, participation, accountability, and deliberative judgment.

What is needed is an *institutional source of reform thinking*, a bipartisan or nonpartisan group of well-respected and experienced politicians, academics, and other experts whose task is to analyze the operations of political and governmental systems and recommend reforms. This National Reform Commission must be a group whose motives are above suspicion, if that is possible, and whose behavior in promoting reform is above reproach. Commission members need to be grounded in an agreed-on theoretical approach or at least understand and articulate alternate approaches and models. The idea is for Congress (or in another version, the national political parties) to rank order the seven (or other) values, articulate broad goals and criteria, and let the commission go to work. Its report should, in the best of worlds, be reasonably comprehensive and include reforms that would benefit as well as hurt all sides. Its work would attract national media attention. The report must be adopted as a whole, a "take it all or leave it all" proposition, lest its delicate balance be jeopardized. In addition, there must be an enforcement mechanism such that if the reform package is not accepted (by, for example, two-thirds of those participating in the decision), something truly bad will occur: members of Congress must resign or be ineligible for re-election, the party leaders must resign, budgets are slashed, or something similar. An action forcing process is essential.

If the Commission were truly distinguished, building broad-based popular, and perhaps even institutional, support for its recommendations might be possible, putting pressure on those who must take the up or down vote. Of course, that pressure would best work on elected officials, but judges, high-ranking executives, and party leaders are not immune to such pressure. Even if fundamental reform is not in the offing, this commission and omnibus reform package approach could be invoked to deal with less comprehensive and more specific clusters of problems: campaign finance, nominations, legislative–executive relations, and so on. The recently established Bipartisan Policy Center has sought to play this role, albeit without formal congressional authorization, establishing a Commission on Political Reform composed of former federal and state government notables. In June 2014, the Commission issued a substantial report advocating many of the reforms concerning elections and Congress discussed in this book.[13] The Center's Democracy Project Director has testified before Congress on the proposals.

Delayed Enactment. To the extent that government officials fear changes in the game they play, leading them to resist reforms that affect them here and now, why not enact reforms and delay their start date for 6 or 8 or 10 years? The average senator or representative serves about 12 years; any given reform with a 6-year delay would affect about half of them; an 8-year delay would apply the reform to fewer. In terms of presidential and congressional candidate selection systems, reforms of this type would hardly make a ripple; only some officials know for sure that they will be candidates for higher office in 6 or 8 years, and they certainly do not know what the political landscape will look like then. A long-term approach makes it easier to discount the potential downsides of rules changes. The same lesson works for the bureaucracy. Top-level officials would be gone, and union–management relations might change in that period of time. There still might be resistance to any reform at any time, but at least some of the pressure would be alleviated.

Trial Runs. It is not beyond imagination that at least some discrete reforms could be instituted on a trial basis or that the rule or law establishing them would have a sunset provision requiring reconsideration after a period of time, maybe four or six years. Granted, short life spans for reforms are not the ideal mechanism and hardly are efficient, but they do have advantages. Members of Congress, the parties, the judiciary, or the executive might exhibit less reticence to support reforms if they know for certain that to continue, some sort of positive action is required. Bad reforms would die naturally, without a vote; good ones would undergo scrutiny and, perhaps, be approved. The likely objection is that some, perhaps many, reforms involve a fundamental shift in political power, structural changes, and costly investments, all of which build pressure not to revise what has been put into place. That is a risk that must be taken.

Scorekeeping. When reforms are adopted, it often is hard to know whether they have the desired effect. For the most part, that task is left to political scientists, economists, and other scholars. What the political system needs is an official scorekeeper, some institution like a National Reform Evaluation Agency—ideally not part of any government institution and not the same commission that recommended the reforms—to evaluate and report on the success or failure of the reform effort. Along with the evaluation could come recommendations for improvement. If combined with a sunset provision on reforms, this scorekeeping activity would enhance the chances that reforms could be enacted and could work.

Dissemination. Reforms at any one level, in any one political or governmental institution, have repercussions. Some are good; some are not. Other institutions, perhaps at other levels of government, often borrow from the original innovator, rather than reinvent a well-traveled wheel. States and cities learn from each other; so do Washington and the states. Among the states, there are several organizations— the National Conference of State Legislatures, National Governors Association, National League of Cites—that facilitate such efforts; and the Office of Public Engagement and Intergovernmental Affairs in the Executive Office of the President dabbles in such activity as well. The U.S. Election Assistance Commission undertakes similar dissemination efforts, and the national political parties' staffs and the federal Judicial Conference serve a similar purpose. A formal means of disseminating reform results, such as the suggested National Reform Evaluation Agency, might prove useful, both in spreading good ideas and in obtaining critical feedback for the scorekeepers. Such an agency could spread "best practices" in election management, voting machine technology, training of election administrators, fraud detection, computerized voting, or election education, doing so with more authority and resources than the U.S. Election Assistance Commission and other public and private bodies.[14]

Changing the Constitution

The really big and interesting reform proposals in this book focus on the institutions of government, on their interrelationships, and on electoral rules. For the most part, these require constitutional changes; laws and rules changes are insufficient. Since only 27 of thousands of constitutional amendments have been approved, it is obvious that prospects for change are slim at best, probably close to zero; but for reformers hope springs eternal. What is required?

Change Article Five. Since the most likely means to institutional change is through the amending process, perhaps the first and most important political reform is to change that process. Currently, amendments may be proposed by a two-thirds vote of both houses of Congress or by a convention called by Congress "on the Application of the Legislatures of two thirds of the several States." They become part of the Constitution "when ratified by the Legislatures of three-fourths of the several States, or by Conventions in three-fourths thereof." That is quite a hurdle to jump when one considers that 13 states representing about 5 percent of the population can block any amendment. But is that number reasonable today, if it ever was? The Senate functions on a 60-vote rule, for all intents and purposes, and the highest vote threshold required in Congress is two-thirds for ratification of treaties. Why could not the amending process be similar, say a three-fifths provision for proposing amendments and two-thirds for ratification? That still stacks the deck against action and protects minority populations and small states, but it makes possible much-needed changes. Without such a change, structural change will be all but impossible; and all constitutional provisions will evolve not according to the will of substantial majorities of American citizens and their representatives but according to the wishes of as few as five members of the Supreme Court engaged in judicial review. If the accountability and responsiveness principles means anything, it should mean that overwhelmingly popular institutional changes should be done democratically, albeit carefully and deliberately. Very different forms of amending are found in the states. For example, some legislatures can enact amendments by passing an amendment by a supermajority (two-thirds) in two successive sessions, separated by an election. Others can propose amendments by a supermajority vote that puts them on referendum ballots where they must be approved by majorities or supermajorities of the voters. In principle, that same model could be followed for the federal Constitution, but small states probably would block such a constitutional change.

The one possible negative to amending Article Five is that it makes piecemeal and narrowly targeted reform easier. The danger is that reformers will use the new amendment to address particularistic problems or currently popular policies, divorced from related issues. That is where unintended consequences flourish.

Call a Convention. One mechanism for amending the Constitution has never been tried: a constitutional convention called by Congress—probably the only mechanism for dealing with thoroughgoing reform. The country came close in the 1960s when 32 states sought to overturn the Supreme Court's 1964 "one man, one vote" decision, and again in the early 1990s when 32 states petitioned for a convention to enact a balanced budget amendment. A convention has advantages over the standard amending process in that it could be more comprehensive in its actions and more deliberative in its judgments.

On the other hand, perhaps wisdom has prevailed in avoiding a convention because there are many questions for which answers are unknown. Larry Sabato, relying in part on questions raised by Professor Laurence Tribe of Harvard Law School and others, has done a superb job in presenting the numerous issues in his book, *A More Perfect Constitution*.[15] There are at least four sets of interrelated questions to be answered: (1) How would the convention be called? (2) Who would the delegates to the convention be and how would they be chosen? (3) Is the convention limited to deal with only the matters that the state legislatures asked for or what Congress mentioned in its legislation establishing the convention? (4) How would it function? No one knows the answers, and no one will until a convention occurs.

The Constitution is silent on precisely how states may petition Congress. Can the application be made by simple majority of both state legislative chambers, or is a supermajority required? Do applications expire after some period of time? May Congress impose a deadline on the convention, and does failure to meet it kill the state applications?

One fear is that if the "wrong" delegates are chosen, the convention could become not a reform caucus but a forum for a political vendetta or policy "coup" in which an array of policy proposals replaced the institutional and procedural reform purposes for which the convention was called. It is not hard to imagine a left- or right-wing majority proposing all sorts of policies, for example, guaranteeing everyone a minimal income, legalizing drug sales, banning gay marriage, or abolishing the income tax. It is not hard to think of genuinely scary assaults on traditional civil rights and liberties. Much depends on the delegates. Do voters in the states elect them? If so, how—by districts or at large, in partisan or nonpartisan elections? Are they appointed by governors with legislative confirmation? How are they apportioned among and within the states? May sitting congressmen or state legislators be delegates? Who decides these questions?

The Constitution provides that Congress may call a convention to deal with amendments, but that limitation may be unenforceable. Unless the law calling the convention is clear and subsequently enforced, the convention could move well beyond the intention of Congress. Suppose the call concerned the federal judiciary—imposing term limits on judges and justices and altering the mode of appointment and confirmation. What prevents delegates from deciding that similar limits should apply to Congress; and, by the way, why not eliminate the Electoral College? Look what happened in 1787 in Philadelphia! If the reforms were reported as a nonamendable package to be ratified or rejected, there could be some strange and unanticipated, perhaps destructive, results. Why not take a cue from the framers and rewrite the entire Constitution? Those who hope for a switch to a parliamentary form of government, the abolition of judicial review, imposition of direct democracy, or an end to federalism will feel their mouths watering at the prospect.

Who presides? Are decisions to be taken by majority or supermajority rule? Are votes taken by state delegations or does the "one person, one vote" principle apply? May the convention call for testimony from elected officials or experts? May they compel attendance?

Should the convention's recommendations be made as a package or as a series of specific amendments? If the former, there is the danger that unrelated items could be squeezed into the package. If the latter, and especially if the specific reforms were logically interconnected, the results could be counterproductive if only one of two closely linked items were ratified. Constitutionally mandating multimember districts for the House of Representatives in one amendment, while undermining the political party system (by taking away its control over nominations, for example) in another, could present problems. Sabato suggests that before their legislatures act to ratify, states should give the voters a chance, via referendums, to opine on the amendments. Is the work of the convention time-limited, or are its proposals available for ratification forever? Recall that the Twenty-Seventh Amendment concerning congressional pay raises, ratified in 1992, was originated in 1789 by James Madison!

These questions are but the tip of the iceberg, and they raise yet others. For example, should the Constitution be amended to require an amending convention every 50 or 100 years?

13.3 CONCLUSION

The argument of this book has been fourfold: (1) that fundamental and comprehensive reform requires thoughtful assessment and prioritization of the values to be advanced and the goals to be achieved; (2) that any attempt at structural reform requires a clear-headed consideration of which elected institution, Congress or the presidency, should be primary, and of what sort of party system best organizes political and governmental action; (3) that all reforms are problematical in that they may not achieve their ends, may have bad consequences, and likely will disappoint; and (4) that really important reforms are, in the end, unlikely to be enacted. It is not a positive message. There simply are too many unknowns and too many roadblocks to allow a positive prediction. Successful reform ultimately depends on three matters.

The first concerns the criteria and values to be emphasized. Which of the criteria identified in chapter 1 are most, and which are least, important? What tradeoffs are to be made? Unless these values are prioritized, and unless the priorities guide the reform process, efforts at comprehensive reform are likely to fail and certain to have negative consequences. The second is a decision on political parties. What kind of system do Americans want: one in which a strong party can take hold of government and act, subject to a popular judgment to renew it or replace it with another party, or a system envisioned by the founders that downplays parties and partisanship, stresses individualism, and relies on structures and procedures that do not depend on party directives? The third consideration is institutional: regardless of party type, which elected institution, Congress or the presidency, should be in the driver's seat? One's judgment depends on how he or she trades off effective and efficient, and thus potentially dangerous, government against government that is safer, more constrained, and less productive, characterized by representativeness, responsiveness to voters, accountability, and maximum citizen participation. Making sure that policy decisions emerge from a careful and deliberative process is important regardless of which model one chooses.

In the end, reform depends on the people in power who have the ability to make changes. Unfortunately, few of them are so inclined, some for good reasons (they doubt the reformist messages or they are too busy trying to govern) and others for bad reasons (self-interest in maintaining or gaining power or sheer disinterest). All of them are primarily concerned with policy, not process or structure. Perhaps the pathway to institutional reform lies, first, in reducing the number of government programs that attract the attention of legislators, presidents, bureaucrats, judges, interest groups, and the media. Not a few scholars of late have questioned the very possibility of government's handling of such a complex, broad, overlapping, and often uncoordinated list of policies and programs—an array that cannot possibly lead to effective or efficient government.[16] Unless such political actors change their views and priorities, anything resembling comprehensive and effective reform will not happen. They must be trusted and held accountable at election time for ensuring that government meets the seven criteria as well as possible; sadly, few voters have reform on their minds when voting. The veteran reformer James Sundquist put it well in framing the issue as a gamble:

> An institutional structure that enables the government to move decisively to do good things will also enable it to move with dispatch to do bad things. . . . To support constitutional reforms, the political players would have to be prepared to

Table 13.1 Assessment of Reform

VALUE TO BE ADVANCED AT NATIONAL LEVEL	REFORMS THAT WILL HAVE:		
	PROBABLE POSITIVE EFFECTS THAT OUTWEIGH NEGATIVES AND COSTS	UNCERTAIN, NEUTRAL, OR MIXED EFFECTS	PROBABLE NEGATIVE EFFECTS AND COSTS THAT OUTWEIGH POSITIVES
Effectiveness			
Accountability			
Efficiency			
Reasoned deliberative judgment			
Representation			
Responsiveness			
Participation (voting turnout)			

gamble. . . . It becomes an axiom of constitutional reform, then, that any structural amendment that would bring major benefits cannot be adopted—again, barring a governmental collapse that can be clearly attributed to the constitutional design— while any measure that stands a chance of passage is likely to be innocuous.[17]

Big reforms are impossible, and little ones often are not worth the effort. That is not to say that there won't be any reforms. There is no shortage of ideas. Sometimes the need is just too obvious and pressing to ignore; sometimes circumstances such as election results cry for modest changes; sometimes political pressures are over-whelming; sometimes reforming structures and processes serve as a substitute for taking tough stands on substantive policy issues. Piecemeal solutions to narrow problems will emerge and be enacted. When it comes to holistic substantive reforms that are likely to make a real difference in governance and politics, however, the American people may have to wait a long time. In the end, the burden falls on the policy makers and on the citizens. Unless they take reform seriously, not much will happen.

QUESTIONS TO CONSIDER

1. Ultimately, what should be the purpose of reforms?
2. Is reforming American government possible? What scenario would make it likely?

EXERCISE

Consider Table 13.1. Fill in the cells with appropriate reforms discussed throughout the book. What do you conclude? Compare your results to those of your colleagues.

NOTES

1. Marcus E. Ethridge, *The Case for Gridlock: Democracy, Organized Power, and the Legal Foundations of American Government* (Lanham. MD: Lexington Books, 2010).
2. E. Scott Adler and John D. Wilkerson, *Congress and the Politics of Problem Solving* (Cambridge, UK, and elsewhere: Cambridge University Press, 2012), chap. 6.
3. Shaun Bowler and Todd Donovan, *The Limits of Electoral Reform* (Oxford: Oxford University Press, 2013), chap. 8.
4. Paul C. Light, *A Government Ill Executed: The Decline of the Federal Service and How to Reverse It* (Cambridge, UK, and London: Harvard University Press, 2008): 182–83.
5. Bowler and Donovan, *Limits of Electoral Reform,* chap. 8.
6. Charles Stewart III, "What Hath HAVA Wrought: Consequences, Intended and Not, of the Post Bush v. Gore Reforms," VTP Working Paper prepared for the conference on "Bush v. Gore, 10 Years Later: Election Administration in the United States," Center for the Study of Democracy, University of California, Irvine, April 16–17, 2011, http://www.vote.caltech.edu/sites/default/files/wp_102_pdf_4dadc8a267.pdf/; Bowler and Donovan, *Limits of Electoral Reform.*
7. Leroy N. Rieselbach, *Congressional Reform* (Washington, D.C.: CQ Press, 1986): 122.
8. Steven M. Gillon, *That's Not What We Meant to Do: Reform and Its Unintended Consequences in Twentieth Century America* (New York and London: Norton, 2000).
9. Bowler and Donovan, *Limits of Electoral Reform*: 134–37.

10. Thomas E. Mann and Norman J. Ornstein, *The Broken Branch: How Congress Is Failing American and How to Get It Back on Track* (Oxford and New York: Oxford University Press, 2006): 155.
11. James L. Sundquist, *Constitutional Reform and Effective Government*, rev. ed. (Washington, D.C.: Brookings, 1992): 334.
12. Adrian Vermeule, "Political Constraints on Supreme Court Reform," *Minnesota Law Review* 90 (2005): 1154.
13. "Governing in a Polarized America: A Bipartisan Blueprint to Strengthen our Democracy," http://bipartisanpolicy.org/wp-content/uploads/sites/default/files/files/BPC%20CPR%20Governing%20in%20a%20Polarized%20America.pdf
14. Trevor Potter and Marianne Holt Viray, "Federal Election Authority: Jurisdiction and Mandates," in Ann N. Crigler, Marion R. Just, and Edward J. McCaffery, *Rethinking the Vote: The Politics and Prospects of American Election Reform* (New York and London: Oxford University Press, 2004): 102–16.
15. Larry J. Sabato, *A More Perfect Constitution: 23 Proposals to Revitalize Our Constitution and Make America a Fairer Country* (New York: Walker & Company, 2007), chap. 7.
16. Peter H. Schuck, *Why Government Fails So Often* (Princeton, NJ: Princeton University Press, 2014); Philip K. Howard, *The Rule of Nobody: Saving American from Dead Laws and Broken Government* (New York and London: Norton, 2014).
17. Sundquist, *Constitutional Reform*: 16, 330.

Index